空中英語教室

STUDIO CLASSROOM

全新修訂版

完勝大考！英語7000單字

初級篇｜1～2500字

空中英語教室編輯群／著

笛藤出版

推薦序

「工欲善其事，必先利其器」是大家耳熟能詳的一句話。舉凡想要自己或期待他人學習與精進英文者，站在坊間一字排開的輔助教材、字典、學習雜誌、模擬考題庫、語言學習 APPs 與名人學習血淚史之前，除了自嘆口袋不夠深、無法將它們全數收編，就是籠罩在『天啊！應該帶誰回家？』的猶豫與無助中。的確，對一個尚未有成功學習經驗的人而言，這樣的茫然再自然不過，同時突顯市面上過剩的工具書無法真正幫助學習者對症下藥的窘境。當學習者未能知悉有效的學習方法與策略時，盲目挑選的工具書不見得能讓他們用對的方法學習，不盡理想的學習效果只是一條注定的不歸路。

學習語言的終極目標是能毫無滯澀地與人溝通，而字彙正是使用語言技巧的磐石；無論聽、說、讀、寫，無一與之絕緣，重要性完全不亞於台灣人最重視的文法觀念。豐富的字彙量讓學習者如虎添翼，加乘他們在聽、說、讀、寫上的表現。當他們無須時時停下來解讀個別字義時，便可全神貫注在更高階的自我表達或是順利接收完整且正確的訊息。反之，因為字彙量不足而屢屢被迫中斷思考的學習者，若不盡早打破僵局，很可能永遠在原地踏步，等不到突飛猛進的一天。再者，大多數單純為了應付考試而學習英文的人，看到生字的第一反應就是拜託 Google 大神、或按下網頁上的翻譯年糕鍵。雖能即時解決眼前的問題，卻留下單字到底該怎麼背的後遺症。當學習者不願意花時間去認識一個字，這個字停留在腦海的時間會跟著縮短。

空中英語教室這次編製的『完勝大考！英語 7000 單字初級篇』突破了上述的盲點。首先，依照教育部公告的初級單字字表來篩選放入書中的英文字彙，是生活中最常被使用的基本英文單字，學習者無須自行搜尋整理這些已由大數據分析過的英文字。另外，英文字彙可能有多種詞性或一詞多義，這些絕非是用手機或電腦輸入單字後跳出的中文翻譯會告訴學習者的事。有如盲人摸象的問題解決方式，會讓學習者只看到冰山一角。本書不僅按照字母排序提供常用字（例如：mouth）的各種詞性與相對應的解釋（n. 嘴 / v. 裝腔作勢地說），還有相關的搭配詞（keep sb's mouth shut）、實用的片語動詞（mouth off about sth & mouth off to/at sth）及它們的中英文例句。如此整合單字及延伸用法的一魚多吃學習方式可強化學習者的字彙掌握度，當再次遇到同樣單字卻屬於不同詞性或字義時，將不似往日般迷惘，或因為只學過片段的字義而鬧笑話。學習者還可隨身攜帶手機 APP 的版本，除了閱覽內容，還可聆聽空中英語教室老師的清楚發音，包括單字、延伸詞彙、例句、重音、連音與變音等等；它能滿足不同學習風格的學習者，也讓所有學習者獲得更全面的輔助。

本書的編排目的、內容設計與行動學習 APP 可讓學習者反覆接觸及容易理解這些常用的初級英文字彙及延伸用法。用對的方式來有效學習英文字彙可幫助學習者盡早將新單字變成舊單字，進而達到靈活運用語言的最終目的。「工欲善其事，必先利其器」說的正是這本『完勝大考！英語 7000 單字初級篇』。

文藻外語大學外語教學系陳思安助理教授

本書特色

1. 本書收錄實用初級字彙，其中包括相同拚法，不同詞性的字彙等約 2987 字。以點、線、面擴展方式學習該單字用法，使用讀者能夠有效率增加字彙量。
2. 收錄進階詞彙，如搭配詞及實用片語等，使讀者快速了解該單字的延伸用法，進而在語言學習上更加活用單字。
3. 本書以單元學習的方式，分為 80 回，以每 25 字歸納為一回，並在每回結束時，設計 10 題練習題，以有效評核學習狀況，使讀者能夠循序漸進的習得單字。
4. 本書字表中收錄 525 個單字，曾出現在歷屆學測，指考及統測考題中。
5. 本書另附有完勝大考 7000 單字雲_初級--專屬序號，幫助讀者學習不間斷，充份利用零碎時間，走到哪聽到哪，走到哪背到哪。

※ 為何搭配詞那麼重要呢？

想要講一句話，但是語塞講不出來，因為「不知道要用什麼字表達心中所想的東西」。有時會覺得自己的英文看似「字字是英文」，但其實「句句不是英文」，不知如何道地、精準地使用英文。有了搭配詞，你不會再害怕開口說英文；出國在外，跟外國人交談再也不用支支吾吾，很順利地就能講出流利的句子。這，就是搭配詞的力量。

※ 完勝大考 7000 單字雲及單字書內容的差異：

1. 單字雲：主要單字及例句，並附音檔。
   - ◆提供多樣互動練習題　◆聽發音猜中文意思
   - ◆聽發音猜英文拚法　◆聽發音猜單字
2. 單字書：提供主要單字及例句，並補充實用片語、搭配詞並搭配詞例句。
   單字書另提供 80 回，每回 10 題，便於讀者更深入學習單字的使用情境。

本書使用導覽

◎ **詞性縮寫**

v. = Verb **動詞**
n. = Noun **名詞**
adj. = Adjective **形容詞**
adv. = Adverb **副詞**
prep. = Preposition **介系詞**
conj. = Conjunction **連接詞**

◎**音標參考** DICT.TW **線上字典** / Macmillan Dictionary / Cambridge Dictionary

同：**同義詞**
搭：**搭配詞**
▶：**例句**
：**學測或指考或統測年度**

103

effort [ˈef.ɚt] *n.* 努力

實用片語與搭配字

make effort 盡一番努力

▶ They put a lot of time and effort into making this movie.
他們花了很多時間和努力在拍攝這部電影。

▶ You have to make effort to learn a new language.
你必須努力才能學習一個新的語言。

目次 Contents

完勝大考 7000 單字雲開通説明

親愛的讀者 您好：

恭喜您獲得【完勝大考 7000 單字雲】專屬 QR Code，請按以下步驟開通：

➡ 請掃下方 QR Code 進入【完勝大考 7000 單字雲服務首頁】，輸入空英官網會員帳號及密碼直接登入。若非空英官網會員，請按【註冊】，並填妥相關欄位成為空英會員。

序號：8q5g2d6P3j9T
對象：購完勝大考7000字初級篇附贈
級別：初

★注意事項：

(1) 完勝大考 7000 單字雲 - 初級服務網址：https://7000wb.studioclassroom.com

(2) 完勝大考 7000 單字雲的音檔服務係為雲端服務，無離線收聽的功能。

(3) 任何可上網的裝置，都可以使用服務網址收聽音檔。

(4) 序號開通後，若書籍轉給他人使用，只能以原帳號接續使用，無法轉移。

若您在操作上有任何疑問，或完勝大考 7000 單字雲無法正常使用，請洽空中英語教室客服專線 (02)2533-9123。

單字
Vocabulary

收錄 2987 字

► 80 回單字（每回 25 字）

每回 25 個實用單字，附上音標、詞性、例句、實用片語與搭配字等説明，循序漸進增加字彙量。

► 80 回練習題（每回 10 題）

每回單字後面皆有練習題，馬上驗收前面所學，加深學習印象。

Unit 1

a [eɪ] *art.* 一個

▶ That is a dog.
那是一隻狗。

---

ability [əˈbɪl.ə.t̬i] *n.* 能力

實用片語與搭配字
have the ability to 具備能力

▶ The abilities of the young athlete were outstanding.
這些年輕運動員的能力非常傑出。

▶ John has the ability to make people believe in themselves.
約翰具備讓他人相信自己的能力。

---

able [ˈeɪ.bəl] *adj.* 能；能做的

實用片語與搭配字
be able to 能夠

▶ I am able to run.
我能跑。

▶ Sam is able to ride a unicycle.
山姆會騎獨輪車。

---

about [əˈbaʊt]

① *prep.* 在…的周圍

② *adv.* 大約

▶ The forest is all about me.
這片森林圍繞在我四周。

▶ The test takes about an hour.
這個考試大約花了一小時。

---

above [əˈbʌv]

① *prep.* 在…上面

② *adv.* 在上面；向上面

③ *adj.* 上文的

▶ There is a tree above us.
在我們上面有一棵樹。

▶ She looks at the sky above.
她看著上面的天空。

▶ There are problems in the above list.
上面的列表有些問題。

---

abroad [əˈbrɑːd] *adv.* 在國外

▶ I think they will move abroad next year.
我想他們明年將會搬到國外住。

---

absence [ˈæb.səns] *n.* 缺席

▶ John's absence in class was noticed by the teacher.
約翰缺課被那位老師注意到了。

97

absent [ˈæb.sənt]

① *adj.* 使不在場（不存在的；缺乏的）

② *v.* 缺席；缺勤；不在

▶ John was absent from class today.
約翰今天沒有去上課。

▶ They absented themselves from the discussion.
他們不參與這場討論。

---

accept [əkˈsept] *v.* 接受

▶ Frank accepted Lisa's invitation to dinner.
法蘭克接受了麗莎的晚宴邀請。

---

according to [əˈkɔːr.dɪŋ ˌtuː] *prep.* 根據

▶ It is true according to the story.
根據這則新聞報導，這是事實。

across [əˈkrɑːs]

① *prep.* 在…的對面；在…的另一邊

② *adv.* 橫過；從一邊到另一邊

實用片語與搭配字

come across 偶然碰見

▶ The store is across the street.
這家店在對街。

▶ I can swim across the river.
我可以游泳橫渡這條河。

▶ I came across an interesting article on dieting yesterday.
昨天我偶然看到一篇關於節食的有趣文章。

---

act [ækt]

① *n.* 所做之事；行為

② *v.* 演出；扮演

實用片語與搭配字

act out 將…表演出來

▶ Carl is in the act of doing his homework.
凱爾正在做他的功課。

▶ She will act in the play.
她會在這齣劇中演出。

▶ Sometimes it is necessary to act out your emotions to relieve stress.
有時把你的情緒發洩出來以緩解壓力是必要的。

action [ˈæk.ʃən] *n.* 行動

實用片語與搭配字

take action 採取行動

▶ The team went into action.
這個團隊開始行動。

▶ To do well in your final tests this year, you have to take action now and start studying.
今年要把期末考考好，你必須現在採取行動，開始唸書。

---

active [ˈæk.tɪv] *adj.* 活躍的；活潑的

▶ The horses were active when I went to feed them this morning.
我今早去餵馬時，牠們很雀躍。

actor / actress [ˈæk.tɚ / ˈæk.trəs]

n. （男）演員 / 女演員

▶ Fred is an actor, and Sandy is an actress.
佛萊德是位男演員，珊蒂是位女演員。

---

add [æd] *v.* 增加

實用片語與搭配字

add a touch / touches of sth 增添

▶ I can add your name to the list.
我可以把你的名字加在這個名單上。

▶ You can add a touch of excitement to your life by joining a hiking group.
參加健行社團能為你的生活增添一點興奮感。

addition [əˈdɪʃ.ən] *n.* 加；附加

▶ There was pie in addition to cake at the party.
在派對中已有派再加上蛋糕。

address [ˈæd.res]

① *n.* 地址

② *v.* 向…發表演說

實用片語與搭配字

address sth to sb 向…發表演說

▶ My address is on Main Street.
我的地址是在主要大街。

▶ The man will address the crowd.
那位男士會向群眾發表演說。

▶ You can address the letter to me and I will give it to Hannah.
你可以把話告訴我，我會再轉達給漢娜。

---

adult [ˈæd.ʌlt]

① *n.* 成年人

實用片語與搭配字

young adult 年輕人

② *adj.* 成人的

▶ Jim is not an adult.
吉姆不是個成年人。

▶ Young adults spend a lot of time on their smartphones every day.
年輕人每天花很多時間在他們的智慧型手機。

▶ He is taking an adult education class.
他正在上成人教育課程。

advance [ədˈvæns]

① *n.* （使）前進；促進

實用片語與搭配字

in advance 預先

▶ The advance of the forest fire caused the people to leave town.
森林大火不斷蔓延促使居民必須離城。

▶ If you order from the restaurant in advance, the food will be ready when you get there.
如果你提前向餐廳預訂，在你到的時候食物就已經準備好了。

make advance in 進一步

② *v.* 使前進

▶ Scientists have made many advances in cancer research in the past decade.
在過去的十年裡，科學家們在癌症研究方面取得了許多進展。

▶ I should advance this chess piece.
我應該要讓這棋子往前移。

101

affair [ə'fer] *n.* 事情；事務

實用片語與搭配字

have an affair with sb 與…發生關係

▶ Organizing my bedroom was an all day affair.
整理我的臥室是一件需要花整天功夫的事情。

▶ The woman divorced her husband after she found out he was having an affair with his secretary.
這女人發現自己的丈夫和祕書有外遇後就離婚了。

---

afraid [ə'freɪd] *adj.* 害怕的

▶ Eva is afraid of the dark.
伊娃害怕黑暗。

---

after ['æf.tɚ]

① *prep.* 在…以後

② *conj.* 在…之後

③ *adv.* 之後；後來

▶ Ted is in line after David.
泰德排在大衛之後。

▶ I went to bed after I read.
我讀完後就上床睡覺。

▶ Jim is following after.
吉姆跟在後頭。

---

afternoon [ˌæf.tɚ'nu:n] *n.* 下午

▶ Allen likes to take naps in the afternoon.
艾倫喜歡在下午睡午覺。

---

again [ə'gen] *adv.* 再一次

▶ Jeff will write the test again.
傑夫會將考卷再寫一次。

Exercise 1

I. Choose and write the correct word. Change the form of the word when necessary.

1	absent (adj.) active (adj.)	The kids must be really hungry; they've been __________ all day with one thing or another.
2	actor (n.) adult (n.)	Children under 6 must be supervised by an __________ at all times.
3	accept (v.) advance (v.)	She ______________ the gift with a big smile, and thanked everyone several times.
4	absence (n.) ability (n.)	He has a lot of natural __________ in sports, but he doesn't work very hard.
5	affair (n.) advance (n.)	What I do in my private life is my _________, so just mind your own business.

II. Multiple choices.

( ) 1. My little sister is _________ of the dark, so she never goes into a haunted house.
(A) scary (B) afraid (C) fear (D) frightened

( ) 2. The new champion will _________ the public at the award ceremony.
(A) advance (B) approach (C) address (D) announce

( ) 3. More and more young people plan to study _________ to gain different cultural experiences from other countries.
(A) abroad (B) absent (C) across (D) aboard

( ) 4. Two of the students were __________ from class due to the flu.
(A) addictive (B) aggressive (C) active (D) absent

( ) 5. She won't be able to __________ to the next level if she doesn't work harder.
(A) address (B) accept (C) advance (D) add

against [ə'genst] *prep.* 反對

▶ Nelson is against the changes.
尼爾森反對這些改變。

---

age [eɪdʒ]

① *n.* 年齡

② *v.* 變老；使…顯得蒼老

▶ Anita is seven years of age.
安妮塔七歲。

▶ Since Laura turned 30, she feels she is aging quickly.
自從蘿拉滿 30 歲，她感覺自己加快顯得蒼老。

---

ago [ə'goʊ] *adv.* 在…以前

▶ Laura started piano three years ago.
蘿拉三年前開始彈鋼琴。

---

agree [ə'griː] *v.* 意見一致

實用片語與搭配字

agree with 認同

▶ Angel and Roy agree about the movie.
安琪和洛伊對這部電影意見一致。

▶ I agree with you that we have to recycle plastic.
我認同你的想法，我們應該要回收塑膠。

agreement [ə'griː.mənt] *n.* 同意書；協定

實用片語與搭配字

reach an agreement 達成共識

▶ Eric will sign the agreement today.
艾瑞克今天會簽下同意書。

▶ The two sides reached an agreement after months of discussions.
經過數個月的討論，兩方達成了共識。

---

ahead [ə'hed] *adv.* 領先；在前面

實用片語與搭配字

go ahead 先走

▶ Carol is ahead of the other students.
凱洛超前其他學生。

▶ Max will be late so let's go ahead and start the meeting.
麥斯將會遲到，所以讓會議先開始吧。

---

aid [eɪd]

① *n.* 幫助；援助

實用片語與搭配字

come to the aid of 援助

▶ The nurse gave aid to one of our team members.
這位護士幫了我們其中一名隊員。

▶ Many countries came to the aid of Japan after the big earthquake.
大地震後，許多國家都來援助日本。

② *v.* 幫助；救助

實用片語與搭配字

aid sb in sth / doing sth
幫助

- The army aided people trying to get away from the flood .
  這支軍隊幫助那些試圖逃離洪水的人們。
- The nurse aided the doctor in treating the patient.
  這位護士協助醫生治療病人。

---

aim [eɪm]

① *n.* 瞄準的對象；目標

① *v.* 瞄準；(使)對準

- Please take accurate aim.
  請精確瞄準目標。
- Mike aimed his gun at the empty bottles.
  麥可用他的槍瞄準了那些空瓶子。

---

air [er] *n.* 空氣

實用片語與搭配字

a breath of fresh air
令人耳目一新的人(或物)

- The air is really clean!
  這個空氣十分清新！
- The new girl in our class was a breath of fresh air because she was so friendly.
  班上新來的女生很友善，真的是讓人耳目一新。

---

aircraft [ˈer.kræft] *n.* 飛機；飛行器

- Look at the number of aircraft at this airport.
  看看這座機場裡飛機的數量。

---

airline [ˈer.laɪn]

n. 航空公司；(飛機的)航線

- The new airline will begin services next week.
  新的航空公司將在下週開始提供服務。

---

airmail [ˈer.meɪl] *n.* 航空郵件

- The letter came by airmail.
  這封信是航空郵件寄到的。

---

airplane / plane [ˈer.pleɪn / pleɪn]

n. 飛機

- I got here by airplane. She got here by plane, too.
  我搭飛機來的，她也搭飛機。

---

airport [ˈer.pɔːrt] *n.* 機場

- Carol works at the airport.
  凱洛在機場工作。

97

alarm [ə'lɑ:rm]

① *n.* 驚慌；擔憂

實用片語與搭配字

false alarm 假警報，虛驚

raise the alarm 發布警訊

② *v.* 令某人擔心或害怕

▶ John expressed alarm when the bear ran towards him.
當熊跑向約翰時，他顯得很驚慌。

▶ We all ran out of the building when someone yelled 'fire', but thank goodness it was a false alarm.
當有人大喊火災的時候，我們從大樓裡跑了出去，不過幸好這只是虛驚一場。

▶ Scientists first raised the alarm on global warming in the 1970s.
科學家在 1970 年代首先發布全球暖化的警訊。

▶ Your behavior alarmed me.
你的行為讓我很擔心。

---

album ['æl.bəm] *n.* 相簿

▶ Place the photo album on the bookshelf.
把相簿放到書架上。

---

alike [ə'laɪk]

① *adj.* 相像的

① *adv.* 相同地

▶ Family members are alike in so many ways.
家庭成員在很多地方都會很相像。

▶ The twins dress alike every day.
這對雙胞胎每天穿著一樣。

alive [ə'laɪv] *adj.* 活著的；有活力的

實用片語與搭配字

keep sb / sth alive 維持生命

▶ The dog was still alive after it fell from the roof.
這隻狗從屋頂跌落後仍活著。

▶ First aid is important to keep someone who is injured alive until the ambulance comes.
急救是重要的，好讓受傷的人維持生命，直到救護車到來。

---

all [ɑ:l]

① *adj.* 所有的

② *adv.* 所有地

③ *pron.* 全部；一切

④ *n.* 所有一切

▶ I closed all the doors.
我關上所有的門。

▶ The juice is all finished.
這果汁全部被喝完了。

▶ All of the students are here.
全部學生都在這裡。

▶ He lost the race, but he gave it his all.
他雖然輸了比賽，但他已盡了全力。

allow [ə'laʊ] *v.* 允許

實用片語與搭配字

allow for 顧及，考慮到

▶ The teacher allowed her students to take their notes to the exam.
這位老師允許學生們考試時可以帶筆記。

▶ Parents must allow for more time to get ready when traveling with young children.
父母必須考量到帶著小朋友旅行需要花更多的時間準備。

---

almond ['ɑːl.mənd] *n.* 杏仁

▶ I would like to eat a handful of almonds.
我想吃一把杏仁。

---

almost ['ɑːl.moʊst] *adv.* 幾乎；差不多

▶ Jeff is almost finished with his project.
傑夫快要完成他的報告了。

---

alone [ə'loʊn]

① *adj.* 單獨的

實用片語與搭配字

leave sb alone 避免打擾某人

② *adv.* 單獨地

▶ Janet was all alone.
珍妮特都是獨自一人。

▶ My brother failed his final exam, so Mom told me to leave him alone.
我哥哥搞砸了期末考，所以媽媽叫我不要去打擾他。

▶ Jim stood alone on the stage.
吉姆單獨地站在台上。

---

along [ə'lɑːŋ]

① *prep.* 沿著

實用片語與搭配字

go along with 同意，支持

② *adv.* 向前

▶ Tina walked along the path.
蒂娜沿著小徑走。

▶ We went along with her plan, even though we didn't think it was a good one.
儘管我們覺得那不是一個很好的計劃，我們還是支持她的計劃。

▶ We biked along the riverside.
我們沿著河邊騎腳踏車。

---

aloud [ə'laʊd] *adv.* 出聲地

▶ Please read the message aloud.
請把訊息大聲地讀出來。

Exercise 2

I. Choose and write the correct word. Change the form of the word when necessary.

1	album (n.) alarm (n.)	Firefighters rushed to the building after the __________ went off.
2	ahead (adv.) alone (adv.)	Look straight __________ and you'll see the post office on your right.
3	airmail (n.) album (n.)	I keep the photographs in an __________.
4	alive (adj.) alone (adj.)	She doesn't know if her husband is __________ or dead.
5	again (adv.) alike (adv.)	The twins look __________, but they differ in temperament.

II. Multiple choices.

( ) 1. He had to perform first __________ on his wife when they were in a car accident.
(A) aim (B) air (C) aid (D) age

( ) 2. The __________ is taking steps to ensure safety on its aircraft.
(A) airport (B) airline (C) airmail (D) aircraft

( ) 3. I __________ didn't recognize her; she'd changed a lot.
(A) almost (B) already (C) alike (D) along

( ) 4. His parents won't __________ him to stay out late.
(A) alarm (B) agree (C) aim (D) allow

( ) 5. __________ was finally reached after a very lengthy discussion.
(A) Almond (B) Aim (C) Agreement (D) Aircraft

Unit 3

alphabet [ˈæl.fə.bet] *n.* 字母表

▶ I often sing the alphabet.
我經常唱字母歌。

---

already [ɑːlˈred.i] *adv.* 已經

▶ I already finished my homework.
我已經完成我的家庭作業了。

---

also [ˈɑːl.soʊ] *adv.* 也；還

▶ Maggie also likes listening to music.
瑪姬也喜歡聽音樂。

97

although [ɑːlˈðoʊ] *conj.* 雖然；儘管

▶ Although the stage looks large, it cannot hold all the musical instruments.
雖然舞台看起來很大，仍無法容納所有的樂器。

---

altogether [ˌɑːl.təˈgeð.ɚ] *adv.* 完全；全部

▶ After a week of rain, the rain stopped altogether.
在下了一整星期的雨後，雨終於全停了。

---

always [ˈɑːl.weɪz] *adv.* 總是；經常

▶ Leon always gets to school early.
黎恩總是很早到校。

---

am [æm / əm]
v. （用於第一人稱單數）是

▶ I am happy.
我很快樂。

101

among [əˈmʌŋ] *prep.* 在…之中

▶ Jim saw Fischer sitting among the students.
吉姆看見費雪坐在這群學生之中。

---

amount [əˈmaʊnt]
① *n.* 總額
② *v.* 合計；總計

▶ The amount of rain from the storm caused a lot of damage.
這次暴風雨的總雨量造成了很大的破壞。

▶ The clothes I bought amounted to US$250.
我買的衣服總計二百五十美元。

---

an [æn] *art.* 一個

▶ This is an apple.
這是一顆蘋果。

ancient [ˈeɪn.ʃənt] *adj.* 古代的

▶ They were able to find the ancient city.
他們有辦法找到古城。

and [ænd / ənd / ən] *conj.* 和；以及

▶ Zoe wants ice cream and cake.
佐伊想要吃冰淇淋和蛋糕。

anger [ˈæŋ.gɚ] *n.* 憤怒；生氣

實用片語與搭配字
be angered by 因…感到生氣

▶ I understand her anger. That wasn't fair.
我了解她的憤怒，那並不公平。

▶ My mom was angered by my brother's refusal to clean his room.
我媽媽因為我哥拒絕打掃房間而感到生氣。

angry [ˈæŋ.gri] *adj.* 生氣的

實用片語與搭配字
be angry with 生氣

▶ Anne gets angry easily.
安很容易生氣。

▶ Kevin was angry with his girlfriend for being two hours late to their date.
凱文對他女朋友約會遲到兩個小時感到很生氣。

animal [ˈæn.ə.məl] *n.* 動物

▶ There are some animals at the zoo.
動物園裡有些動物。

ankle [ˈæŋ.kəl] *n.* 腳踝

▶ Your ankle looks quite red. What did you do?
你的腳踝看起來很紅，你做了什麼？

another [əˈnʌð.ɚ]

① *adj.* 另一個的
② *pron.* 另一個

▶ I'd like another vacation.
我還想要去度另一個假期。

▶ One student's score was better than another.
這個學生的成績比另一個好。

answer [ˈæn.sɚ]

① *n.* 答案；回答
② *v.* 答覆

▶ What is the answer?
這個答案是什麼？

▶ Please answer the question.
請回答這個問題。

ant [ænt] *n.* 螞蟻

▶ The ant is working hard.
這隻螞蟻很努力工作。

any [ˈen.i]

① *adj.* 所有的；盡可能多的

② *pron.* 無論哪個；任何一個

③ *adv.* 根本；絲毫

► I'll eat any extra rice.
我會吃所有多的飯。

► Any of these students can do it.
無論哪一個學生都可以做到。

► The storm can't get any worse.
這暴風雨強度已達到極限。

---

anybody [ˈen.iˌbɑː.di] *pron.* 任何人

► If anybody talks during class, they will be asked to leave.
如果有任何人在課堂上講話，就會被要求離開。

---

anyhow [ˈen.i.haʊ] *adv.* 無論如何；不管怎樣

► It may rain, but I will go shopping anyhow.
有可能會下雨，但無論如何我都要去購物。

---

anyone [ˈen.i.wʌn]

pron. 無論誰（用於肯定句）；任何人（用於否定句和疑問句）

► Anyone is welcome to join us.
無論誰，我們都很歡迎加入。

---

anyplace [ˈen.i.pleɪs] *adv.* 隨便哪地方

► Just put your books down anyplace.
把你的書隨便放在什麼地方都可以。

---

anything [ˈen.i.θɪŋ]

pron. 任何事物；無論什麼事情

► I don't see anything.
我什麼都沒看到。

Exercise 3

I. Choose and write the correct word. Change the form of the word when necessary.

1	among (prep.) amount (n.)	The secretary has a large __________ of mail to answer every day.
2	ankle (n.) animal (n.)	She sprained her __________ while playing squash.
3	altogether (adv.) always (adv.)	In this world there's __________ danger for those who are afraid of it.
4	already (adv.) although (con.)	I've __________ seen that film, so I'd rather see another one.
5	another (adj.) among (prep.)	Peer pressure is strong __________ young people.

II. Multiple choices.

(　　) 1. __________ she is very poor, she's not lost her dignity.
(A) Altogether　(B) Although　(C) Also　(D) Anyhow

(　　) 2. The __________ temple ruined in the war will be reconstructed soon.
(A) another　(B) anyplace　(C) ancient　(D) ankle

(　　) 3. She scolded him in great __________ because he made the same mistake again.
(A) answer　(B) ankle　(C) amount　(D) anger

(　　) 4. A human can think and talk, but an __________ cannot.
(A) ankle　(B) anybody　(C) animal　(D) anyone

(　　) 5. The train went slower and slower until it stopped __________.
(A) altogether　(B) although　(C) also　(D) always

Unit 4

anytime [ˈen.i.taɪm] *adv.* 在任何時候

▶ Anytime you want to talk, I'm here for you.
你想談話的任何時間，我都可以陪你。

---

anyway [ˈen.i.weɪ] *adv.* 無論如何；反正

▶ Please finish the job anyway you can.
無論如何，請你完成工作。

---

anywhere [ˈen.i.wer]
adv. 在（或去）任何地方

▶ Anywhere you want to live sounds good to me.
無論你想住哪裡我都可以。

---

apartment [əˈpɑːrt.mənt] *n.* 公寓

▶ I would enjoy living in that apartment.
我會非常樂意住在那棟公寓。

---

ape [eɪp]
① *n.* 猿猴
② *v.*（拙劣地）模仿

▶ The ape climbed the tree.
那隻猿猴爬上了樹。

▶ Please don't ape his behavior. That's rude.
請不要模仿他的動作，那樣很沒禮貌。

104
appear [əˈpɪr] *v.* 出現

▶ Then the rabbit will appear in the hat!
然後那隻兔子會出現在這頂帽子裡！

98
appearance [əˈpɪr.əns] *n.* 出現

▶ Please make an appearance this evening.
今天晚上請來露個面吧。

---

appetite [ˈæp.ə.taɪt] *n.* 胃口

▶ My appetite is never satisfied.
我的胃口從來沒有被滿足過。

---

apple [ˈæp.əl] *n.* 蘋果

實用片語與搭配字
The Big Apple (nickname for NYC)
紐約市

▶ The apple tastes good.
這顆蘋果好吃。

▶ In a month's time I am off to the Big Apple and I can't wait to visit the Statue of Liberty.
再一個月我就要前往紐約市了，我迫不及待想造訪自由女神像。

apply [ə'plaɪ] *v.* 塗；敷；放在…上面

實用片語與搭配字

apply to; apply for

向某個單位或機關提出申請；透過申請的過程取得想要的東西

▶ Please apply this medicine to your mosquito bite.
請把這藥塗在你被蚊子咬的地方。

▶ John is applying for a new job after he lost his old one.
約翰在丟了舊工作之後，申請了一個新的工作。

April ['eɪ.prəl] *n.* 四月

實用片語與搭配字

April Fool's Day　愚人節

▶ I'm going to Hong Kong in April.
我四月要去香港。

▶ Many people like to play tricks on others on April Fool's Day.
許多人喜歡在愚人節當天捉弄人。

---

apron ['eɪ.prən] *n.* 圍裙

▶ I always wear an apron when I cook so my clothes don't get dirty.
我煮飯時都會穿上圍裙，這樣我的衣服就不會弄髒。

---

are [ɑ:r / ər]

v. 是（用於第二人稱或第三人稱複數）

▶ They are high school students.
他們是高中生。

---

area ['er.i.ə] *n.* 區域

▶ That's a big area.
那是個很大的區域。

---

argue ['ɑ:rg.ju:] *v.* 爭吵；辯論

實用片語與搭配字

argue for; argue with

為…爭辯或說理；與某人爭辯或說理

▶ Sarah and Beth love to argue.
莎拉和貝絲很愛爭辯。

▶ The lawyer has spent the past decade argueing for women's rights.
這位律師過去十年一直在爭取婦女的權益。

argument ['ɑ:rg.jə.mənt]

n. 爭論；爭吵；爭辯

實用片語與搭配字

make argument　做出論證

▶ The argument continued all day long.
這場爭論持續了一整天。

▶ During the debate, you have to make argument for and against free education.
辯論的時候，你必須提出論點去贊成與反對免費的教育。

---

arm [ɑ:rm]

① *n.* 手臂

▶ I hurt my arm playing baseball.
我在打棒球的時候傷了我的手臂。

實用片語與搭配字

cost an arm and a leg 一大筆錢

② *v.* 裝備；武裝

▶ The luxury bag costs an arm and a leg.
這名牌包包要價不斐。

▶ Arm yourself before entering the woods.
進入樹林前要先把你自己武裝好。

---

armchair [ˈɑːrm.tʃer] *n.* 扶手椅（常是單人椅）

▶ I would like to buy a large armchair.
我想要買一張大扶手椅。

---

army [ˈɑːr.mi] *n.* 陸軍；軍隊

實用片語與搭配字

an army of 一大群

▶ He is a soldier in the army.
他是陸軍中的士兵。

▶ An army of people arrived at the beach on Saturday to help clean up the trash.
星期六有一大群人到海灘淨灘。

---

around [əˈraʊnd]

① *adv.* 到處

實用片語與搭配字

look around 遊覽，逛

② *prep.* 圍繞

▶ The students are sitting around.
學生們坐在那裡。

▶ When you are lost, the best thing to do is look around for a police station to ask for help.
當你迷路的時候，最好的辦法就是尋找警察局，向他們請求協助。

▶ There is a fence around the yard.
有道籬笆圍繞著這個院子。

98

arrange [əˈreɪndʒ] *v.* 整理；安排

實用片語與搭配字

arrange for 為…做安排

▶ Please arrange these books neatly on the shelf.
請把這些書整齊地排在書架上。

▶ I called the taxi company to arrange for a taxi to the airport.
我打電話到計程車公司，叫了一輛車到機場。

99 95

arrangement [əˈreɪndʒ.mənt]

n. 約定；安排；準備工作

▶ I need to make arrangements with my boss about when to take a vacation.
我需要和我的老闆約個時間討論何時休假。

arrest [əˈrest]

① *v.* 逮捕

實用片語與搭配字

be arrested for doing sth 因…遭逮捕

② *n.* 逮捕；拘留

實用片語與搭配字

under arrest 逮捕

- ▶ The police arrested the thief.
  警察逮捕了小偷。
- ▶ The thief was arrested for stealing the diamonds.
  小偷因偷竊鑽石而被逮捕了。
- ▶ The arrest of the little boy made the whole community angry .
  那個小男孩被逮捕讓整個社區都感到憤怒。
- ▶ The police put the thief under arrest.
  警察逮捕了小偷。

---

arrive [əˈraɪv] *v.* 到達

實用片語與搭配字

arrive in 抵達

- ▶ Jane arrived at 10:00 for the meeting.
  珍在十點鐘抵達會議。
- ▶ Jane arrived in New York on Monday.
  珍在週一抵達紐約。

---

arrow [ˈer.oʊ] *n.* 箭

- ▶ See that arrow flying through the air!
  看那支箭劃過了天空！

Exercise 4

I. Choose and write the correct word. Change the form of the word when necessary.

1	apply (v.) appear (v.)	The first dinosaur __________ around 225 or 230 million years ago.
2	argue (v.) arrive (v.)	We have sent you a package which should __________ within a couple of days.
3	appetite (n.) appearance (n.)	I lost my __________ for meat after seeing a television program about the treatment of animals on some farms.
4	arrest (v.) arm (v.)	The bank was robbed this afternoon by a man __________ with a large knife.
5	arrangement (n.) argument (n.)	He and his girlfriend split up after having a big __________ at the party.

II. Multiple choices.

(　) 1. I __________ with my roommate because she always takes too long in the shower.
(A) applied　(B) appeared　(C) argued　(D) armed

(　) 2. The average rent for a two-bedroom __________ in this city is probably about $700 a month now.
(A) apartment　(B) apron　(C) appetite　(D) area

(　) 3. We are quite busy today, but I'll see if I can __________ a meeting for sometime tomorrow morning.
(A) appear　(B) apply　(C) arrest　(D) arrange

(　) 4. I hope they'll __________ the guy that has been breaking into cars all over the neighborhood soon.
(A) arrange　(B) arrest　(C) arrive　(D) argue

(　) 5. There are a number of different __________ in the city where crime has become a serious problem.
(A) aprons　(B) armchairs　(C) areas　(D) arrows

Unit 5

art [ɑːrt] *n.* 藝術品；藝術

實用片語與搭配字

work of art 藝術品

▶ That painting is a beautiful piece of art.
這幅畫是一件美麗的藝術品。

▶ This museum is filled with beautiful works of art.
這座博物館盡是美麗的藝術品。

---

article [ˈɑːr.t̬ɪ.kəl] *n.* 文章；論文

實用片語與搭配字

write an article / articles on
針對…寫文章

▶ Kurt has written many articles for the newspaper.
科特在報紙上寫了許多文章。

▶ The newspaper has asked me to write an article on my favorite holiday places.
報社邀請我寫一篇關於我最喜歡的度假地點的文章。

---

artist [ˈɑːr.t̬ɪst] *n.* 藝術家

▶ The artist painted for hours each day.
這位畫家每天都作畫好幾個鐘頭。

---

as [æz / əz]

① *adv.* 和…一樣地
② *conj.* 像…一樣
③ *prep.* 作為；以…的身分
④ *pron.* 與…相同的人、事、物

▶ He did as well as he could.
他竭盡所能做好。

▶ It's not so bad as you think.
這不是像你所想的那麼糟。

▶ I'm acting as a judge in this case.
我在這情況下扮演著像法官一樣的角色。

▶ I got the same book as you bought.
我和你買同樣的書。

---

ask [æsk] *v.* 問

實用片語與搭配字

ask for 要求

▶ Can I ask you a question?
我可以問你一個問題嗎？

▶ You should ask for help if you don't know how to do the homework.
如果你不知道作業怎麼做，你應該請求協助。

---

asleep [əˈsliːp] *adj.* 睡著的

▶ Missy was asleep on the train and missed her stop.
蜜西在火車上睡著，錯過了她該下車的站。

實用片語與搭配字

fall asleep 睡著

▶ I was so tired I fell asleep on the bus.
我太累而在公車上睡著了。

---

assistant [əˈsɪs.tənt] *n.* 助手

▶ Your assistant should do that for you.
你的助手應該幫你做那件事。

---

at [æt] *prep.* 從事於；忙於；處於

▶ Jane is at work.
珍在工作。

attack [əˈtæk]

① *v.* 進攻；襲擊

② *n.* 攻擊

實用片語與搭配字

attack on; attack by
向…發動攻擊；遭受攻擊

▶ My cat attacked my dog when he was asleep.
我的貓趁著我的狗睡著時攻擊牠。

▶ They said the attack lasted over an hour.
他們說攻擊持續了超過一個小時。

▶ Tom was attacked by bees when he stepped on the bee hive.
湯姆踩在蜂巢上時，被蜜蜂襲擊了。

---

attend [əˈtend] *v.* 出席；參加

實用片語與搭配字

attend to sb; be attended by
處理，照顧，關心；受到照顧

▶ I would love to attend that rock concert.
我會很樂意去參加那場搖滾音樂會。

▶ The basketball game was attended by many celebrities.
這場籃球賽受到許多名人的關注。

attention [əˈten.ʃən] *n.* 注意；注意力

實用片語與搭配字

pay attention to 注意

▶ You will learn more in class if you pay attention.
如果你專心，將會在課堂上學到更多。

▶ Pay attention to your teacher. She is going over what will be covered in the final exam.
注意聽老師說，她會提到期末考要考的內容。

August [ɑːˈɡʌst] *n.* 八月

▶ I'm on vacation in August.
我八月的時候在度假。

---

aunt [ænt] *n.* 姑姑；阿姨；嬸嬸；伯母

▶ My aunt Liz is coming to visit.
我的姑姑麗姿要來看我。

autumn ['ɑː.t̬əm] *n.* 秋天

▶ My birthday is in the autumn.
我的生日在秋天。

---

99 95

avoid [ə'vɔɪd] *v.* 避免

▶ Remember to avoid the holes in the road when you're driving.
當你在開車時，記得閃避路上的那些坑洞。

---

away [ə'weɪ] *adv.* 離開

實用片語與搭配字

walk away 離開

▶ Tim will be away for two weeks.
提姆將會離開兩個星期。

▶ It's best to walk away from an argument as you may say something you'll regret.
爭吵的當下，最好的方式就是離開，因為你有可能會說出讓自己後悔的話。

---

baby ['beɪ.bi] *n.* 嬰兒

實用片語與搭配字

have a baby 生孩子

▶ Sean isn't a baby. He's three years old!
西恩不是個嬰兒，他已經三歲了！

▶ Stan and his wife don't want to have babies.
斯坦和他的妻子不想生孩子。

---

babysit ['beɪ.bi.sɪt] *v.* 當臨時保母

▶ I like to babysit my little sister.
我喜歡當我妹妹的保母。

---

babysitter ['beɪ.bi͵sɪt̬.ɚ] *n.*（臨時）保母

▶ I work as a babysitter.
我的工作是保母。

---

back [bæk]

① *n.* 背部

② *adj.* 後面的；後部的

③ *adv.* 回原處

實用片語與搭配字

come back 回來

④ *v.* 使倒退

▶ I hurt my back playing basketball.
我在打籃球的時候傷了我的背。

▶ Jim sat in the back seat of the car.
吉姆坐在這輛車的後座。

▶ He ran back to the car.
他跑回那部車裡。

▶ The elderly movie star made a successful come back after her award-winning performance.
老牌的電影明星在她的演出得獎後成功的回歸了。

▶ We need the driver to back the car up.
我們需要這位駕駛將車倒退。

實用片語與搭配字

back sb up 支持

▶ Starting a business is not easy and you need friends to back you up to get through difficult times.

創業很不容易，你需要朋友支持以度過難關。

---

backward [ˈbæk.wɚd]

① *adj.* 向後的

實用片語與搭配字

backward glance 向後看

② *adv.* 向後

實用片語與搭配字

move backward 倒退

▶ I need to face backward in the elevator in order to fit.

為了擠進電梯，我需要在電梯裡面向後方。

▶ After being fired from her job, Susan left without a backward glance.

蘇珊被開除後，她頭也不回的離開。

▶ The baby climbed backward down the stairs.

這個寶寶倒退著爬下樓梯。

▶ Many people wish they could move backward in time so that they can fix their mistakes.

許多人都希望時光能倒轉，好讓他們彌補過去所犯的錯誤。

---

bad [bæd] *adj.* 壞的

▶ I don't want a bad score on the test.

我不想要在這個考試得個壞成績。

---

bag [bæg] *n.* 袋子

▶ Shane has a new bag.

顯恩有一個新包包。

---

bake [beɪk] *v.* 烘烤

實用片語與搭配字

bake for 為…烘培

▶ Shaun loves to bake cookies in her free time.

希恩喜歡在她空閒的時候烤餅乾。

▶ Our school has asked moms to bake for the sports day, anything from cake to pies.

我的學校請媽媽們為運動會烘焙點心，從蛋糕到派，什麼都有。

---

bakery [ˈbeɪ.kɚ.i] *n.* 麵包店；烘焙坊

▶ This bakery has the best bread in the whole town.

這家麵包店有著整個城裡最好吃的麵包。

Exercise 5

I. Choose and write the correct word. Change the form of the word when necessary.

1	assistant (n.) article (n.)	Don't throw the newspaper away; there's an __________ in it about a friend of mine.
2	attend (v.) avoid (v.)	Please let the teacher know if you are unable to __________ the class.
3	babysitter (n.) assistant (n.)	My __________ will help you if I am busy with another client.
4	asleep (adj.) backward (adj.)	She's not __________; her eyes are open.
5	avoid (v.) attack (v.)	The bees will __________ anyone who gets near their hive.

II. Multiple choices.

( ) 1. You can't __________ doing your homework, so you might as well get started now.
(A) attend (B) attack (C) arrive (D) avoid

( ) 2. These latest paintings show how the __________ has really grown in maturity.
(A) arrow (B) artist (C) autumn (D) art

( ) 3. The car passed over the body twice, once __________ and then forward.
(A) backward (B) back (C) away (D) asleep

( ) 4. The smell of fresh bread from the __________ made him hungry, but he didn't stop.
(A) babysitter (B) attention (C) bakery (D) attack

( ) 5. Maple leaves turn red in the __________.
(A) August (B) autumn (C) attention (D) assistant

Unit 6

balcony [ˈbæl.kə.ni] *n.* 陽台

▶ Susan loves to spend each morning drinking her tea on the balcony.
蘇珊喜歡每天早晨在陽台喝茶。

---

ball [bɑːl]

① *n.* 球

② *v.* 呈球狀

▶ Throw the ball!
丟球吧！

▶ Don't ball up that paper!
不要把紙揉成一團！

---

balloon [bəˈluːn]

① *n.* 汽球

② *v.* （在大小、重量或重要性上）激增

▶ The little girl has a balloon.
這個小女孩有一顆氣球。

▶ The cost of the party is ballooning.
這場派對的花費如同氣球般激增。

---

bamboo [bæmˈbuː] *n.* 竹子

▶ I have a chair made of bamboo.
我有一把用竹子製成的椅子。

---

banana [bəˈnæn.ə] *n.* 香蕉

▶ Neil is eating a banana.
尼爾正在吃香蕉。

---

band [bænd] *n.* 樂團

實用片語與搭配字

band together 攜手，團結，聯合

▶ Jimmy and Jack are starting a band.
吉姆與傑克創始了一個樂團。

▶ The students banded together to convince their teacher not to give them any homework.
學生們聯合起來說服老師不要給他們任何作業。

---

bank [bæŋk]

① *n.* 堤；岸

② *n.* 銀行

③ *v.* 存款於銀行

▶ Jade slid down the bank by the river.
潔德從河堤滑落。

▶ I put my money in the bank.
我把錢存在銀行。

▶ Sara has banked here for 20 years.
莎拉在這家銀行儲蓄已經有二十年。

B

banker [ˈbæŋ.kɚ] *n.* 銀行家；銀行業者

▶ The banker helped me decide what to do with my money.
這位銀行員幫助我決定如何處理我的錢。

---

bar [bɑːr]

① *n.* 棒子

② *v.* 閂上、閂住某物（尤指使某物緊閉）

實用片語與搭配字

be barred from 遭到阻饒

▶ I tripped on the bar.
我被這根棒子絆倒了。

▶ Help me bar the door!
幫我閂上這個門！

▶ After John and Marcus started a fight in the restaurant, they were barred from going back there.
自從約翰和馬克斯在餐廳打架之後，他們再也不能進去那家店了。

---

barbecue / BBQ [ˈbɑːr.bə.kjuː]

① *n.* 烤肉架；烤肉

② *v.*（在戶外）烤（肉）

▶ Please move the barbecue to the backyard.
請把烤肉架挪到後院去。

▶ The best way to cook steak is to barbecue it.
烹調牛排最好的方式就是用烤的。

---

barber [ˈbɑːr.bɚ] *n.* 理髮師

▶ The barber is cutting Willie's hair.
這位理髮師正在剪韋利的頭髮。

---

bark [bɑːrk]

① *n.* 狗吠叫聲

② *v.* 咆哮；怒吼

③ *n.* 樹皮

▶ That dog's bark is very loud.
那隻狗吠聲很大。

▶ The famous cook barked orders to the other cooks.
這位有名的廚師對著其他廚師大聲點餐。

▶ Check out the bark on that tree.
看看那棵樹的樹皮。

---

base [beɪs]

① *n.* 底部；底層

② *v.* 把…放在基礎上

▶ We camped at the base of the mountain.
我們在山底下露營。

▶ The movie is based on a popular novel.
這部電影是根據一本暢銷書改編而成。

---

baseball [ˈbeɪs.bɑːl] *n.* 棒球

▶ Dora loves playing baseball.
朵拉喜愛打棒球。

basement [ˈbeɪs.mənt] *n.* 地下室	▶ Your basement is damp and dark. 你的地下室又潮濕又黑暗。
basic [ˈbeɪ.sɪk] *adj.* 基礎的	▶ This is a basic English class. 這是一堂基礎英文課。
basics [ˈbeɪ.sɪks] *n.* 基礎；基本原理	▶ I now know the basics of grammar. 我現在知道文法的基本原則了。
101 **basis** [ˈbeɪ.sɪs] *n.* 基礎；根據	▶ This is the basis of the argument. 這就是這個論點的基礎。
basket [ˈbæs.kət] *n.* 籃子	▶ Put the oranges in the basket. 把橘子放進籃子裡。
basketball [ˈbæs.kət.bɑːl] *n.* 籃球	▶ Becky wants to play basketball. 貝琪想要打籃球。
bat [bæt] ① *n.* 球棒；球拍 ② *v.* 用球棒打球 ③ *n.* 蝙蝠	▶ He hit the ball with the bat. 他用那個球棒擊球。 ▶ I will bat next. 下一位該我打球。 ▶ Tanya is scared of the bat. 坦雅害怕蝙蝠。
bath [bæθ] *n.* 泡澡；洗澡	▶ I need a hot bath. 我需要泡一個熱水澡。
bathe [beɪð] *v.* 洗澡；沐浴	▶ Remember to bathe every day. 記得要每天洗澡。
bathroom [ˈbæθ.ruːm / ˈbæθ.rʊm] *n.* 浴室	▶ The bathroom is next to the kitchen. 這間浴室在廚房的隔壁。

battle [ˈbæt̬əl]

① *n.* 戰役

② *v.* 與…作戰

實用片語與搭配字

battle against 與…作戰

▶ The battle that won the war was fought in this town.
贏得這場戰爭的戰役是在這個鎮上打的。

▶ Both teams battled for the basketball.
兩隊都為籃球而戰。

▶ Many people today battle against cancer and other diseases caused by unhealthy lifestyles.
現今許多人都在對抗因不健康的生活習慣所導致的癌症和其他疾病。

Exercise 6

I. Choose and write the correct word. Change the form of the word when necessary.

1	bakery (n.) balcony (n.)	He stood on the __________ looking down into the courtyard.
2	barbecue (n.) barber (n.)	He went to the hair salon to have his favorite __________ cut his hair.
3	barbecue (v.) bank (v.)	If the weather is fine, we'll __________ at the ranch.
4	basis (n.) bath (n.)	We're going to be meeting there on a regular __________.
5	bark (v.) bar (v.)	Our dog __________ a lot; but he's just being friendly. He would never actually bite anyone.

II. Multiple choices.

(　　) 1. Firefighters are __________ to save the town from the forest fire coming towards it.
(A) barbecuing　(B) barking　(C) battling　(D) bathing

(　　) 2. The panda's natural habitat is the __________ forest.
(A) balloon　(B) bamboo　(C) barbecue　(D) barber

(　　) 3. She used her family's history as a __________ for her novel.
(A) base　(B) bank　(C) banana　(D) ball

(　　) 4. On hot days, we sometimes __________ or shower twice a day.
(A) bat　(B) base　(C) bar　(D) bathe

(　　) 5. We consult an senior __________ about our money.
(A) banker　(B) barber　(C) balloon　(D) bathroom

be [biː / bi / bɪ] *v.* 是

▶ The little boy wants to be a doctor.
這個小男孩將來想要當醫生。

beach [biːtʃ]

① *n.* 海灘；沙灘

② *v.* 將（船等）拖上岸

▶ I love sitting on the beach.
我喜愛坐在海灘上。

▶ If the boat has a hole, you can beach it.
如果這艘船有個洞，你可以將船拖上岸。

bead [biːd]

① *n.*（有孔）珠子

② *v.* 用珠裝飾

▶ I want to save that bead for a necklace I am making.
我想要保留那顆珠珠給我正在做的一條項鍊。

▶ I beaded her dress in a lovely pattern.
我用珠子以漂亮的花樣裝飾她的洋裝。

bean [biːn] *n.* 豆子

▶ The bean was planted in the garden.
這顆豆子被種在園子裡。

bear [ber]

① *n.* 熊

② *v.* 承擔；忍受

實用片語與搭配字

bear in mind 記住

▶ Ann has a toy bear.
安有隻玩具熊。

▶ Please bear with me on this explanation.
請容忍我對此所做的解釋。

▶ If you go to Europe during the holidays, bear in mind that the weather over there is much cooler, so bring something warm with you.
如果你去歐洲度假，記住那裡的天氣冷多了，所以要帶點保暖的衣物。

beard [bɪrd] *n.* （下巴上的）鬍鬚；山羊鬍

▶ Your beard is very long.
你的鬍鬚很長。

beat [biːt]

① *v.*（接連地）打；擊

實用片語與搭配字

beat up; beat around the bush
打擊；說話拐彎抹角

▶ Dora likes to beat the drum.
朵拉喜歡打鼓。

▶ My father is a very direct man and does not beat around the bush when he wants to say something.
我爸是個很直接的人，他說話不拐彎抹角。

② *n.* （音樂的）節拍；拍子

▶ You can feel the beat of the music.
你可以感受到音樂的節拍。

beautiful [ˈbjuː.t̬ə.fəl] *adj.* 美麗的

▶ That is a beautiful flower.
那是一朵美麗的花。

beauty [ˈbjuː.t̬i] *n.* 美好的事物；美景；美人

▶ There is a lot of beauty in the park.
在公園裡有很多美好的事物。

實用片語與搭配字

natural beauty 自然景觀

▶ Yellowstone Park has much natual beauty.
黃石公園有許多自然景觀。

because [bɪˈkɑːz] *conj.* 因為

▶ I'm happy because it is sunny.
因為天氣晴朗，我很開心。

become [bɪˈkʌm] *v.* 成為

▶ He'll become a good runner if he practices.
如果他練習的話，他會成為一個很棒的跑者。

bed [bed] *n.* 床

▶ Please put the clothes on the bed.
請把衣服放在床上。

bedroom [ˈbed.ruːm / ˈbed.rʊm] *n.* 臥室

▶ I love an organized bedroom.
我喜歡整潔的臥室。

bee [biː] *n.* 蜜蜂

▶ That bee is trying to sting me!
這隻蜂蜜一直要叮我！

beef [biːf] *n.* 牛肉

▶ The farmer is taking his beef to sell at the market next week.
農夫下週會將他的牛肉帶去市場銷售。

beep [biːp]

① *n.* 嗶嗶聲

② *v.* 發嗶嗶聲

▶ There is a beep coming from your phone.
你的手機發出嗶嗶聲。

▶ Please do not beep your horn, it is bothering all the other drivers.
請不要鳴喇叭，這會打擾到所有其他的駕駛。

beer [bɪr] *n.* 啤酒

▸ The beer has been kept cold.
這啤酒已經冷藏了。

beetle [ˈbiː.t̬əl] *n.* 甲蟲

▸ I am very scared of beetles.
我非常怕甲蟲。

before [bɪˈfɔːr]

① *conj.* 在…之前

實用片語與搭配字

before long 不久

② *prep.* 在…前面（到某事之前）

③ *adv.* 以前；在前

▸ I want to see you before you go home.
我想在你回家之前跟你見個面。

▸ Many students hate school life, but before long it will be over and they have to take responsibility for their own lives.
許多學生不喜歡校園生活，但這不久就會結束，他們也必須為他們的人生負起責任。

▸ That happened before school started.
那件事發生在開學以前。

▸ She called me before the movie.
她在電影開始前打電話給我。

beg [beg] *v.* 乞討；請求

▸ I always beg my father for help with my homework.
我總是懇求父親協助我的作業。

begin [bɪˈgɪn] *v.* 開始

實用片語與搭配字

begin with 開始

▸ Duncan will begin his final project soon.
鄧肯快要開始他最後一個研究。

▸ To tell you the story of my life, let me begin with the place where I was born.
我的人生故事，要從我出生的地方開始講起。

beginner [bɪˈgɪn.ɚ] *n.* 初學者

▸ She is a beginner in that particular sport.
她在那個特定運動項目上是個初學者。

beginning [bɪˈgɪn.ɪŋ] *n.* 開始；起點

實用片語與搭配字

mark the beginning of sth 開始某件事

▸ She started from the beginning of the story.
她從故事的一開頭說起。

▸ The discovery of gold in America marks the beginning of many big cities.
在美國，黃金的發現是許多大城市的開端。

behind [bɪˈhaɪnd]

① *prep.* 在（…的）後面

實用片語與搭配字

leave behind 留下

② *adv.* 落後；在背後

► The table is behind her.
那張桌子在她背後。

► My mom told me that to be successful in the future you cannot leave behind your past.
我媽媽告訴我未來要成功，就不能遺忘過去。

► We swam behind the other people.
我們游泳落後於其他人。

belief [bɪˈliːf] *n.* 相信；信念；信仰

► My belief in this judge has always been strong.
我對這位法官一直都很有信心。

Exercise 7

I. Choose and write the correct word. Change the form of the word when necessary.

1	bead (n.) beard (n.)	He has decided to grow a ________ and a mustache.
2	beat (v.) bear (v.)	She was afraid she wouldn't be able to ________ the pain.
3	beetle (n.) beep (n.)	He saw a shiny green ________ on the leaf.
4	behind (prep.) before (conj.)	Don't try to walk ________ you can crawl.
5	beer (n.) beef (n.)	What's the best method of cooking ________?

II. Multiple choices.

(   ) 1. It is my ________ that we'll find a cure for cancer for cancer in the next ten years.
(A) beginning (B) beep (C) belief (D) beauty

(   ) 2. ________ the eggs before you add the sugar.
(A) Bear (B) Beat (C) Bead (D) Become

(   ) 3. As a ________, everything is very new to him.
(A) beginner (B) beauty (C) beetle (D) belief

(   ) 4. She went to her neighbor to ________ for some milk to feed her baby.
(A) begin (B) become (C) beep (D) beg

(   ) 5. We never know the love of the parents until we ________ parents ourselves.
(A) beat (B) bead (C) become (D) bear

Unit 8

believable [bɪˈliː.və.bəl] *adj.* 可相信的

▶ The speaker is very believable.
這位演講者可信度很高。

believe [bɪˈliːv] *v.* 相信

實用片語與搭配字

believe in 相信

▶ They believe they are right.
他們相信他們是對的。

▶ You should believe in yourself then you can achieve anything you want to.
你應該要相信自己，便能達到任何你想要的。

bell [bel] *n.* 鈴；鐘

▶ The bell is ringing. I need to go.
鈴聲響起，我必須走了。

belong [bɪˈlɑːŋ] *v.* 屬於

實用片語與搭配字

belong with 屬於

▶ The umbrella belongs to Jane.
這把傘是珍的。

▶ The white sock doesn't belong with the black sock.
這支白色的襪子並不屬於那支黑色的襪子。

below [bɪˈloʊ]

① *prep.* 在…之下

② *adv.* 在下面

▶ The book is below the cupboard.
那本書在碗櫃下。

▶ I sit below the tree.
我坐在樹下。

belt [belt]

① *n.* 腰帶

實用片語與搭配字

under sb's belt 達到的，已獲得的

② *v.* 用帶子束緊

▶ I bought a new leather belt while on vacation.
我在度假時買了一條新皮帶。

▶ Matt just finished climbing another mountain; that is the fourth one under his belt.
麥特剛爬完另一座山，這是他爬的第四座山。

▶ You need to belt your pants before they fall off.
你需要在褲子掉下來以前用皮帶繫緊。

bench [bentʃ] *n.* 長凳

▶ I would appreciate a long bench in front of this store.
如果這個店門口能有張長凳可坐，我會很感謝。

102

bend [bend]

① *v.* 使彎曲

實用片語與搭配字

bend over backwards 竭力，盡力

② *n.* 彎；曲

▶ The road bends to the right just before you get to my house.
在你快到我家前，路會彎向右邊。

▶ Ken is a nice person and will be bend over backwards to help you.
肯是個很好的人，他會竭盡所能幫你。

▶ There is a bend in the road up ahead, so drive carefully.
前面的路會有一個彎道，所以要小心駕駛。

103

beside [bɪˈsaɪd] *prep.* 在旁邊

▶ She is sitting beside Chris.
她正坐在克里斯旁邊。

besides [bɪˈsaɪdz]

① *prep.* 除…之外還有；而且

② *adv.* 除…之外還有；而且

▶ He was given a trophy besides the gold medal.
除了這個金牌，他還得了一個獎盃。

▶ I heard the water, the birds, and something else besides.
我聽到了水聲、鳥聲，還有其他的聲音。

best [best]

① *adj.* 最好的

② *adv.* 最好的

③ *n.* 最好的人（或事物）

④ *v.* 擊敗；戰勝

▶ This is the best book I have ever read.
這是我讀過最好的一本書。

▶ The best reader is John.
約翰是最好的讀者。

▶ That car is the best.
這台車是最棒的車。

▶ I'll best you in the next race.
我會在下次的賽跑中贏過你。

bet [bet]

① *v.* 以（錢、物）打賭

實用片語與搭配字

bet on 對…下注

② *n.* 打賭；賭注

▶ I bet that Mary would win the race.
我打賭瑪莉會贏得這場賽跑。

▶ I am surely going to win this spelling competition because I have been practicing for months; you can bet on it.
我肯定會贏得這場拼字比賽，因為我已經練習好幾個月了，你可以相信我。

▶ I put a bet on Mary to win the race.
我把賭注押在瑪莉會贏得這場賽跑。

實用片語與搭配字

make a bet; take a bet 打賭

▶ All the students want to make a bet that their class will win the first place in the basketball contest.
所有學生都想要賭他們班會在籃球比賽得第一名。

better [ˈbetə]

① *adj.* 較佳的
② *adv.* 更好地
③ *n.* 較令人滿意的工作；更好的待遇；較好者
④ *v.* 改善；改進

▶ This picture is better than my last one.
這張照片比我上次那張更好。

▶ James dances better than Mia.
詹姆士跳舞跳得比米雅好。

▶ This work is better.
這個工作比較好。

▶ Wait and see. I'll better my situation!
等著瞧，我將會改善我的處境的！

between [bɪˈtwin]

① *prep.* 在…之間
② *adv.* 在（兩個或兩個以上的人或事）之間

▶ The car is between the house and the fence.
這輛車位於房子與籬笆之間。

▶ I used the library between classes.
我用課堂之餘去了圖書館。

beyond [biˈjɑ:nd]

① *prep.* 在…那一邊；越過
② *adv.* 非…所能及；令…無法理解

▶ It is just beyond the traffic circle.
它就在圓環的另一邊。

▶ That is beyond my ability.
那不是我的能力所能及的。

bicycle / bike [ˈbaɪ.sə.kəl / baɪk] *n.* 腳踏車

▶ You can use my bicycle.
你可以用我的腳踏車。

big [bɪg] *adj.* 大的

▶ That is a big dog.
那隻狗很大。

bill [bɪl]

① *n.* 帳單

▶ This is the bill from all we spent on our trip.
這張帳單是我們旅途中所有的花費。

實用片語與搭配字

pay bill 付帳

▶ Tim always pays the bill when he and his girlfriend go out to eat.
提姆和他的女友出去吃飯的時候，都是他付帳。

② *v.* 給…開帳單

▶ Please bill my father for the flowers.
請將這些花的帳單開給我爸爸。

bind [baɪnd] *v.* 把…裝訂成冊；綑紮

實用片語與搭配字

bind together 綁在一起

▶ Jason will bind his articles into a book.
傑森將會把他的文章匯集成一本書。

▶ Bind the papers together, or you will lose some.
把這疊紙綁在一起，否則你會搞丟一些。

---

bird [bɝːd] *n.* 鳥

▶ There is a bird outside my window.
我的窗外有一隻鳥。

95

birth [bɝːθ] *n.* 出生

實用片語與搭配字

give birth to 生孩子，分娩

▶ The baby's birth was very exciting.
這個嬰孩的出生很令人興奮。

▶ Amy will give birth to twins soon and she is very excited.
艾美很快就會生下雙胞胎，她對此感到很興奮。

---

birthday [ˈbɝːθ.deɪ] *n.* 生日

▶ My birthday is October 11.
我的生日是十月十一日。

---

bit [bɪt] *n.* 少許；少量；小塊

▶ I need a bit of luck.
我需要一點點的運氣。

---

bite [baɪt]

① *v.* 咬

② *n.* 一口之量

▶ The snake tried to bite me.
這條蛇想要咬我。

▶ Ken took a bite of my pizza.
肯恩吃了一口我的比薩。

98

bitter [ˈbɪt̬.ɚ] *adj.* 苦的

實用片語與搭配字

bittersweet 苦中帶甜的

▶ That fruit is very bitter.
那水果味道非常苦。

▶ Emily's last day at the company was bittersweet. She is excited to start a new job, but sad to leave her friends.
艾蜜莉在公司的最後一天是苦中帶甜的，她期待新工作的開始，但也對於要離開朋友而感到悲傷。

Exercise 8

I. Choose and write the correct word. Change the form of the word when necessary.

1	believable (adj.) bitter (adj.)	We'll be able to judge which candidate is more __________ after listening to their speeches.
2	belt (n.) bench (n.)	She chose a __________ beside the pond and then sat down.
3	bind (v.) bend (v.)	Superman is able to __________ a steel bar in half with his bare hands.
4	between (adv.) beyond (adv.)	This problem is __________ my understanding; would you explain it to me again?
5	bill (n.) birth (n.)	Our average electricity __________ might go up $500 - $1000 per month during summer.

II. Multiple choices.

(   ) 1. There's nothing which has not been __________ before being ripe.
(A) bitter (B) better (C) best (D) big

(   ) 2. I think she has many good qualities __________ being very beautiful.
(A) between (B) below (C) besides (D) bet

(   ) 3. Does anyone know who this cell phone __________ to? It was left in the classroom.
(A) bends (B) belongs (C) bets (D) binds

(   ) 4. You cannot __________ a couple together and make them husband and wife.
(A) bend (B) bite (C) bill (D) bind

(   ) 5. You've worked for 15 hours without a break; I __________ you're very tired.
(A) bend (B) bet (C) beg (D) belong

Unit 9

black [blæk]

① *adj.* 黑的

② *n.* 黑色

▶ The phone is black.
這支手機是黑色的。

▶ Diane doesn't like black. She likes bright colors.
黛安不喜歡黑色，她喜歡明亮的顏色。

---

blackboard [ˈblæk.bɔːrd] *n.* 黑板

▶ Please write your sentences on the blackboard.
請把你的這些句子寫在黑板上。

---

blank [blæŋk]

① *adj.* 空白的

② *n.* 空白

▶ I need to hang some pictures on these blank walls.
我需要掛一些畫在這些空白的牆上。

▶ You must fill in the blanks.
你必須要填寫這些空格。

---

blind [blaɪnd]

① *adj.* 眼盲的

實用片語與搭配字

blind eye 視而不見

② *v.* 使變瞎；使失明

▶ The elderly woman has become blind.
這位老婦人眼睛已經瞎了。

▶ Many people turn a blind eye to the terrible things happening in the world today because they do not want to know.
許多人都對現今世界上發生的壞事視而不見，因為他們並不想要知道。

▶ He was blinded while playing baseball.
他在打棒球時被弄瞎了眼睛。

block [blɑːk]

① *n.* 在轉彎的路口；街區

實用片語與搭配字

building block 基礎

② *v.* 堵塞；阻擋

▶ You can stand on that block.
你可以站在那個街口。

▶ A good education is the most important building block of a person's life.
良好的教育是成就一個人最重要的基礎。

▶ Your car is blocking the road.
你的車堵住了路。

實用片語與搭配字

block out
擋住（光線或噪音）；不去想（不愉快的往事）

► After being lost in the desert for a week, Janet just wanted to block out the bad experience and not think about it again.
珍妮特在沙漠中迷路一週後，她只想要阻隔不好的回憶，不想再回想起那些事。

---

blood [blʌd] *n.* 血

► There is blood on the tissue.
這張衛生紙上有血。

---

bloody [ˈblʌd.i] *adj.* 流血的；血腥的

► John ran water over his bloody hand before he put medicine on it.
約翰在擦藥以前先用水沖他流血的手。

---

blow [bloʊ]

① *v.* 吹；吹動

實用片語與搭配字

blow up 勃然大怒

② *n.* 強風；暴風

► The wind blew hard.
這風吹得很大。

► My boss gets angry quickly and he can blow up at you over the smallest mistake.
我的老闆很容易發火，他會因為很小的錯誤而對你發脾氣。

► The tree fell down during the blow.
這棵樹在強風吹襲時倒了。

---

blue [bluː]

① *adj.* 藍色的

② *n.* 藍色

► The door is blue.
這扇門是藍色的。

► Luke's favorite color is blue.
路克最愛的顏色是藍色。

---

board [bɔːrd]

① *n.* 木板

② *v.* 用木板封閉（門窗）

► The board needs to be cut shorter.
這塊木板需要裁短一些。

► I need to board up that basement window.
我需要用木板把地下室那片窗戶給封住。

---

boat [boʊt] *n.* 小船

► There is a boat on the river.
這條河上有艘船。

95

body [ˈbɑː.di] *n.* 身體

► You should take care of your body.
你應該照顧好你的身體。

boil [bɔɪl]

① *v.* 煮沸

實用片語與搭配字

boil down to 歸結為

② *n.* 沸騰

▶ Boil the water in the pot.
用這個壺煮開水。

▶ The company's problems boil down to one thing - lack of money.
公司的問題總歸於一件事情：資金的缺乏。

▶ Mary brought the water to a boil.
瑪麗把水燒開了。

---

bomb [bɑːm]

① *n.* 炸彈

② *v.* 轟炸

▶ The bomb was placed in the basement of the apartment.
炸彈被放在這棟公寓的地下室裡。

▶ London was bombed many times during World War II.
第二次世界大戰中，倫敦多次被轟炸。

---

bone [boʊn] *n.* 骨頭

▶ Ken broke a bone in his leg.
肯恩的腿斷了一根骨頭。

---

bony [ˈboʊ.ni] *adj.* 骨頭的；多骨的

▶ Rosa doesn't like to eat bony fish.
羅莎不喜歡吃多刺的魚。

---

book [bʊk]

① *n.* 書

② *v.* 預訂；預約

實用片語與搭配字

book for 預訂

▶ I found a book to read.
我找到一本書讀。

▶ I booked a ticket to France.
我訂了一張票去法國。

▶ Sunday is my mother's birthday and I will book a table for our whole family at her favorite restaurant.
星期天是我媽媽的生日，我會在她最喜歡的餐廳為全家人訂位。

---

bookcase [ˈbʊk.keɪs] *n.* 書櫃

▶ I need to buy an attractive bookcase.
我需要買一個好看的書櫃。

98

bored [bɔːrd] *adj.* 感到無聊的；厭煩的

實用片語與搭配字

be bored with sb 感到無聊

▶ My bored brother sat for a long time.
我那覺得無聊的哥哥坐著很久了。

▶ The audience was so bored with the speaker that many of them left the room.
觀眾覺得講者太無趣，所以許多人都離席了。

boring [ˈbɔː.rɪŋ] *adj.* 令人厭煩的；乏味的

- I do not want to watch another boring movie!
  我不想再看另一部無聊乏味的電影！

---

born [bɔːrn] *adj.* 天生的；命中註定的

- Eddy was born to run.
  艾迪天生是跑步高手。

---

borrow [ˈbɑːr.oʊ] *v.* 借（入）

- Could I please borrow your dictionary?
  我可以借你的字典嗎？

實用片語與搭配字

borrow from 借

- Many languages borrow from each other and that is why some words sound familiar in another language.
  許多語言會向其他語言互相借字，這就是為什麼不同的語言仍有許多字聽起來相近的原因。

---

both [boʊθ]

① *adj.* 兩個…（都）

- Both guests arrived at our house.
  這兩位客人都已經抵達我家。

② *pron.* 兩者（都）

- We are both students.
  我們兩人都是學生。

---

bottom [ˈbɑː.t̬əm]

① *n.* 底部；底層

- The ball is at the bottom of the hill.
  這顆球掉在山丘底下。

實用片語與搭配字

rock bottom 最低點

- Mark hit rock bottom after he was laid-off, but he never gave up and now has his own successful business.
  馬克被裁員後就處於低潮，但他從不放棄，現在他擁有成功的事業。

② *adj.* 最低的；最後的，最下的

- The dictionary is on the bottom level of the bookshelf.
  那本字典在書架的最底層。

實用片語與搭配字

bottom line 底線

- Many large companies today do not really care about their employees because their bottom line is profit.
  現在許多公司都不在乎他們的員工，因為他們的底線是利潤。

③ *v.* 到達底部；降至最低點（+out）

- The boat bottomed on the big rock.
  這艘船的底部撞到了那塊大岩石。

---

bowl [boʊl] *n.* 碗；缽

- I put some soup in the bowl.
  我盛了一些湯在碗裡。

實用片語與搭配字

a bowl of sth 一碗…

- In winter, I usually eat a bowl of soup with a slice of toast for dinner.
  冬天的時候，我通常喝一碗湯配一片吐司當晚餐。

Exercise 9

I. Choose and write the correct word. Change the form of the word when necessary.

<table>
<tr><td rowspan="2">1</td><td>bookcase (n.)</td><td rowspan="2">He stood at the __________ of the stairs and called up to me.</td></tr>
<tr><td>bottom (n.)</td></tr>
<tr><td rowspan="2">2</td><td>boring (adj.)</td><td rowspan="2">I stared in horror at his __________ mouth.</td></tr>
<tr><td>bloody (adj.)</td></tr>
<tr><td rowspan="2">3</td><td>block (v.)</td><td rowspan="2">He put his hands over his ears to __________ out the noise.</td></tr>
<tr><td>blow (v.)</td></tr>
<tr><td rowspan="2">4</td><td>blank (adj.)</td><td rowspan="2">A __________ man cannot judge colors.</td></tr>
<tr><td>blind (adj.)</td></tr>
<tr><td rowspan="2">5</td><td>bomb (n.)</td><td rowspan="2">Several people were injured in a __________ explosion.</td></tr>
<tr><td>block (n.)</td></tr>
</table>

II. Multiple choices.

( ) 1. The __________ can easily be assembled with a screwdriver.
(A) bone (B) bomb (C) bookcase (D) blood

( ) 2. He turned to a __________ page in his notebook, and began to write.
(A) blind (B) block (C) bloody (D) blank

( ) 3. After the volcano erupted, __________ lava poured down the side of the mountain.
(A) boiling (B) boring (C) bloody (D) bony

( ) 4. I don't want to __________ money from the bank to buy a car; I'd rather pay for it in cash.
(A) boil (B) bomb (C) borrow (D) blow

( ) 5. This job is so __________; I wish I could do something more creative.
(A) bottom (B) boring (C) blue (D) bored

Unit 10

box [bɑːks]

① *n.* 盒子；箱子

② *v.* 把…裝箱；把…置於容器內

▶ My shoes are in a box.
我的鞋子在盒子裡。

▶ I boxed up my old books.
我把我的舊書裝箱。

---

boy [bɔɪ] *n.* 男孩

▶ Carl and Sandy have a baby boy.
卡爾跟珊蒂有一個男嬰。

---

boyfriend [ˈbɔɪ.frend] *n.* 男朋友

▶ Her boyfriend is a respectful person.
她的男朋友是一個有禮貌的人。

brave [breɪv] *adj.* 勇敢的

▶ Peter is very brave.
彼得非常勇敢。

---

bread [bred] *n.* 麵包

▶ The bread is delicious.
這塊麵包非常美味。

break [breɪk]

① *v.* 打破；損壞

實用片語與搭配字

make or break；break off
不成則敗的；分開，絕交，終止

② *n.* 裂縫；破損

▶ He's going to break the window.
他要打破這扇窗。

▶ Meg's boyfriend cheated on her and she decided to break off their relationship of 10 years.
梅格的男朋友劈腿了，她決定要結束這十年的戀情。

▶ The break in the door is big.
門上的這條裂縫很大。

---

breakfast [ˈbrek.fəst]

① *n.* 早餐

實用片語與搭配字

bed and breakfast
（私人住宅或小型飯店提供的）住宿和早餐

② *v.* 吃早餐

▶ This breakfast is delicious.
這頓早餐很好吃。

▶ Travelers today do not like to stay in hotels, but prefer the more personal bed and breakfast guesthouses.
現今的遊客並不喜歡住在飯店，他們傾向去只提供床和早餐的小型旅店。

▶ I'm going to breakfast with my family.
我要跟我家人吃早餐。

bridge [brɪdʒ]

① *n.* 橋

② *v.* 在…上架橋

▶ He is standing on the bridge.
他正站在橋上。

▶ We're trying to bridge the river.
我們試著要架橋於這條河上。

---

bright [braɪt] *adj.* 光亮的；明亮的

▶ That is a bright light.
那道光很亮。

---

brightly [ˈbraɪt·li] *adv.* 明亮地

▶ The light shone brightly.
這道光明亮地閃耀著。

---

bring [brɪŋ] *v.* 攜帶

實用片語與搭配字

bring about; bring up; bring back
引起，導致；提起；帶回

▶ I will bring a salad.
我會帶沙拉來。

▶ One day when I have children, I will bring them up to respect all life on earth.
當我有孩子時，我會要他們尊重地球上的萬物。

---

brother [ˈbrʌð.ɚ] *n.* 兄或弟

▶ My brother's name is Willy.
我哥哥的名字是威利。

---

brown [braʊn]

① *adj.* 褐色的

② *n.* 褐色

③ *v.* （把食物）炒成褐色

▶ The brown house is nice.
這棟褐色的房子很棒。

▶ I don't like red, but I do like brown.
我不喜歡紅色，但我很喜歡棕色。

▶ Carla is browning the bread by the fire.
卡兒拉正在火爐旁把麵包烤成焦黃色。

---

bug [bʌg]

① *n.* 昆蟲；小蟲子

② *v.* 煩擾；使…擔心

▶ I saw a big bug.
我看到一隻大蟲。

▶ Don't bug your brother!
不要煩你的哥哥！

---

build [bɪld] *v.* 建造

實用片語與搭配字

build on; build up 以…為基礎；增強

▶ They want to build a house.
他們想蓋一間房子。

▶ It is not easy to build up a company from scratch, but you can do it if you believe in yourself.
要從頭開始創建一家公司並不容易，但只要相信自己，就一定可以辦到。

building [ˈbɪl.dɪŋ] *n.* 房屋；建築物

▶ That building looks beautiful.
那棟建築物看起來很美麗。

---

bus [bʌs]

① *n.* 公車

實用片語與搭配字
take a / the bus; bus stop
搭公車；公車站

② *v.* 用公車(校車)運送

▶ George is on the bus.
喬治在公車上。

▶ I take the bus to work every day because I can read my book and not worry about the traffic.
我每天搭公車上班，因為這樣可以看書，而且不用煩惱交通。

▶ We bus our children to school.
我們讓小孩子坐校車去上學。

---

businessman [ˈbɪz.nɪs.mən] *n.* 商人

▶ That businessman is very busy with his work.
那位商人非常忙於他的工作。

---

busy [ˈbɪz.i]

① *adj.* 忙碌的

實用片語與搭配字
be busy with; keep sb busy
因…而忙碌；讓…忙碌

② *v.* 使忙於…

▶ I had a busy day.
我今天很忙。

▶ Henry was so busy with his new job that he hardly had time for his friends anymore.
亨利忙於新的工作，所以他很難安排時間和他的朋友見面。

▶ You can busy yourself with paperwork.
你可以先處理文書資料。

---

but [bʌt / bət]

① *conj.* 但是

② *prep.* 除…以外

③ *adv.* 只；僅僅

▶ I like movies, but I don't like cartoons.
我喜歡看電影，但是我不喜歡看卡通。

▶ No one knew about the meeting but me.
除了我以外，沒有人知道這個會議。

▶ It will hurt for but a second.
那只會痛一下下。

---

butter [ˈbʌt̬.ɚ]

① *n.* 奶油；牛油

② *v.* 塗奶油於…

▶ I love butter on my toast.
我喜歡我吐司上的奶油。

▶ Wait. I need to butter my toast.
等等，我需要塗奶油在我的吐司上。

實用片語與搭配字
butter sb up 奉承（某人）

▶ Sarah wanted to ask her mother to go to the summer camp, but she tried to butter her up first with flowers and candy.
莎拉想要媽媽同意讓她去夏令營，所以她先買了花和糖果討好她。

---

butterfly [ˈbʌt̬.ɚ.flaɪ] *n.* 蝴蝶

▶ There is a butterfly on the table.
有一隻蝴蝶在桌上。

---

buy [baɪ]

① *v.* 買

▶ Ann wants to buy a picture.
安想要買一張畫。

實用片語與搭配字
buy sth from 向…買東西

▶ You can buy something from the online store, but be careful when you use your credit card.
你可以在網路商店買東西，但使用信用卡時要小心。

② *n.* 購買

▶ That picture was a great buy.
那張畫很值得買。

---

by [baɪ]

① *prep.* 在…旁邊，在…附近

▶ The window is by the door.
這扇窗在這扇門旁邊。

② *adv.* 經過

▶ I'll drop by the store on my way home.
我回家的路上會經過那家店。

---

cage [keɪdʒ]

① *n.* 籠子

▶ There is a cage in the truck.
卡車上有一只籠子。

② *v.* 把（鳥或動物）關進籠子裡

▶ Help me cage this cat before it runs away.
趁這隻貓跑走前，幫我把牠關進籠子裡。

Exercise 10

I. Choose and write the correct word. Change the form of the word when necessary.

1	bright (adj.) brightly (adv.)	The sun shines __________ on the swimmers at the beach.
2	break (n.) bridge (n.)	The island is joined to the mainland by a __________.
3	bread (n.) bridge (n.)	I had three pieces of __________ for breakfast this morning.
4	bright (adj.) busy (adj.)	Sandy is a very __________ teenager; she leaves for school at 7 in the morning and arrives home at 9 at night.
5	butterfly (n.) butter (n.)	She had only a slice of bread and __________ for breakfast.

II. Multiple choices.

( ) 1. When I was little, my dad was my hero because he seemed so big and strong and __________.
(A) bright (B) brown (C) busy (D) brave

( ) 2. They're __________ a new school in the village.
(A) building (B) bugging (C) breaking (D) caging

( ) 3. We have to __________ into the house as we've lost the key.
(A) build (B) break (C) bring (D) bridge

( ) 4. In the zoo we saw many monkeys running around the __________.
(A) bug (B) building (C) cage (D) bread

( ) 5. The rich __________ gave his whole fortune to the hospital.
(A) building (B) cage (C) businessman (D) butterfly

cake [keɪk] *n.* 蛋糕

► We should buy a birthday cake.
我們應該買個生日蛋糕。

---

call [kɑ:l]

① *v.* （給…）打電話

實用片語與搭配字

call for; call in
需要，(去某地)接(某人); 叫…進來

② *n.* 一通電話

實用片語與搭配字

make call 打電話

► I'll call Ken.
我會打電話給肯恩。

► During the meeting the manager called for ideas on how to promote the new product.
在會議當中，經理需要行銷新產品的點子。

► I got a call from Ken.
我接到肯恩打來的電話。

► I excused myself from the meeting to make a call to my husband to cancel our dinner date.
我為了打電話給我丈夫取消晚餐約會而離開會議。

---

camel [ˈkæm.əl] *n.* 駱駝

► The camel is sleeping under the tree.
這隻駱駝在樹底下睡覺。

102

camera [ˈkæm.rə] *n.* 照相機

► I took a picture with my camera.
我用我的照相機照了張照片。

104

camp [kæmp]

① *n.* 營地

實用片語與搭配字

concentration camp 集中營

② *v.* 露營；紮營

實用片語與搭配字

camp out 露營

► Duncan is still at the camp by the lake.
鄧肯還在湖邊的營地。

► During World War II, many people died in Nazi concentration camps.
二次大戰時，許多人死於納粹集中營。

► I'll camp at the lake this weekend.
我這週末會在湖邊露營。

► As children we loved to camp out with Dad, but these days it is not safe anymore.
小時候我們很喜歡和父親一起去露營，但現在已經不再那麼安全了。

can [kæn / kən]

① *aux. v.* 能夠；可以

② *n.* （食物）罐頭

③ *v.* 把（食物、飲料）裝罐

▶ I can carry your bag.
我可以提你的袋子。

▶ I have a can of tomato.
我有一罐番茄。

▶ My mother will can these vegetables.
我媽媽會把這些蔬菜裝罐。

---

candy / sweet [ˈkæn.di / swiːt]

n. 糖果；甜食

▶ I bought a bag of candy. Would you like a sweet?
我買了一包糖果，你想吃一顆糖嗎？

---

cap [kæp]

① *n.* （有帽舌的）便帽；帽子

② *v.* 覆蓋於…；覆蓋某物的頂部

▶ Don't wear your cap in the house.
在房子裡不要戴帽子。

▶ I'll cap this bottle when I'm finished.
當我喝完我會把瓶子蓋起來。

---

car [kɑːr] *n.* 汽車

▶ He has a red car.
他有一輛紅色的車。

---

card [kɑːrd] *n.* 卡片

▶ This is a birthday card.
這是一張生日卡片。

---

care [ker]

① *n.* 擔心；煩惱；憂慮

實用片語與搭配字

take care; take care of 保重；照顧

② *v.* 關心；在乎

實用片語與搭配字

care for 照顧

▶ He is young. He has no cares.
他還年輕，沒有什麼煩惱。

▶ Traveling by yourself is a lot of fun, but you also have to take care of yourself.
一個人去旅行很有趣，但也必須把自己照顧好。

▶ Jane cares about the environment.
珍很關心環境。

▶ Parents will pay a lot of money for kindergartens to care for their children while they are at work.
父母願意花大把錢把小孩子送到幼稚園，只為了在上班時小孩子有人照顧。

---

careful [ˈker.fəl] *adj.* 小心的

▶ Please be careful. The steps are wet.
請小心，這個樓梯很濕。

實用片語與搭配字

be careful about; be careful with
當心

▶ Please be careful with those boxes; if anything breaks you have to pay for it.
請當心這些箱子，有任何東西破損的話，你必須賠償。

---

careless [ˈker.ləs] *adj.*
粗心的；疏忽的；漫不經心的

▶ You do not want to be a careless student!
你不會想當一個粗心大意的學生吧！

---

carry [ˈker.i] *v.* 搬；提；運送

▶ I can carry the big box.
我可以搬這個大箱子。

實用片語與搭配字

carry on; carry with 繼續進行；帶著

▶ Life is not always easy, but we have to carry on and find the good things in each day.
人生並不容易，但每天我們仍必須持續前進，去找尋美好的事物。

---

case [keɪs]

① *n.* 案子；病例；事件

▶ This is an interesting case.
這是一個有趣的案子。

② *n.* 盒子；箱

▶ The watch is in its case.
那隻錶在它的盒子裡。

實用片語與搭配字

in case 以防萬一

▶ In case you cannot remember what your homework is, I have sent you an email to remind you.
以防你忘了回家作業有哪些，我已經寄了一封電子郵件提醒你了。

③ *v.* 把…裝箱

▶ I'll case up the art and return it.
我會把這件藝術品裝箱並歸還。

---

cat [kæt] *n.* 貓

▶ That is a cute cat.
那是一隻很可愛的貓。

---

catch [kætʃ]

① *v.* 抓住；接住

▶ Chris can catch the dog later.
克里斯稍後會抓住這隻狗。

實用片語與搭配字

catch sb's eye; catch up with
引起（某人）的注意；趕上（某人或某事）

▶ I am looking forward to our school reunion to catch up with my classmates I have not seen in years.
我期待著我們的返校日，好與許多不見的同學敘舊。

② *n.* 接球；抓住

▶ That was a great catch. You're good at baseball.
那球接得好，你很會打棒球。

cause [kɑːz]

① *n.* 原因

實用片語與搭配字

cause and effect 有因果關係的

② *v.* 使（不好的事情）發生；導致；造成

實用片語與搭配字

be caused by; cause sb to
因（不好的事）而受影響；使（某人）因（不好的事）造成影響

▶ What was the cause of the fire?
這場火災的原因是什麼？

▶ One's actions always have results and this cause and effect might affect our future.
一個行為總會伴隨後果，而這可能會影響到我們的未來。

▶ Willy caused the accident.
威利讓這場意外發生。

▶ The tsunami was caused by the earthquake.
這海嘯是地震造成的。

---

cent [sent] *n.* 一分（硬幣）

▶ That costs 99 cents.
那要花九十九分錢。

---

center [ˈsen.t̬ɚ]

① *n.* 中央；中心

② *v.* 將…放在中央，使置中

▶ Wayne stood in the center of the room.
韋恩站在這間房間的中央。

▶ Olivia centered her cup on the desk.
奧利維亞把她的杯子放在書桌的正中央。

certain [ˈsɝː.tən]

① *adj.* 某種（或一定）程度的

實用片語與搭配字

be certain of 對…有把握

② *pron.* 一些；某幾個

▶ I will save a certain amount of money each week.
我每個禮拜會固定存一些錢。

▶ Before you accuse someone of doing something wrong, you have to be certain of your facts.
在你指責某人做錯事之前，你必須確定這是事實。

▶ Certain of the cups were broken.
有幾個杯子被打破了。

---

chair [tʃer]

① *n.* 椅子

② *v.* 主持（會議等）

實用片語與搭配字

be chaired by 主持（會議等）

▶ I sat on the chair.
我坐在椅子上。

▶ Melody chaired the meeting.
美樂蒂主持這場會議。

▶ The meeting will be chaired by our president, so we know it's going to be important.
這會議將由主席主持，所以我們知道這將是重要的會議。

chance [tʃæns]

① *n.* 機會

實用片語與搭配字

give chance to; by chance
把機會給他人；偶然，碰巧

② *v.* 碰巧；偶然發生

▶ You might still have a chance.
你還是可以有機會的。

▶ Twenty years ago, I met my husband by chance after he crashed his car into mine.
二十年前，因為他的車擦撞了我的車，使我偶然遇見我的丈夫。

▶ Michael chanced to meet Nina at the party.
麥可碰巧在派對上見到了妮娜。

---

chart [tʃɑːrt]

① *n.* 圖表；示意圖

② *v.* 繪製…的圖表；標示

▶ I looked at the chart.
我看著這個圖表。

▶ Jeff will chart the river this summer.
傑夫這個夏天會繪製這條河的流向圖表。

---

chase [tʃeɪs]

① *v.* 追趕；追逐；追捕

實用片語與搭配字

chase after 追趕，追求，努力爭取

② *n.* 追捕；追趕；追逐

▶ Sandy chases the dog.
珊蒂追著這隻狗跑。

▶ It is better to be happy with what you have than to chase after the things you cannot have.
對自己擁有的東西感到快樂比追逐那些你不能擁有的事物更好。

▶ I saw the chase on TV.
我在電視上看見那個追捕畫面。

Exercise 11

I. Choose and write the correct word. Change the form of the word when necessary.

1	camp (v.) care (v.)	Don't spend time with someone who doesn't __________ about spending it with you.
2	center (n.) cause (n.)	The police are still trying to determine the __________ of the fire.
3	carry (v.) case (v.)	The box is too heavy to __________ down the slope; we'll have to drag it down.
4	chase (v.) cap (v.)	The top of the mountain is snow - __________ all year round.
5	chance (n.) chart (n.)	There's a __________ on the classroom wall showing the relative heights of all the students.

II. Multiple choices.

(　　) 1. This cup is very full, so be __________ with it.
(A) careless　(B) care　(C) careful　(D) carry

(　　) 2. The train is just drawing into the station; if we hurry, we can __________ it.
(A) catch　(B) check　(C) chase　(D) care

(　　) 3. She enjoyed the __________ to speak with someone who spoke her language.
(A) case　(B) chart　(C) chick　(D) chance

(　　) 4. Don't forget the __________ before you leave for the trip.
(A) cap　(B) chance　(C) camera　(D) case

(　　) 5. There were a __________ number of people at the meeting who didn't agree with the decision.
(A) certain　(B) careless　(C) careful　(D) chance

Unit 12

check [tʃek]

① *v.* 檢查；核對；查核

- I'm going to check the kitchen.
  我要去檢查廚房。

實用片語與搭配字

check out
辦理退房手續，退房離開，打量（某人）

- You have to check out of the hotel before 11 am.
  您必須在上午 11 點前退房。

② *n.* 檢查

- The check at the airport isn't too hard.
  那個機場的安檢不會太嚴。

---

chick [tʃɪk] *n.* 小雞

- The hen has three baby chicks.
  這隻母雞生了三隻小雞。

---

chicken [ˈtʃɪk.ɪn] *n.* 雞

- The chickens are enjoying the sunshine.
  這群雞正在享受陽光。

實用片語與搭配字

chicken out 臨陣退縮

- Jack went bungee jumping with his friends, but as soon as they tied the rope around his waist, he chickened out and could not do it.
  傑克和他的朋友一起去高空彈跳，但是當他們把繩子綁在他的腰上時，他卻臨陣退縮，不敢做了。

---

chief [tʃi:f]

① *adj.* 首要的；最重要的；最主要的

- Penny is the chief researcher.
  佩妮是首席研究者。

② *n.* 首領；領導人；頭目；酋長

- The chief is a good guy.
  這位首領是一個好人。

---

child [tʃaɪld] *n.* （一個）小孩

- They have a child.
  他們有一個小孩。

Christmas [ˈkrɪs.məs] *n.* 聖誕節

- Christmas is my favorite holiday.
  聖誕節是我最喜愛的節日。

---

church [tʃɝ:tʃ] *n.* 教堂

- Henry is going to church on Sunday.
  亨利星期天要去教堂。

---

city [ˈsɪt̬.i] *n.* 城市

- This is a small city.
  這是一個小城市。

class [klæs]

① *n.* 班級

② *v.* 把…歸類；把…分級

▶ Kim and I are in the same class.
金和我在同一班。

▶ Jimmy was classed as a good student.
吉姆被歸類為好學生。

classmate [ˈklæs.meɪt] *n.* 同班同學

▶ I walk to school with my classmate.
我和我的同學一起走路上學。

classroom [ˈklæs.ruːm / ˈklæs.rʊm] *n.* 教室

▶ Our class always decorates our classroom to show what we are learning.
我們班上總是會將我們學到的事物布置在教室裡。

clean [kliːn]

① *adj.* 乾淨的

② *v.* 把…弄乾淨

實用片語與搭配字

clean up; clean after
清理；打掃（某人）弄髒的地方，解決（某人）製造的問題

③ *adv.* 乾淨地

▶ That is a clean bedroom.
那是間乾淨的臥房。

▶ I can clean the living room.
我可以把客廳打掃乾淨。

▶ In our house, whoever cooks does not need to clean up after.
在我們家，做飯的人餐後不用打掃。

▶ Jason washed the floor clean.
傑森將地板洗得很乾淨。

clear [klɪr]

① *adj.* 純淨的；透明的；清澈的

實用片語與搭配字

make clear; crystal clear
把…弄清楚；清澈透明的，清楚明瞭的

② *v.* 清理；移走；清除；清掃；疏通

實用片語與搭配字

clear up （天氣）轉晴，清理

③ *adv.* 清晰地

▶ There is clear air up here.
這上面的空氣很清新。

▶ My father made it crystal clear to me that if I stayed out so late, he would not let me go out with my friends anymore.
我父親很清楚地告訴我，如果我再晚歸，他就不讓我和朋友出去了。

▶ I'll clear the table.
我會清理這張桌子。

▶ After raining for days, the sky finally cleared up and the sun appeared.
雨下了好幾天之後，天空終於放晴，太陽也露臉了。

▶ He's speaking loud and clear.
他說得很清楚也很大聲。

C

climb [klaɪm]

① *v.* 攀爬

實用片語與搭配字

climb up 攀升，攀登

② *n.* 攀登；爬升

▶ Tommy can climb the tree.
湯米可以爬這棵樹。

▶ In order for you to quickly climb up the corporate ladder, you need friends in high places.
為了迅速升遷到管理階層，你需要有身在管理核心的朋友。

▶ That was a hard climb.
那裡很難爬。

---

climbing [ˈklaɪ.mɪŋ] *n.* 攀岩；登山

▶ The climbing was a great work-out.
那次攀岩是很棒的健身方式。

---

clock [klɑːk] *n.* 時鐘

▶ You can see the time on the clock.
你可以在那時鐘上看時間。

---

close [kloʊs]

① *adj.* 近的；接近的

實用片語與搭配字

close with;
keep a close eye on sb / sth
親近（某人）; 密切關注（某人或某事）

② *adv.* 靠近地

▶ We are close to success.
我們離成功很接近了。

▶ If you bring your kids to the crowded park, make sure to keep a close eye on them.
如果你把孩子帶到人多擁擠的公園，一定要留心注意他們。

▶ Let's stay close to the house.
讓我們靠近這房子一點吧。

close [kloʊz] *v.* 關閉

實用片語與搭配字

close down 關閉，（使）倒閉，（使）停業

▶ Please close the door.
請關上門。

▶ The opening of a big department store next door forced the store to close down last month.
隔壁大型百貨的開張迫使那家店上個月停業了。

close [kloʊs / kloʊz] *n.* 結束

▶ The close of the meeting was quick.
這場會議結束得很快。

---

cloud [klaʊd]

① *n.* 雲

▶ I see the cloud in the sky.
我看見天空上的雲。

② *v.* （使）變得模糊；（使）變得黯然

實用片語與搭配字

cloud over 烏雲密佈；愁容滿面

▶ Evan clouded the window with his breathing.
伊凡在窗戶上呵氣讓玻璃變得霧濛濛模糊一片。

▶ James' face clouded over when he received a rejection letter from his top choice university.
當詹姆士收到他首選大學的不錄取通知書，他看起來愁容滿面。

---

coast [koʊst] *n.* 海岸

▶ Let's drive along the coast.
我們沿著海岸行駛吧。

---

coat [koʊt]

① *n.* 外套

② *v.* 給…塗上一層；使覆蓋上一層

▶ It's cold. Put on your coat.
天冷了，穿上你的外套。

▶ Eva coated the stairs with paint.
伊娃為這樓梯塗上一層油漆。

---

cocoa [ˈkoʊ.koʊ] *n.* 可可粉；可可飲料

▶ I'd like to drink some cocoa.
我想要喝一點熱可可。

---

coffee [ˈkɑː.fi] *n.* 咖啡

▶ This coffee is too hot to drink.
這杯咖啡太燙還不能喝。

---

cola / Coke [ˈkoʊ.lə / koʊk]

n. 可樂；碳酸類飲料 / 可口可樂

▶ Can I offer you a cola? It's Coke.
我可以請你喝一杯可樂嗎？是可口可樂喔。

---

cold [koʊld]

① *adj.* 冷的

② *n.* 寒冷；低溫

▶ This is a very cold day.
今天天氣非常冷。

▶ You can feel the cold through the window.
你可以透過這扇窗感受到外面的寒冷。

---

color [ˈkʌl.ɚ]

① *n.* 顏色

實用片語與搭配字

skin color 膚色

② *v.* 塗顏色於…

▶ What color is the door?
這扇門是什麼顏色？

▶ This make-up brand is good for people of all skin colors.
這家彩妝品牌適用於各種膚色的人。

▶ I'm going to color this picture.
我要將這張圖片塗上顏色。

Exercise 12

I. Choose and write the correct word. Change the form of the word when necessary.

1	chick (n.) check (n.)	Please __________ your answers with those in the back of the book.
2	church (n.) chief (n.)	A new __________ of this team has just been appointed.
3	clear (adj.) close (adj.)	The two countries have always maintained __________ relations.
4	clear (v.) close (v.)	They always __________ up their bedrooms before they go out.
5	coat (n.) coast (n.)	They live in a town along the east __________.

II. Multiple choices.

( ) 1. The children went into the __________ to greet their teacher.
(A) coast (B) classroom (C) classmate (D) coat

( ) 2. They began to __________ down the mountain when it was dark.
(A) clear (B) clean (C) close (D) climb

( ) 3. A good strong cup of __________ is what I need now.
(A) coffee (B) chance (C) coat (D) cloud

( ) 4. Make sure your hands are __________ before you have dinner.
(A) close (B) cold (C) chief (D) clean

( ) 5. Our family enjoy going to __________ and worshipping God.
(A) coast (B) church (C) classroom (D) city

Unit 13

come [kʌm] *v.* （向或跟隨說話人）來；過來

實用片語與搭配字

come up with; come along; come across; come from; first come, first serve

想出，提出（主意或計畫）；跟隨；表現得，讓人覺得；來自；先到先得

▶ I'll come home after school.

我放學後會回家。

▶ The beautiful painting is for sale, but it is first come, first serve, so I am going over there right now to buy it.

這幅漂亮的畫可出售，但它是先到先得，所以我現在就去買它。

95

common [ˈkɑː.mən] *adj.* 普通的；常見的

實用片語與搭配字

have in common; common sense

有共通之處；常識

▶ This is a very common food.

這是非常普通的食物。

▶ Tammy and her husband have a lot in common, they both like to watch movies, play sports, and cook.

譚美和她老公有很多共通之處，他們都喜歡看電影、運動及下廚。

98

continue [kənˈtɪn.juː] *v.* 繼續

實用片語與搭配字

continue until

繼續（直到因某人或某事而停止）

▶ Let's continue with our reading.

繼續看我們的書吧。

▶ This project will continue until the end of the year.

這個專案將持續到年底。

---

cook [kʊk]

① *v.* 烹調

實用片語與搭配字

cook for 為…下廚

② *n.* 廚師

▶ Jim wants to cook dinner tomorrow.

吉姆明天想要煮晚餐。

▶ If you want to be a chef in the army, you have to cook for thousands of soldiers every day.

如果你想當一名部隊伙房，你必須每天為數以千計的士兵做飯。

▶ Angel was the cook last night.

安琪是昨晚的廚師。

---

cookie [ˈkʊk.i] *n.* （甜）餅乾

▶ There is a cookie on the table.

這張桌子上有一塊餅乾。

---

cooking [ˈkʊk.ɪŋ] *n.* 烹飪

▶ We are eating my mother's cooking for dinner.

我們正在吃我媽媽煮的晚餐。

C

cool [kuːl]

① *adj.* 涼快的

實用片語與搭配字

keep cool 保持冷靜

② *n.* 涼快；涼爽

③ *v.* （使）冷卻；（使）變涼；（使）涼爽

實用片語與搭配字

cool sb down （使）（某人）冷靜下來

▶ The weather is cool today.
今天的天氣很涼快。

▶ The best thing to do in a bad situation is to keep cool. If you panic, you might not survive.
在不好的情況下，最好的做法是保持冷靜。如果你驚慌，可能無法生存下去。

▶ He wears a jacket in the cool of the night.
他在夜晚涼意中穿起夾克。

▶ Let the pie cool before you eat it.
讓這派變涼，你再吃。

▶ After an argument with my father, I went for a walk to cool down.
和父親爭論之後，我去散步冷靜一下。

---

corn [kɔːrn] *n.* 玉米

▶ Eat your corn. It's good for you.
吃玉米，這對你很好。

---

correct [kəˈrekt]

① *adj.* 正確的

② *v.* 改正；更正；糾正

▶ That is the correct answer.
這是正確答案。

▶ The teacher will correct your work.
這位老師會改正你的作業。

102

cost [kɑːst]

① *n.* 價格

② *v.* 花費

實用片語與搭配字

cost up to 費用高達（金額）

▶ The car has a high cost.
這輛車的價格很高。

▶ This car cost me a lot of money.
這輛車花了我不少錢。

▶ University education is not cheap and in some countries, it can cost up to a million dollars.
大學教育所費不貲，在某些國家可能要花費高達百萬美元。

---

could [kʊd / kəd] *aux. v.* 能；可以

▶ If I had the tools, I could fix this computer.
如果我有工具，我就能修電腦。

---

count [kaʊnt]

① *v.* 數數；計算

▶ I'm counting the chickens.
我正在算雞的數量。

實用片語與搭配字

count as 以…計算

② *n.* 總計；計數

▶ If you participate in the speech competition, it will count as an extra point for your final grade.

如果你參加演講比賽，它將算作期末成績的額外分數。

▶ Right now, the count is ten.

現在，總計是十。

95

country [ˈkʌn.tri] *n.* 國家

▶ What country are you from?

你來自哪個國家？

course [kɔːrs]

① *n.* 課程

② *v.* 追逐

▶ I have chosen my course.

我已經選好課程了。

▶ The dogs coursed across the field.

這群狗在田野中追逐著。

104

cover [ˈkʌv.ɚ]

① *v.* 蓋上；覆蓋；遮蔽

實用片語與搭配字

cover sth up 掩蓋，掩飾，隱瞞

② *n.* 蓋子；罩子；遮蓋物；覆蓋物

實用片語與搭配字

don't judge a book by its cover

不要以貌取人

▶ Don't cover the cup.

別蓋上這個杯子。

▶ John tried to cover up his past by moving to a different country.

約翰搬到另一個國家，企圖要隱藏他的過去。

▶ Where is the cover for this jar?

這個罐子的蓋子在哪裡？

▶ Joe might look sloppy, but he is very intelligent. Don't judge a book by its cover.

喬可能看起來邋遢，但其實他很聰明。不要以貌取人。

cow [kaʊ] *n.* 乳牛

▶ There are three cows on the farm.

這個農場裡有三頭乳牛。

cowboy [ˈkaʊ.bɔɪ] *n.* 牛仔

▶ The cowboy is chasing the cow.

這個牛仔正在追趕那隻牛。

crow [kroʊ] *n.* 烏鴉

▶ The crow just flew off the fence.

這隻烏鴉剛從籬笆飛走了。

C

crowded [ˈkraʊ.dɪd]

adj. 擁擠的；擠滿人群的

實用片語與搭配字

be crowded with （某處）擠滿（群眾）

▶ There was no room in the crowded subway train.
在這個擁擠的地鐵車廂裡沒有什麼空間。

▶ The mall will be crowded with people during the holidays.
過節時，購物中心將擠滿了人。

---

cry [kraɪ]

① *v.* 哭泣

實用片語與搭配字

cry out 大叫，大喊

② *n.* 哭聲；叫喊聲

▶ Jim cries when he is sad.
吉姆傷心的時候會哭。

▶ You can cry out for help if you get scared during the swimming lesson.
如果你在游泳課時感到害怕，你可以大聲呼救。

▶ I heard the cry of the baby.
我聽到嬰孩的哭聲。

---

cub [kʌb] *n.* 幼獸；幼崽

▶ Don't stand between the mother bear and her cub.
不要站在母熊和幼熊之間。

---

cup [kʌp]

① *n.* 杯子

② *v.* 使（手）成杯狀

▶ Please pass the cup.
請把杯子傳過來。

▶ I can cup a lot of water in my hands.
我可以徒手盛起很多水。

---

cut [kʌt]

① *v.* (用刀) 剪，切，割，砍，削，剁

實用片語與搭配字

cut in; cut off 插隊，插話；打斷（某人的話）

② *n.* 傷口

▶ Let's cut this paper together.
我們一起剪這張紙吧。

▶ It is rude to cut in when another person is talking.
在別人談話時插話是不禮貌的。

▶ That cut looks bad. You should see a doctor.
這個傷口看起很糟，你應該去看醫生。

cute [kjuːt] *adj.* 可愛的

▶ That dog is really cute.
那隻狗真的很可愛。

---

dad / daddy / papa [dæd / ˈdæd.i / ˈpɑː.pə]

n. 爸爸

▶ My dad works in a factory.
我爸爸在工廠工作。

Exercise 13

I. Choose and write the correct word. Change the form of the word when necessary.

1	common (adj.) correct (adj.)	Earthquakes are so ________ in Japan that people often don't pay attention to them.
2	count (v.) cover (v.)	We'd better ________ up the food until we start eating; otherwise, the flies will get into it.
3	cookie (n.) cooking (n.)	I don't mind eating in if you do the ________.
4	cowboy (n.) crow (n.)	He dressed up as a ________ for the party.
5	count (v.) cost (v.)	The child can ________ from one to a hundred.

II. Multiple choices.

( ) 1. Regardless of how often I ________ him, he always makes the same mistake.
(A) count (B) cost (C) cover (D) correct

( ) 2. If you ________ to miss classes, you'll fail the course.
(A) continue (B) course (C) come (D) cover

( ) 3. I dropped one of my ________ because I didn't have time to do all the homework.
(A) cookies (B) colors (C) cooks (D) courses

( ) 4. It's good to meet people from different parts of the ________.
(A) country (B) cold (C) cook (D) cooking

( ) 5. The train was very ________, and we had to stand.
(A) cold (B) cute (C) common (D) crowded

Unit 14

D

dance [dæns]

① *v.* 跳舞

實用片語與搭配字

dance with 與…跳舞

② *n.* 舞蹈

▶ I love this song. Let's dance.
我好愛這首歌，我們一起跳舞吧。

▶ David likes dangerous sports, but he has danced with death several times.
大衛喜歡危險的運動，但他曾多次與死神共舞。

▶ This is the last dance.
這是最後一支舞。

---

dancer [ˈdæn.sɚ] *n.* 舞蹈演員；跳舞者

▶ Laura is an excellent dancer.
蘿拉是一位優秀的舞者。

---

dancing [ˈdæn.sɪŋ] *n.* 跳舞

▶ There was dancing and singing at the party.
在派對上有跳舞和唱歌。

---

danger [ˈdeɪn.dʒɚ] *n.* 危險

實用片語與搭配字

in danger 置身危險之中

▶ There is a danger of fire.
有火災的危險。

▶ The project is in danger of being canceled because the company is bankrupt.
由於公司破產，該專案面臨被取消的危險。

---

dark [dɑːrk]

① *adj.* 昏暗的；黑暗的

② *n.* 暗處

實用片語與搭配字

keep sb in the dark （使某人）蒙在鼓裡

▶ I found the book in a dark corner.
我在一個暗暗的角落發現了這本書。

▶ He sat alone in the dark.
他獨自坐在暗處。

▶ My friends kept me in the dark about plans for my birthday.
我的朋友們暗中計劃我的生日。

100

date [deɪt]

① *n.* 日期；日子

② *v.* 在…上寫上日子，在…上標明日期

▶ What is the date today?
今天是幾號？

▶ Don't forget to date your letter.
別忘記在你的信件上註明日期。

daughter [ˈdɑː.t̬ɚ] *n.* 女兒

▶ Eva has two daughters.
伊娃有兩個女兒。

---

day [deɪ] *n.* 一天

▶ This is a beautiful day.
今天是美好的一天。

---

dead [ded] *adj.* 死亡的

實用片語與搭配字

be dead meat （某人）死定了

▶ I think that snake is dead.
我覺得那條蛇已經死了。

▶ I am dead meat when I get home; I borrowed my dad's car without asking and he found out.
我回家的時候發現大事不妙，因為父親發現我未經允許就開了他的車。

deal [diːl]

① *v.* 分牌；發牌

實用片語與搭配字

deal with 處理

② *n.* 交易

實用片語與搭配字

make a deal / deals with 達成交易

▶ Melody will deal the cards.
美樂蒂會發紙牌。

▶ If you deal with problems the moment they appear, your life will be so much easier.
如果你在問題出現時就立即處理，那生活會順遂許多。

▶ Don't talk during the deal.
不要在交易中交談。

▶ Simon made a deal with his father to get good grades.
賽門為了取得好成績，和他父親達成了協議。

---

dear [dɪr]

① *adj.* 親愛的

② *n.* 親愛的（人）

③ *adv.* 疼愛地

▶ You are my dear friend.
你是我親愛的朋友。

▶ Hello, dear. How are you?
嗨，親愛的，你好嗎？

▶ He holds his children dear.
他非常疼愛他的小孩。

---

death [deθ] *n.* 死亡

▶ The cat's death was very sad.
這隻貓的死讓人感到非常難過。

December / Dec. [dɪˈsem.bɚ] *n.* 十二月

▶ Christmas is in December.
聖誕節在十二月。

decide [dɪˈsaɪd] *v.* 決定

實用片語與搭配字

decide on sth / sb 決定

▶ I will decide after school.
我下課後會決定。

▶ It is difficult to decide on what to buy my brother for his birthday because he is so picky.
因為我的哥哥很挑剔，所以很難決定生日要買什麼送他。

95

deep [di:p]

① *adj.* 深的

② *adv.* 深遠地

▶ That is a deep hole.
那個洞很深。

▶ You'll have to dig deep to find it.
你需要挖得很深才找得到。

---

deer [dɪr] *n.* 鹿

▶ The deer is hiding in the forest.
這隻鹿藏在森林裡。

102

delete [dɪˈli:t] *v.* 刪除

▶ We must delete some files to create more space.
我們必須刪除一些檔案來清出更多的空間。

---

desk [desk] *n.* 書桌

▶ The paper is on the desk.
這份報告在書桌上。

---

die [daɪ] *v.* 死亡

實用片語與搭配字

die of 因…而死亡

▶ You'll die if you fall off the cliff.
你若摔下懸崖是會死的。

▶ I didn't eat breakfast and if we don't find something to eat right now, I am going to die of hunger.
我沒有吃早飯，如果我們現在沒有找到吃的東西，我會餓死的。

97

different [ˈdɪf.ɚ.ənt] *adj.* 不同的

▶ Pens and pencils are different.
鋼筆和鉛筆是不同的。

---

difficult [ˈdɪf.ə.kəlt] *adj.* 困難的

▶ The test is difficult.
這個考試好難。

dig [dɪg]

① *v.* 挖掘

實用片語與搭配字

dig into 探究，細查

② *n.* 刺；戳；碰

▶ Steve can dig a hole.
史帝夫可以挖一個洞。

▶ Sandra dug into our bag and found a pen.
桑德拉翻我們的包包，找到了一支筆。

▶ He gave it a quick dig but found nothing.
他很快地戳了一下，並沒有發現什麼。

---

digit [ˈdɪdʒ.ɪt] *n.* 數字

▶ The last digit on the telephone number was 3.
電話號碼上的最後一個數字是三。

---

dinner [ˈdɪn.ɚ] *n.* 晚餐

▶ Dinner is at 5:00.
晚餐是在五點。

direct [dəˈrekt, daɪˈrekt]

① *adj.* 直接的

② *v.* 指揮；管理；領導

▶ Don't take the direct route.
不要走這條直達的路線。

▶ You can help direct traffic.
你可以幫忙指揮交通。

Exercise 14

I. Choose and write the correct word. Change the form of the word when necessary.

1	dancer (n.) danger (n.)	In war, life is full of __________ for everyone.
2	deal (v.) date (v.)	Our teacher always __________ the communication book while signing her name.
3	different (adj.) difficult (adj.)	There are __________ categories of books in the library.
4	digit (n.) dinner (n.)	His phone number differs from mine by one __________.
5	decide (v.) delete (v.)	They couldn't __________ whether to have chocolate or vanilla ice cream.

II. Multiple choices.

( ) 1. You can __________ the files by dragging them into your files.
(A) direct (B) decide (C) delete (D) dig

( ) 2. His father's __________ gave him a whole new perspective on life.
(A) death (B) deal (C) dark (D) dance

( ) 3. Everyday is a beginning; take a __________ breath and start again.
(A) dark (B) deep (C) dear (D) difficult

( ) 4. Some animals have the power to see in the __________.
(A) deal (B) date (C) dancer (D) dark

( ) 5. __________ is the twelfth month of the year.
(A) November (B) December (C) September (D) October

Unit 15

directly [daɪˈrekt.li / dɪˈrekt.li] *adv.* 筆直地

▶ He went directly to the store.
他直接走到了這家店。

---

dirty [ˈdɝː.t̬i]

① *adj.* 骯髒的

② *v.* 弄髒

▶ His pants are all dirty.
他的褲子都髒了。

▶ Put on an apron or you'll dirty your shirt.
穿上圍裙，不然你會弄髒你的衣服。

discover [dɪˈskʌv.ɚ]

v. （尤指首次）發現；找到

實用片語與搭配字

discover in 發現，找到

▶ Sherry is trying to discover a new type of fish.
雪莉嘗試著發現新品種的魚。

▶ The earliest human remains were discovered in Africa.
最早的人類遺骸是在非洲被發現的。

---

dish [dɪʃ] *n.* 盤子；碟子

▶ He dropped the dish.
他把盤子掉在地上。

---

do [də / du / duː]

① *v.* 做；實行

實用片語與搭配字

dos and don'ts 可做與不可做之事

② *aux. v.* 助動詞

▶ Andy will do his homework after school.
安迪放學後會做功課。

▶ If you want to be safe when you travel alone, there are many dos and don'ts that you have to learn.
如果你想要安全的獨自旅行，那麼你必須學習許多的準則。

▶ Do you know what you have done?
你知道你做了什麼嗎？

Doctor / Dr. [ˈdɑːk.tɚ]

① *n.* 醫生

② *n.* 醫生；博士

▶ Jimmy wants to be a doctor.
吉姆想要當醫生。

▶ I made an appointment with Dr. Kim for next Tuesday.
我掛了下星期二金醫師的約診。

dog [dɑːg] *n.* 狗

▶ That's a nice dog.
那是一隻很棒的狗。

---

doll [dɑːl] *n.* 洋娃娃

▶ I gave Eva a doll for her birthday.
我送伊娃一個洋娃娃當她的生日禮物。

---

dollar [ˈdɑː.lɚ]
n. （美、加等國的錢幣單位）元

▶ Laura found a dollar on the floor.
蘿拉在地上發現一塊錢。

---

door [dɔːr] *n.* 門

▶ Please close the door.
請關上門。

---

double [ˈdʌb.əl]
① *n.* 兩倍（量）
② *v.* 使加倍；變成兩倍

▶ Do we get paid double for working on holidays?
我們在假日工作會拿到兩倍的薪水嗎？

▶ Please double the sugar when you make the cake.
當你做這個蛋糕時，請放雙倍的糖。

doubt [daʊt]
① *n.* 疑慮；懷疑

實用片語與搭配字
without doubt 毫無疑慮

② *v.* 懷疑

▶ Kelly is having doubts about marrying Albert.
凱莉對於是否要嫁給亞伯心懷疑慮。

▶ Iceland is without a doubt the most beautiful place I have ever visited.
毫無疑問，冰島是我去過最美麗的地方。

▶ I doubt she'll ever have children.
我懷疑她將來是否會生小孩。

---

doughnut [ˈdoʊ.nʌt] *n.* 甜甜圈

▶ Let's go to the bakery and buy some doughnuts for the party.
我們一起去麵包店為這個派對買些甜甜圈吧！

---

dove [dʌv] *n.* 鴿子

▶ The dove flew across the yard.
鴿子從院子飛過。

---

down [daʊn]
① *adv.* 向下

▶ He walked down the hill.
他走下山丘。

實用片語與搭配字

break down

（機車或車輛）出故障，（人）崩潰

► When your car breaks down on the highway, you should phone the police and tell them where you are.

當你的車在高速公路上拋錨，你應該報警並告知你的位置。

② *prep.* 在…下方

③ *adj.* 下行的；向下的

④ *v.* 使墜下；使掉下

⑤ *n.* 失敗；倒楣事

► The school is down the hill.

這間學校在山丘下。

► This is the down elevator.

這電梯是往下的。

► The airplane was downed.

這架飛機墜機了。

► The downs of life can be hard to handle.

生命中的低潮有時很難面對。

實用片語與搭配字

ups and downs 盛衰，心情高低起伏

► Despite the many ups and downs of being a reporter, it is still an interesting job.

儘管作為一名記者有許多起伏，但它仍然是一個有趣的工作。

---

downstairs [ˌdaʊnˈsterz]

① *adv.* 向樓下

② *adj.* 樓下的

③ *n.* 樓下

► Sean ran downstairs.

西恩跑下樓。

► It's in the downstairs bathroom.

那在樓下的浴室裡。

► I want to go downstairs.

我想要去樓下。

---

downtown [ˌdaʊnˈtaʊn]

① *adv.* 在城市的商業區

② *adj.* 在市中心的

③ *n.* 商業區；鬧區

► Jason goes downtown twice a week to visit his grandmother.

傑森一星期去城裡探望他的祖母兩次。

► Did you go to the downtown store last week?

你上週去了位在市中心的那家商店嗎？

► Our city is small, so it doesn't really have a downtown.

我們的城市很小，所以沒有什麼繁華的商業區。

---

dozen [ˈdʌz.ən] *n.* （一）打

► He bought a dozen.

他買了一打。

D

drag [dræg]

① *v.* 拖；拉

實用片語與搭配字

drag sb into sth
硬讓某人捲入（不愉快或困難局面）

② *n.* 拖曳；緩慢的前行（拖曳機）

▶ Don't drag the blanket on the floor, or it will get dirty!
別把毯子拖在地上，會弄髒的！

▶ If you get caught doing something illegal, do not drag me into it. I will not help you.
假如你犯了法而被逮，別把我捲入，因為我幫不了你。

▶ Sometimes the farmer may stand on the drag while it is being used.
有時候農夫會站在犁上面操作農事。

---

dragon [ˈdræg.ən] *n.* 龍

實用片語與搭配字

dragon boat festival 端午節

▶ He fought the angry dragon until it died.
他與憤怒的龍戰鬥直到牠死去。

▶ We like to watch dragon boat races during the Dragon Boat Festival.
我們喜歡在端午節的時候看龍舟比賽。

---

dragonfly [ˈdræg.ən.flaɪ] *n.* 蜻蜓

▶ The dragonfly landed on my shoulder.
這隻蜻蜓停在我肩膀上。

---

drama [ˈdræm.ə] *n.* 戲劇；劇本

▶ I like to watch dramas at the theater.
我喜歡到劇院看戲劇表演。

---

draw [drɑː]

① *v.* 畫圖

實用片語與搭配字

draw attention 吸引注意

② *n.* 抽獎；抽籤

▶ Benjamin can draw very well.
班傑明畫圖畫得很好。

▶ It is not a good idea to draw attention to yourself when you are a tourist in another country.
當你去別的國家旅行，不要太引人注意。

▶ I won this prize in a draw.
我在抽獎中贏得了這個獎項。

---

drawer [drɔr] *n.* 抽屜

▶ Put the keys back in the bottom drawer.
請把鑰匙放回最下面的抽屜。

---

drawing [ˈdrɑː.ɪŋ] *n.* 繪圖；素描

▶ My aunt gave me a beautiful drawing of a rose.
阿姨畫了一幅美麗的玫瑰送我。

Exercise 15

I. Choose and write the correct word. Change the form of the word when necessary.

1	drag (v.) draw (v.)	I find it difficult to __________ myself away from the computer.
2	downtown (adv.) downstairs (adv.)	She came __________ after her shower, wrapped in a towel.
3	dragon (n.) drawer (n.)	He opened the __________ and took out a pair of socks.
4	doubt (n.) doughnut (n.)	There's no __________ at all that we did the right thing.
5	Drama (n.) Dove (n.)	__________ is an art that is traditionally performed in a theater.

II. Multiple choices.

( ) 1. You can order the book __________ from the publisher.
(A) down (B) doubt (C) double (D) directly

( ) 2. The body of the victim was __________ in a lake near the murderer's home.
(A) done (B) dragged (C) discovered (D) drown

( ) 3. Apples are on special for a dollar a __________ this week.
(A) dove (B) dozen (C) doughnut (D) doll

( ) 4. The __________ listened to his breathing and checked his pulse.
(A) doctor (B) dollar (C) dozen (D) dove

( ) 5. I work __________, but I live in the suburbs.
(A) downstairs (B) down (C) downtown (D) directly

Unit 16

dream [driːm]

① *n.* 夢；睡夢；夢境

② *v.* 夢想；想像

實用片語與搭配字

dream come true 夢想成真

▶ That dream was very real.
那個夢非常真實。

▶ Ben dreams of becoming a pilot.
班夢想成為一位機師。

▶ Megan's dream came true when she got accepted to Harvard University.
當梅根被哈佛大學錄取時，她的夢想成真了。

---

dress [dres]

① *n.* 禮服；洋裝

② *v.* 穿衣；打扮

實用片語與搭配字

dress up 盛裝

▶ She wore a long dress that was black and white.
她穿著一件黑白相間的長禮服。

▶ My daughter dressed herself for the first time this morning!
我女兒今天早上第一次自己穿衣服！

▶ I like to dress up for weddings in beautiful clothes and high heels.
我喜歡穿著漂亮的衣服和高跟鞋參加婚禮。

---

drink [drɪŋk]

① *v.* 喝

② *n.* （一杯）飲料

▶ She needs to drink more water.
她需要多喝水。

▶ Have a drink.
喝一杯飲料。

---

drive [draɪv]

① *v.* 駕駛

實用片語與搭配字

drive sb away 將（某人）趕走

② *n.* 駕車路程；（開車）兜風

▶ Jay drives to work every morning.
杰伊每天早上開車去上班。

▶ Jenny's constant complaining drove all her friends away.
珍妮不停地抱怨，把她所有的朋友都趕走了。

▶ Cindy enjoys the drive to school.
辛蒂很享受去上學的這段車程。

---

driver [ˈdraɪ.vɚ] *n.* 司機

▶ The wealthy family has two drivers.
這個有錢人家有兩名司機。

drop [drɑːp]

① *v.* 使滴下；掉落

▶ Why is water dropping from the ceiling?
為什麼有水從天花板滴下來？

實用片語與搭配字

drop sb / sth off
（通常指用汽車）捎帶⋯（至某地）

▶ I need a big favor; could you drop this package off at the post office on your way to work?
我需要你幫個大忙；你能在上班的路上順便把這個包裹送到郵局嗎？

② *n.* （一）滴

▶ Add a few drops of cooking oil into the bowl and mix.
加幾滴食用油到碗裡，然後混和攪拌一下。

---

drug [drʌg]

① *n.* 藥品

▶ The doctor gave him drugs to help ease the pain.
醫生開給他一些藥幫助他減輕疼痛。

實用片語與搭配字

take drug 服藥

▶ Do not take drugs when you know you are going to drive because they might make you feel sleepy.
當你知道你會開車時不要吃藥，因為它可能會讓你感到昏昏欲睡。

② *v.* 使施用藥物

▶ To ease the pain, she was drugged with pain killers.
為了減輕疼痛，為她施用了止痛藥。

---

drugstore [ˈdrʌg.stɔːr] *n.* 藥房

▶ Do you need anything from the drugstore?
你需要在藥房買些什麼嗎？

---

drum [drʌm]

① *n.* 鼓

▶ My sister can play the drums, but I can't.
我姊姊會打鼓，但我不會。

② *v.* 打鼓

▶ Someone needs to tell him he is drumming too loud.
要有人告訴他，他打鼓打得太大聲了。

---

dry [draɪ]

① *adj.* 乾燥的

▶ He wants some dry socks.
他想要一些乾的襪子。

② *v.* （使）變乾，（使）乾燥；晾乾，烘乾

▶ Sherry is going to dry the laundry.
雪莉要烘乾衣物。

實用片語與搭配字

dry up （河流、湖泊等）乾涸，（指資源或供應）耗盡，枯竭

▶ The party was quite boring and after an hour the conversation dried up, so we went home.
這個派對很無聊，過了一個小時就沒話聊，所以我們就回家了。

D

---

dryer [ˈdraɪ.ɚ] *n.* 烘乾機；吹風機

▶ Honey, can you put the wet clothes in the dryer for me ?
親愛的，你可以幫我把這些濕衣服放進烘乾機嗎？

---

duck [dʌk]

① *n.* 鴨子

② *v.* 突然低下（頭、身子）

▶ There is a duck in the pond.
有一隻鴨子在這個池塘裡。

▶ The roof is low. Duck your head.
這個屋頂很低，請低下你的頭。

---

duckling [ˈdʌk.lɪŋ] *n.* 小鴨

▶ There are three cute ducklings in the yard.
在這個院子裡有三隻可愛的小鴨。

---

dull [dʌl]

① *adj.* 乏味的；單調的

② *v.* 使緩和；使遲鈍

▶ The movie was so dull that people were leaving one by one.
這部電影實在太乏味，以至於觀眾一個個離開。

▶ Take this medicine to dull the pain.
吃這個藥讓疼痛減緩。

---

dumb [dʌm] *adj.* 啞的

▶ Todd was born deaf and dumb, but he is able to do many things.
泰德生來就聾啞，但他能夠做很多事情。

---

dumpling [ˈdʌm.plɪŋ] *n.* 水餃

▶ Dumplings taste best when eaten with soy sauce.
水餃沾醬油吃是最棒的。

---

during [ˈdʊr.ɪŋ]

prep. 在…的整個期間；在…期間的某個時候

▶ I was coughing during the movie.
我在看電影的時候一直咳嗽。

97

duty [ˈduː.t̬i] *n.* 責任；義務

▶ It's his duty as a police officer to protect the people of this town.
身為一名警察，他的責任就是要保護這個鎮上的居民。

實用片語與搭配字

on duty 值班

▶ I will be on duty at the hospital from 8pm to 8am; bring me a coffee if you have time.
我將從早上八點在醫院值班到晚上八點，如果你有空，帶杯咖啡給我。

---

each [iːtʃ]

① *adj.* （兩個或兩個以上人或物）每個的；各自的
② *pron.* （視作單數）每個；各個
③ *adv.* 各個（地）；各自（地）；每一個（地）

▶ There is one pencil for each student.
每個學生有一支鉛筆。

▶ Each person has a vote.
每個人有一票。

▶ I'll give you ten dollars each.
我會給你們每個人各美金十元。

---

eagle [ˈiː.gəl] *n.* 老鷹

▶ The eagle is flying.
這隻老鷹在飛翔。

---

ear [ɪr] *n.* 耳朵

▶ I hurt my ear.
我傷了我的耳朵。

---

early [ˈɝː.li]

① *adj.* 早的
② *adv.* 提早；早地

▶ The early morning is quiet.
這個清晨是寧靜的。

▶ I came to school early.
我提早到校。

96

earn [ɝːn] *v.* 賺（錢）；掙得

實用片語與搭配字

earn a living 謀生

▶ How much money do you earn an hour working at the theater?
你在戲院工作一個小時賺多少錢？

▶ It does not matter how you earn a living as long as you don't steal money.
只要你不偷竊，你怎麼謀生都無所謂。

---

earth [ɝːθ] *n.* 地球；土地

實用片語與搭配字

move heaven and earth 竭盡全力

▶ The earth is an amazing place.
我們這個地球是個充滿驚奇的地方。

▶ You have to move heaven and earth to make your dreams come true.
你必須竭盡全力來實現你的夢想。

---

earthquake [ˈɝː.θ.kweɪk] *n.* 地震

▶ The earthquake killed hundreds of people.
這次地震導致數百人喪生。

Exercise 16

I. Choose and write the correct word. Change the form of the word when necessary.

1	dream (n.) drug (n.)	Much of the crime in this area is related to the ________ abuse.
2	drive (v.) drop (v.)	People who ________ litter can be fined in some cities.
3	duty (n.) drum (n.)	It is the ________ of every citizen to respect the law.
4	early (adv.) each (adv.)	He was forced to retire ________ from teaching because of ill health.
5	dress (v.) dry (v.)	How should I ________ for the dancing party this Saturday night?

II. Multiple choices.

(　　) 1. ________ my lifetime, I haven't got around to much traveling.

(A) Duckling　(B) During　(C) Dumpling　(D) Drum

(　　) 2. The book was so ________ that I didn't finish it.

(A) dry　(B) dumb　(C) dull　(D) early

(　　) 3. After the ________, only a few houses were left standing.

(A) earth　(B) duty　(C) drugstore　(D) earthquake

(　　) 4. The hotel's bedrooms are equipped with a telephone and a hair ________.

(A) dryer　B) drugstore　(C) drum　(D) duck

(　　) 5. There was an accident here yesterday; a car hit the tree and the ________ was killed.

(A) dryer　(B) driver　(C) dumpling　D) duckling

Unit 17

ease [iːz]

① *n.* 安逸自在；舒適；容易不費力

② *v.* 減輕；放鬆

▶ He is living at ease.
他生活過得無憂無慮。

▶ The doctor tried to ease her pain.
醫生試著減輕她的痛楚。

---

east [iːst]

① *n.* 東方

② *adj.* 東部的

③ *adv.* 向東方；朝東部

▶ We need to go east.
我們要往東方走。

▶ I like the east coast.
我喜歡東岸。

▶ Bonita is ready to drive east.
玻妮塔準備往東開。

---

eastern [ˈiː.stɚn] *adj.* 東部的

▶ The city of Hualien is located in eastern Taiwan.
花蓮市位於東台灣。

---

easy [ˈiː.zi] *adj.* 容易的；不費力的

▶ The puzzle is easy.
這拼圖很容易。

---

eat [iːt] *v.* 吃

▶ Let's eat lunch.
一起吃午餐吧。

---

edge [edʒ]

① *n.* 邊緣

實用片語與搭配字

on edge 如坐針氈的；惴惴不安的；煩躁的

② *v.* 使鋒利；將（刀）開刃

▶ The edge is sharp.
這邊緣很銳利。

▶ Everybody was on edge after the earthquake, not knowing whether more would occur.
地震後，大家都很緊張，不知道是否會再發生。

▶ I'm edging the knife.
我正在磨刀。

---

education [ˌedʒ.əˈkeɪ.ʃən] *n.* 教育

▶ A college education is necessary if you want to become a teacher.
如果你想成為一位老師，大學教育是必要的。

實用片語與搭配字

higher education; education system
高等教育；教育體制

▶ Many education systems in the world require that students complete at least 9 years of schooling.
世界上許多教育體制要求學生完成至少九年的學業。

E

---

effect [əˈfekt]

① *n.* 效果；影響

實用片語與搭配字

come into effect 生效

② *v.* 產生；招致

▶ She took some medicine for her cold, but it didn't have any effect.
她因為感冒吃了一點藥，但沒有任何效果。

▶ New laws to protect animals will come into effect in January.
保護動物的新法律條文將於一月生效。

▶ This year, our boss wants to effect some changes in the office.
今年，我們老闆想要在辦公室裡作些改變。

99

effective [əˈfek.tɪv] *adj.* 有效的

▶ Green tea is effective for losing weight.
綠茶對於減肥是有效的。

103

effort [ˈef.ɚt] *n.* 努力

實用片語與搭配字

make effort 盡一番努力

▶ They put a lot of time and effort into making this movie.
他們花了很多時間和努力在拍攝這部電影。

▶ You have to make effort to learn a new language.
你必須努力才能學習一個新的語言。

---

egg [eg] *n.* （食用的）蛋（尤指雞蛋）

▶ Anne ate two eggs for lunch.
安午餐吃了兩顆蛋。

---

eight [eɪt]

① *n.* 八

② *adj.* 八個的；八的；八歲的

▶ I like the number eight.
我喜歡八這個數字。

▶ There are eight students.
這裡有八個學生。

---

eighteen [ˌeɪˈtiːn]

① *n.* 十八

② *adj.* 十八個的；十八的；十八歲的

▶ Eighteen is my lucky number.
十八是我的幸運數字。

▶ I saw eighteen cars.
我看到十八輛車。

eighty [ˈeɪ.t̬i]

① *n.* 八十

② *adj.* 八十歲的；八十個的；八十的

▶ Eighty is a big number.
八十是個很大的數字。

▶ He is eighty years old.
他八十歲。

---

either [ˈiː.ðɚ / ˈaɪ.ðɚ]

① *adj.* （只能）兩者擇一的；非此即彼的

② *pron.*（兩者中的）任何一個

③ *conj.*（兩種可能性的選擇）不是…就是…；要？…要？…；或者…或者…

② *adv.* （用於否定句）也

▶ Eat either meal.
吃其中一餐。

▶ Either dessert will be fine.
任何一個甜點都好。

▶ Either we go now, or we stay all night.
我們要不現在去，或者整晚留下來。

▶ If you aren't going, I'm not either.
如果你不去，我也不去。

---

elder [ˈel.dɚ]

① *adj.* 年長的

② *n.* 年長者

▶ They are twins, but Jamie is the elder sister.
她們是雙胞胎，但潔咪是姊姊。

▶ It's important to respect your elders.
尊敬你的長輩是很重要的。

---

elect [iˈlekt]

① *v.* 選舉

② *adj.* 當選的

▶ Abe was elected president of the class this year.
艾比被選為今年的學生會長。

▶ An elect group of classmates was chosen to attend the meeting.
這群當選的同學們被選去參加這次的會議。

98

element [ˈel.ə.mənt] *n.* 元素

▶ The ceremony had all the elements of a perfect wedding.
這場典禮具備了所有完美婚禮的元素。

---

elephant [ˈel.ə.fənt] *n.* 大象

▶ George sat on the elephant.
喬治坐在大象上。

---

elevator [ˈel.ə.veɪ.t̬ɚ] *n.* 電梯

▶ Take the elevator up to the seventh floor to get to the theater.
搭電梯到七樓就能抵達戲院。

eleven [əˈlev.ən]

① *n.* 十一

② *adj.* 十一個的；十一的；十一歲的

▶ What is three plus eleven?
三加十一是多少？

▶ There are eleven pencils on the desk.
桌上有十一枝鉛筆。

---

else [els] *adv.* 其他；另外（用於以 any-，every-，no- 和 some- 開頭的詞後面，或用於 how，what，where，who，why 之後，但不用於 which 之後）

▶ I don't know how else to do it.
我不知道怎麼用其他方法做。

emotion [ɪˈmoʊ.ʃən] *n.* 情感

▶ He never shows any emotions, so I was surprised when I saw him crying.
他從未表現出情緒，所以當我看到他哭泣時非常驚訝。

encourage [ɪnˈkɝː.ɪdʒ] *v.* 鼓勵；激發

▶ My mom always encouraged me to go after my dreams.
我母親總是鼓勵我去追求夢想。

---

encouragement [ɪnˈkɝː.ɪdʒ.mənt] *n.* 鼓勵

實用片語與搭配字

give encouragement 鼓勵（他人）

▶ Without the encouragement from my family, I wouldn't be where I am today.
如果沒有我家人的鼓勵，我不可能有今天的成就。

▶ Instead of complaining about your daughter, you should give encouragement to help her do better.
與其抱怨你的女兒，不如鼓勵她做得更好。

Exercise 17

I. Choose and write the correct word. Change the form of the word when necessary.

1	effect (n.) edge (n.)	Global warming has had a significant __________ on our climate over the last few years.
2	ease (v.) elect (v.)	The candidate promised to lower taxes if he got __________, but no one trusted him.
3	emotion (n.) element (n.)	Protein is an essential __________ for growth and repair of the human body.
4	elder (adj.) either (adj.)	The boy agrees that his __________ sister is much more clever than him.
5	effort (n.) elevator (n.)	We got stuck in the __________ for about 20 minutes after my son pushed all the buttons at once.

II. Multiple choices.

( ) 1. I think your essay would be more __________ if you make it shorter and more direct.

(A) easy (B) either (C) effective (D) elect

( ) 2. It is important to have at least a grade 12 __________ if you want to get a good job.

(A) emotion (B) education (C) element (D) effort

( ) 3. You have to put in a lot more __________ if you really want to improve your English.

(A) effort (B) effect (C) element (D) elder

( ) 4. The coach always takes time to praise all the members of the team before a game in order to __________ them.

(A) elect (B) ease (C) edge (D) encourage

( ) 5. I don't eat meat, and my husband doesn't, __________.

(A) either (B) elder (C) elevator (D) easy

Unit 18

end [end]

① *n.* 末端；盡頭；最後部分；末尾

實用片語與搭配字

come to an end 完結，結束

② *v.* （使）結束；（使）停止

實用片語與搭配字

end up with 以…告終

▶ That's the end.
那就是終點了。

▶ This year will come to an end in about a month, and I can't wait for Christmas.
今年再過一個月就要結束，我等不及要過聖誕節了。

▶ I'm going to end this fighting.
我要結束這場爭執。

▶ You should stop buying shoes or you will end up with too many pairs, and then you have to give them away.
你應該停止買鞋子，否則你將會因為太多鞋子，而必須把它們送人。

---

ending [ˈen.dɪŋ] *n.* 結局；結尾

▶ The movie did not have a happy ending.
這部電影沒有快樂的結局。

102

enemy [ˈen.ə.mi] *n.* 敵人

▶ They've been enemies ever since their big fight.
自從那次大吵之後，他們就成了敵人。

---

102 100 96 95

energy [ˈen.ɚ.dʒi] *n.* 活力；精力

▶ Since I started exercising, I have a lot more energy.
自從我開始運動以後，我就擁有更多活力。

English [ˈɪŋ.glɪʃ]

① *n.* 英語

② *adj.* 英格蘭的；英國的

▶ I speak English.
我說英語。

▶ This is an old English story.
這是一個古老的英格蘭故事。

96

enjoy [ɪnˈdʒɔɪ] *v.* 享受；欣賞

▶ Everyone enjoyed the party!
每個人都很開心享受這場派對！

---

enjoyment [ɪnˈdʒɔɪ.mənt] *n.* 樂趣；享受

▶ I get no enjoyment from watching sports.
觀賞運動對我來說不是一種樂趣。

enough [əˈnʌf]

① *adj.* 足夠的

② *n.* 足夠；充分

③ *adv.* 十分地；足夠地

▶ I have enough bottles.
我有足夠的瓶子。

▶ Thanks. That's enough.
謝謝，這樣夠了。

▶ The steak is cooked enough.
這個牛排煎夠熟了。

---

enter [ˈen.t̬ɚ] *v.* 進入

實用片語與搭配字

enter into 進入（某地）

▶ Chris entered the building.
克里斯進了這棟樓。

▶ Be careful before you enter into agreement to buy a house -- once you sign, it's done.
在你同意買房子之前要小心， 一旦你簽了，就完成了。

---

entire [ɪnˈtaɪr] *adj.* 全部的

▶ She can eat an entire pizza by herself.
她可以自己吃下一整個披薩。

---

entrance [ˈen.trəns] *n.* 入口

▶ I'll meet you by the south entrance of this building.
我會在這棟大樓的南面入口跟你會合。

---

envelope [ˈɑːn.və.loʊp] *n.* 信封

▶ Carol went to the stationery store to buy some envelopes.
卡蘿去文具店買了一些信封。

---

environment [ɪnˈvaɪ.rən.mənt] *n.* 環境

▶ We must keep our environment clean by not littering.
我們不亂丟垃圾以維持環境整潔。

---

equal [ˈiː.kwəl]

① *adj.* （地位、待遇）平等的，相當的；（數量、大小）相等的

實用片語與搭配字

be equal to 能勝任…; 等於…

② *n.* （地位等）相同的人

③ *v.* 等於

▶ The two students are equal.
這兩名學生能力相當。

▶ John was equal to Peter in their ability to complete the project.
約翰和彼得在專案能力上並駕其驅。

▶ He has met his equal.
他遇到和他旗鼓相當的人。

▶ Three times three equals nine.
三乘以三等於九。

E

eraser [ɪˈreɪ.sɚ] *n.* 橡皮擦

▶ Can I borrow one of your erasers for the test?
我可以借你的一個橡皮擦去考試嗎？

error [ˈer.ɚ] *n.* 錯誤；過失

▶ There were some spelling errors, but that's about all.
只有些拼字的錯誤，沒有其他錯了。

103 97

especially [ɪˈspeʃ.əl.i] *adv.* 尤其；特別

▶ My mother loves desserts, especially French desserts.
我母親喜愛甜點，尤其是法式點心。

essay [ˈes.eɪ] *n.* 文章；短文

▶ Your essay was very interesting to read.
你的文章讀起來很有趣。

even [ˈiː.vən]

① *adv.* （用於強調比較）甚至更；愈加；還
② *adj.* 平坦的；平滑的
③ *v.* 使平均；使平衡；使相等

▶ This dessert tastes even better.
這個甜點嚐起來更好吃。

▶ The top of the rock is quite even.
這塊岩石上頭蠻平的。

▶ The teacher tried to even the score.
這位老師試著把分數弄平均。

evening [ˈiːv.nɪŋ] *n.* 傍晚

▶ I'll meet you in the evening.
我傍晚會跟你碰面。

event [ɪˈvent] *n.* 事件；（比賽）項目

▶ Each person attending the event must pay sixty dollars.
每個參加這活動的人都要交六十美元。

ever [ˈev.ɚ] *adv.* 究竟；到底

▶ Will this ever finish?
這究竟會有結束的一天嗎？

every [ˈev.ri] *adj.* 每個的

▶ I go to school every day.
我每天去上學。

everybody [ˈev.ri͵bɑː.di] *pron.* 每個人

▶ Everybody in the room stood up together.
房間裡的每個人一起站了起來。

everyday [ˋev.ri.deɪ] *adj.* 每天的；日常的

實用片語與搭配字

everyday life 日常生活

▶ The everyday traffic on the freeway is bad.

高速公路上每天的交通都很糟。

▶ Getting up early for school is just part of everyday life.

早起上學只是日常生活的一部分。

Exercise 18

I. Choose and write the correct word. Change the form of the word when necessary.

1	energy (n.) enjoyment (n.)	May the Christmas be a time of laughter and real __________ for you.
2	even (adj.) equal (adj.)	A dollar is __________ to one hundred cents.
3	entire (adj.) every (adj.)	He was so tired that he slept through the __________ movie.
4	error (n.) essay (n.)	You should check your homework before handing it in so that you can find your own __________.
5	end (v.) enter (v.)	His eyes brightened when he saw her __________ his room.

II. Multiple choices.

( ) 1. There are many things you can do in your everyday life to help protect the __________, such as recycling or riding a bicycle.

(A) entrance (B) essay (C) environment (D) ending

( ) 2. The men quickly searched the forest for signs of __________ soldiers.

(A) essay (B) enemy (C) every (D) eraser

( ) 3. After working all day, she simply didn't have the __________ to go out dancing at the party.

(A) energy (B) event (C) envelope (D) entrance

( ) 4. We'll meet at the main __________ of the building of our department.

(A) essay (B) event (C) evening (D) entrance

( ) 5. The discovery by Columbus was quite an __________ in the world.

(A) end (B) enough (C) event (D) envelope

Unit 19

everyone [ˈev.ri.wʌn] *pron.* 每個人

▶ I was happy to see everyone working hard.
我很開心看到每個人都認真工作。

---

everything [ˈev.ri.θɪŋ] *pron.* 每件事

▶ She found everything she needed in the kitchen.
她在廚房裡找到了每一樣她需要的東西。

---

everywhere [ˈev.ri.wer] *adv.* 到處

▶ The sky lanterns were everywhere in the sky!
這些天燈滿布天空中！

---

exact [ɪɡˈzækt] *adj.* 確切的

▶ This is the exact location where the president gave his speech.
這裡是總統發表演說的確切地點。

---

examination / exam
[ɪɡˌzæm.əˈneɪ.ʃən / ɪɡˈzæm] *n.* 考試

實用片語與搭配字
pass exam 通過考試

▶ I'm studying for the examination.
我正為了這場考試在讀書。

▶ In order for Bill to go to a good university, he needs to pass an exam first.
比爾需要先通過考試，才能進一所好的大學。

examine [ɪɡˈzæm.ɪn]
v. （仔細地）檢查；調查

實用片語與搭配字
examine in 檢查，細查

▶ Diego examined the picture.
底耶戈仔細地檢查了這幅畫。

▶ Students will be examined in all their subjects, so you should start studying early.
學生需要通過所有科目的考試，所以你應該盡早開始念書。

---

example [ɪɡˈzæm.pəl] *n.* 例子

實用片語與搭配字
give an example 舉例

▶ That's a great example.
那是個很好的例子。

▶ When you write an essay, give an example to support your main points.
當你寫文章的時候，舉一個例子來支持你的論點。

97

excellent [ˈek.səl.ənt] *adj.* 出色的；極好的

▶ This restaurant has excellent food.
這家餐廳有很棒的菜餚。

E

101

except [ɪkˈsept] *v.* 把…除外；不計

▶ Children are excepted from paying tax.
小孩不需要賦稅。

excepting [ɪkˈsep.tɪŋ] *prep.* 除…之外

▶ Everyone is going excepting me.
除了我之外，大家都會去。

101 100

excite [ɪkˈsaɪt] *v.* 使興奮

▶ Thinking of going back to college next year really excites me.
一想到明年能回到大學念書，就讓我很興奮。

excited [ɪkˈsaɪ.t̬ɪd] *adj.* 感到興奮的

實用片語與搭配字

be excited about 因（某事某人）感到興奮

▶ The excited dog ran to greet its master.
這隻興奮的狗跑向牠主人打招呼。

▶ Mary was so excited about her trip to Australia that she could not sleep for a week.
瑪麗對她去澳洲的旅行感到非常興奮，以至於她一週都睡不好。

excitement [ɪkˈsaɪt.mənt] *n.* 興奮；激動

▶ John was full of excitement as Sharon walked toward him.
當雪倫走向約翰的時候，他滿心興奮。

101 98

exciting [ɪkˈsaɪ.t̬ɪŋ] *adj.* 刺激的；令人興奮的

▶ Basketball is a very exciting sport!
棒球是一項非常刺激的運動！

102 95

excuse [ɪkˈskjuːs] *n.*（辯解的）理由；藉口

實用片語與搭配字

make excuses 表示歉意；找藉口

▶ Do you have an excuse for being late?
你對於遲到有什麼理由嗎？

▶ I always have to make excuses for my brother because he is so rude to everyone.
我總是要為我弟弟對別人的魯莽找藉口。

excuse [ɪkˈskjuːz] *v.* 原諒

▶ Please excuse me from the dinner table; I must take this call.
請原諒我離開餐桌，我得接這通電話。

exercise [ˈek.sɚ.saɪz]

① *n.* 運動；練習

② *v.* 運動；練習

▶ I don't have time for exercise every day.
我沒有時間每天運動。

▶ I try to exercise every day.
我試著每天運動。

---

exist [ɪgˈzɪst] *v.* 存在

實用片語與搭配字

exist in 存在

▶ Dinosaurs existed millions of years ago.
恐龍存在於數百萬年前。

▶ Dragons and fairies only exist in your imagination.
龍和精靈只存在在你的想像當中。

103

expect [ɪkˈspekt] *v.* 預計；期待

實用片語與搭配字

expect sth from sb 對（某人）抱有期望

▶ We expect you to be home by 10 p.m.
我們預計你會在晚上十點到家。

▶ I expect loyalty from my boyfriend because that is more important than anything else.
我希望我的男朋友對我忠誠，因為這比其他任何事情都重要。

expensive [ɪkˈspen.sɪv] *adj.* 昂貴的

▶ Don't buy that dress; it's too expensive.
別買那件洋裝，太貴了。

---

experience [ɪkˈspɪr.i.əns]

① *n.* 經驗

② *v.* 體驗；經歷

▶ Do you have any experience teaching students?
你有任何教學的經驗嗎？

▶ Have you ever experienced the pain of breaking your leg?
你曾體驗過斷腿的痛嗎？

---

expert [ˈek.spɝːt]

① *n.* 專家

② *adj.* 專家的；有經驗的

▶ Dana is an expert in training animals.
戴娜是訓練動物的專家。

▶ Please give me your expert opinion.
請給我你的專業意見。

---

explain [ɪkˈspleɪn] *v.* 解釋

▶ The teacher explained the poem to her students.
這位老師向學生解釋這首詩。

express [ɪk'spres]

① *v.* 表達

實用片語與搭配字

express in 以…表達

② *adj.* 直達的；快速的

③ *adv.* 以快遞方式服務地

④ *n.* 快遞；快運

- ▶ If you don't agree, feel free to express your opinion.
  如果你不贊同，請不用客氣表達你的意見。
- ▶ Ruth does not like to talk to people, but she can express herself well in her drawings.
  露絲不喜歡和人說話，但在她的圖畫中能充份表達。
- ▶ Mary took the express bus to the airport.
  瑪麗搭了直達車去機場。
- ▶ Send these boxes express.
  用快遞寄出這些箱子。
- ▶ Make sure to send this package by express.
  請確保用快遞寄出這個包裹。

---

extra ['ek.strə]

① *adj.* 額外的

② *adv.* 特別地；非常地

③ *n.* 附加費用

- ▶ Kelly earned extra money for working overtime.
  凱莉因為加班賺了額外的錢。
- ▶ David likes his bacon extra crispy.
  大衛想要他的培根特別酥脆。
- ▶ Sarah was unhappy with the hotel for adding so many extras on the bill.
  莎拉對這家旅館在帳單上加了這麼多額外的費用感到不滿。

---

eye [aɪ]

① *n.* 眼睛

② *v.* 注視；看；審視

- ▶ You have blue eyes.
  你有一雙藍眼睛。
- ▶ Wade has been eying a new car.
  韋德一直在注意一輛新車。

Exercise 19

I. Choose and write the correct word. Change the form of the word when necessary.

1	exam (n.) example (n.)	The company is an outstanding ________ of a small business that grew into a big one.
2	excite (v.) except (v.)	I know nothing about it ________ what I have read in the papers.
3	exact (adj.) excellent (adj.)	The ________ number of people carrying the virus is unknown.
4	experience (n.) express (n.)	He's sure to get the job because he has over 5 year's ________ in similar jobs.
5	exist (v.) expect (v.)	Sometimes I wonder if intelligent life ________ on other planets, or even on our planet.

II. Multiple choices.

( ) 1. The baby's first step caused great ________ in the family.
(A) exercise (B) excuse (C) excitement (D) example

( ) 2. When learning new vocabulary, in addition to translating it in your notebook, try ________ the word in English.
(A) experiencing (B) expecting (C) explaining (D) excusing

( ) 3. We can't do this by ourselves; we need to get some advice from the ________.
(A) extra (B) exercise (C) exam (D) expert

( ) 4. Detectives ________ the body to see if there were any clues to the cause of the death.
(A) examined (B) excused (C) experienced (D) excited

( ) 5. The children made up all kinds of ________ to avoid doing housework.
(A) excitements (B) examples (C) eyebrows (D) excuses

Unit 20

eyebrow / brow [ˈaɪ.braʊ / braʊ] *n.* 眉毛

▶ Marian's eyebrows have a nice shape.
瑪麗安的眉毛形狀很好看。

---

face [feɪs]

① *n.* 臉

② *v.* 正視；必須對付（難題）；面對

實用片語與搭配字

face with 面對

▶ He has a round face.
他有一張圓臉。

▶ You need to face your problems.
你必須正視你的問題並解決。

▶ If you are faced with a dangerous situation, stay calm and think clearly.
如果你面對危險的情況，保持冷靜，思路清楚。

---

fact [fækt] *n.* 事實；實際情況

實用片語與搭配字

in fact 事實上

▶ There are two important facts.
有兩個重要的事實。

▶ Traveling is great, in fact, I can think of many reasons why people should travel.
旅行是好的，事實上，我可以想到人們應該旅行的許多原因。

---

factory [ˈfæk.tɚ.i] *n.* 工廠

▶ Mike works in a factory.
麥可在工廠工作。

fail [feɪl]

① *v.* 失敗

實用片語與搭配字

fail in 失敗

② *n.* 不及格

▶ During Allison's first month in New York, she failed to find a job.
艾莉森待在紐約的第一個月並沒有找到工作。

▶ If you fail in school, it does not mean you will fail in life -- it depends on your attitude.
如果你在學校失敗，並不意味著你會在生活中失敗 -- 這取決於你的態度。

▶ Rosa received four passes and two fails on her exams.
蘿莎的考試有四科通過，兩科不及格。

---

failure [ˈfeɪ.ljɚ] *n.* 失敗

▶ Jessica's surprise party was a complete failure.
潔西卡的驚喜派對完全失敗了。

fair [fer]

① *adj.* 公平的

② *adv.* 公平地；公正地

實用片語與搭配字

have one's fair share of sth

遭遇許多（或過多）（壞事情）

③ *n.* 展覽會

▶ Gabe is a fair and wise boss.
蓋伯是位公平又有智慧的老闆。

▶ Remember to stick to the rules and play fair.
記得要遵守規則，公平地競賽。

▶ The writer had his fair share of failures before he became a famous author.
這位作家在成名之前，曾經歷許多次失敗。

▶ Ben bought seven books at the book fair.
班恩在書展買了七本書。

---

fall [fɑːl]

① *n.* 秋天；跌倒

② *v.* 落下；跌倒

實用片語與搭配字

fall in 落入

▶ Fall is my favorite season.
秋天是我最喜歡的季節。

▶ The pencil is going to fall.
這支鉛筆快掉了。

▶ It is easy to fall in love, but staying together is not easy.
墜入愛河不難，但維持關係很不容易。

---

false [fɑːls] *adj.* 錯誤的

▶ Is this true or false?
這是對的還是錯的？

---

family [ˈfæm.əl.i] *n.* 家庭

▶ There are three people in my family.
我家有三個人。

famous [ˈfeɪ.məs] *adj.* 著名的；出名的

▶ The city of Philadelphia is famous for its cheese steaks.
費城以起司牛排著名。

---

fan [fæn]

① *n.* 電扇；扇子

② *v.* 搧（風）

▶ Turn off the fan when you leave.
當你離開的時候要關電扇。

▶ Melody fanned herself with the paper.
美樂蒂用紙給自己搧風。

---

far [fɑːr]

① *adv.* 遠地；遙遠地；久遠地

▶ Did you drive far?
你開得很遠嗎？

② *adj.* 遠的；遙遠的

實用片語與搭配字

far from 遠為…

- ▶ It happened in a far off country.
  這發生在一個遙遠的國家。
- ▶ James told us he was sick, but that is far from the truth; he actually went to see a baseball game.
  詹姆斯告訴我們他病了，但這完全不是真的；其實他去看了棒球比賽。

farm [fɑːrm]

① *n.* 農場

② *v.* 耕作；種植；養殖

- ▶ Tom is visiting the farm.
  湯姆要去參觀這座農場。
- ▶ He's going to farm that land.
  他要耕作這塊田。

---

farmer [ˈfɑːr.mɚ] *n.* 農夫

- ▶ Tom will be a farmer.
  湯姆將會成為農夫。

fast [fæst]

① *adj.* 快速的；敏捷的

② *adv.* 快速地；迅速地

- ▶ That is a fast car.
  那部車跑得很快。
- ▶ You drive really fast.
  你開車開得很快。

---

fat [fæt]

① *adj.* 肥胖的

② *n.* 脂肪

實用片語與搭配字

high in fat 高熱量

- ▶ That dog is really fat.
  那隻狗真的很胖。
- ▶ Please cut the fat off my steak.
  請幫我切掉牛排上的肥油。
- ▶ Fried chicken is extremely high in fat and very unhealthy.
  炸雞有非常高的熱量且非常不健康。

---

father [ˈfɑː.ðər / ˈfɑː.ðɚ]

① *n.* 父親

② *v.* 成為…的父親

- ▶ He is my father.
  他是我的父親。
- ▶ Jeff fathered two children.
  傑夫是兩個小孩的爸爸。

---

fault [fɑːlt]

① *n.* 缺點；錯誤

② *v.* 挑…的錯；犯錯

- ▶ People all have faults and weaknesses.
  大家都有缺點和弱點。
- ▶ He faulted the doctor for not saving his daughter's life.
  他怪罪醫師沒有挽救他女兒的性命。

favor [ˈfeɪ·vər]

① *n.* 善意的行為；恩惠

實用片語與搭配字

ask a favor 請人幫忙

② *v.* 偏愛；偏袒

實用片語與搭配字

in favor of 偏袒

- ▶ Could you do me a favor and take out the garbage?
  你可以幫我個忙把垃圾拿出去嗎？
- ▶ I need to ask a favor. Could you lend me some money?
  請你幫我一個忙。能借給我一些錢嗎？
- ▶ She always felt that her parents favored her younger sister.
  她總是覺得父母偏愛妹妹。
- ▶ Dennis is in favor of traveling by train because he has a fear of flying.
  丹尼斯偏好坐火車旅行，因為他害怕飛行。

favorite [ˈfeɪ.vər.ət]

① *adj.* 最喜愛的

② *n.* 特別喜愛的人、物

- ▶ Shirley wore her favorite dress to the opera.
  雪莉穿上她最喜愛的禮服到歌劇院。
- ▶ Chocolate chip cookies are my favorite!
  巧克力脆片餅乾是我的最愛！

---

fear [fɪr]

① *n.* 懼怕；擔憂

② *v.* 害怕；畏懼；懼怕

實用片語與搭配字

have a fear of; fear for 害怕；為⋯擔心

- ▶ Fear can be very dangerous.
  懼怕會是非常危險的。
- ▶ I don't fear them.
  我不怕他們。
- ▶ Many people have a fear of spiders, however, I think they are pretty cool.
  許多人害怕蜘蛛，不過，我認為牠們很酷。

fearful [ˈfɪr.fəl] *adj.* 害怕的

- ▶ He's fearful that his boss will fire him.
  他很怕他的老闆會開除他。

February / Feb. [ˈfeb.ruː.er.i] *n.* 二月

- ▶ The weather is cold in February.
  二月的時候天氣很冷。

fee [fiː] *n.* 費用

- ▶ There may be a transfer fee if you send money to a different country.
  如果你想匯錢到別的國家，可能需要付轉帳費。

feed [fi:d]

① *v.* 餵養；給（人、團體或動物）提供食物

② *n.* 動物飼料；（嬰兒的）一餐

► I need to feed the chickens.

我必需餵這群雞。

► I'll buy more feed for the chickens tonight.

我今晚會多買一些飼料給雞吃。

F

Exercise 20

I. Choose and write the correct word. Change the form of the word when necessary.

1	favor (n.) failure (n.)	The hospital has a backup generator in case there's a power __________.
2	fear (v.) feed (v.)	They suffer from health problems and __________ the long term effects of radiation.
3	false (adj.) fair (adj.)	He tried to give the police a __________ name and address when they stopped him for speeding.
4	fail (v.) face (v.)	No matter how hard it is, just keep going because you only __________ when you give up.
5	family (n.) fault (n.)	Don't put the blame on him; it's not all his __________.

II. Multiple choices.

(　　) 1. He got a job working in his uncle's leather __________ punching holes in belts and shoes.
(A) failure　(B) factory　(C) fault　(D) family

(　　) 2. There are lots of good internet sites which give __________ about all different kinds of animals.
(A) faults　(B) fairs　(C) facts　(D) favors

(　　) 3. This __________ doctor has operated on many important people.
(A) famous　(B) far　(C) false　(D) fearful

(　　) 4. Let's go to the football game and cheer for our __________ team.
(A) fearful　(B) fair　(C) favorite　(D) fast

(　　) 5. Our teacher isn't __________; she always gives the highest marks to her favorites.
(A) fault　(B) false　(C) fair　(D) favor

Unit 21

F

feel [fiːl]

① *v.* 覺得；感到；體會到

實用片語與搭配字

feel like; feel for 意欲；同情

② *n.* 感覺；氣氛

▶ I feel sad.
我感到難過。

▶ I feel like having pizza tonight at that new restaurant.
我今晚想去那間新開的餐廳吃比薩。

▶ There was the feel of rain in the air.
空氣中有種要下雨的感覺。

103

feeling [ˈfiː.lɪŋ]

n. （感官的）感覺；感情；情緒

實用片語與搭配字

gut feeling; mixed feeling
直覺；複雜的感受

▶ That was a terrible feeling.
那感覺真的很糟。

▶ I have a gut feeling it is going to rain tomorrow, so you should take an umbrella with you.
我的直覺告訴我明天會下雨，所以你應該要帶傘出門。

feelings [ˈfiːlɪŋz] *n.* 情感；感受

▶ Her feelings were hurt.
她的情感受了傷。

fellow [ˈfel.oʊ] *n.* 人；傢伙

實用片語與搭配字

fellow student 同學

▶ This fellow right here is my son.
站在這裡的這個人是我的兒子。

▶ At university, it is good to respect your fellow students, then they will respect you.
在大學裡應該尊重你的同學，這樣他們也會尊重你。

female [ˈfiː.meɪl]

① *adj.* 女的

② *n.* 女性

▶ The female lion ran away from the male lion.
這頭母獅子從那頭公獅子的身邊跑開。

▶ Our company needs workers - both male and female.
我們公司需要員工，男性和女性都需要。

fence [fens]

① *n.* 籬笆

▶ He put up a wooden fence to keep his dog from running away.
他架起木籬笆來阻止他的狗逃離。

② *v.* 把…用籬笆圍起

▶ We fenced in our garden to protect the flowers from the dogs.
我們用籬笆圍起花園，來保護花朵不被這些狗摧殘。

---

festival [ˈfes.tə.vəl] *n.* 節日；節慶

▶ The food festival in Singapore last year was wonderful.
去年新加坡的美食節超棒的。

---

fever [ˈfiː.vɚ] *n.* 發燒

▶ Terri stayed home from work today due to a high fever.
泰芮今天因為發高燒待在家裡沒去上班。

---

few [fjuː]

① *adj.* 一些的；幾個的

實用片語與搭配字

a few 一些的

② *pron.* 很少；不多；幾個

▶ There are few cookies left.
還剩下幾塊餅乾。

▶ Employees at our company only have a few vacation days every year.
我們公司裡的員工每年只有幾天假。

▶ Few students passed the test.
沒有幾個學生通過這個考試。

---

field [fiːld] *n.* 原野；田地

▶ The horses ran quickly across the field.
馬群快速地跑過原野。

---

fifteen [ˌfɪfˈtiːn]

① *n.* 十五

② *adj.* 十五個的；十五的

▶ That is number fifteen.
那是十五。

▶ There are fifteen candles.
有十五支蠟燭。

---

fifty [ˈfɪf.ti]

① *n.* 五十

② *adj.* 五十個的；五十的

▶ Fifty is after forty-nine.
五十在四十九之後。

▶ I'll buy fifty apples.
我會買五十顆蘋果。

---

fight [faɪt]

① *v.* 與…打架；吵架；失和

實用片語與搭配字

fight for; fight against
為…而戰；與…作戰

▶ The boys fight all the time.
這群男孩總是在打架。

▶ My sister loves animals and she fights for animal rights whenever she can.
我的妹妹很喜歡動物，她會盡可能為牠們爭取權益。

② *n.* 吵架；打架

實用片語與搭配字

put up a fight 奮戰

▶ Ivy was in a fight.
艾薇剛剛和人吵架。

▶ When the robber grabbed the woman's bag, she put up a fight and he gave up.
當搶匪抓住那個女人的包包時，她奮力抵抗逼得他最後放棄。

---

fighter [ˈfaɪ.t̬ɚ] *n.* 戰士；鬥士；拳擊手

▶ By the final round, both fighters were ready to drop.
最後一輪的時候，兩邊的拳擊手都快累垮了。

101

figure [ˈfɪg.jɚ]

① *n.* 數字

② *v.* 計算

實用片語與搭配字

figure out 計算出；理解

▶ Add the final figures together and that number will be your final score.
把最後的數字加起來，得出的數字就是你的最後總分。

▶ She's still figuring the cost of the items.
她還在計算這些物品的費用。

▶ If you can't figure out your math problem, you should ask your teacher for help.
如果你算不出這個數學題，就應該尋求老師的協助。

96

fill [fɪl]

① *v.* 裝滿

實用片語與搭配字

fill in; fill with 填滿；充滿

② *n.* 可應付的量；需要的量

▶ Elaine filled the jar with oil.
伊蓮把這個罐子裝滿了油。

▶ I was sick yesterday, so I asked a co-worker to fill in for me at the school where I work.
昨天我病了，所以請一位同事在我工作的學校裡替我代班。

▶ Eat your fill of hotdogs.
你可以盡情吃熱狗吃個夠。

---

film [fɪlm]

① *n.* 電影

② *v.* 拍成影片

▶ I love to watch funny films.
我愛看喜劇片。

▶ The director filmed her latest movie in Iceland.
這位導演在冰島拍攝了她最新的一部電影。

final [ˈfaɪ.nəl]

① *adj.* 最後的

② *n.* 決賽

▶ This is the final race.
這是最後一場比賽。

▶ We're going to watch the final.
我們要去看這場決賽。

finally [ˈfaɪ.nəl.i] *adv.* 最後；終於

▶ The baseball season has finally ended.
棒球季終於結束了。

find [faɪnd]

① *v.* 找到

實用片語與搭配字

find out 找出；查明

② *n.* 發現物；被發現的人（尤指有價值或有用者）

▶ Alysa can't find her shoes.
雅莉莎找不到她的鞋子。

▶ Please find out whether we get a day off tomorrow due to the typhoon.
請確認明天是否會因為颱風而放假。

▶ That shirt was a great find.
那件衣服是很棒的戰利品。

---

fine [faɪn]

① *adj.* 美好的

② *adv.* 很好地；令人滿意地

③ *n.* 罰款；罰金

④ *v.* 處…以罰款

▶ This is a fine day.
今天是美好的一天。

▶ She is doing fine.
她過得很好。

▶ I need to pay a parking fine.
我需要付一筆停車罰金。

▶ The police officer fined the driver.
警察開了張罰單給這位駕駛。

---

finger [ˈfɪŋ.gɚ]

① *n.* 手指

② *v.* 用手指觸碰；撫摸

▶ He has five fingers.
他有五隻手指。

▶ Catherine fingered the cloth.
凱薩琳用手指摸了那塊布料。

finish [ˈfɪn.ɪʃ]

① *v.* 結束；完成

實用片語與搭配字

finish with; finish off
完成，與…斷絕關係；結束，擊敗

② *n.* （比賽的）結果；（某事的）最後階段

▶ I will finish my work in five minutes.
我會在五分鐘內完成我的工作。

▶ The soccer players were so hungry after the game that they finished off their dinner in ten minutes.
比賽結束後足球隊員們都很餓，十分鐘內就吃完晚餐了。

▶ The race had an exciting finish.
這場比賽有個令人興奮的結果。

fire [faɪr]

① *n.* 火災；火

實用片語與搭配字

open fire; play with fire 開火；玩火

② *v.* 開火；射擊

實用片語與搭配字

fire at 向…開火

③ *v.* 解僱；開除

▶ There is a fire in the house.
這間房子鬧火災。

▶ If you drink and drive, you play with fire because you can hurt or kill someone.
如果你酒後駕車，這是玩火自焚，因為你可能因此傷害或殺了某人。

▶ The men fired from the roof of the house.
這些男人從這棟房子的屋頂上開火。

▶ The soldiers fired at the house where the enemy was hiding.
那些士兵向一棟藏著敵軍的住宅開槍。

▶ The lazy worker was fired.
那個懶惰的工人被解僱了。

---

fireman / firewoman

[ˈfaɪr.mən / ˈfaɪr.wʊm.ən / ˈfī(-ə)r-ˌwu̇-mən]

n. （男）消防隊員／女消防隊員

▶ The brave fireman rescued the girl from the burning fire.
那位勇敢的消防隊員將女孩從火場中救出。

Exercise 21

I. Choose and write the correct word. Change the form of the word when necessary.

1	feeling (n.) fence (n.)	The __________ marks the boundary between my land and hers.
2	field (n.) fight (n.)	The cattle got out of the __________ through an opening in the fence.
3	few (adj.) final (adj.)	The __________ exam for this class will be on May 1 st .
4	figure (v.) find (v.)	It took them about a month to __________ out how to start the equipment.
5	finally (adv.) fine (adv.)	The lost boy was __________ reunited with his parents.

II. Multiple choices.

(　　) 1. There is a big music __________ in Quebec City each summer.

(A) final　(B) festival　(C) fence　(D) fellow

(　　) 2. We must __________ the task before the deadline by all means.

(A) film　(B) fight　(C) finish　(D) fill

(　　) 3. __________ kangaroos carry their young in pouches that are external to their bodies.

(A) Female　(B) Fellow　(C) Final　(D) Fighter

(　　) 4. This old __________ has never been knocked down by an opponent.

(A) finger　(B) feeling　(C) fight　(D) fighter

(　　) 5. If you have a __________, you should drink plenty of liquid.

(A) fellow　(B) figure　(C) fever　(D) film

Unit 22

firm [fɝːm]

① *adj.* 堅定的；穩固的

② *adv.* 堅定不移地；穩固地

③ *v.* 使穩固

實用片語與搭配字

firm up （透過鍛煉）使（身體部位）結實，（使）緊實

- It's important for parents and teachers to be firm with their children.
  父母和老師對孩子要有堅定的態度是很重要的。
- Martha has always stood firmly behind women's rights.
  瑪莎在女權議題上態度始終堅定。
- After firming the soil, water the plant.
  將土鋪穩之後，再為植物澆水。
- Lifting weights is a good way to firm up your muscles.
  舉重是讓肌肉變結實的好方法。

first [ˈfɝːst]

① *adj.* 第一的

② *n.* 第一

③ *adv.* 第一；首先

- He is first in the line.
  他是隊伍中的第一個人。
- This prize is for first.
  這是第一名的獎品。
- Melody arrived first.
  美樂蒂首先抵達。

fish [fɪʃ]

① *n.* 魚

② *v.* 釣魚；捕魚

實用片語與搭配字

fish for 設法用間接手段得到

- Jean caught a big fish.
  珍捉了一條大魚。
- Olivia is going fishing.
  奧莉薇雅要去釣魚。
- My boyfriend likes to fish for compliments. He loves hearing me tell him how smart he is.
  我男朋友喜歡得到稱讚。他愛聽我說他有多聰明。

fisherman [ˈfɪʃ.ɚ.mən] *n.* 漁夫

- The fisherman caught a fish and cooked it for dinner.
  這個漁夫捕了一條魚，並煮來當晚餐吃。

fishing [ˈfɪʃ.ɪŋ] *n.* 釣魚；捕魚

- Fishing is a relaxing thing to do.
  釣魚是一件令人放鬆的事。

F

fit [fɪt]

① *adj.* 適合的；合身的

實用片語與搭配字

fit for 適合

② *v.* 合身；適合

實用片語與搭配字

fit in 相處融洽，使適應

③ *n.* 適合

- She's not fit for this job, so we can't hire her.
  她並不適合這份工作，所以我們無法聘僱她。
- This house was damaged in the typhoon and is not fit for living.
  這間房子因颱風受損，已不適合居住。
- These pants don't fit me anymore!
  這件褲子我穿起來不再合身了！
- I think Jeremy is the perfect fit for our team.
  我想傑瑞米是最適合我們團隊的人了。

---

five [faɪv]

① *n.* 五

實用片語與搭配字

high five 舉手擊掌

② *adj.* 五的；五個的

- Four plus one equals five.
  四加一等於五。
- When people high five each other, it usually means they are happy.
  當人們相互擊掌，意味著他們很開心。
- I've lived here for five years.
  我住這裡住了五年。

---

fix [fɪks]

① *v.* 修理；校準

實用片語與搭配字

fix up 修理，安排，改進

② *n.* 困境

- The engineer could not fix my computer, so I had to buy a new one.
  這位工程師無法修好我的電腦，所以我必須買一台新的。
- I am going to fix up my house by the lake and turn it into a beautiful vacation home.
  我將要把那棟湖邊的房子整修成一間美麗的度假小屋。
- Give him a hand; he is in a bad fix.
  拉他一把吧，他已陷入了困境。

---

flag [flæg]

① *n.* 旗幟

實用片語與搭配字

red flag; wave flag
示警紅旗；表示擁護支持，搖旗吶喊

② *v.* 標示；打旗號表示

實用片語與搭配字

flag down 揮手示意某人停車

- There were flags all over town.
  整個城鎮飄滿了旗幟。
- Flag all the photos that you will use in your talk.
  在你演講中會用到的照片都標記出來。
- Her car broke down and she had to flag down a motorist who stopped and helped her.
  因為車子壞了，她揮手示意一位駕駛停下來協助她。

flash [flæʃ]

① *v.* 使閃光

實用片語與搭配字

flash on 靈機一動

② *n.* 閃光

實用片語與搭配字

camera flash 相機閃光燈

- ▶ Don't flash the light in my eyes!
  別對著我的眼睛閃燈。
- ▶ After thinking about my project for a while, I suddenly flashed on a great idea.
  在苦思專案一段時間後，我突然靈機一動想到一個好主意。
- ▶ She saw a flash of light hit the tree.
  她看見一道閃電擊中了那棵樹。
- ▶ When you take a photograph at night, it is a good idea to use a camera flash to provide light.
  當你在晚上拍照，最好使用閃光燈來補光。

---

flashlight [ˈflæʃ.laɪt] *n.* 手電筒

- ▶ The lights went out during the storm, so we used flashlights.
  這場暴風雨中停電了，所以我們用手電筒。

---

flat [flæt]

① *adj.* 平坦的

② *adv.* 平坦地

③ *n.* 平地；低窪地

④ *v.* 使平坦

- ▶ Most of the houses in this country have flat roofs.
  這個國家大部分的房子屋頂都是平的。
- ▶ I tripped and fell flat on my face! How embarrassing!
  我絆倒而且跌個狗吃屎！好尷尬！
- ▶ I love walking through the flats around my uncle's farm.
  我喜歡散步穿過我舅舅農場附近的平地。
- ▶ Sarah uses the flipper to flat the pancakes.
  莎拉用鍋鏟將煎餅弄平。

---

flight [flaɪt] *n.* 飛行；飛機航程

實用片語與搭配字

catch flight 趕上飛機

- ▶ I have to go to the airport. My flight is at 2:00.
  我需要去機場，我的飛機時間是兩點。
- ▶ I have to catch a flight to Canada tonight, so I am not sure if I can finish my work on time.
  由於今晚要搭飛機去加拿大，所以我不確定能否按時完成工作。

flood [flʌd]

① *n.* 水災

② *v.* 淹沒

▶ The typhoon caused a serious flood in our county.
這個颱風在我們國家造成很嚴重的水災。

▶ Water flooded onto the floor when she sat in the bathtub.
當她坐進浴缸裡，水就淹滿到地上了。

---

floor [flɔːr]

① *n.* 地板

② *v.* 在…鋪設地板

▶ Ophelia likes the wooden floor.
奧菲莉雅喜歡這個木地板。

▶ Jim floored the room last weekend.
吉姆上週末將這個房間鋪好地板。

---

flour [ˈflaʊ.ɚ]

① *n.* 麵粉

② *v.* 灑粉於…

▶ How much flour do we need for this cake?
做這個蛋糕需要多少麵粉？

▶ You should flour your hands before you mix this dough.
你應該在揉麵團前先灑些麵粉在手上。

---

flow [floʊ]

① *v.* 流動；飄垂

實用片語與搭配字

flow from 從…流出

② *n.* 流動；（向某方向）移動

實用片語與搭配字

cash flow 資金流動

▶ The Colorado River flows through seven U.S. states.
科羅拉多河流經美國七個州。

▶ Inventions flow from everyday problems which people find solutions for.
新的發現總是出現在解決問題的過程中。

▶ We need to find something to stop the flow of blood on this cut.
我們必須找個東西止住這個傷口的出血。

▶ The company went bankrupt after several months of cash flow problems.
這家公司經歷數個月資金周轉的問題後破產了。

---

flower [ˈflaʊ.ɚ]

① *n.* 花

② *v.* 開花

▶ The flowers are blue.
這些花是藍色的。

▶ The trees will flower in April.
這些樹會在四月開花。

---

flu [fluː] *n.* 流行性感冒

▶ Angela stayed home from school today because she has the flu.
安琪拉因為得了流行性感冒，所以今天沒上學留在家裡。

flute [flu:t]

① *n.* 長笛

② *v.* 刻凹槽於…

▶ Annie has been playing the flute since she was six years old.
安妮從六歲就開始吹長笛。

▶ The little boy fluted on a piece of wood.
這個小男孩在一塊木頭上刻洞。

F

---

fly [flaɪ]

① *n.* 蒼蠅

② *v.* 飛行

實用片語與搭配字

fly away 飛走

▶ There is a fly in my soup.
我的湯裡有一隻蒼蠅。

▶ Birds can fly.
鳥可以飛行。

▶ If you speak too loudly, the bird will fly away.
若你說話太大聲，那隻鳥可能會飛走。

focus [ˈfoʊ.kəs]

① *n.* 焦點；焦距

② *v.* 調節（相機、顯微鏡等）的焦距

▶ Jim's focus at work lately is to finish this project.
吉姆最近的工作焦點是要完成這個專案。

▶ Can you please show me how to focus this camera?
你可以教我如何調這台照相機的焦距嗎？

---

fog [fɑ:g]

① *n.* 霧

② *v.* 被霧籠罩；布滿霧氣

▶ There was fog on the mountain.
那座山上有霧。

▶ The mountain fogged over.
這座山被霧籠罩著。

---

foggy [ˈfɑ:.gi] *adj.* 多霧的

▶ Drive slowly on the mountain roads, as they can be quite foggy.
在山路上開車要緩慢，因為那裡可能濃霧瀰漫。

follow [ˈfɑ:.loʊ] *v.* 跟隨

實用片語與搭配字

follow up; follow by 後續（行動），跟進（行動）; 被…跟隨

▶ The dog is following you.
這隻狗正跟著你。

▶ When you learn new vocabulary in school, you should follow up at home by reviewing the words.
當你在學校學了新的單字，你應該要回家複習當天所學的內容。

Exercise 22

I. Choose and write the correct word. Change the form of the word when necessary.

<table>
<tr><td rowspan="2">1</td><td>fisherman (n.)</td><td rowspan="2">One local ________ was drowned when his boat caught fire and burned.</td></tr>
<tr><td>fishing (n.)</td></tr>
<tr><td rowspan="2">2</td><td>fit (adj.)</td><td rowspan="2">Cockroaches have ________ bodies, so they can squeeze under things to hide.</td></tr>
<tr><td>flat (adj.)</td></tr>
<tr><td rowspan="2">3</td><td>fix (v.)</td><td rowspan="2">A driver isn't supposed to ________ his lights at the oncoming vehicles.</td></tr>
<tr><td>flash (v.)</td></tr>
<tr><td rowspan="2">4</td><td>flu (n.)</td><td rowspan="2">I came down with the ________ and was unable to go to work.</td></tr>
<tr><td>flute (n.)</td></tr>
<tr><td rowspan="2">5</td><td>flow (v.)</td><td rowspan="2">We should always learn from everything; we should ________ in order to learn more.</td></tr>
<tr><td>focus (v.)</td></tr>
</table>

II. Multiple choices.

( ) 1. More water ________ out of the Amazon River than any other river in the world.
(A) flies (B) fires (C) flashes (D) flows

( ) 2. They often have ________ after a heavy rainfall in summer.
(A) floors (B) flour (C) flows (D) floods

( ) 3. Don't ________ others' steps when making your own trip.
(A) focus (B) follow (C) flow (D) flat

( ) 4. It was so ________ that the driver could hardly make out the way ahead.
(A) foggy (B) firm (C) flat (D) first

( ) 5. The bridge provides a ________ platform for bungee jumpers.
(A) five (B) firm (C) foggy (D) flu

Unit 23

following [ˈfɑː.loʊ.ɪŋ]

① *prep.* 在…以後

② *n.* 擁護者；追隨者

③ *adj.* 接著的

► There will be drinks and snacks outside following the talk.
會談之後外面會有飲料與點心。

► That boy band has a large following around the world.
那個男孩樂團在世界各地有很多的擁護者。

► We'll fly into Paris and drive to the countryside the following day.
我們會飛到巴黎，並且隔天開車到鄉下。

95

food [fuːd] *n.* 食物

► Please have some food.
請享用一些食物。

---

fool [fuːl]

① *n.* 傻子

實用片語與搭配字

make a fool of
愚弄（某人），令（某人）出洋相

② *v.* 欺騙；愚弄

實用片語與搭配字

fool around 遊手好閒，閒蕩

► You're a fool if you really think you can pass that test without studying.
如果你認為沒有讀書就可以通過那個考試，那你就是個傻子。

► You will make a fool of yourself if you go shopping in your pajamas.
若你穿著睡衣出門逛街，一定會出洋相。

► Sara was fooled by the smooth-talking salesman.
莎拉被那位花言巧語的銷售員騙了。

► When you fool around during exam time, you will get bad grades.
你在考試時間閒晃不好好作答，你的成績將會很差。

---

foolish [ˈfuː.lɪʃ] *adj.* 愚蠢的

► It was really foolish of Erin to not get gas before leaving on the car trip.
愛玲在開車去旅行前沒有加油，真的很愚蠢。

---

foot [fʊt]

① *n.* 腳

② *v.* 步行；走

► I hurt my foot.
我傷了我的腳。

► The soldiers footed up the mountain.
這隊士兵步行上山。

football [ˈfʊt.bɑːl] *n.* 足球

▶ I played football in high school, but I didn't continue in college.
我在高中的時候踢足球，但是到大學時就沒有再繼續了。

---

for [fɔːr / fɚ]

① *prep.* 為贏得；為了…

② *conj.* 因為；由於…的緣故

▶ Lillian wants to run for president.
莉莉安想要競選總統。

▶ I am lucky for I work hard.
我很幸運是因為我認真工作。

---

force [fɔːrs]

① *n.* 力氣；力量

實用片語與搭配字

join force; come into force
聯合以達到共同的目標；(使法律、規則等）生效，開始執行

② *v.* 強行打開；用力移動

實用片語與搭配字

force into 強迫，迫使

▶ It takes a lot of force to move that box.
搬運那個箱子需要花很大的力氣。

▶ The government made a new law and it will come into force next month.
政府訂定的新法將在下個月生效。

▶ Helen forced the door open.
海倫硬把門打開。

▶ In some poor countries, young girls are forced into marriages by their families.
在一些貧困的國家，年輕女孩受家庭壓迫而結婚。

---

foreign [ˈfɔːr.ən] *adj.* 外國的

實用片語與搭配字

be foreign to 對（某人）而言是陌生的

▶ Emily is from a foreign country.
艾蜜莉來自國外。

▶ Marcus has never been abroad and the whole idea of traveling by plane is foreign to him.
馬可斯從來沒有出過國，搭飛機旅行這件事對他來說很陌生。

---

foreigner [ˈfɔːr.ə.nɚ] *n.* 外國人

▶ Let's plan an activity for the foreigners living in our city.
我們為那些住在本地的外國人辦一個活動吧。

---

forest [ˈfɔːr.ɪst] *n.* 森林

▶ Jane likes sitting in the forest.
珍喜歡坐在森林裡。

---

forget [fɚˈget] *v.* 忘記

▶ Don't forget to do your homework.
不要忘記做你的功課。

實用片語與搭配字

forget about 忘記，不再想

▶ After getting poor grades on my three subjects, I can forget about getting the scholarship.
在我考砸了三個科目之後，我就不用再想拿到獎學金了。

---

forgive [fɚˈɡɪv] *v.* 原諒

▶ I'm sorry I missed our meeting today. Can you please forgive me?
我很抱歉我錯過了今天的會議。可以請你原諒我嗎？

實用片語與搭配字

forgive for; forgive and forget
原諒；不念舊惡

▶ It may not always be easy, but to forgive and forget is the best way to get over a bad experience.
選擇不念舊惡並不容易，但它卻是擺脫壞經驗的最佳方法。

---

fork [fɔːrk]

① *n.* 叉子

② *v.* 叉起；用叉挖

▶ My fork is dirty.
我的叉子髒了。

▶ Can you fork some pork onto my plate?
你可以用叉子放一些豬肉到我盤子裡嗎？

---

100 97

form [fɔːrm]

① *n.* 形式；形狀

② *v.* 形成；構成

▶ From our tent, we could see the form of a bear.
從我們的帳篷，似乎看到一隻熊的樣子。

▶ The company formed a group to plan social events for employees.
這家公司組了一個小組為員工計畫交流活動。

---

formal [ˈfɔːr.məl]

adj. 適合正式場合的；莊重的

▶ Carol needs to get a formal dress for the wedding on Saturday.
凱洛需要為星期六的婚禮找一件正式的禮服。

---

former [ˈfɔːr.mɚ] *adj.* 以前的；較早的

▶ I don't have Andrew's phone number, but I can ask one of my former coworkers.
我沒有安德魯的手機號碼，但是我可以詢問一位以前的同事。

---

forty [ˈfɔːr.t̬i]

① *n.* 四十

② *adj.* 四十個的；四十的

▶ Eight times five equals forty.
八乘以五等於四十。

▶ There are forty balloons.
那裡有四十顆汽球。

forward ['fɔːr.wɚd]

① *adj.* 前面的

▶ The forward journey will be quite difficult, so I hope you're ready.
前面的旅程將會很困難，所以我希望你已經準備好了。

② *adj.* 未來的

▶ This advertising company has many forward ideas.
這家廣告公司有許多前瞻性的構想。

③ *n.* 前鋒

▶ There are two forwards on a football team who are often star players.
一個足球隊裡的兩名前鋒通常都是明星球員。

④ *adv.* 向前

▶ Please face forward when you take the photo.
照相時請往前看。

實用片語與搭配字

lean forward 向前傾身

▶ The spy leaned forward to get closer to the two men to hear what they were talking about.
為了要得到兩位男士的對話內容，那名間諜朝著他們的方向傾身偷聽。

⑤ *adv.* 向將來

▶ We need to look forward now and forget about the past.
我們現在需要忘記背後努力向前看。

---

four [fɔːr]

① *n.* 四

▶ Four plus one equals five.
四加一等於五。

② *adj.* 四個的；四的

▶ I like four different colors.
我喜歡四種不同的顏色。

---

fourteen [͵fɔːr'tiːn]

① *n.* 十四

▶ Fourteen is less than fifteen.
十四小於十五。

② *adj.* 十四的；十四個的

▶ She is fourteen years old.
她十四歲。

---

fox [fɑːks] *n.* 狐狸

▶ Shauna looked out the window and was surprised to see a little fox.
紹娜往窗外看去，意外地看見一隻小狐狸。

---

frank [fræŋk] *adj.* 坦白的

▶ To be frank, I think your plan is going to fail.
坦白說，我覺得你的計劃會失敗。

free [friː]

① *adj.* 免費的

▶ Amber gave me a free ticket.
安柏給我一張免費的票。

② *adv.* 自由地；無拘束地

▶ The chickens ran free.
這群雞自由地到處跑。

實用片語與搭配字

break free 掙脫，脫離

▶ Miriam wanted to break free from her boring life, so she quit her job and went traveling for a year.
為了脫離枯燥無味的生活，米瑞安決定辭職去旅行一年。

② *v.* 釋放；使自由

▶ I'm going to free that poor turtle.
我要放那隻可憐的烏龜自由。

實用片語與搭配字

free sb from / of sth; be free from
使（某人）擺脫；免於，無…之憂

▶ It is impossible to be completely free from responsibility in today's complicated world.
在當今複雜的世界裡，完全擺脫責任是不可能的。

F

---

freedom [ˈfriː.dəm] *n.* 自由

▶ The soldiers fought for freedom.
這些士兵為自由奮戰。

Exercise 23

I. Choose and write the correct word. Change the form of the word when necessary.

1	food (n.) fool (n.)	I felt like a ________ when I realized my mistake.
2	forgive (v.) forget (v.)	He left a box of chocolate at the door, hoping that she would ________ him for his fault.
3	former (adj.) formal (adj.)	Although he had had little ________ education, he could read and write well.
4	frank (adj.) free (adj.)	To be ________ with you, I think your son has little chance of passing this exam.
5	form (n.) forest (n.)	Breast cancer is the most common ________ of cancer among women in this country.

II. Multiple choices.

( ) 1. Her parents are very liberal and allow her a lot of ________.
(A) forest (B) form (C) force (D) freedom

( ) 2. Why don't you put your chair ________ to get a better view?
(A) forward (B) free (C) following (D) foreign

( ) 3. It is very difficult to live in a ________ country when you don't speak the language.
(A) former (B) formal (C) foreign (D) foolish

( ) 4. You think you're clever; on the contrary, I assure that you're very ________.
(A) foolish (B) following (C) forward (D) free

( ) 5. The hunters camped in the midst of the thick ________.
(A) force (B) freedom (C) forest (D) form

Unit 24

F

freezer [ˈfriː.zɚ] *n.* 冷凍庫

▶ Can you please put this meat in the freezer?
可以請你將這塊肉放進冷凍庫嗎？

---

fresh [freʃ] *adj.* 新鮮的

實用片語與搭配字

fresh from 剛從…來的

▶ The fresh air is good for you.
新鮮的空氣對你身體很好。

▶ You can buy vegetables fresh from the market every morning if you can get up early.
如果你可以早起，就可以買到每天早上剛從市場來的蔬果。

Friday [ˈfraɪ.deɪ] *n.* 星期五

▶ Friday is my favorite day of the week.
一週中我最愛的一天是星期五。

---

friend [frend] *n.* 朋友

實用片語與搭配字

be friends with 為（某人）的朋友

▶ Neil is my friend.
尼爾是我的朋友。

▶ It is hard to be friends with a bully, but a friend is sometimes all they need.
和一個惡霸做朋友很難，但有時他們才最需要朋友。

---

friendly [ˈfrend.li] *adj.* 友善的；親切的

實用片語與搭配字

be friendly with 對…友善

▶ All of my new classmates were friendly.
我所有的新同學都很友善。

▶ You do not have to like your co-workers, but it costs nothing to be friendly with them in the office.
你不需要喜歡你的同事，但在辦公室對他們友善不會有任何損失。

---

fright [fraɪt] *n.* 驚駭

實用片語與搭配字

stage fright （初上舞台的）怯場

▶ Andy, you gave me a fright! Don't scare people like that!
安迪，你嚇到我了！不要這樣嚇人！

▶ The singer suffers from stage fright every time she has to do a performance in front of a large crowd.
每當要上台面對眼前的觀眾表演時，那位歌手總是為之怯場。

frighten [ˈfraɪ.tən] *v.* 使害怕

實用片語與搭配字

frighten sb / sth away / off
把…嚇跑

▶ Laura is frightened of dogs because one chased her when she was little.
蘿拉很怕狗，因為她小時候曾經被狗追。

▶ The dog's barking frightened the thief away.
狗狗的叫聲嚇跑了那個小偷。

---

frog [frɑːg] *n.* 青蛙

▶ There is a frog on the road.
這條路上有隻青蛙。

---

from [frɑːm] *perp.* 從…開始；始於

▶ Shawn is walking home from school.
尚恩正從學校走回家。

---

front [frʌnt]

① *n.* 正面；前面
② *adj.* 前面的；前部的
③ *v.* （建築物或地方）朝向；面向

▶ The front of the house looks great.
這房子的正面看起來很棒。

▶ Jack is sitting in the front row.
傑克正坐在前排。

▶ The store fronts the beach.
這家店朝向海灘。

---

fruit [fruːt]

① *n.* 水果
② *v.* 結果實

▶ Apples are a delicious fruit.
蘋果是一種美味的水果。

▶ All the trees have fruited.
所有的樹都結了果子。

---

full [fʊl] *adj.* 裝滿的；充滿的

實用片語與搭配字

full of 充滿的

▶ This box is full. There is no more room.
這個盒子是滿的。沒有多餘的空間。

▶ After winning the beauty contest, Judy is really full of herself and only wants to talk about her win.
在贏得選美比賽後，茱蒂顯得自以為是，她只想談論她勝出的事情。

---

fun [fʌn] *n.* 樂趣

▶ We had fun at the party.
我們在派對玩得很開心。

---

function [ˈfʌŋk.ʃən]

① *n.* 功能；作用

▶ My new smartphone has a lot of functions; I can use it for everything!
我的新智慧型手機有很多功能，所有事情我都能用！

② *v.* 運作

▶ Steven Brown will function as the mayor until the next election takes place.
史蒂芬．布朗將繼續擔任市長直到下一次選舉之前。

---

funny [ˈfʌn.i] *adj.* 有趣的；滑稽可笑的

▶ That movie was funny. I laughed a lot.
那部電影很有趣，我一直大笑。

F

---

further [ˈfɝː.ðɚ]

① *adv.* 更遠地

② *adj.* 較遠的

實用片語與搭配字

go further 促進，推進

③ *v.* 推動；增進

▶ Amy can run further than Kellie, so she will be on the track team.
艾美比凱莉跑得更遠，所以她會進田徑隊。

▶ I saw Jeff and Shirley at the further end of the campus earlier today.
今天較早時，我在校園較遠的盡頭看見傑夫與雪莉。

▶ If you want to go further in life, you have to work hard and continue to study.
若想在人生中更上一層樓，你必須努力工作，並且繼續學習。

▶ What else can we do to further our building plans?
還有什麼事是我們可以做的，來推動大樓營建計畫？

---

future [ˈfjuː.tʃɚ]

① *n.* 未來

實用片語與搭配字

near future; look to the future; in the future 不久的將來；考慮、計畫將來；未來

② *adj.* 未來的

實用片語與搭配字

future generation 未來的世代

▶ Looking at my newborn baby, I began to imagine her future.
看著我新出生的寶寶，我開始想像著她的未來。

▶ Many people look to the future for a better life instead of appreciating everything they have today.
許多人計劃更好的未來，卻忘記珍惜當下。

▶ Now that you've finished from college, what are your future plans?
現在你已大學畢業了，你未來的計劃是什麼？

▶ The future generation is going to have bigger problems with global warming if we do not do anything today.
如果我們現在不正視全球暖化，未來的世代將會面臨更大的問題。

100

gain [geɪn]

① *v.* 得到；獲益

實用片語與搭配字

gain from; gain experience; gain knowledge 從…獲得；獲得經驗；獲得知識

② *n.* 收益；獲利

實用片語與搭配字

weight gain 增加體重

▶ I've gained a lot of knowledge from this course; I'm glad I took it!
我從這堂課獲得很多知識，真高興我上了這堂課！

▶ Working at a convenience store lets you gain experience that you can use one day.
在便利商店打工獲得的經驗能在未來派上用場。

▶ Be careful of people who are only looking for personal gain.
對那些只求個人利益的人要小心防範。

▶ Sudden weight gain or weight loss can both be symptoms of serious diseases.
體重突然增加或減少都可能是嚴重疾病的徵兆。

---

game [geɪm] *n.* 遊戲

▶ Let's play a game!
讓我們來玩個遊戲吧！

---

garage [gəˈrɑːʒ]

① *n.* 車庫

② *v.* 把車送入車庫或修理廠

▶ The house we want to buy has a garage big enough for two cars.
我們要買的那間房子有一個足夠停兩輛車的車庫。

▶ Eve had to garage her car because it ran out of gas.
伊芙不得不把車停放在車庫裡，因為車子沒油了。

---

garbage [ˈgɑːr.bɪdʒ] *n.* 垃圾

▶ Dear, can you please take out the garbage tonight?
親愛的，可以請你今晚把垃圾拿出去嗎？

---

garden [ˈgɑːr.dən]

① *n.* 花園

② *v.* 從事園藝；在園中種植

▶ Look at the flowers in that garden!
看看那花園裡的花！

▶ Gertrude gardens on the weekends.
葛楚德每個週末都在做園藝。

---

gardener [ˈgɑːr.dən.ɚ] *n.* 園丁；花匠

▶ Richard is a gardener who plants many kinds of flowers.
理查是個園丁，他種植許多不同種類的花。

gas [gæs]

① *n.* 氣體；氣

實用片語與搭配字

greenhouse gas 溫室氣體（尤指二氧化碳）

② *v.* 用氣體處理；放出氣體

▸ Steam is a type of gas.
蒸氣是一種氣體。

▸ A greenhouse gas like methane is one of the biggest causes of global warming.
溫室氣體像鉀烷是造成全球暖化最重要的原因之一。

▸ The house was gassed to kill the cockroaches.
這棟房子被放置滅蟑氣體來除滅蟑螂。

---

gate [geɪt] *n.* 柵欄門；圍牆門；大門

▸ Don't forget to close the gate when you leave the yard.
當你離開後院時，不要忘記關上門。

Exercise 24

I. Choose and write the correct word. Change the form of the word when necessary.

1	freezer (n.) fright (n.)	I had a terrible __________ this morning when I saw a snake in the backyard.
2	further (adj.) fourteen (adj.)	We expect to see __________ improvement over the coming year.
3	frighten (v.) gain (v.)	He fired into the air, hoping that the noise would __________ the bears off.
4	garden (n.) garbage (n.)	He always puts his __________ in a trash can because he doesn't want to be a litterbug.
5	funny (adj.) full (adj.)	The classroom was __________ of activities; every child was busy.

II. Multiple choices.

(   ) 1. The __________ of the heart is to pump the blood through the body.
(A) fright (B) function (C) future (D) gain

(   ) 2. He is a very nice person, always pleasant and __________.
(A) friendly (B) future (C) full (D) front

(   ) 3. Our car broke down and we had to drive it to the __________.
(A) garden (B) function (C) freezer (D) garage

(   ) 4. You can store the coffee beans in the __________ to keep them fresh.
(A) gain (B) future (C) freezer (D) garage

(   ) 5. He had a holiday job as a __________ when he was a student.
(A) gardener (B) fun (C) gain (D) frog

Unit 25

gather [ˈgæð.ɚ] *v.* 聚集；招集

實用片語與搭配字

gather around 集合

▶ Please gather all of the workers together for lunch.
請集合所有員工吃午餐。

▶ On Christmas day the whole family gathers around the fireplace and sing Christmas carols.
在聖誕節，全家人會圍聚在爐火邊唱聖誕頌歌。

general [ˈdʒen.ər.əl]

① *adj.* 總的；普遍的

實用片語與搭配字

in general 一般來說，通常

② *n.* 將軍；上將

▶ What is the general idea of this book?
這本書整體的概念是什麼？

▶ In general the company is doing well, but there are some problems that need to be solved.
公司營運狀況大致良好，但還是有些問題需要解決。

▶ General Patton helped the United States win World War II.
巴頓將軍幫助美國贏得第二次世界大戰。

generous [ˈdʒen.ər.əs] *adj.* 慷慨的；大方的

▶ Thank you for your generous gift!
謝謝你這麼慷慨豐盛的禮物！

---

gentle [ˈdʒen.t̬əl] *adj.* 溫和的

實用片語與搭配字

be gentle with 對…溫和

▶ Sharon will always remember her grandmother's gentle voice.
雪倫將會永遠記得她祖母溫柔的聲音。

▶ The painting is very valuable, so please be gentle with it when you move it.
這幅畫很珍貴，搬動它時請小心。

---

gentleman [ˈdʒen.t̬əl.mən] *n.* 紳士

▶ A gentleman should always open doors for ladies.
紳士應該總是為女士開門。

96

geography [dʒiˈɑː.grə.fi] *n.* 地理

▶ We are learning about Africa in our geography class.
我們在地理課上學習了解非洲。

G

get [get] *v.* 得到

實用片語與搭配字

get out of 從…中出來

► Damon got a lot of presents for his birthday.
戴蒙得到了很多生日禮物。

► After the new year's fireworks, it was hard to get out of downtown.
跨年煙火放完之後，會很難離開市中心。

---

ghost [goʊst] *n.* 鬼；幽靈

► Gina is afraid of ghosts.
吉娜怕鬼。

---

giant [ˈdʒaɪ.ənt]

① *n.* 巨人

② *adj.* 巨大的

► There are stories that a giant lives in these woods.
有許多關於一個巨人住在這座森林裡的故事。

► Jill asked her mom for a giant ice cream cone.
吉兒跟媽媽要了一個特大的冰淇淋甜筒。

---

gift [gɪft] *n.* 禮物

實用片語與搭配字

gift from sb; wrap gift
來自…的禮物；包禮物

► Grandma gave Gabe a gift for his birthday.
奶奶給蓋伯一份生日禮物。

► The expensive vase was a gift from my boss when I left my job after 30 years.
這個貴重的花瓶是我工作三十年離開公司時，老闆送給我的禮物。

---

giraffe [dʒɪˈræf] *n.* 長頸鹿

► Derek's favorite animal at the zoo is the giraffe.
德瑞克在動物園最喜愛的動物是那隻長頸鹿。

---

girl [gɝːl] *n.* 女孩

► Alicia is a beautiful girl.
艾莉莎是個美麗的女孩。

---

give [gɪv] *v.* 給予

實用片語與搭配字

give away; give and take
贈送，分發；互相忍讓，雙方遷就

► Robbie's parents give him money every month.
羅比的父母每個月給他錢。

► In any relationship, you have to give and take so both people feel valued.
在一段關係裡，必須互相忍讓，這樣雙方都能感到被重視。

glad [glæd] *adj.* 高興的

實用片語與搭配字

be glad of 慶幸

- I'm glad Arnold is feeling better.
  我很高興阿諾身體比較好了。
- I have been working non-stop for the past week, so I was glad of my new colleague's help.
  過去一週我一直不停地工作，所以我很慶幸新來的同事給我的協助。

---

glass [glæs] *n.* 玻璃

實用片語與搭配字

glass ceiling
無形的限制 （通常專指女性在工作中升級時遇到的無形障礙，使她無法晉升到較高階層）

- Be careful with that vase. It is made of glass.
  小心那花瓶，它是玻璃做的。
- In the 21st Century, women still face the glass ceiling and it is still difficult for them to get top jobs.
  在二十一世紀，女人還是面臨許多無形的限制，以致於很難獲得職場高位。

---

glasses [ˈglɑːsɪz] *n.* 眼鏡

- Linda can't see well. She needs glasses.
  琳達無法看清楚，她需要眼鏡。

---

glove [glʌv] *n.* 手套

- My hands are cold, so I want to get some new gloves.
  我的手很冷，所以我想要買新的手套。

---

glue [gluː]

① *n.* 膠水

② *v.* 使黏牢

- Can I borrow some glue to make this craft?
  我可以跟你借一些膠水做這個手工嗎？
- All you need to do is glue the pieces of paper together.
  你需要做的只是將這些紙片黏起來。

---

go [goʊ]

① *v.* 去（參加）

實用片語與搭配字

go away; go ahead; come and go
走開，離開；開始做，（用於給別人許可）進行，開始；時來時去，變化不斷

② *n.* 輪到的機會

- I can go to the party.
  我可以去參加派對。
- Acquaintances may come and go, but a good friend will always be by your side.
  熟悉的人可能來了又走，但一個好朋友總是會在你身邊。
- It's your go, Carolyn. What are you going to do?
  凱洛琳，這是妳的機會。妳想要怎麼做？

goal [goʊl] *n.* 目標；終點

實用片語與搭配字

set goal; achieve goal
建立目標；達成目標

▶ What are your goals for next year?
你明年的目標是什麼？

▶ If you want to be successful, you should set clear goals.
如果你想成功，你應該設定明確的目標。

---

goat [goʊt] *n.* 山羊

▶ Look out the window! I see some goats on the mountain.
往窗外看！我看到那座山上有一些羊。

---

god / goddess [gɑːd / ˈgɑː.des]
n. 神 / 女神

實用片語與搭配字

thank God 感謝上帝，謝天謝地

▶ Christians worship God in church.
基督徒在教會敬拜上帝。

▶ "Thank God I survived that terrible accident," Mary said when she woke up in the hospital.
瑪莉在醫院醒來時說：「經歷那場可怕的意外後，感謝上帝我還活著！」

---

gold [goʊld]

① *n.* 黃金

② *adj.* 金（製）的

▶ This coin is made of gold.
這枚錢幣是黃金做的。

▶ Avery wears a gold ring on her finger.
艾弗莉的手指上戴著一枚金戒指。

---

golden [ˈgoʊl.dən] *adj.* 黃金的；金黃色的

實用片語與搭配字

silence is golden 沉默是金

▶ Thomas gave his wife a golden necklace for her birthday.
湯姆士在他妻子生日時送了她一條金項鍊。

▶ After a busy day at work talking to many people, the silence of my home is golden.
結束了忙碌的一天，和許多人說話之後，我覺得家裡的寧靜很珍貴。

---

golf [gɑːlf] *n.* 高爾夫球

▶ Harvey plays golf every weekend in the summer.
哈維在夏天的每個週末都打高爾夫球。

Exercise 25

I. Choose and write the correct word. Change the form of the word when necessary.

1	general (adj.) gentle (adj.)	There's a __________ presumption that fatty foods are bad for your heart.
2	gift (n.) giant (n.)	This tall man looks scary, but he's really a gentle __________.
3	glue (v.) give (v.)	The workers are __________ the tiles to the floor with contact cement.
4	goat (n.) goal (n.)	If you're going to achieve a high __________, you have to take some chances.
5	glad (adj.) golden (adj.)	I didn't enjoy marking those papers and I was __________ to be rid of them.

II. Multiple choices.

( ) 1. It was very __________ of you to share the food with me on such a cold day.
(A) general (B) gentle (C) generous (D) giant

( ) 2. My favorite subjects at school are history and __________.
(A) general (B) geography (C) golf (D) gift

( ) 3. Cows tend to __________ together at one end of the field when it's going to rain.
(A) glue (B) give (C) gate (D) gather

( ) 4. To get the plant out of the pot, turn it upside down and give it a __________ knock.
(A) general (B) giant (C) gentle (D) gold

( ) 5. Everything is a blur when I take my __________ off.
(A) glass (B) glasses (C) glove (D) golf

good [gʊd]

① *adj.* 好的

實用片語與搭配字

sounds good 聽起來不錯

② *n.* 利益；好處

③ *adv.* 很好地；非常

實用片語與搭配字

put … to good use 善用…

► Ashley is a good student. She gets good grades.
艾胥莉是個好學生，她都拿好成績。

► When you watch commercials on TV, every product sounds good.
當你看著電視上的廣告時，會覺得每樣產品都不錯。

► Take this medicine. It's for your good.
吃下這藥，這對你是好的。

► The business is doing good.
這生意做得很好。

► During the holidays, I put my time to good use by studying English.
我在假期中好好利用時間學英文。

---

goodbye / bye [gʊdˋbaɪ / baɪ] *n.* 再見

實用片語與搭配字

say goodbye to 對…說再見

► Goodbye! I'll see you next time.
再見！下次再會了。

► I shouted at my boss the other day and now I can say goodbye to the promotion he promised me.
那天我對老闆大吼，現在我可以對他承諾的晉升說再見了。

---

goose [gu:s] *n.* 大雁；鵝

► Do you see the geese flying in the sky?
你看到天上飛的大雁嗎？

98

govern [ˋgʌv.ɚn] *v.* 統治；管理

實用片語與搭配字

be governed by 被…統治

► The president governed the country for 8 years.
這位總統治理這個國家長達八年。

► People need to be governed by rules, or the world will be in total chaos.
人們需要受到法規管理，不然世界會陷入一片混亂。

---

government [ˋgʌv.ɚn.mənt] *n.* 政府

► The government has made a statement explaining the new law.
政府做了一個解釋新法的聲明。

grade [greɪd]

① *n.* 等級；成績

② *v.* 打分數；分等級

▸ I'm not happy with my math grade, so I need to study harder.
我不滿意我的數學成績，因此我需要更加努力讀書。

▸ The teacher spent all night grading her students' essays.
老師整晚都在為她學生的文章打分數。

---

grand [grænd] *adj.* 巨大的；雄偉的

▸ The trees in this forest are grand!
這個森林裡的樹都很巨大雄偉！

---

grandchild [ˈgræn.tʃaɪld] *n.* （外）孫子女

▸ Irma has five grandchildren.
爾瑪有五個孫子女。

---

granddaughter [ˈgræn.dɑː.t̬ɚ]

n. （外）孫女

▸ John loves to play with his granddaughter.
約翰喜歡和他的孫女玩。

---

grandfather / grandpa

[ˈgræn.fɑː.ðɚ / ˈgræn.pɑː / ˈgræm.pɑː] *n.* 祖父；外公

▸ Christian is Jeremiah's grandpa.
克里斯汀是傑若麥亞的祖父。

---

grandmother / grandma

[ˈgræn.mʌð.ɚ / ˈgræn.mɑː / ˈgræm.mɑː] *n.* 祖母；外婆

▸ Grandma is my mother's mother.
外婆是我媽媽的媽媽。

---

grandson [ˈgræn.sʌn] *n.* （外）孫子

▸ Brandon loves watching his grandsons grow up.
布蘭登喜愛看著他的孫子們長大。

---

grape [greɪp] *n.* 葡萄

▸ Can I please have some grape juice with my lunch?
我中餐可以配一點葡萄汁喝嗎？

---

grass [græs] *n.* （青）草

▸ The children love playing in the grass.
這些孩子喜歡在草地上玩耍。

---

grassy [ˈgræs.i]

adj. 長滿青草的；覆蓋著青草的

▸ My dog loves to run in the grassy hills near our house.
我的狗喜歡在我家附近滿是青草的山丘上奔跑。

gray / grey [greɪ]

① *adj.* 灰色的

② *n.* 灰色

實用片語與搭配字

grey hair 白頭髮

③ *v.* 成為灰色（或灰白）

▶ Gabe is wearing a gray shirt.
蓋伯正穿著一件灰色襯衫。

▶ Mark's shirt is a dark gray.
馬克的襯衫是深灰色的。

▶ Grey hair is in fashion these days so many young people dye their hair grey.
現在白髮是時尚趨勢，許多年輕人把頭髮染白。

▶ David's hair is graying.
大衛的頭髮變灰白了。

great [greɪt]

① *adj.* 極好的

② *n.* 偉人；大人物

▶ This restaurant is great! Let's come back again!
這間餐廳很棒！我們找一天再來吧！

▶ Michael Jordan is a basketball great.
麥可喬丹是一個籃球名將。

greedy [ˈgriːˌdi] *adj.* 貪婪的；貪吃的

▶ Don't be greedy, Leo, save some cake for others!
里歐，別貪心！留些蛋糕給別人吧！

---

green [griːn]

① *adj.* 綠色的

② *n.* 綠色

③ *v.* 成為綠色

▶ Everyone should eat more green vegetables.
大家都應該多吃些綠色蔬菜。

▶ Hope's eyes are a beautiful green.
荷普的眼睛是美麗的綠色。

▶ In the spring, the grass greens.
在春天，草地都變成綠色。

greet [griːt] *v.* 迎接；問候

▶ The owner greeted guests at the entrance.
這位主人在入口處迎接客人。

---

ground [graʊnd]

① *n.* 地面

實用片語與搭配字

common ground
（興趣、信仰或觀點上的）共通點

▶ Let's sit on the ground.
我們坐在地上吧。

▶ Alice and her boyfriend argued over getting a dog, but then later reached common ground and decided to get a cat.
原本艾莉絲和她的男朋友對於養狗有些爭吵，但之後達成共識決定養貓。

② *v.* （船）擱淺；（飛機）停飛

▶ The ship was grounded near an island.
這艘船在一座島嶼附近擱淺。

---

group [gru:p]

① *n.* 群體

② *v.* 把…分組（或歸類）

實用片語與搭配字

group together 把…放在同一組

▶ A group of us are going to the movies together.
我們這群人要一起去看電影。

▶ The teacher grouped her students in teams.
老師把她的學生分成小組。

▶ At parties people who know each other will usually group together.
通常在派對裡相識的人會聚在一起。

104

grow [groʊ] *v.* 長大；成長

實用片語與搭配字

grow up; grow out of
長大；（孩子）長大而穿不下（原來合身的衣服），（隨著年齡增長而）戒除

▶ The children are growing quickly.
孩子們長得很快。

▶ Don't buy expensive clothes for your children because they will grow out of them very quickly.
別買太昂貴的童裝，因為小孩長大的速度很快，常穿不下那些衣服。

---

growth [groʊθ] *n.* 成長

實用片語與搭配字

rapid growth; economic growth
迅速成長；經濟成長

▶ Children drink milk to help their bone growth.
孩子喝牛奶是為了幫助他們骨骼的成長。

▶ Poor countries need economic growth so their people can live more comfortable lives.
貧窮的國家需要經濟的成長，才能讓人民過更舒適的生活。

---

guard [gɑ:rd]

① *n.* 衛兵；看守者

實用片語與搭配字

security guard; on guard 警衛；提防

② *v.* 守衛；防範

▶ There are always four guards at the gate of the castle.
這個城堡的大門總是有四個衛兵站崗。

▶ When traveling in Rome, you need to be on guard because there are pickpockets.
你在羅馬旅行時必須要小心提防，因為那裡會有扒手。

▶ There are two men guarding the wealthy businessman's house.
有兩個男人守衛著這名富商的家。

實用片語與搭配字

guard against 防止，防範

▶ Always guard against saying hurtful words, because you cannot take back your words.

永遠不要說傷人的話，因為你不能收回你的話。

Exercise 26

I. Choose and write the correct word. Change the form of the word when necessary.

1	government (n.) grade (n.)	The __________ has issued a new document mapping out its policies on education.
2	great (adj.) greedy (adj.)	He's a __________ man; he only married her because her family is quite wealthy.
3	guard (v.) grow (v.)	The mother cat was __________ her kittens from the other cats.
4	ground (n.) growth (n.)	He threw the ball to me, but I missed it and it landed on the __________.
5	grassy (adj.) gray (adj.)	It was such a beautiful day; they sat and had their lunch on a __________ hillside.

II. Multiple choices.

( ) 1. My job is to __________ them by letter and put them in order.
(A) ground (B) guard (C) group (D) grow

( ) 2. He is the only party leader who's competent enough to __________ this country.
(A) grade (B) guess (C) ground (D) govern

( ) 3. In some cultures, people traditionally __________ each other by rubbing noses.
(A) greet (B) group (C) ground (D) govern

( ) 4. Her son is a quick student and always has high __________.
(A) good (B) grades (C) group (D) grass

( ) 5. My parents are so delighted because they've had their first __________.
(A) ground (B) grade (C) grandchild (D) government

Unit 27

guava [ˈgwɑː.və] *n.* 芭樂

▶ Leah eats a guava every morning for breakfast.
麗雅每天早餐都吃一顆芭樂。

---

guess [ges]

① *v.* 猜測

② *n.* 猜想；推測

實用片語與搭配字
make a guess / guesses 猜測

▶ Guess what's in the box!
猜猜盒子裡有什麼！

▶ Your guess is as good as mine.
你的推測和我的一樣好。

▶ I don't know, but if I have to make a guess, I would say there are about 200 countries in the world.
我不知道，但假如一定要猜，我會說這世界上大約有 200 個國家。

---

guest [gest]

① *n*. 客人

② *v.* 當特別來賓；當特約演員

▶ Justine had 20 guests at her party.
喬絲汀的派對上有二十位客人。

▶ Who will guest on tonight's show?
今晚的節目誰會來當特別來賓？

guide [gaɪd]

① *n.* 嚮導

實用片語與搭配字
travel guide 旅遊指南

② *v.* 為…領路

實用片語與搭配字
guide sb through
引領（某人）走出（生命關卡，正在經歷的事件）

▶ Jason works as a New York tour guide.
傑森擔任紐約導遊的工作。

▶ Read a travel guide before you visit a country for the first time.
第一次造訪某個國家前，可以先閱讀旅遊指南。

▶ Can you guide me to the nearest bathroom?
你可以帶我去最近的洗手間嗎？

▶ My brother is a computer expert and he will guide me through the computer class I am taking.
我哥哥是個電腦專家，他會從旁指導我正在上的電腦課程。

---

guitar [gɪˈtɑːr] *n.* 吉他

▶ I'm learning how to play the guitar in my spare time.
我在空閒時學習彈吉他。

gun [gʌn]

① *n.* 槍

實用片語與搭配字

gun shot 槍聲

② *v.* 向…開槍

▶ Don't play with guns. They're dangerous.
不要玩槍，那很危險。

▶ I heard the gun shot, and I immediately called the police.
我一聽見槍聲就立刻報警。

▶ The soldier gunned down his enemy.
這名士兵開槍擊倒他的敵人。

G

---

guy [gaɪ] *n.* 傢伙；人；朋友

▶ Who is that guy over there? I don't recognize him.
在那邊的男子是誰？我不認識他。

---

habit [ˋhæb.ɪt] *n.* 習慣

實用片語與搭配字

habit of 習慣

▶ You shouldn't make a habit of checking your smartphone in bed.
你不應該養成在床上用智慧型手機的習慣。

---

hair [her] *n.* 頭髮；毛髮

▶ Andrea has long curly hair.
安卓雅有一頭長捲髮。

---

haircut [ˋher.kʌt] *n.* 理髮；剪髮

▶ Steve went to the salon for a haircut.
史提夫到理髮廳去剪頭髮。

---

half [hæf]

① *n.* 一半

② *adj.* 一半的

③ *adv.* 一半地；部分地

▶ The second half of the game was really exciting.
這場比賽的下半場非常刺激。

▶ Thirty minutes is half an hour.
三十分鐘是半小時。

▶ Cindy got half the answers right on the quiz.
辛蒂在這次小考只寫對了一半。

---

hall [hɑ:l] *n.* 走廊；大廳

▶ Don't run in the halls at school.
不要在學校的走廊上跑步。

---

ham [hæm] *n.* 火腿

▶ Would you like a ham sandwich?
你要吃個火腿三明治嗎？

hamburger / burger

[ˈhæmˌbɝː.gɚ / ˈbɝː.gɚ] *n.* 漢堡

▶ I'd like a hamburger with French fries and a drink, please.
請給我一個漢堡、薯條和一杯飲料。

---

hammer [ˈhæm.ɚ]

① *n.* 鎚子；榔頭

② *v.* 鎚打

▶ I need a hammer to fix this table.
我需要一個鎚子來修理這張桌子。

▶ My neighbors have been hammering all morning, I think they're fixing their house.
我的鄰居整個早上都在敲敲打打，我想他們在整修房子。

---

hand [hænd]

① *n.* 手

② *v.* 傳遞；給；面交給…

▶ The baby eats with her hands.
嬰兒用她的手吃東西。

▶ Can you hand me the salt?
你可以把鹽遞給我嗎？

---

handkerchief [ˈhæŋ.kɚ.tʃiːf] 手帕

▶ Grandpa used a handkerchief to wipe the sweat off of his face.
祖父用手帕將他臉上的汗水擦去。

handle [ˈhæn.dəl]

① *n.* 柄；把手

② *v.* 處理；操作

▶ The handle on Susie's suitcase broke, so she had to push it instead.
蘇西行李上的把手壞了，所以她只好用推的。

▶ Linda is a travel agent who handles a lot of cases each day.
琳達是一個旅遊仲介，每天要處理很多案件。

---

handsome [ˈhæn.səm] *adj.* 英俊的

▶ Which actor do you think is most handsome?
你覺得那一位男演員最英俊？

---

hang [hæŋ] *v.* 懸掛；把…吊起

▶ Let's hang that picture on the wall!
將那張照片掛在牆上吧！

---

hanger [ˈhæŋ.ɚ] *n.* 衣架

▶ Can you pass me a hanger? I need to hang up this sweater to dry.
你可以給我一個衣架嗎？我需要把這件毛衣掛起來晾乾。

happen [ˈhæp.ən] *v.* 發生

▶ What happened at school today?
學校今天發生了什麼事？

happy [ˈhæp.i] *adj.* 快樂的

▶ The baby smiles when she's happy.
這個寶寶開心時就會笑。

hard [hɑːrd]

① *adj.* 硬的

② *adv.* 努力地；艱苦地

▶ This rock is hard.
這塊石頭很硬。

▶ Carrie studies hard to do well in school.
凱莉努力用功要在學校裡有好表現。

hardly [ˈhɑːrd.li] *adv.* 幾乎不

▶ The concert was so short, I hardly had time to enjoy it.
這場演唱會太短，我還沒好好享受就結束了。

H

Exercise 27

I. Choose and write the correct word. Change the form of the word when necessary.

1	guess (v.) guide (v.)	If you don't have a compass, use the stars to __________ you.
2	guava (n.) guitar (n.)	He plays the __________ and sings folk songs in the town band.
3	half (adj.) handsome (adj.)	He was a real nerd in high school; I can't believe he's so __________ now.
4	hard (adv.) hardly (adv.)	There were so many people in the doorway that we could __________ get out.
5	happen (v.) handle (v.)	People differ from one another in their ability to __________ their stress.

II. Multiple choices.

( ) 1. We've fallen into the __________ of getting up late on Sunday mornings.
(A) happen (B) hammer (C) habit (D) hanger

( ) 2. We need a bigger __________ to pound these large nails into the beam.
(A) hammer (B) handle (C) hanger (D) hamburger

( ) 3. Do not wait for good things to __________ to you, but you need to walk toward happiness.
(A) handle (B) hammer (C) guess (D) happen

( ) 4. We're always taught to __________ the meaning of the words we don't know from the text.
(A) hang (B) guess (C) happen (D) handle

( ) 5. His motive for working so __________ is that he needs money for studying abroad.
(A) hardly (B) half (C) hard (D) handsome

Unit 28

H

hat [hæt] *n.* 帽子

實用片語與搭配字

hat off to sb 向（某人）致敬

▶ Alex is wearing a hat on his head.
艾力克斯的頭上戴著一頂帽子。

▶ I take my hat off to woman who have full-time jobs but take care of young children.
我向每個有全職工作又同時照顧孩子的女人致敬。

---

hate [heɪt]

① *v.* 厭惡；憎恨

② *n.* 厭惡；反感；仇恨

實用片語與搭配字

love-hate relationship 愛恨交加的關係

▶ I really hated that movie. It was really bad.
我非常厭惡那部電影，那演得太糟了。

▶ Drew has a real hate for math.
茱兒真的很討厭數學。

▶ Sara has a love-hate relationship with living in the city. She likes the convenience, but hates the noise.
莎拉對於這座城市又愛又恨，她喜歡城市的便利，但討厭它的吵雜。

---

hateful [ˈheɪt.fəl] *adj.* 可惡的；令人討厭的

▶ I can't believe Vivian would say such hateful things to you!
我不敢相信薇薇安會對你說這麼可惡的話！

---

have [hæv]

① *v.* 擁有

② *aux. v.* 已經（加過去分詞，構成完成式）

▶ The two brothers have a lot of problems at school.
兩兄弟在學校有很多的問題。

▶ We have been here before.
我們以前來過這裡。

---

he [hiː] *pron.* 他

▶ He is my father.
他是我的父親。

---

head [hed]

① *n.* 頭

② *v.* 率領

▶ The baby has no hair on his head.
這個寶寶的頭上沒有頭髮。

▶ The boss heads the company.
這位老闆領導著這公司。

實用片語與搭配字

head for 朝…前進

▶ Schools just closed for the holidays and I will head for the beach soon.
學校剛放假，我很快就要去海邊玩了。

---

headache [ˈhed.eɪk] *n.* 頭痛

▶ My headache is bothering me a lot.
我的頭痛非常困擾我。

health [helθ] *n.* 健康

實用片語與搭配字

health care 醫療保健

▶ Exercise is good for your health.
運動有益你的健康。

▶ Health care is very important and governments must make sure everyone can afford it.
醫療保健是非常重要的，政府必須確保每個人都負擔得起。

healthy [ˈhel.θi] *adj.* 健康的

▶ Having a healthy diet is the best way to lose weight.
最佳的瘦身方式是健康的飲食。

---

hear [hɪr] *v.* 聽見

實用片語與搭配字

hear of 聽說

▶ Did you hear Caleb's story?
你聽過迦勒的故事嗎？

▶ I am looking for a new second-hand car, so if you hear of anything, let me know.
我在找一輛新的二手車，如果你聽到任何消息再告訴我。

---

heart [hɑːrt] *n.* 心；心臟

實用片語與搭配字

break heart 使（某人）心碎

▶ Ian's heart beats fast after he runs.
伊恩在跑步之後心跳跳得很快。

▶ My best friend moved away when we were in elementary school and it broke my heart.
我最好的朋友在念小學時搬家，讓我很心碎。

---

heat [hiːt]

① *n.* 高溫；熱度

② *v.* 變熱

實用片語與搭配字

heat up 加熱

▶ The heat is really high during the summer.
夏天時溫度非常高。

▶ Mom heated the food over the fire.
媽媽在爐火上加熱食物。

▶ If you want to heat up the competition, you should get better players.
如果你想讓比賽更精彩，就必須找到更優秀的球員。

heater ['hiːtə] *n.* 暖氣機（暖爐）；加熱器

▶ It's cold in here! Can you turn on the heater?
這裡好冷！你可以打開暖氣嗎？

97

heavy ['hev.i] *adj.* 重的

實用片語與搭配字

heavy rain 大雨；暴雨

▶ This box is heavy. There are a lot of things in it.
這個箱子很重，有很多東西在裡面。

▶ Despite heavy rain, we still went on our camping trip in the mountains.
儘管下了大雨，我們還是去山上露營。

height [haɪt] *n.* 高度

▶ My brother reached the height of 180cm by age 16.
我弟弟在十六歲時身高已達一百八十公分。

---

hello [he'loʊ] *n.* 哈囉（打招呼）

▶ Say hello to your mother for me.
替我跟你母親打個招呼。

---

help [help]

① *v.* 給予幫忙

實用片語與搭配字

help with 幫忙…

② *n.* 幫助

▶ Zach helped his mom wash the dishes after dinner.
查克在晚餐後幫媽媽洗碗盤。

▶ My math teacher is very kind and has offered to help with my homework.
我的數學老師很和藹，願意協助我完成作業。

▶ Zach is a big help to his mom and dad.
查克幫了他的父母很大的忙。

---

helpful ['help.fəl] *adj.* 有幫助的

▶ My children are very helpful doing work around the house.
我的孩子們在家會幫忙做事。

---

hen [hen] *n.* 母雞

▶ Let's go outside and see if the hen has laid any eggs.
我們到外面去看看那隻母雞是否已經下蛋了。

---

her(s) [hɝ(z)]

pron. 她的（she 的所有格）

▶ Linda really loves her children.
琳達非常愛她的孩子。

---

here [hɪr]

① *adv.* 在這裡

▶ Let's sit here and eat.
我們坐在這裡吃吧。

H

② *n.* 這裡

▶ The mall is a five-minute walk from here.
購物中心離這裡走路五分鐘。

---

hero / heroine [ˈhɪr.oʊ / ˈherəʊɪn]
n. 英雄 / 女英雄

▶ Batman is my favorite comic book hero. What about you?
蝙蝠俠是我最喜愛的漫畫英雄。你呢？

---

herself [hɝːˈself] *pron.* 她自己

▶ She likes to treat herself to coffee.
她喜歡給自己來杯咖啡。

---

hey [heɪ] *(interj.)* 嗨；喂

▶ Hey! Look at that fancy car.
嗨！看看那輛豪華大車。

---

hide [haɪd] *v.* 躲藏；隱藏

實用片語與搭配字

hide behind 躲在後面

▶ The puppy ran to hide when he heard the children coming downstairs.
那隻小狗一聽到小孩下樓的聲音就跑去躲起來。

▶ Some students hide behind their busy schedules as an excuse not to read.
有些學生把功課繁忙當作不閱讀的藉口。

Exercise 28

I. Choose and write the correct word. Change the form of the word when necessary.

1	heater (n.) health (n.)	I turned on the __________ in the hall to take the chill off the house.
2	hateful (adj.) healthy (adj.)	She looks so __________ with her red cheeks and bright eyes.
3	hero (n.) height (n.)	When I was little, my father was my __________ because he seemed so strong and brave.
4	heat (v.) head (v.)	Combine the eggs with a little flour and __________ the mixture gently.
5	heavy (adj.) helpful (adj.)	It's always __________ to learn from your mistakes because then your mistakes seem worthwhile.

II. Multiple choices.

( ) 1. I tried taking tablets for the __________ but they didn't have any effect.
(A) heater (B) heat (C) head (D) headache

( ) 2. I think the people who said those __________ things about him owe him an apology.
(A) healthy (B) heavy (C) hateful (D) helpful

( ) 3. The boy wanted to __________ behind the door to startle the little girl.
(A) help (B) hide (C) heat (D) hear

( ) 4. The suitcase looks __________, but actually it's very light.
(A) heavy (B) helpful (C) healthy (D) high

( ) 5. I'm not worried about her because she can take care of __________.
(A) Hers (B) here (C) herself (D) hero

Unit 29

high [haɪ]
① *adj.* 高的
② *n.* 高峰；高水準
③ *adv.* 在高處

▶ This chair is high. My feet don't touch the ground.
這把椅子很高，我的腳碰不到地。

▶ Summer temperatures are at a high this year.
今年夏天氣溫達到高峰。

▶ April lives high in that building.
艾菩兒住在那棟大樓的高樓層。

---

highway [ˈhaɪ.weɪ] *n.* （快速）公路

▶ Will these driving directions take us onto the highway?
這些方向指標會帶我們上快速公路嗎？

---

hiking [ˈhaɪ.kɪŋ]
n.（在鄉間或山上）健行；徒步旅行

▶ My husband and I enjoy hiking.
我先生和我喜歡健行。

---

hill [hɪl] *n.* 小山；丘陵

▶ Amanda's house is on top of that hill.
亞曼達的房子位在那座山丘頂上。

---

him [hɪm]
pron. 他（he 的受格）

▶ Who is that man? I don't know him.
那位男士是誰？我不認識他。

---

himself [hɪmˈself] *pron.* 他自己

▶ He sees himself in the mirror every morning.
他每天早上在鏡子裡看自己。

---

hip [hɪp] *n.* 臀部；屁股

▶ Grandma broke her hip when she fell down. I hope she'll be ok!
祖母跌倒時摔斷了臀骨，我希望她沒事！

---

hippopotamus / hippo
[ˌhɪp.əˈpɑː.t̬ə.məs / ˈhɪp.əʊ / ˈhɪp.oʊ] *n.* 河馬

▶ Although it looks cute, the hippopotamus is a deadly animal.
雖然河馬看起來很可愛，但是牠是非常危險的動物。

hire [haɪr]

① *v.* 僱用

實用片語與搭配字

hire sb to do v-ing; hire for; hire out
僱用…做事；以…原因被僱用；出租

② *n.* 租用（物）；雇用（人）

▶ Our company is hiring three new salespeople this month.
我們公司這個月要僱用三位新的業務員。

▶ We decided to hire out our car to tourists during the summer to earn extra money.
夏季時，我們決定把車子租給觀光客來賺外快。

▶ Who is going to train the new hires?
誰要去訓練這些新進員工？

---

his [hɪz]

pron. 他的（he 的所有格）

▶ Kai loves to play with his children.
凱喜歡和他的孩子們玩耍。

---

history [ˈhɪs.t̬ɚ.i] *n.* 歷史

▶ Albert really loves to study history.
亞伯非常喜歡研讀歷史。

99

hit [hɪt]

① *v.* 撞；打

實用片語與搭配字

hit by 被…撞

② *n.* 擊中；打擊

▶ Mark hit his head on the shelf.
馬克的頭撞到架子了。

▶ Tom was hit by a car when he crossed the busy street.
湯姆在通過交通繁忙的路口時被車撞了。

▶ Gabe took a hit on the head.
蓋伯的頭被擊中了。

---

hobby [ˈhɑː.bi] *n.* 嗜好

▶ Alex's hobby is collecting stamps from around the world.
艾力克斯的嗜好是收集世界各地的郵票。

---

hold [hoʊld]

① *v.* 握著

實用片語與搭配字

hold on; hold up
緊握，繼續，堅持；延遲，支撐

② *n.* 可以手攀（或腳踏）的東西

▶ The teacher told the children to hold hands.
那位老師叫孩子們手牽手。

▶ Please finish your report on time or you will hold up the whole project.
請準時完成你的報告，否則你將會拖延整個專題計劃。

▶ Take a hold of this handle and don't let go.
握著這個把手不要放開。

holder ['hoʊl.dɚ] *n.* 支撐物；支托物

▶ I'm glad these seats have cup holders. I can put my drink down.
我很高興這些座位有杯座，讓我可以把飲料放下來。

---

hole [hoʊl]

① *n.* 洞；孔

實用片語與搭配字

black hole 黑洞

② *v.* 鑿洞於；穿孔於

▶ Alicia dug a hole in the sand.
艾莉莎在沙子裡挖了個洞。

▶ Many people have lost millions of dollars in the black hole of the stock market.
許多人在股票市場這個黑洞已損失了上百萬。

▶ The painting got holed by the boys.
這幅畫被那些男孩弄破了個洞。

---

holiday ['hɑː.lə.deɪ] *n.* 假日

實用片語與搭配字

on holiday 休假；度假

▶ Josh's favorite holiday is Christmas.
聖誕節是喬許最喜歡的節日。

▶ I will be going on holiday to France in a couple of weeks.
我將在幾個星期後去法國度假。

---

home [hoʊm]

① *n.* 家

實用片語與搭配字

home sweeet home; bring home
溫暖的家；帶…回家

② *adj.* 家庭的

③ *adv.* 在家

③ *v.* 為…提供住處

▶ What time will you be at home today?
你今天幾點會在家？

▶ Scientists have tried for years to bring home the idea of global warming to governments, but no one listens.
多年來科學家們一直試圖把地球暖化的訊息帶回給政府，但是沒有人聽。

▶ Kai really loves his mom's home cooking.
凱非常喜歡他媽媽做的家常菜。

▶ Linda goes home for lunch every day.
琳達每天都回家吃午餐。

▶ The dogs have all been homed.
這些狗都已經被安置住處了。

---

homesick ['hoʊm.sɪk] *adj.* 想家的；思鄉的

▶ Do you often get homesick when you are traveling abroad?
當你出國旅行時會常常想家嗎？

homework [ˈhoʊm.wɝːk] *n.* 功課；家庭作業

▶ The teacher gave his students a lot of homework.

老師給了他的學生很多功課。

---

honest [ˈɑː.nɪst] *adj.* 誠實的；真誠的

實用片語與搭配字

be honest with 誠實以對

▶ If you want your marriage to succeed, it is important to be honest.

如果你希望你的婚姻成功，誠實是很重要的。

▶ You have to be honest with yourself and decide whether you should stay at a company with no future.

你必須誠實面對自己，並決定是否要待在一個沒未來的公司。

---

honey [ˈhʌn.i] *n.* 蜂蜜

▶ I like my tea with a little honey in it.

我喜歡加一點點蜂蜜在我的茶裡。

---

hop [hɑːp]

① *v.* 單足跳

② *n.* 跳躍

▶ For the next race, you all have to hop on one foot across the finish line.

下一場賽跑，你們都要單腳跳到終點線。

▶ You're almost there! Just one more hop!

你快到了！只需要再跳一步！

---

hope [hoʊp]

① *v.* 希望

實用片語與搭配字

hope for 希望

② *n.* 期望；希望

▶ I hope I can finish my work in time today.

我希望我今天可以準時完成我的工作。

▶ I have not studied hard this semester and the best I can hope for is to pass all my subjects.

這學期我沒有認真念書，我只期望所有的科目都能及格。

▶ Lamont has a lot of hopes and dreams.

拉蒙特有著許多的期望和夢想。

---

horse [hɔːrs] *n.* 馬

▶ Wilma often rides horses at a ranch on the weekends.

葳瑪經常在週末去牧場騎馬。

Exercise 29

I. Choose and write the correct word. Change the form of the word when necessary.

1	highway (n.) hobby (n.)	They're trying to blast away the hill to pave the way for the new ________.
2	homesick (adj.) honest (adj.)	If you aren't ________ in business, any success you achieve will be meaningless.
3	hold (v.) hire (v.)	It'll be very difficult to ________ that many new staff in such a short time span.
4	holder (n.) holiday (n.)	This suitcase is big enough for you to take clothes with you on your ________.
5	hop (v.) hope (v.)	How long can you ________ on your right foot?

II. Multiple choices.

(　　) 1. The guild book points out the main facts of early American ________.

(A) homesick　(B) history　(C) hole　(D) hobby

(　　) 2. As she read the letter from her mother, she began to feel more and more ________.

(A) holiday　(B) holder　(C) history　(D) homesick

(　　) 3. He needs a ________ to keep him busy and stop him from getting into mischief.

(A) holiday　(B) hope　(C) holder　(D) hobby

(　　) 4. There's a ________ in the bottom of the water tank, and the water has been leaking away.

(A) hole　(B) home　(C) hold　(D) hit

(　　) 5. Patrick likes doing active things like canoeing, ________ and bungee jumping.

(A) home　(B) hiking　(C) highway　(D) holder

Unit 30

hospital ['hɑː.spɪ.t̬əl] *n.* 醫院

▶ After the car accident, Emily had to stay in the hospital for a week.
這場車禍後，艾蜜莉需要住院一個星期。

---

host / hostess [hoʊst / 'hoʊ.stɪs]
n. 男主人 / 女主人

▶ Adam and Erin are the host and hostess of this party.
亞當和艾玲是這個派對的男女主人。

---

hot [hɑːt] *adj.* 熱的；溫度高的

▶ Don't touch that! It's hot!
不要碰那個！那是燙的！

實用片語與搭配字

hot and cold 冷熱

▶ When you twist your ankle, hot and cold treatment is the best way to take away the pain.
當你扭傷腳踝，冷熱療法是消除疼痛最好的方法。

---

hotel [hoʊ'tel] *n.* 旅館；飯店

▶ I'm looking for a hotel near the beach for our vacation.
我正為我們的假期尋找一間靠近海邊的旅館。

---

hour [aʊr] *n.* 小時

▶ Eli works eight hours a day.
伊萊一天工作八小時。

---

house [haʊs] *n.* 房子

▶ Joanne lives in a big house.
喬安住在一棟大房子裡。

house [haʊz] *v.* 住

▶ That building houses many students.
那棟大樓裡住著許多學生。

---

how [haʊ] *adv.* 怎麼；如何（指方法）

▶ How do you use this machine?
你怎麼使用這個機器？

---

103 97

however [ˌhaʊ'ev.ɚ] *adv.* 然而；無論如何

▶ I agree with your point, however, I'd like to add one thing.
我同意你的看法，然而，我想再加上一點意見。

H

huge [hjuːdʒ] *adj.* 巨大的

實用片語與搭配字

huge amount of 大量的

► An elephant is a huge animal.

大象是一個巨大的動物。

► Following our year-end party, there was a huge amount of food left which we gave to the poor.

年終聚餐結束後留下好多的剩菜，我們打包給窮人。

---

hum [hʌm]

① *v.* 哼（音樂）

② *n.* 嗡嗡聲；持續低沉的噪音

► If you don't know the words to the song, you can just hum along.

如果你不知道這首歌的歌詞，可以跟著旋律哼。

► Where is that hum coming from? It's really bothering me!

那嗡嗡聲是從哪裡來的？真的很煩人！

---

human [ˈhjuː.mən]

① *adj.* 人的

② *n.* 人

實用片語與搭配字

human being 人類

► Doctors know a lot about human bodies.

醫生對人體非常了解。

► There are over 7 billion humans in the world today.

現今世界上有超過七十億人口。

► Every human being deserves love and kindness.

所有人都值得被愛以及友善相待。

humble [ˈhʌm.bəl]

① *adj.* 謙虛的；謙遜的

② *v.* 使…感到自慚；使謙卑

► It's not easy to find a humble person in this business.

在這個行業裡要找到謙虛的人真是不容易。

► Jack humbled himself and apologized to his son.

傑克低聲下氣地向他的兒子道歉。

---

humid [ˈhjuː.mɪd] *adj.* 潮濕的

► The weather on this island is extremely humid, especially in the spring.

這島上的天氣極度潮濕，尤其是在春天。

---

humor [ˈhjuː.mɚ] *n.* 幽默感

► I want to date someone with a good sense of humor.

我想要跟一個很有幽默感的人交往。

hundred [ˈhʌn.drəd]

① *n.* 一百

② *adj.* 一百的

▶ Hundreds of people work in Taipei 101.

有很多人在台北 101 大樓裡工作。

▶ Gabe has seen that movie a hundred times.

那部電影蓋伯已經看了一百次。

---

hunger [ˈhʌŋ.gɚ] *n.* 飢餓

實用片語與搭配字

hunger strike 絕食抗議

▶ This money will go toward ending hunger in Africa.

這筆錢會幫助結束非洲的饑荒。

▶ The prisoners went on a hunger strike for 20 days before the government listended to their complaints.

在政府聽見他們的請求前，這些犯人進行了 20 天的絕食抗議。

---

hungry [ˈhʌŋ.gri] *adj.* 飢餓的

實用片語與搭配字

hungry for 渴望…

▶ I'm hungry. Let's eat.

我肚子餓，我們吃東西吧。

▶ Throughout your life, you should remain hungry for knowledge and adventure.

在你的一生中，你應該持續對知識和冒險的渴求。

---

hunt [hʌnt]

① *v.* 搜尋；尋找

② *n.* 搜尋；尋找；打獵

▶ Grandma hunted for her glasses for 20 minutes.

祖母找眼鏡找了二十分鐘。

▶ Let's have an egg hunt this Easter! It will be fun!

今年復活節一起去找復活蛋吧！會很好玩的！

---

hunter [ˈhʌn.t̬ɚ] *n.* 獵人

▶ The hunter knelt down behind a tree and watched the deer.

這名獵人跪在樹後觀察那隻鹿的動向。

101

hurry [ˈhɝː.i]

① *v.* （使）加快；催促

② *n.* 匆忙

▶ Hurry up! The show is about to start.

快一點！表演即將開始了。

▶ Why are you in such a hurry? We don't have class until 10:00.

你為什麼這麼匆忙呢？我們十點才有課。

hurt [hɝːt]

① *v.* 傷害

② *n.* 創傷；痛苦

▶ Mikey hurt his leg when he fell.

米奇摔下來時傷了他的腿。

▶ Holly will never forget the hurt of a broken heart.

荷莉不會忘記心碎的痛苦。

---

husband [ˈhʌz.bənd] *n.* 丈夫

▶ Joy loves her husband. They've been married for 10 years.

喬伊愛她的丈夫，他們已經結婚十年了。

I [aɪ] *pron.* 我（第一人稱單數主格）

▶ I love you.

我愛你。

---

ice [aɪs] *n.* 冰塊；冰

實用片語與搭配字

break the ice 打破僵局，打開話題

▶ Can you put some ice in my drink?

你可以在我的飲料裡放點冰塊嗎？

▶ Martha broke the ice by starting the meeting with a really funny joke.

馬莎用笑話來做為會議的開場。

---

idea [aɪˈdiː.ə] *n.* 主意；想法；點子

▶ I have no idea how to finish this project.

我不知道要如何完成這份專案。

Exercise 30

I. Choose and write the correct word. Change the form of the word when necessary.

1	huge (adj.) human (adj.)	It takes the ________ eyes some time to adapt completely to seeing in the dark.
2	hurry (n.) hunger (n.)	Several hundreds of people in this town are dying of ________ every day.
3	hurt (v.) hunt (v.)	Bats sleep in the daytime and come out to ________ for food at night.
4	humid (adj.) humble (adj.)	He's very ________ even though he got the top mark on the test.
5	hunter (n.) husband (n.)	She complained that her ________ spends too much time playing games on his phone.

II. Multiple choices.

( ) 1. If we don't ________, we'll miss the start of the game.
(A) hunt (B) hurt (C) hurry (D) hum

( ) 2. The ________ machine was moved to the new position on the rollers.
(A) honest (B) huge (C) humid (D) human

( ) 3. Many thanks to the host and ________ for such a wonderful dinner.
(A) humor (B) house (C) hotel (D) hostess

( ) 4. This little boy is recovering in ________ after a serious attack by a stray dog.
(A) hospital (B) hotel (C) hurry (D) hunt

( ) 5. The sticky ________ weather made people feel uncomfortable; they even showered twice a day.
(A) humor (B) humid (C) hurry (D) hungry

Unit 31

if [ɪf] *conj.* 假如

▶ If you finish your homework, then you can watch a movie.
如果你寫完功課，你就可以看電影。

ignore [ɪgˈnɔːr] *v.* 不理會；忽視

實用片語與搭配字
be ignored by sb; ignore the fact
被忽略；無視事實

▶ I tried to ignore the noise outside my window because I wanted to sleep.
我試著不理會窗外的噪音，因為我想要睡覺。

▶ We cannot ignore the fact that we are destroying the planet with our own greed.
不可忽略的事實是我們的貪念正在破壞這個地球。

---

ill [ɪl]

① *adj.* 生病的

② *adv.* 壞；惡劣地

實用片語與搭配字
fall ill 生病

③ *n.* 壞；傷害

▶ Peggy was feeling quite ill after work so she went straight to bed.
佩吉下班後覺得很不舒服，所以她直接上床睡覺了。

▶ Our vacation days were ill-chosen; everywhere we went was packed.
我們度假的日期選得不好，去哪裡都爆滿。

▶ You will fall ill if you walk around in the cold without wearing enough clothes.
在這寒冷的天氣裡，若你外出衣服穿得太少，就會生病。

▶ I wish no ill of my former boss.
我希望我前老闆平安無事。

---

illness [ˈɪl.nəs] *n.* 疾病；身體不適

▶ The doctor gave me medicine for my illness.
這位醫生為我的病開了藥。

imagine [ɪˈmædʒ.ɪn] *v.* 想像

▶ Imagine winning the lottery! What would you buy?
想像你中了樂透！你會買什麼？

---

importance [ɪmˈpɔːr.təns] *n.* 重要性

▶ Kids should learn the importance of protecting the environment.
孩子應該學習環境保護的重要性。

96

important [ɪmˈpɔːr.tənt] *adj.* 重要的

▶ The students have an important test next week.
這些學生下週有個重要的考試。

impossible [ɪmˈpɑː.sə.bəl]
adj. 不可能的；辦不到的

實用片語與搭配字
impossible for 不可能的

▶ Who can sing that impossible song?
誰能唱那首超難的歌？

▶ It is impossible for me to go on holiday with you because I have too much work.
因為工作太多，我沒辦法和你一起去度假。

improve [ɪmˈpruːv] *v.* 改善；改進

實用片語與搭配字
improve on; improve quality
進步；改善品質

▶ If you want to improve your English, you should try to practice every day.
如果你英文要進步，應該試著每天練習。

▶ You need to improve on time management if you want to keep your job.
如果你想要保住這個工作，你就必須做好時間管理。

improvement [ɪmˈpruːv.mənt]
n. 改善處；改進

實用片語與搭配字
show improvement 顯示改善

▶ Steven is making a lot of improvements around his house.
史蒂芬在他家做了很多修繕的工作。

▶ Peter has been studying hard this year and his grades shows improvement.
今年彼得很認真學習，他的成績進步了。

---

in [ɪn]
① *prep.* 在…之內
② *adv.* 在裡頭
③ *adj.* 在裡頭的

▶ Albert put his computer in his bag.
亞伯把電腦放進他的包包裡。

▶ Please come in!
請進！

▶ When we came to the restaurant, no one was in.
當我們到這家餐廳時，裡面沒有人。

---

inch [ɪntʃ]
① *n.* 英寸
② *v.* 緩慢的移動

▶ Alison cut 5 inches off her hair.
艾莉森把她的頭髮剪掉了五英寸。

▶ The cars inched forward in the traffic jam.
這些車輛在車陣中緩緩移動。

include [ɪnˈkluːd] *v.* 包含

▶ Emily's afterschool activities include ballet and soccer.
艾蜜莉的課後活動包含芭蕾舞和足球。

---

income [ˈɪn.kʌm] *n.* 收入；所得

實用片語與搭配字

earn income; increase income
賺取收入；增加收入

▶ Doctors receive a higher income than nurses.
醫生的收入比護士高。

▶ After he quit his job, John did not earn income for nearly a year.
在約翰離職後，他將近一年都沒有收入。

increase [ɪnˈkriːs]

① *v.* 增大；增加；增強

實用片語與搭配字

increase by; increase in
增加（數量或尺寸的多寡）; 在…方面增加

② *n.* 增加；增大

▶ How can we increase our sales this year?
我們今年要如何增加業績？

▶ The temperature on earth has increased by 2 degrees Celsius over the past decades.
過去十年來，地球的溫度增加了攝氏兩度。

▶ There was an increase in car accidents after the speed limit was raised.
在行車速限提高後，車禍數量也增加了。

---

independence [ˌɪn.dɪˈpen.dəns] *n.* 獨立

▶ Today is the day our country celebrates its independence.
今天是國家慶祝獨立的日子。

---

independent [ˌɪn.dɪˈpen.dənt] *adj.* 獨立的

▶ Michael is independent enough to travel by himself.
麥可已經夠獨立可以自己去旅行。

indicate [ˈɪn.də.keɪt] *v.* 顯示；表明

實用片語與搭配字

be indicated by 指示

▶ This letter indicates that you will be in class 2B next year.
這封信指出你明年會在 2B 班。

▶ His illness was indicated by the fact that he was tired all the time.
他的病是平時的勞累所致。

101

industry [ˈɪn.də.stri] *n.* 工業；企業

▶ There are a lot of jobs available in the car industry here.
這裡的汽車產業有很多工作機會。

influence ['ɪn.flu.əns]

① *n.* 影響（力）；作用

實用片語與搭配字

have influence; under influence
擁有影響力；在…的影響之下

② *v.* 影響

實用片語與搭配字

be influenced by; influence over
受到…的影響；影響

▶ Donald's wife has a lot of influence over him.
唐納德的太太對他有很大的影響力。

▶ The man was under the influence of alcohol when he caused the accident.
這個人受酒精影響而發生事故。

▶ I won't try to influence your decision; you should do what you think is best.
我不會去影響你的決定，你應該做你認為最好的事。

▶ Mark had influence over his boss because he was married to the boss' sister.
馬克能夠影響他的老闆，因為他娶了老闆的妹妹。

---

ink [ɪŋk]

① *n.* 墨水

② *v.* 給…上油墨；用墨水寫

▶ Oh no! I got ink on my white shirt!
糟糕！我的白衣服沾到墨水了！

▶ Please ink the stamp before you use it.
在使用這個印章之前請你先用印泥。

---

insect ['ɪn.sekt] *n.* 昆蟲

▶ Tim spent all afternoon by the river catching insects.
提姆花了整個下午的時間在河邊抓昆蟲。

inside [ɪn'saɪd]

① *n.* 內部；裡面

實用片語與搭配字

inside out; know sth inside out
裡面朝外的，徹底地；對…瞭若指掌

② *adj.* 裡面的

③ *adv.* 在裡面

④ *prep.* 在…的裡面

▶ The inside of the jacket is a different color.
這件夾克的襯裡是不一樣的顏色。

▶ My brother has fixed cars for years; he knows cars inside out.
我哥哥修理車子多年，他對車子相當了解。

▶ Eva and Jack are sitting at an inside table.
伊娃和傑克正坐在裡面的桌子。

▶ The children stayed inside during the storm.
孩子們在暴風雨時待在裡頭。

▶ We can finish this project inside a week.
我們能夠在一週內完成這項專案。

insist [ɪnˈsɪst] *v.* 堅持

實用片語與搭配字

insist on doing sth 堅持

- ▶ When stopped by the police officer, Yvonne insisted she wasn't speeding.
  當依芳被警察攔下來時，她堅持她沒有超速。
- ▶ Nicole insisted on paying for the bill, even though we offered to pay for our own food.
  儘管我們提出各付各的，妮可還是堅持要付帳。

97

instance [ˈɪn.stəns]

① *n.* 實例；情況

實用片語與搭配字

in instance; for instance
在（某種、某些）情況下；例如

② *v.* 引證；舉例

- ▶ An instance of courage was when Tom saved the woman's life.
  湯姆救了那個女人的命是一個勇氣的實例。
- ▶ There are many different kinds of jobs, for instance, doctor, nurse, teacher.
  有不同類型的職業，例如：醫生、護士、老師。
- ▶ Doris instanced the latest surveys in her speech.
  桃樂絲在她的演講中舉了最近的調查作例子。

Exercise 31

I. Choose and write the correct word. Change the form of the word when necessary.

1	imagine (v.) improve (v.)	We need more feedback from the consumers in order to ________ our goods.
2	important (adj.) impossible (adj.)	Your attitude plays a far more ________ role in your success or failure than your capacity.
3	illness (n.) income (n.)	If you're spending more than your ________, you'll need to tighten your belt.
4	influence (n.) instance (n.)	Movie stars and sports celebrities have always had a lot of ________ on what young people wear.
5	indicate (v.) increase (v.)	He ________ to the map on the wall and asked the students to show him where they were from.

II. Multiple choices.

(   ) 1. This grammar book ________ lists of irregular verbs, phrasal verbs, and spelling rules.
(A) imagines (B) insists (C) includes (D) ignores

(   ) 2. I can't ________ why Sally went to the party when she doesn't know anyone there, and she hates drinking.
(A) include (B) imagine (C) improve (D) influence

(   ) 3. Aaron is in love with a girl in his chemistry class, but she just completely ________ him every time he tries to talk to her.
(A) ignores (B) includes (C) improves (D) increases

(   ) 4. We were going to go home, but the hostess ________ that we stay for supper.
(A) imagined (B) insisted (C) indicated (D) influenced

(   ) 5. If you need any help, with your grammar homework for ________, don't be afraid to ask for assistance.
(A) independence (B) influence (C) instance (D) increase

Unit 32

instant [ˈɪn.stənt]

① *adj.* 立即的

② *n.* 頃刻間

▶ My brother eats instant noodles every day after school.
我弟弟每天放學後都吃泡麵。

▶ Take this medicine and you will feel better in an instant.
吃了這個藥你就會立即感到比較好。

98

instrument [ˈɪn.strə.mənt] *n.* 樂器；儀器

▶ Do you play any musical instruments?
你會彈奏任何樂器嗎？

95

interest [ˈɪn.trɪst]

① *n.* 興趣

實用片語與搭配字

take interest in 對…關心、想了解

② *v.* 使發生興趣

▶ Albert has an interest in history.
亞伯對歷史感興趣。

▶ If you want to become a doctor you should take more interest in your studies and improve your grades.
如果你想成為一位醫生，你就必須多用心在學習上，並且提升自己的成績。

▶ The salesman tried to interest me to buy a more expensive car.
這名銷售員試圖說服我買一台更貴的車。

---

interested [ˈɪn.trɪs.tɪd] *adj.* 感興趣的

實用片語與搭配字

be interested in 對…有興趣

▶ The interested boy tried something new.
這個感興趣的男孩試了一些新的玩意。

▶ Tammy is interested in art of the 19th century.
譚美對十九世紀的藝術感興趣。

---

interesting [ˈɪn.trɪs.tɪŋ]

adj. 有趣的；引起興趣的

▶ That chef always cooks interesting dishes.
那位主廚總是烹煮有趣的料理。

---

international [ˌɪn.t̬ɚˈnæʃ.ən.əl] *adj.* 國際的

▶ The international organization is trying to help people wherever they are.
這個國際組織正嘗試幫助人們，無論他們身在何處。

interview [ˈɪn.tɚ.vjuː]

① *n.* 面試；會見

實用片語與搭配字

conduct interview; an interview with
進行面談；與…進行面試

② *v.* 採訪；進行面試

實用片語與搭配字

be interviewed by 被（某人）面試或採訪

▶ I'm so nervous about my job interview tomorrow!
我對明天的工作面試感到好緊張！

▶ Our company is hiring new staff and I have to conduct interviews with the candidates.
我們公司正在招募新職員，而我需要和應徵者進行面談。

▶ Melody is excited to interview a famous musician on her show.
美樂蒂對要在她的節目上訪問一位有名的音樂家感到很興奮。

▶ The movie star was interviewed by the reporter after she decided to quit making movies.
那位電影明星在決定不拍電影後，接受記者的訪問。

---

into [ˈɪn.tuː] *prep.* 到…裡面（表動作的方向）

▶ Sharon walked into the store and ordered a coffee.
雪倫走進店裡點了一杯咖啡。

96

introduce [ˌɪn.trəˈduːs] *v.* 介紹

▶ Can you introduce me to that girl over there?
你可以介紹我給那邊那個女孩認識嗎？

103

invent [ɪnˈvent] *v.* 發明；創造

▶ Thomas Edison invented things that changed people's lives.
湯馬斯・愛迪生發明的東西改變了人們的生活。

---

invitation [ˌɪn.vəˈteɪ.ʃən] *n.* 邀請（函）；請帖

實用片語與搭配字

accept invitation 接受邀請

▶ Thank you for the invitation to your birthday party!
謝謝你生日派對的邀請！

▶ Once you accept an invitation to attend a friend's wedding, you have to go.
一旦你答應了要參加朋友的婚宴，你就必須要去。

95

invite [ɪnˈvaɪt]

① *v.* 邀請

▶ Do you think they will invite her ex-boyfriend to the wedding?
你想他們會邀請她的前男友參加婚禮嗎？

I

② *n.* 邀請（函）

▶ I didn't get the invite until it was too late, so I missed the event.
我太晚才收到邀請函，以致錯過了那場活動。

---

iron [aɪrn]

① *n.* 鐵（金屬）
② *adj.* 鐵的
③ *v.* 熨（衣）；燙平

▶ Iron is a strong metal.
鐵是一種堅固的金屬。

▶ Tina uses iron pots for cooking.
緹娜用鐵鍋來烹飪。

▶ Robbie ironed his shirts after he washed them.
羅比洗完襯衫後把它們燙平。

---

is [ɪz / z / s]

v. （用於第三人稱單數）是

▶ Kaitlyn is a very cute baby.
凱特琳是一個非常可愛的寶寶。

---

island [ˈaɪ.lənd] *n.* 島

▶ I'm planning to take a vacation on a small island.
我計畫到一個小島上度假。

---

it [ɪt] *pron.* 它

▶ What is it?
這是什麼？

---

item [ˈaɪ.t̬əm] *n.* 項目；品項

▶ If you spend more than $100, you can choose one item from this shelf.
如果你消費超過一百元，你可以從架上選一件東西。

---

its [ɪts] *pron.* 它的（it 的所有格）

▶ The dog is playing with its toy.
這隻狗正在玩牠的玩具。

---

itself [ɪtˈself] *pron.* 它自己

▶ Each day will take care of itself.
一天的難處一天當就好。

---

jacket [ˈdʒæk.ɪt] *n.* 夾克；外套

▶ It's windy today, so don't forget your jacket!
今天風大，不要忘記帶你的夾克！

---

jam [dʒæm]

① *n.* 果醬

▶ Richard put some jam on his toast.
理查放了些果醬在他的烤麵包上。

② *v.* 把…塞入

③ *n.* 擁擠；堵塞

實用片語與搭配字

traffic jam 交通阻塞

▶ We jammed ten people into the car to go to the beach.
我們車子裡塞了十個人一起去海邊。

▶ The jam of cotton in his ears did not block out the sound.
塞在他耳朵裡的棉花並不能擋住聲音。

▶ It is very common in cities these days to see traffic jams because there are too many cars on the road.
都市裡塞車是很常見的事，因為路上有太多車了。

January / Jan. [ˈdʒæn.ju.er.i] *n.* 一月

▶ Jeff's birthday is January 31.
傑夫的生日是一月三十一日。

---

jazz [dʒæz] *n.* 爵士樂

▶ Let's go see a jazz concert this weekend.
這個週末一起去參加爵士音樂會吧。

---

jeans [dʒiːnz] *n.* 牛仔褲

▶ Ariel wants to buy some new jeans at the mall.
愛瑞兒想在購物中心買幾件新的牛仔褲。

---

jeep [dʒiːp] *n.* 吉普車

▶ A jeep is great for driving in the mountains.
在山中很適合開吉普車。

Exercise 32

I. Choose and write the correct word. Change the form of the word when necessary.

1	invite (v.) introduce (v.)	The day after they moved into their house, their new neighbors came by to __________ themselves.
2	interview (n.) invitation (n.)	I was really nervous during the job __________, so I don't think they'll hire me.
3	interested (adj.) interesting (adj.)	If you're __________ in the job, I'll send you all the details.
4	iron (v.) jam (v.)	I'd better __________ my pants before we go out; they're all wrinkled.
5	island (n.) item (n.)	The only __________ of furniture he has in his bedroom is a bed.

II. Multiple choices.

( ) 1. The little boy __________ his hands in his pockets, and walked away angrily.
(A) ironed (B) joined (C) jogged (D) jammed

( ) 2. He's such a creative teacher that he can always __________ an interesting game for his class.
(A) invents (B) invites (C) instances (D) interviews

( ) 3. It's not a good idea to pressure children into playing a musical __________.
(A) instrument (B) invitation (C) interview (D) interest

( ) 4. __________ coffee just doesn't compare with freshly ground coffee.
(A) Instant (B) International (C) Iron (D) Interested

( ) 5. Why don't you text all your friends and __________ them to your party?
(A) invent (B) interest (C) invite (D) interview

Unit 33

job [dʒɑːb] *n.* 工作

▶ Lisa has a great job as a doctor.
作為一位醫生，莉莎有份很好的工作。

---

jog [dʒɑːg]

① *v.* 慢跑

② *n.* 慢跑

▶ Matt turned on his music and jogged away.
麥特打開他的音樂去慢跑。

▶ David gets up at 6 a.m. every day to go for a jog.
大衛每天早上六點起床去慢跑。

---

join [dʒɔɪn]

① *v.* 一起做；加入

實用片語與搭配字

join in 加入，參加

② *n.* 接合點

▶ Everyone joined hands and prayed.
大家拉起手來一起禱告。

▶ The opera singer was in the middle of her song when someone with a loud voice from the audience joined in.
歌劇歌手唱到一半的時候，有觀眾發出了巨大的聲音。

▶ Where is the join? I can't see it.
接縫在哪裡？我看不到。

---

joint [dʒɔɪnt]

① *n.* 關節；接縫

② *adj.* 共同的；共有的

③ *v.* 連接；接合

▶ Yoga can help prevent sore and stiff joints.
瑜珈可以幫助防止關節的痠痛和僵硬。

▶ It was a joint project between two departments.
這是兩個部門共同合作的專案。

▶ The robot can move because its arms and legs are jointed.
這個機器人可以動是因為他的手和腳是連接在一起的。

---

joke [dʒoʊk]

① *n.* 笑話

實用片語與搭配字

make jokes 開玩笑

② *v.* 開玩笑；戲弄

▶ Robin likes to tell funny jokes.
羅賓喜歡講有趣的笑話。

▶ I wish John would be more serious and stop making jokes about everything.
我希望約翰能夠正經一點，不要一直亂開玩笑。

▶ Kai likes to joke with his friends.
凱喜歡和他的朋友們開玩笑。

實用片語與搭配字
joke about 拿…開玩笑

▶ You should never joke about a person's weight or age.
你不應該拿一個人的體重或年紀來開玩笑。

---

joy [dʒɔɪ] *n.* 喜悅；高興

▶ Sue's grandchildren bring her a lot of joy.
蘇的孫子們帶給她許多快樂。

103

judge [dʒʌdʒ] *n.* 法官；裁判

▶ The judge spent all night thinking about his final decision in the case.
這位法官花了一整晚的時間細想這件案子最後的決定。

---

judgment [ˈdʒʌdʒ.mənt] *n.* 審判；判斷（力）

▶ Many people believe that there will be a day of judgment after we die.
許多人相信在死後會有審判的一天。

實用片語與搭配字
pass judgement; make judgment; in sb's judgement
做判斷；在（某人）看來

▶ Beware of passing judgment on another person because you do not know their situation and you may be wrong.
評論其他人要謹慎，因為你不知道他們的情況，你有可能判斷錯誤。

---

juice [dʒuːs] *n.* 果汁

▶ Alicia likes to drink orange juice for breakfast.
艾莉莎喜歡早餐喝柳橙汁。

---

juicy [ˈdʒuː.si] *adj.* 多汁的

▶ These mangoes are so sweet and juicy.
這些芒果又甜又多汁。

July [dʒʊˈlaɪ] *n.* 七月

▶ America's birthday is July 4.
美國的國慶是七月四日。

---

jump [dʒʌmp]

① *v.* 跳；跳躍

▶ Kangaroos can jump very high.
袋鼠能跳很高。

實用片語與搭配字
jump the gun
（尤指不經仔細考慮）過早地採取行動

▶ We wanted to keep our decision to get married secret, but my sister jumped the gun and told everyone.
我們想要在結婚前守住秘密，但我姐姐太早告訴大家了。

② *n.* 跳躍

▶ How high is a kangaroo's jump?
袋鼠能跳多高？

June [dʒu:n] *n.* 六月

▶ Yvonne's birthday is June 22.
依芳的生日是六月二十二日。

just [dʒʌst]

① *adj.* 公正的；正直的

② *adv.* 剛好

▶ King David was a fair and just ruler.
大衛王是一位公平公正的統治者。

▶ This shirt fit Phil just right.
菲爾穿這件襯衫剛剛好。

keep [ki:p]

① *v.* 保留；保有

實用片語與搭配字

keep sth / sb out of sth;
keep an eye on
（使）不參加；（使）置身於…之外；留意，照看

② *n.* 撫養；照顧

▶ You can keep the book. It's yours!
你可以留著那本書，送給你！

▶ My mother went out shopping and asked me to keep an eye on my younger sister.
我媽媽去購物，並要求我照顧好妹妹。

▶ The child is in the keep of his grandparents.
這孩子是由他的祖父母撫養照顧。

keeper [ˈki:.pɚ] *n.* 飼養者；保管人

▶ Gary works as a zoo keeper.
蓋瑞的工作是動物園飼養員。

ketchup / catsup [ˈketʃ.ʌp / ˈkæt.səp]

n. 番茄醬

▶ Michelle put ketchup on her French fries.
米雪兒在她的薯條上加番茄醬。

key [ki:]

① *n.* 鑰匙

實用片語與搭配字

key to …的答案

② *v.* 鎖上

③ *adj.* 關鍵的

▶ The door is locked. Do you have a key?
這門是鎖著的，你有鑰匙嗎？

▶ The key to happiness is not in money or things, it is inside of you.
通往快樂的答案不是錢或物質，而是在自己的心中。

▶ How do you key this kind of lock?
你是怎麼鎖上這種鎖的？

▶ The speaker had three key points to his speech.
這位演說家在他的演講中有三大重點。

kick [kɪk]

① *v.* 踢

實用片語與搭配字

kick out of; kick off
趕出去；（活動的）開始

② *n.* 踢

▶ The soccer player kicked the ball with his foot.
這位足球員用他的腳踢球。

▶ The music festival kicked off with a brilliant fireworks show.
音樂節以精彩的煙火秀拉開序幕。

▶ The player's kick sent the ball flying.
這個球員的一踢，讓球飛了起來。

---

kid [kɪd]

① *n.* 小孩

② *v.* 戲弄；取笑

▶ Linda has two kids in elementary school.
琳達有兩個在小學唸書的小孩。

▶ This is not a good time to kid.
現在不是開玩笑的時候。

---

kill [kɪl]

① *v.* 殺死；弄死

② *n.* 被捕殺的動物；獵物；捕殺

▶ Mandy killed the cockroach with her shoe.
曼蒂用她的鞋子打死了蟑螂。

▶ The lion moved in for the kill.
這頭獅子逼近那隻獵物。

---

kind [kaɪnd]

① *adj.* 親切的

實用片語與搭配字

be kind to 對⋯友善

② *n.* 種類

▶ Grandma Doris is kind and loving.
桃樂絲奶奶親切又有愛心。

▶ Be kind to all people whether rich or poor.
不論富有或貧窮，都要友善對待所有人。

▶ How many kinds of animals are in the zoo?
這個動物園裡有幾種動物？

---

kindergarten [ˈkɪn.dɚˌɡɑːr.tən] *n.* 幼稚園

▶ Melissa is going to kindergarten next year.
馬莉莎明年要上幼稚園了。

---

king [kɪŋ] *n.* 國王

▶ Prince William will one day be king.
威廉王子有一天會當上國王。

---

kingdom [ˈkɪŋ.dəm] *n.* 王國

▶ Once upon a time in a magic kingdom, there was a dragon.
很久很久以前在神奇王國裡有一隻巨龍。

Exercise 33

I. Choose and write the correct word. Change the form of the word when necessary.

1	jog (v.) join (v.)	We only need one more player for this game; can you tell your sister to ________ in?
2	kindergarten (n.) kingdom (n.)	After the old king died, his son ruled over the ________.
3	kind (adj.) key (adj.)	He is a gentle man, always ________ and considerate.
4	joke (v.) kick (v.)	The fireman had to ________ the door in to get into the burning building.
5	judgement (n.) judge (n.)	You must not let your let your personal reactions interfere with your professional ________.

II. Multiple choices.

( ) 1. We want a double hamburger with cheese, mayonnaise, and ________.
(A) keeper (B) juice (C) ketchup (D) joy

( ) 2. Summer is a pleasant season for all kinds of cold foods and ________ fruits.
(A) just (B) juicy (C) key (D) kind

( ) 3. The ________ sentenced the the thief to five years in prison.
(A) judge (B) judgement (C) joke (D) key

( ) 4. Most children know how to count by the time they start ________.
(A) kingdom (B) keeper (C) kid (D) kindergarten

( ) 5. There are many ________ ventures between Japanese and American companies.
(A) join (B) just (C) joint (D) juicy

Unit 34

kiss [kɪs]

① *v.* 親吻；接吻

② *n.* 吻

▶ The parents kissed their baby on the cheek.
這對父母親了寶寶的臉頰。

▶ Josh gave his wife a kiss before he left for work.
喬許上班前給了他的妻子一個吻。

---

kitchen [ˈkɪtʃ.ən] *n.* 廚房

▶ Henry is cooking in the kitchen.
亨利正在廚房煮東西。

---

kite [kaɪt] *n.* 風箏

▶ Let's go fly a kite in the park!
我們去公園放風箏吧！

---

kitten / kitty [ˈkɪt̬.ən / ˈkɪt̬.i] *n.* 小貓

▶ Sally's cat just had five kittens.
莎莉的貓剛生了五隻小貓。

---

knee [niː]

① *n.* 膝蓋

實用片語與搭配字

on sb's knee 在（某人）的膝上

② *v.* 用膝蓋碰（撞）

▶ Grandpa's knees hurt after he walks.
爺爺走路後覺得膝蓋疼痛。

▶ When Jason was young, he used to sit on his grandfather's knee and listen to stories.
傑森小的時候常常坐在爺爺的腿上聽故事。

▶ You can knee your attacker in the stomach.
你可以用膝蓋撞襲擊者的肚子。

---

knife [naɪf]

① *n.* 刀

② *v.* 用刀切

▶ Robbie cut the apple with a knife.
羅比用刀切蘋果。

▶ The thief tried to knife the officer in the chest.
這名小偷試著用刀刺向警察的胸口。

---

knock [nɑːk]

① *v.* 敲（門）；撞擊

▶ Jeff knocked on the door, but no one answered.
傑夫敲了敲門，但沒有人回應。

② *n.* 敲；撞

實用片語與搭配字

knock on effect 連鎖反應

▶ I was just about to go to bed when there was a knock on my door.
就在我要去睡時，有人敲我的門。

▶ If you fail to complete the project on time, there will be a knock on effect because many other things will be delayed.
如果你沒能如期完成報告，許多事情都會因此受到影響而耽擱。

---

know [noʊ] *v.* 知道

▶ Albert knows a lot about science.
亞伯對科學博學多聞。

102

knowledge [ˈnɑː.lɪdʒ] *n.* 知識

實用片語與搭配字

gain knowledge 獲得知識

▶ Professor Lin has a lot of knowledge about world history.
林教授有許多關於世界歷史的知識。

▶ There are many ways to gain knowledge; for example, studying, traveling and reading.
有許多管道可以汲取知識，例如讀書、旅行和閱讀。

---

koala [koʊˈɑː.lə] *n.* 無尾熊

▶ Koalas are from Australia, and so are kangaroos.
無尾熊來自澳洲，袋鼠也是。

---

lack [læk]

① *n.* 欠缺…；沒有…

② *v.* 缺乏；缺少

實用片語與搭配字

lack in 缺乏…

▶ A lack of education is a big problem in poor countries.
在貧窮國家，教育資源缺乏是個大問題。

▶ He lacked the money to take his dream vacation.
他沒有足夠的錢去度他夢想中的假期。

▶ Gina's boyfriend lacks in looks, but he has a kind heart.
吉娜的男朋友長得不是特別好看，但他有一顆善良的心。

---

lady [ˈleɪ.di] *n.* 女士；小姐

▶ Mrs. Pang is a kind lady.
彭小姐是位仁慈的女士。

---

ladybug [ˈleɪ.di.bʌg] *n.* 瓢蟲

▶ Nathan showed his mom a ladybug he found in the yard.
納森將他在花園裡發現的瓢蟲拿給媽媽看。

lake [leɪk] *n.* 湖泊

▶ Kaylah and Ryan went fishing on the lake.
凱拉和萊恩去了湖上釣魚。

---

lamb [læm]

① *n.* 羔羊

② *v.* 產羊羔，生小羊

▶ The lamb was born in the spring.
這隻小羊在春天出生。

▶ The farmer's sheep have lambed.
農夫的羊已經生了小羊。

---

lamp [læmp] *n.* 燈

▶ Can you turn on the lamp? We need some light.
你可以開燈嗎？我們需要一些燈光。

---

land [lænd]

① *n.* 土地；陸地

② *v.* 著陸

實用片語與搭配字

land on 降落在…

▶ This house is on a large piece of land.
這棟房子座落在一大片土地上。

▶ The airplane landed safely.
這架飛機安全地著陸了。

▶ People say when a four-leaf clover lands on your head, you will be lucky.
據說一朵四葉草掉到你頭上的話，你會獲得好運。

---

lane [leɪn] *n.* 巷

▶ Tammy lives just down the lane from Ashley.
譚美就住在艾胥莉家的巷尾。

---

language [ˈlæŋ.gwɪdʒ] *n.* 語言

實用片語與搭配字

body language; use language
肢體語言；使用語言

▶ How many languages do you speak?
你會說多少種語言？

▶ If you cannot speak a language, then body language is a good way to tell people what you want.
若你不會說一個語言，那肢體語言就是告訴別人你要什麼的好方法。

---

lantern [ˈlæn.tɚn] *n.* 燈籠

▶ I bought a beautiful lantern for my living room.
我買了一個美麗的燈籠放在我的客廳。

---

lap [læp] *n.* 膝部；（坐時的）大腿上側

▶ Derek sits on his grandma's lap to hear a bedtime story.
德瑞克坐在祖母的腿上聽睡前故事。

large [lɑːrdʒ] *adj.* 大的

▶ The blue whale is the largest animal on Earth.
藍鯨是地球上最大的動物。

---

last [læst]

① *adj.* 最後的

② *adv.* 最後地

實用片語與搭配字

at last 終於，最終

③ *n.* 最後的人或物

④ *v.* 持續

實用片語與搭配字

last for 持續…

▶ Jeremy quit his job. Tomorrow is his last day.
傑瑞米辭了他的工作，明天是他上班最後一天。

▶ At a wedding, the bride always walks in last.
在婚禮上，新娘總是最後走進來。

▶ I have worked hard the whole year and at last, I can take my well-deserved vacation.
我辛苦工作了一整年，終於可以好好放個假了。

▶ Peter is always the last to be chosen for sports teams.
彼得總是最後一個被選進球隊裡的人。

▶ How long did the party last?
這個派對持續了多久？

▶ That leather jacket is of good quality and will last you for many years.
皮外套的材質相當好，可以持續穿好幾年。

L

late [leɪt]

① *adj.* 遲到的

② *adv.* 遲到；來不及

實用片語與搭配字

better late than never
亡羊補牢猶未晚（遲做總比不做好）

▶ Jim missed the beginning of the movie because he was late.
吉姆因為遲到而錯過了電影的開頭。

▶ If you arrive late, you won't be able to get on the plane.
如果你晚到了，就會無法上飛機。

▶ I was late for the party, but better late than never.
我參加派對遲到了，但總比沒到來的好。

---

later [ˈleɪ.t̬ɚ] *adv.* 較晚地；後來

▶ My sister arrived later than my brother.
我的姊姊比哥哥更晚抵達。

latest [ˈleɪ.t̬ɪst] *adj.* 最近的；最新的

▶ Have you heard the latest news about Shelly?
你是否聽到了關於雪莉最近的消息？

Exercise 34

I. Choose and write the correct word. Change the form of the word when necessary.

1	knife (n.) knee (n.)	Steven won't be racing in the final due to his __________ injury.
2	knock (v.) lack (v.)	She won't get promoted to a manager because she __________ the ability to make difficult decisions.
3	last (adj.) late (adj.)	We hope your family and my family can get together for a celebration like __________ year.
4	lake (n.) lane (n.)	In the beautiful park, there's a path winding along the __________.
5	latest (adj.) large (adj.)	These __________ paintings show how the artist has really grown in maturity.

II. Multiple choices.

( ) 1. Travelling to different countries can really broaden one's __________ of the world.
(A) knock (B) land (C) lack (D) knowledge

( ) 2. She enjoyed the chance to converse with someone who spoke her __________.
(A) lane (B) language (C) lantern (D) lamb

( ) 3. She bumped into his tray, knocking the food onto his __________.
(A) lap (B) lamp (C) lamb (D) lady

( ) 4. Because of the snow, the pilot had to __________ the plane at an airport in another city.
(A) last (B) lack (C) land (D) knock

( ) 5. Although the good shoes cost more, they __________ much longer than cheap ones.
(A) land (B) last (C) lack (D) know

laugh [læf]

① *v.* 大笑；笑

② *n.* 笑聲

實用片語與搭配字

for a laugh 取樂，開玩笑

▶ Justin laughed at the funny movie.
賈斯汀看這部有趣的電影時大笑。

▶ Eva has a very loud laugh.
伊娃笑起來很大聲。

▶ Mika does not like dressing up for Halloween, but this year he did it for a laugh.
米卡不喜歡萬聖節變裝，但今年他為了好玩變裝了。

---

law [lɑː] *n.* 法律

實用片語與搭配字

break the law; under the law
犯法；根據法律的規定

▶ Carolyn always follows the traffic laws when she drives.
凱洛琳開車的時候總是遵守交通規則。

▶ Under the law, it is illegal for teenagers younger than 16 to have a full-time job.
法律規定，未滿十六歲的青少年做全職工作是違法的。

---

lawyer [ˈlɑː.jɚ] *n.* 律師

▶ Zoe is studying to be a lawyer.
佐伊正在為將來要成為一位律師而努力讀書。

---

lay [leɪ] *v.* 放置

實用片語與搭配字

lay on 躺在…

▶ Alicia lay her baby down to sleep.
艾莉莎將寶寶放下讓他睡覺。

▶ You can lay on the charm as much as you like, but I know you are just trying to get what you want.
你可以盡可能運用你的魅力，但我知道你只是想要獲得你所要的。

---

lazy [ˈleɪ.zi] *adj.* 懶惰的

▶ Lazy students rarely get good grades.
懶惰的學生很少會拿到好成績。

97

lead [liːd]

① *v.* 帶領

▶ The teacher led her students down the hall.
這位老師帶著她的學生到走廊上。

實用片語與搭配字

lead the way 帶路

② *n.* 榜樣

實用片語與搭配字

take the lead 帶頭

▶ I knew the city well so my friends asked me to lead the way to the museum.
我對這座城市很熟悉，所以我朋友叫我帶他們到博物館。

▶ Asher is in the lead. He might win the race!
亞瑟現在領先，他可能會贏得這場比賽！

▶ The singer started singing a well-known song and we took his lead and joined in.
歌手開始唱著一首知名的歌曲，我們也跟著一起加入。

---

leader [ˈliː.dɚ] *n.* 領導者

實用片語與搭配字

the leader of …的領導者

▶ A boss must be a good leader.
一個老闆必須要是一個好的領袖。

▶ The leader of the country was good to his people and they loved him.
國家領導人善待他的人民，人民也很愛戴他。

98

leadership [ˈliː.dɚ.ʃɪp] *n.* 領導能力；領導

▶ The technology company did very well under the leadership of the new CEO.
這家科技公司在新執行長的領導下表現得很好。

---

leaf [liːf]

① *n.* 葉片

② *v.* 匆匆翻閱

▶ Leaves fall off the trees in the fall.
葉子在秋天時會從樹上落下。

▶ I like to leaf through the books when I visit a bookstore.
當我去書店時，我喜歡把書拿起來翻閱。

---

learn [lɝːn] *v.* 學習

實用片語與搭配字

learn from; learn one's lesson
向…學習；汲取教訓

▶ Mavis wants to learn Spanish.
麥維斯想要學西班牙文。

▶ Jack learned his lesson after the teacher caught him cheating during the exam.
在老師抓到傑克段考作弊後，他為此學到了教訓。

103

least [liːst]

① *adj.* 最少的；最小的

▶ The chicken dish costs the least amount on the menu.
這道雞肉料理是菜單上價錢最便宜的。

② *pron.* 最小；最少；最不

③ *adv.* 最小；最少；最不

▶ The least you can do is be on time.
準時是你至少能做到的。

▶ Of all the students in the class, Tim talks least.
在班上所有學生裡面，提姆最少講話。

---

leave [liːv]

① *v.* 離開

實用片語與搭配字

leave sb / sth behind 撇下，丟下

② *n.* 休假

實用片語與搭配字

take leave 告別，告辭

▶ What time do we need to leave the house?
我們什麼時候需要離開住處？

▶ Following her divorce, Lillian left everything behind and went traveling around the world.
莉莉安離婚後，她拋下一切去環遊世界。

▶ Stephanie is on leave today. She's not at work.
史黛芬妮今天休假，她沒有上班。

▶ My father became ill and I had to take leave from work to take care of him.
父親生了重病後，我必須辭職照顧他。

---

left [left]

① *adj.* 左邊的

② *adv.* 在左邊

③ *n.* 左方

▶ Alison wears a ring on her left hand.
艾莉森的左手上戴著一枚戒指。

▶ Please turn left at the next street.
請在下一條街左轉。

▶ Richard's house is on the left.
理查的家在左邊。

---

leg [leg] *n.* 腿

▶ Simon is tall. He has long legs.
賽門很高，他有雙長腿。

---

legal [ˈliː.ɡəl] *adj.* 法律的；法律方面的

實用片語與搭配字

legal age; legal aid 法定年齡；法律援助

▶ Do you know any lawyers? I need some legal advice.
你認識任何律師嗎？我需要一些法律上的建議。

▶ If you want to get a credit card, you have to be legal age.
你必須要到法定年齡才能申辦信用卡。

---

lemon [ˈlem.ən] *n.* 檸檬

▶ Adding a few slices of lemon to a glass of water will make it taste fresh.
在一杯水中加幾片檸檬會讓水喝起來更清爽。

101

lemonade [ˌlem.əˈneɪd] *n.* 檸檬水（甜的）

▶ In order to make lemonade, you need water, sugar, ice and lemons.
做檸檬水，你需要水、糖、冰塊和檸檬。

lend [lend] *v.* 借（出）

實用片語與搭配字
lend a hand; lend sth to sb
幫助；借（東西）給（某人）

▶ Can you please lend me a pen? I need to fill out this form.
可以借我一枝筆嗎？我需要填寫這張表格。

▶ My co-worker is always there to lend a hand when I have too much work.
當我工作量很大時，同事總會伸出援手協助我。

length [leŋθ]
n. （距離）長度；（時間）長短

▶ Andrea has had the same hair length since she was a teenager.
從安卓雅青少年起，她的頭髮都維持一樣的長度。

leopard [ˈlep.ɚd] *n.* 豹

▶ The leopard is a member of the cat family.
豹是貓科動物的一種。

less [les]

① *adj.* 較少的

實用片語與搭配字
less than 少於

② *adv.* 較少地；較小地

③ *pron.* 更少的數（量、額）

實用片語與搭配字
more or less 多少有些，大約

④ *prep.* 減去；扣除

▶ There are less people here today than usual.
今天這裡人比平常還少。

▶ In many jobs, women still earn less than their male colleagues.
在許多職場中，女性還是比他們的男性同事賺得少。

▶ You should try to spend less.
你應該試著少花點錢。

▶ I've had better meals for less.
我用比較低的價錢吃到了更好的餐點。

▶ There are more or less seven billion people in the world. It is hard to get an exact number.
現今世界上大約有七十億人口，很難知道確切的數量有多少。

▶ Ten less six is four.
十減去六等於四。

lesson [ˈles.ən] *n.* （一節）課；課程

▶ There are 50 lessons in this book.
這本書裡有五十課。

let [let] *v.* 讓；允許

▶ Camellia's parents let her borrow the car tonight.
卡蜜拉的父母今晚將車子借她開。

實用片語與搭配字

let go 放手

▶ Kerry had to let go of her fear of failure to apply for a new job.
凱蕊必須要放下害怕失敗的恐懼才能去應徵新工作。

---

letter [ˈletə]

① *n.* 字母

② *n.* 書信

▶ The first letter of the alphabet is "A".
字母表的第一個字母是 A。

▶ Pat wrote a letter to his mother.
派特寫了封信給他的母親。

---

lettuce [ˈletɪs] *n.* 生菜；萵苣

▶ Caroline is cutting up some lettuce for her salad.
凱洛琳正在切沙拉裡的生菜。

Exercise 35

I. Choose and write the correct word. Change the form of the word when necessary.

1	lawyer (n.) leader (n.)	He has passed his law examinations and is now practising as a __________.
2	least (adj.) left (adj.)	He's the best teacher, even though he has the __________ experience.
3	lay (v.) leave (v.)	Please make sure that the house is locked before you __________.
4	length (n.) lesson (n.)	The __________ of the paragraph depends on the information it conveys.
5	lend (v.) let (v.)	The bank will only __________ me money if my parents guarantee the loan.

II. Multiple choices.

(　　) 1. A tour guide will __________ you through the museum and will answer any questions you have.
(A) leave　(B) learn　(C) lead　(D) lay

(　　) 2. She was too __________ to make herself a sandwich and salad, and decided to just have some instant soup.
(A) lazy　(B) least　(C) left　(D) legal

(　　) 3. Put a bed of __________ in a serving bowl and add the tomato and cucumber.
(A) lemonade　(B) leaf　(C) lettuce　(D) lemon

(　　) 4. The first __________ on the timetable for Monday morning is history.
(A) length　(B) lesson　(C) letter　(D) leave

(　　) 5. Under his __________ the army had marched from one victory to another.
(A) leadership　(B) lesson　(C) leader　(D) length

Unit 36

100

level [ˈlev.əl]

① *n.* 級別；層次

② *adj.* 平的；水平的

▶ These words are low level.
這些字是初階程度。

▶ This counter is level.
這個工作檯是平整的。

---

library [ˈlaɪ.brer.i] *n.* 圖書館

實用片語與搭配字

public library 公立圖書館

▶ Dan works in the library at his school in the evenings.
丹恩每個晚上會在學校的圖書館工作。

▶ The public library in our town is the best place to sit and read because it is quiet.
鎮上的公立圖書館是坐下來看書的好地方，因為那裡很安靜。

---

lick [lɪk]

① *v.* 舔；舔食

② *n.* 舔

▶ The friendly dog licked Elijah's hand.
這隻友善的狗舔了舔伊利亞的手。

▶ Would you like a lick of my ice cream cone?
你要舔一口我的甜筒冰淇淋嗎？

---

lid [lɪd] *n.* 蓋子

▶ Keep the lid on the honey in order to avoid ants getting into it.
將蜂蜜的蓋子蓋好以免螞蟻跑進去。

---

lie [laɪ]

① *n.* 謊話

實用片語與搭配字

white lie 善意的謊言

② *v.* 躺臥

實用片語與搭配字

lie in 位於，睡懶覺

▶ He never tells the truth; he always tells lies.
他從來不說真話，他總是說謊。

▶ Phil told a white lie when his pregnant wife asked him if she was fat.
當他懷孕的妻子問他是否肥胖時，菲爾說了一個善意的謊言。

▶ Mom is lying down for a nap.
媽媽躺下來小睡片刻。

▶ My mom and dad like to lie in on Sunday morning and wait for us to bring them breakfast in bed.
我父母親喜歡在星期天早上在床上窩著，等我們把早餐送過去。

L

life [laɪf] *n.* 生命

實用片語與搭配字

be a matter of life or / and death
是生死攸關的事

▶ Gertrude has lived a long life.
葛楚德很長壽。

▶ It could be a matter of life or death if you don't wear your seat belt when driving.
如果駕駛時不繫安全帶，可能是生死攸關的問題。

---

lift [lɪft]

① *v.* 抬起；舉起

實用片語與搭配字

lift up 舉起，抬起

② *n.* 提；吊；升

▶ I can't lift this box. It's too heavy.
我無法抬起這箱子，太重了。

▶ We all like to watch movies that can lift up our moods.
我們都喜歡看可以提振心情的電影。

▶ Can you give me a lift, so I can reach that book?
你能不能把我舉起來，這樣我就能拿到那些書？

---

light [laɪt]

① *n.* 光線

實用片語與搭配字

come to light 真相大白

② *v.* 點燃

③ *adj.* 明亮的

④ *adj.* 輕的

⑤ *adv.* 輕裝地；輕地

▶ There isn't a lot of light in here. I can't see very well.
這裡沒有太多光線，我無法看得很清楚。

▶ The corruption in our government came to light after someone gave some documents to the newspaper.
在有人向報社爆料之後，政府的貪腐終於真相大白。

▶ Mom will light the candles on the birthday cake.
媽媽會在生日蛋糕上點蠟燭。

▶ The room is very light when the curtains are open.
當窗簾打開的時候，這個房間很亮。

▶ A feather is very light.
一根羽毛非常輕。

▶ John likes to travel light.
約翰喜歡輕便旅行。

---

lightning [ˈlaɪt.nɪŋ] *n.* 閃電；電光

▶ The lightning storm caused the neighborhood to lose power.
這雷雨導致這鄰近區域斷電。

like [laɪk]

① *prep.* 像；如

② *v.* 喜歡

③ *n.* 愛好

▶ Alicia is like her dad. They both love music.
艾莉莎像她爸爸，他們都喜歡音樂。

▶ Did you like the movie?
你喜歡那部電影嗎？

▶ What are some of your likes?
你的愛好有哪些？

likely [ˈlaɪ.kli]

① *adj.* 很可能的；可能要發生的

② *adv.* 可能；多半

▶ Babies who are hungry are likely to cry.
肚子餓的寶寶很可能會哭。

▶ The guests will likely arrive soon.
客人們有可能很快就會抵達。

---

lily [ˈlɪl.i] *n.* 百合花

▶ Henry bought his wife a dozen lilies.
亨利買了十二朵百合花給他的妻子。

limit [ˈlɪm.ɪt]

① *n.* 限制；上限；限額

實用片語與搭配字

within the limits 有限制

② *v.* 限制；限定

▶ There is a two-hour time limit at this restaurant because it is so popular.
因為這家餐廳很受歡迎，所以限定用餐時間為兩小時。

▶ Connie lets her little boy play by himself within the limits of the house.
康妮讓小男孩自己在房子內玩耍。

▶ You shouldn't limit yourself to jobs within 15 minutes of your house.
你不該限制自己只找離家十五分鐘路程內的工作。

---

line [laɪn]

① *n.* 直線

實用片語與搭配字

bottom line; draw the line; cross line
底線，最重要的事實；絕不去做；跨越界線（泛指侵犯禁忌或淺規則，做了不該做的事）

② *v.* 排隊

實用片語與搭配字

line up 排隊

▶ The shortest distance between two points is a straight line.
兩點之間最短的距離是一直線。

▶ Kristy crossed the line when she yelled at her boss at the company meeting.
克莉絲蒂在公司會議上對著她的老闆大吼，觸犯到了底線。

▶ People lined the street to see the president.
人們在街上排隊要見總統。

▶ The children lined up to order their lunches at the cafeteria.
孩子們在餐廳排隊買午餐。

link [lɪŋk]

① *n.* 關聯；關係

② *v.* 連接；聯合

▶ There is a definite link between air pollution from cars and global warming.
來自汽車的空氣汙染與地球暖化之間有明確的關聯。

▶ The teammates linked their hands together and ran down the field.
隊友們牽起彼此的手一起跑到球場。

---

lion [ˈlaɪ.ən] *n.* 獅子

▶ The lion is the king of the jungle.
獅子是叢林之王。

---

lip [lɪp] *n.* 嘴唇

▶ Kaitlyn wiped her lips after she ate.
凱特琳吃完東西後擦了她的嘴唇。

---

liquid [ˈlɪk.wɪd] *n.* 液體

▶ Drink lots of liquid and eat more fruit so you won't catch a cold.
喝大量液體和多吃些水果，這樣你才不會感冒。

list [lɪst]

① *n.* 名單

實用片語與搭配字

on list 在名單上

② *v.* 把…編列成表

▶ Do you have a list of guests coming to the party?
你有要來參加派對的賓客名單嗎？

▶ The famous writer was on the short-list for the prize, but someone else won the prize.
那位知名作家在為數不多的入圍名單上，但獲獎者另有其人。

▶ Larry listed his goals for the year on a piece of paper.
賴瑞在一張紙上把他的年度目標列出來。

---

listen [ˈlɪs.ən] *v.* 聽；傾聽

▶ Ray loves to listen to music in the evenings.
瑞伊喜歡在晚上聽音樂。

---

listener [ˈlɪs.ən.ɚ] *n.* 聆聽者

▶ All of Carmen's friends say she is a very good listener.
所有的朋友都說卡門是個很好的聆聽者。

---

little [ˈlɪt̬.əl]

① *adj.* 少的；小的；幼小的；年幼的

▶ When Sam was little, he lived in Spain.
當山姆小的時候，他住在西班牙。

實用片語與搭配字

little bit 很少的

② *adv.* 很少；不多

③ *n.* 少量，少許；不足

▶ If you can wait a little bit, I will be able to help you. I need to finish this job quickly.
如果你能稍微等一下，我就能夠幫你。我需要盡快完成我的工作。

▶ New parents sleep very little in the first few months.
新手爸媽在前幾個月都睡得很少。

▶ If you want some food, there's a little in the kitchen.
如果你想要吃點東西，廚房裡有一些。

100

live [laɪv] *adj.* 活的

▶ You can see many live animals at the zoo.
你可以在動物園看到許多活生生的動物。

live [lɪv] *v.* 住；居住

▶ John and Sue live in New York.
約翰和蘇住在紐約。

---

loaf [loʊf] *n.* 一條或一塊（麵包）

▶ Wanda buys a loaf of French bread at the bakery every day.
汪達每天在這家麵包店買一條法國麵包。

---

local [ˈloʊ.kəl]

① *adj.* 當地的；本地的

② *n.* 本地人

▶ Check your local theater for movie dates and times.
查看一下你當地電影院的電影日期與時間。

▶ If you want to find a good restaurant, ask one of the locals where they like to eat.
如果你要找一個好餐廳，問一個本地人他們喜歡去哪裡吃。

L

Exercise 36

I. Choose and write the correct word. Change the form of the word when necessary.

1	lick (v.) lie (v.)	You can enjoy all the water sports, or simply __________ on the beach.
2	library (n.) lightening (n.)	In the __________, new books have to be classified before they are put on shelves for readers' use.
3	limit (v.) light (v.)	Please __________ the time you spend on the computer to 30 minutes so that other students can use it.
4	live (adj.) local (adj.)	We can check the __________ paper to find out what is happening in town this weekend.
5	link (n.) list (n.)	The __________ between smoking and cancer is too strong to ignore.

II. Multiple choices.

( ) 1. The little boy doesn't have strength to __________ up the heavy box.
(A) light (B) lie (C) lift (D) like

( ) 2. If you add too much __________, the mixture will not be thick enough.
(A) lick (B) liquid (C) link (D) list

( ) 3. Please __________ your educational qualifications and work experience on the application form.
(A) line (B) listen (C) link (D) list

( ) 4. These words are specifically pointed out in the speech so that the __________ can be in no doubt.
(A) listener (B) loaf (C) list (D) link

( ) 5. Research suggests that children whose parents split up are more __________ to drop out of high school.
(A) little (B) likely (C) live (D) like

Unit 37

locate [loʊˈkeɪt] *v.* 位於；坐落在…

實用片語與搭配字

locate in 位於…

▶ Vancouver Island is located off the west coast of Canada.
溫哥華島位於加拿大的西岸。

▶ The company's head office is located in North America, but its factories are all in Asia.
這間企業的總公司位於北美洲，但工廠全部都設在亞洲。

---

lock [lɑːk]

① *n.* 鎖

② *v.* 鎖上

實用片語與搭配字

lock sb up 將（某人）關入監獄、精神病院

▶ Cindy put a lock on her diary so her brother wouldn't read it.
辛蒂將日記上鎖，這樣她哥哥就無法偷看。

▶ Don't forget to lock the doors before you leave.
在你離開家前，不要忘記鎖上門。

▶ The police locked the criminal up to make sure that he does not escape.
警方把罪犯關起來，以確保他不會逃跑。

---

log [lɑːg]

① *n.* 圓木；原木

② *v.* 伐木

實用片語與搭配字

log on （電腦）登入

▶ Dad is in the woods cutting some logs for our fire tonight.
為了我們今晚的營火，爸爸在樹林裡砍些木材。

▶ The company logged so much that many animals in this area lost their homes.
這間公司伐木太多使得這區域的動物失去了牠們的家。

▶ Many people in our company share the same computer, so you have to log on with your name every time you use it.
我們公司許多人共用一台電腦，所以每次使用的時候，都必須輸入你的名字來登入。

---

lone [loʊn] *adj.* 孤單的

▶ The lone wolf stood on top of the hill.
這隻孤單的狼站在山頂上。

103

lonely [ˈloʊn.li] *adj.* 寂寞的；孤獨的

▶ Hope felt lonely, so she called her best friend.
荷普覺得很寂寞，所以她打電話給她最好的朋友。

實用片語與搭配字

be lonely without 因…不在而感到孤單

▶ The old lady would be very lonely without her dog.
沒有了她的狗，老婦人會感到很寂寞。

---

long [lɑːŋ]

① *adj.* 長的

② *adv.* 長時間地；長久地

實用片語與搭配字

last long 持久

③ *v.* 渴望

實用片語與搭配字

long for 渴望…

▶ Mikayla has very long hair.
米凱拉有著一頭很長的頭髮。

▶ How long is grandma staying?
奶奶會待多久？

▶ This good weather won't last long because there is another cold spell coming.
這好天氣不會持續太久，因為有另一波寒流要來了。

▶ After living abroad for three years, Naomi really longs to return home.
在國外住了三年之後，娜俄米非常渴望回家。

▶ All I long for after a hard day's work, is to go home and relax in front of the TV.
結束一天辛苦的工作之後，我只想回家看電視放鬆。

---

look [lʊk]

① *v.* 看；注視

實用片語與搭配字

look up to; look for 向（某人）看齊；尋找

② *n.* 瞥；看

▶ Look at this picture. It is beautiful.
看看這張畫，它很漂亮。

▶ The young boy looks up to his father and he wants to grow up to be just like him.
小男孩向父親看齊，他長大之後想要成為像他父親一樣。

▶ Jeremiah took one look and fell in love with Alexandra.
傑瑞麥雅對雅麗珊卓一見鍾情。

---

lose [luːz] *v.* 輸掉；失去

▶ Now that our star player is hurt, I'm worried that we are going to lose the game.
現在我們的明星球員受傷了，我擔心我們可能會輸了這場比賽。

---

loser [ˈluː.zɚ] *n.* 失敗者；失主

▶ You are not a loser just because you failed one test!
你不會因為一次考試不及格就變成失敗者！

loss [lɑːs] *n.* 喪失；損失；失敗

實用片語與搭配字

loss for / of 喪失

▶ The loss of her dog made Kate sad for a long time.
凱特失去她的狗，讓她傷心了很久。

▶ When Joan told me the bad news, I was at a loss for words and did not know what to say.
當瓊安告訴我這個壞消息時，我無言以對，不知道該說什麼才好。

---

lot [lɑːt] *n.* 很多；大量

▶ Alicia has a lot of toys.
艾莉莎有很多玩具。

---

loud [laʊd]

① *adj.* 吵鬧的；大聲的

② *adv.* 大聲地；響亮地

▶ That music is loud. Can you turn it down?
那音樂很吵，你能關小聲嗎？

▶ Why are you speaking so loud? I'm right here.
你為什麼講話要這麼大聲？我就在這兒。

---

love [lʌv]

① *n.* 愛

實用片語與搭配字

in love 戀愛中

② *v.* 愛；疼愛

▶ Cam has a lot of love for his daughters.
肯慕很愛他的女兒們。

▶ Hannah was so in love with her new boyfriend that she did not want to believe anything bad about him.
漢娜和她的新男友熱戀中，她不相信任何關於她男友不好的傳言。

▶ Cam loves his wife very much.
肯慕非常愛他的妻子。

---

lovely [ˈlʌv.li] *adj.* 美麗的；可愛的

▶ You look lovely tonight, are you going on a date?
你今晚看起來很美麗，你要去約會嗎？

---

lover [ˈlʌv.ɚ] *n.* 戀人；情人

▶ Mario always says, "I'm a lover, not a fighter."
馬力歐總是說：「我是個情人，不是個戰士。」

---

low [loʊ]

① *adj.* 低的

② *n.* 低點；低水平

▶ Jason is sitting in a low chair.
傑森正坐在一張低矮的椅子上。

▶ The temperature is at a new low today.
今天溫度達到新低點。

③ *adv.* 向下地

▶ Steve bent low to get through the door.
史提夫彎低身體通過那道門。

lower [ˈloʊ.ɚ] *v.* 降低；減少

實用片語與搭配字

lower sb's voice; lower cost
降低音量；降低成本

▶ You can lower the hospital bed to make it easier for the patient to get out.
你可以降低醫院的床，讓病人比較容易下床。

▶ When you enter the museum, you have to lower your voice and not speak loudly.
當你進到博物館，你必須要降低音量，說話不能太大聲。

---

luck [lʌk] *n.* 幸運；運氣

實用片語與搭配字

with luck; good luck v-ing sth
好運；祝好運

▶ I'm going to buy a lottery ticket; wish me luck!
我要去買樂透彩券；祝我好運！

▶ We are planning a picnic and with luck this good weather will last until Sunday.
我們計畫要去野餐，幸運的是，好天氣會持續到星期天。

---

lucky [ˈlʌk.i] *adj.* 幸運的

實用片語與搭配字

lucky charm 幸運星

▶ You are so lucky to have that job.
你很幸運可以擁有那份工作。

▶ In some countries, a four-leaf clover is a lucky charm.
有些國家認為四葉草是幸運的象徵。

---

lunch [lʌntʃ]

① *n.* 午餐

實用片語與搭配字

lunch break 午餐時間；午休時間

② *v.* 吃午餐

▶ Daphne eats lunch at 12:00 every day.
黛芬妮每天中午十二點吃午餐。

▶ I usually go out walking during my lunch break to get some fresh air.
為了呼吸新鮮空氣，我經常在午休時間去散步。

▶ Let's lunch together sometime next week.
我們下週找個時間一起吃午餐。

---

machine [məˈʃiːn]

① *n.* 機器

② *v.* 用機器做

▶ Smartphones are amazing machines.
智慧型手機是令人驚嘆的機器。

▶ We can't machine this because the computer is broken.
我們不能用機器操作，因為電腦壞了。

mad [mæd] *adj.* 非常憤怒的；十分惱火的

▶ Derrick's parents are mad at him for coming home late last night.
德瑞克的父母因為他昨晚太晚回家，對他大發雷霆。

---

magazine [ˌmæg.əˈziːn] *n.* 雜誌；期刊

▶ Cara likes to read fashion magazines.
卡拉喜歡看時裝雜誌。

---

magic [ˈmædʒ.ɪk]

① *n.* 神奇力量；魔法；魔術戲法

② *adj.* 魔術的；神奇的

▶ Do you believe there is magic in this world?
你相信這世界上有神奇的力量嗎？

▶ The kids want to go to a magic show this weekend, can you take them?
孩子們這週末想要看魔術秀，你可以帶他們去嗎？

---

magician [məˈdʒɪʃ.ən] *n.* 魔術師

▶ Larry is a great magician! His shows are so entertaining.
賴瑞是個很棒的魔術師！他的表演很有趣。

Exercise 37

I. Choose and write the correct word. Change the form of the word when necessary.

1	lonely (adj.) loud (adj.)	She must be feeling very __________ after the loss of her husband.
2	loser (n.) loss (n.)	Many parents feel a sense of __________ when their children leave home.
3	lock (v.) long (v.)	If you keep valuables in your house, __________ them away somewhere safe.
4	lower (v.) locate (v.)	Our office is __________ just across the street from the fitness center.
5	machine (n.) magic (n.)	If I'm not home when you phone, just leave a message on the answering __________.

II. Multiple choices.

(　) 1. The __________ smiled at his audience, and then slowly drew a pigeon out of his sleeve.
(A) magic　(B) magazine　(C) mailman　(D) magician

(　) 2. The __________ covers a broad range of subjects, from sewing to psychology.
(A) magic　(B) machine　(C) magazine　(D) luck

(　) 3. The children were __________ to survive the fire which destroyed their home.
(A) magic　(B) low　(C) mad　(D) lucky

(　) 4. As soon as I met Nick, he attracted me because he has a __________ voice.
(A) lovely　(B) lucky　(C) lonely　(D) long

(　) 5. There was a __________ crash of thunder and large drops of rain started falling.
(A) loud　(B) lovely　(C) lone　(D) low

Unit 38

M

mail [meɪl]

① *n.* 郵件

實用片語與搭配字

mail order; by mail 郵購；透過郵寄

② *v.* 郵寄

▶ Darren delivers mail to people in his neighborhood.
達倫在他的鄰里間分送信件。

▶ These days shopping is so convenient you can buy almost anything by mail order.
現在購物變得相當方便，你幾乎可以透過郵購買到任何東西。

▶ Jared mailed some postcards to his friends while on vacation.
傑瑞德在度假時寄了些明信片給他的朋友。

---

mailman [ˈmeɪl.mæn] *n.* 郵差

▶ The mailman comes on time every day.
郵差每天都很準時到來。

---

main [meɪn]

① *adj.* 主要的

實用片語與搭配字

main reason 主要原因

② *n.* （輸送水、煤氣的）總管道；（鐵、公路的）幹線

▶ Our main dish tonight will be fresh fish with rice.
我們今晚的主餐是新鮮的魚和飯。

▶ The main reason why the air is so polluted is there are too many cars on the road.
空氣會受到汙染的主要原因是路上有太多車子。

▶ A water main broke and flooded the road in front of our house.
有條主要水管破裂且淹水淹到我家門前的路。

---

100 99

maintain [meɪnˈteɪn] *v.* 維持

實用片語與搭配字

be maintained by; maintain in
（使）維持；保持

▶ What should you do in order to maintain a healthy weight?
你應該怎麼做來保持健康的體重？

▶ The beautiful gardens around the park was maintained by the local government at great cost.
當地政府花了大筆錢維護公園周邊的美麗花園。

---

make [meɪk] *v.* 製造

▶ Children, stop making so much noise!
孩子們，停止製造那麼多噪音！

實用片語與搭配字

make-or-break; be made in; be made of

不成則敗的；被製造

▶ Peter knew it was a make-or-break decision, but he had no choice.
彼得知道這是一個孤注一擲的決定，但他沒有選擇。

---

maker [ˈmeɪ.kɚ] *n.* 製造者

▶ The maker of this guitar is very good.
做這把吉他的師傅很不錯。

---

male [meɪl]

① *adj.* 公的；男性的

② *n.* 男性

▶ I used to have two male dogs, but they fought all the time.
我以前養過兩隻公狗，但牠們總是在打架。

▶ The suspect is a white male, about 170cm tall.
這個嫌疑犯是個白人男子，約一百七十公分高。

---

man [mæn]

① *n.* 男人

② *v.* 操縱

▶ Peter is a man.
彼得是個男人。

▶ There are 10 people manning this boat.
有十個人操縱這艘船。

Mandarin [ˈmæn.dɚ.ɪn] *n.* 國語；普通話

▶ Lauren went to Taipei to study Mandarin for one year.
蘿倫到台北學一年的國語。

---

mango [ˈmæŋ.goʊ] *n.* 芒果

▶ Peggy cut up the mango and put it on her salad.
佩吉切些芒果放進她的沙拉裡。

102

manner [ˈmæn.ɚ] *n.* 方式；態度；禮貌

▶ Why did Kevin talk to you in such a rude manner?
為什麼凱文用這麼粗魯的態度對你說話？

---

many [ˈmen.i]

① *adj.* 許多的

② *pron.* 許多人

▶ Doris has lived in Asia for many years.
桃樂絲已經在亞洲住了很多年了。

▶ Many will receive help from the government this year.
許多人今年將接受來自政府的補助。

map [mæp]

① *n.* 地圖

② *v.* 在地圖上標示出

▶ Are we on the right road? Check the map.
我們在正確的路上嗎？查一下地圖。

▶ Amanda mapped out the way to her new office before work.
亞曼達在上班前先劃出到她新辦公室的路線。

March / Mar. [mɑːrtʃ] *n.* 三月

▶ Andrea's favorite month is March.
三月是安卓雅最喜歡的月份。

---

mark [mɑːrk]

① *v.* 標明；留痕跡於…

實用片語與搭配字

be marked out as sth
被區分（或識別）出是

② *n.* 記號；痕跡

▶ The sports fan marked his face with the colors of his favorite team.
這個運動迷在他臉上畫了他最愛的球隊的代表顏色。

▶ The young man's efforts to save his friend was marked out as courageous.
那位年輕人為了救朋友而做出的努力，被視為是很有勇氣的。

▶ What is the mark of a good leader?
一個好的領導者的特點是什麼？

M

---

marker [ˈmɑːr.kɚ] *n.* 書籤；標識；馬克筆

▶ I placed a marker inside my book.
我在我的書裡放了一個書籤。

---

market [ˈmɑːr.kɪt]

① *n.* 市場

實用片語與搭配字

free market; market share
自由市場；市場佔有率

② *v.* 購買或賣出

▶ John goes to the market every day to buy vegetables.
約翰每天去市場買蔬菜。

▶ There are many brands competing for market share in the mobile phone market.
手機市場上有很多品牌在爭奪市場佔有率。

▶ Farmers market their fruits to customers at the fair.
農夫們在市集銷售他們的水果給消費者。

marriage [ˈmer.ɪdʒ] *n.* 婚姻

▶ The average age for marriage in this country is 27-32.
在這國家的平均結婚年齡是二十七到三十二歲。

實用片語與搭配字

arranged marriage
包辦婚姻（父母之命，媒妁之言的婚姻）

▶ Many cultures still believe in arranged marriages and young people cannot choose who they want to marry.
許多文化仍相信媒妁之言，年輕人沒辦法選擇結婚的對象。

---

marry [ˈmer.i] *v.* 娶；嫁；(和…) 結婚

實用片語與搭配字

be married to （與某人）已婚

▶ Caleb married Victoria on Saturday.
迦勒星期六娶了維多麗亞。

▶ My father has been married to my mother for 50 years and they are still very happy.
我父母結婚五十年了，他們依然很幸福。

---

mask [mæsk]

① *n.* 面具；口罩

② *v.* 掩飾；偽裝

▶ In Chinese opera, people wear beautiful masks with special meanings.
在國劇中，人們戴著有特別意義的美麗面具。

▶ Eve tried to mask her anger, but everyone could see that she was upset.
伊芙試著掩飾她的憤怒，但每個人都看得出來她心情很不好。

mass [mæs] *n.* 大量；大批；眾多

▶ A mass of people waited at the train station.
有一大群人在火車站裡等火車。

---

master [ˈmæs.tɚ]

① *n.* 主人

② *v.* 精通

▶ The dog always obeys its master.
這隻狗總是順從牠的主人。

▶ Yvonne mastered English in one year.
伊芳在一年內就精通了英語。

---

mat [mæt] *n.* 地墊；地毯

▶ Please wipe your feet on the mat before you come into the house.
請你在進房子之前先在地墊上將你的腳擦乾淨。

match [mætʃ]

① *n.* 火柴

② *n.* 比賽；對手

▶ Stanley started a fire with a match.
史丹利用一根火柴點火。

▶ Who won the soccer match last night?
昨晚誰贏了這場足球比賽？

③ *v.* 使比賽；使較量

實用片語與搭配字

match sb against sb

使（某人）與（某人）較量

▶ My two favorite tennis players will be matched against each other in the final.

我最愛的兩名網球選手將在決賽中彼此對打。

▶ The coach matched the students against the teachers for a fun race at the sports day.

在運動會上，教練讓學生與老師進行了一場有趣的比賽。

---

mate [meɪt]

① *n.* 同伴；配偶

② *v.* 使成配偶；使交配

▶ Male birds have colorful feathers in order to attract a mate.

雄鳥有彩色的羽毛是為了要吸引配偶。

▶ The zoo hopes the two pandas will mate soon.

動物園希望這兩隻貓熊能盡快交配。

Exercise 38

I. Choose and write the correct word. Change the form of the word when necessary.

1	maintain (v.) mark (v.)	Combining physical activity with a healthy diet is the best way to ________ a healthy body weight.
2	manner (n.) maker (n.)	The idea of polite ________ has changed a lot between my parents' generation and my children's.
3	male (adj.) main (adj.)	The ________ streets in the center of the city are always very congested.
4	match (v.) master (v.)	Penny was able to ________ the basics of computer programming in a very short time.
5	mask (n.) mass (n.)	As a teacher, I usually have a ________ of students' homework on my desk, waiting to be marked.

II. Multiple choices.

( ) 1. The ________ propped his bicycle up against the wall and put the mail into the mailbox.
(A) monster (B) mark (C) mailman (D) males

( ) 2. If you see a traffic accident, make sure to ________ down the license of the car.
(A) mark (B) man (C) make (D) mail

( ) 3. After twelve years of ________, the two people began to drift apart.
(A) match (B) mask (C) master (D) marriage

( ) 4. They were carrying several baskets of vegetables to the ________.
(A) market (B) mat (C) marker (D) mate

( ) 5. Because of the weather, the football ________ will have to be delayed for a few days.
(A) marker (B) mask (C) match (D) mate

Unit 39

104 99

material [mə'tɪr.i.əl] *n.* 物質；原料

實用片語與搭配字

material world; raw material
物質世界；原料

▶ What material was used to make that cell phone case?
這手機殼是用什麼材質做的？

▶ Many African countries export raw materials to other countries for manufacturing.
許多非洲國家出口原物料給其他國家製作生產。

---

matter ['mæt̬.ɚ]

① *n.* 事情

② *v.* 要緊；有關係

▶ I have an important matter to discuss with you.
我要和你討論一件重要的事情。

▶ Does it matter what we wear to the party?
我們穿什麼去參加派對很重要嗎？

May [meɪ]

① *n.* 五月

② *aux. v.* 可能

▶ In many countries, the second Sunday in May is Mother's Day.
在很多國家，母親節在五月的第二個星期日。

▶ I may be able to go to the movie.
我可能可以去看電影。

---

maybe ['meɪ.bi] *adv.* 也許

▶ Maybe we can see the movie this weekend.
也許我們可以在這週末去看電影。

---

me [miː / mi] *pron.* 我（受格）

▶ Can you pass that book to me?
你可以把那本書傳給我嗎？

---

meal [mɪəl] *n.* 餐；一頓飯

實用片語與搭配字

mealtime 吃飯時間

▶ Deborah wants everyone to share a meal with her for her birthday.
黛博拉希望每個人都能和她一起分享她的生日。

▶ Don't skip mealtimes because it's not good for your health if you don't eat regularly.
不要省略吃飯時間，沒有規律的吃飯對你的健康不好。

M

103

mean [miːn]

① *v.* 有…的意思

② *adj.* 兇惡的；不友善的

▶ What do you mean?
你這話是什麼意思？

▶ Jeffrey, don't be mean to your brother.
傑弗瑞，不要對你弟弟那麼兇。

---

meaning [ˈmiː.nɪŋ] *n.* 意義；意思

▶ What is the meaning of this letter you sent me?
你寄給我的這封信有什麼特別意義嗎？

---

means [miːnz] *n.* 方法；手段；工具

實用片語與搭配字

provide means 提供方法

▶ My job pays too little. I wish I had the means to do more traveling.
我的薪水太少，我希望我有辦法更常去旅行。

▶ A good job can provide the means for you to afford a comfortable life.
一份好的工作能讓你有辦法負擔得起舒適的生活。

---

measurable [ˈmeʒ.ɚ.ə.bəl]

adj. 可測量的；顯著的

▶ Set measurable goals for yourself.
為你自己設可達到的目標。

measure [ˈmeʒ.ɚ] *v.* 測量；記量

實用片語與搭配字

be measured by; take measure
以…測量；採取措施

▶ The tailor measured James for a suit.
這位裁縫師測量詹姆斯的尺寸好幫他作一套西裝。

▶ During a typhoon you have to take measure that everything is secure and safe to decrease damage.
颱風來襲時，你必須做好防颱措施，確保所有東西都固定好，以減少損失。

measurement [ˈmeʒ.ɚ.mənt] *n.* 測量；尺寸

實用片語與搭配字

measurement of; make measurement of / on
…的測量；做測量

▶ The tailor will do some measurements for your suit.
這位裁縫師會為你的西裝測量尺寸。

▶ The measurement of a man is not in how much money he has, but how he treats others.
衡量一個人並不在於他有多少錢，而在於他如何對待他人。

---

meat [miːt] *n.* 肉

▶ Carolyn doesn't eat meat.
凱洛琳不吃肉。

medicine [ˈmed.ɪ.sən] *n.* 藥物

▶ Did you remember to take your medicine before lunch?
你午餐前是否記得吃藥？

meet [miːt]

① *v.* (與…) 相識

實用片語與搭配字

meet with sb; meet up
與 (某人) 見面；碰頭，相聚，會面

② *n.* 集會

▶ Justin met his wife at a wedding.
賈斯汀在一個婚禮上認識了他的妻子。

▶ After the concert, we will meet up with some friends for dinner.
演唱會結束後，我們會和一些朋友聚餐。

▶ The athletes are having a meet and greet with some fans.
這些運動員有個見面會和一些粉絲打招呼。

95

meeting [ˈmiː.t̬ɪŋ] *n.* 會議

實用片語與搭配字

at meeting; attend meeting
開會中；出席會議

▶ Jeremy has a meeting in Taipei tomorrow.
傑瑞米明天在台北有個會議。

▶ All the employees must attend the company meeting today.
所有公司職員都必須出席今天的會議。

melody [ˈmel.ə.di] *n.* 旋律；曲調

▶ I can't remember the melody of that song. Can you sing it for me?
我不記得這首歌的旋律，你可以幫我唱一下嗎？

melon [ˈmel.ən] *n.* 甜瓜；瓜

▶ Rita loves to eat fresh melon in the summer.
瑞塔夏天喜歡吃新鮮的甜瓜。

member [ˈmem.bɚ] *n.* 成員；會員

▶ This band has four members.
這個樂團有四名成員。

memory [ˈmem.ər.i] *n.* 記憶力；記性

實用片語與搭配字

memory of; erase memory
…的回憶；抹去記憶

▶ Eating certain "superfoods" can help improve your memory.
吃某些「超級食品」可以幫助你增強記憶力。

▶ In memory of all the soldiers who died in the war, the president will donate money to their families.
為了紀念在戰場上身亡的軍人，總統將會捐款給他們的家屬。

M

menu [ˈmen.juː] *n.* 菜單

▶ The menu at that restaurant looks great; let's go there next time!
那家餐廳的菜單看起來很棒，我們下次去吧！

---

104 98

message [ˈmes.ɪdʒ] *n.* 口信；信息

實用片語與搭配字

send message; message from sb
傳訊息；來自…的訊息

▶ I'm sorry, I didn't get your message until it was too late.
很抱歉，我很晚才收到你的訊息。

▶ During the war, soldiers would send message to their generals with pigeons.
打仗的時候，軍人會用鴿子來傳遞訊息給長官。

metal [ˈmet̬.əl]

① *n.* 金屬

實用片語與搭配字

heavy metal 重金屬（搖滾樂）

② *adj.* 金屬的

▶ What kind of metal is that box made out of?
這盒子是用什麼金屬做的？

▶ Gold is a heavy metal because it has very high density and it weighs a lot.
黃金是重金屬，因為它有很高的密度及重量。

▶ Our boat has a metal bottom and wooden sides.
我們的船有金屬的底部和木材做的側邊。

---

meter [ˈmiː.t̬ɚ] *n.* 公尺

▶ Please measure out 2 meters of cloth for the shirt.
請測量兩公尺的布來做這件襯衫。

Exercise 39

I. Choose and write the correct word. Change the form of the word when necessary.

1	material (n.) matter (n.)	You can recycle various __________ instead of putting them in the garbage can.
2	measure (v.) mean (v.)	We need to do regular evaluations in order to __________ our students' progress in English.
3	member (n.) meeting (n.)	She has been an important __________ of the chess club ever since she joined.
4	metal (adj.) mean (adj.)	A __________ grid has been placed across the hole to stop people falling in.
5	message (n.) memory (n.)	There is an important __________ for you from work on the answering machine.

II. Multiple choices.

(　　) 1. You can always tell the __________ of a word from the context.

(A) melody　　(B) member　　(C) meaning　　(D) meal

(　　) 2. The success of a popular composer depends on his __________.

(A) melody　　(B) meeting　　(C) matter　　(D) memory

(　　) 3. Grandma has a good __________; she can remember things which happened many years ago.

(A) matter　　(B) means　　(C) memory　　(D) meaning

(　　) 4. The little boy was stamping his feet and refusing to take his __________.

(A) means　　(B) medicine　　(C) meaning　　(D) matter

(　　) 5. Your job is to attend the __________ and report to the board of the Directors.

(A) medicine　　(B) meeting　　(C) meaning　　(D) measure

method [ˈmeθ.əd] *n.* 方法

▶ There are two different methods for completing this math problem.
這個數學題有兩種不同的解法。

---

middle [ˈmɪdl]

① *adj.* 中間的
② *n.* 中央；中間
③ *v.* 放在中間

▶ Gloria is the middle child. She has an older and younger sister.
葛莉雅排行中間，她有一個姊姊和一個妹妹。

▶ Don't walk in the middle of the road.
不要走在路中央。

▶ Please middle the soccer ball to start the game.
請將足球放在球場中間來開球。

---

midnight [ˈmɪd.naɪt] *n.* 午夜；半夜十二點鐘

▶ My uncle sleeps before midnight.
我的叔叔都在午夜前睡覺。

---

mile [maɪl] *n.* 英里

▶ Sharon lives two miles from school.
雪倫住在離學校兩英里的地方。

military [ˈmɪl.ə.ter.i]

① *adj.* 軍事的

實用片語與搭配字

military service 兵役

② *n.* 軍人；軍隊

▶ Leaders should think about their military strength before they go to war.
領導者應該在他們作戰之前想想他們的軍力。

▶ In many countries, young men must finish their military service before they can start a career.
許多國家的年輕男性在就業之前都必須完成兵役。

▶ America has one of the largest militaries in the world.
美國是世界上擁有最大兵力的國家之一。

---

milk [mɪlk]

① *n.* 牛奶
② *v.* 擠奶

▶ Caitlyn loves to drink milk for breakfast.
凱特琳早餐喜歡喝牛奶。

▶ The farmer milked the cow.
農夫為乳牛擠奶。

million [ˈmɪl.jən] *n.* 百萬

實用片語與搭配字

thanks a million 非常感謝

▶ I won a million dollars in the lottery yesterday! I'm so excited!
我昨天贏了一百萬的樂透彩！我超級興奮！

▶ You did me such a big favor. Thanks a million!
你幫了我一個大忙，真的非常感謝！

---

mind [maɪnd]

① *n.* 頭腦

實用片語與搭配字

put sb's mind to sth; bear in mind
用心去(做好事情); 牢記在心

② *v.* 介意；反對

▶ What's on your mind?
你在想什麼？

▶ When traveling to another country, you have to bear in mind the customs and traditions of the people there.
到另外一個國家旅行時，你必須將當地的風俗民情謹記在心。

▶ Do you mind if we stay home tonight?
你介意我們今晚待在家裡嗎？

---

mine [maɪn]

① *n.* 礦；礦山

② *v.* 採礦

③ *pron.* 我的（所有格）；屬於我的（東西）

▶ Most people in this town work in the nearby mine.
這城裡大部分的人都在附近的礦山工作。

▶ These machines are used to mine the gold.
這些機器是用來採金礦的。

▶ The blue shirt is yours, and the red one is mine.
那件藍色襯衫是你的，而這件紅色的是我的。

---

minus [ˈmaɪ.nəs]

① *prep.* 減去；少

② *n.* 缺點；不利條件

③ *adj.* 負的

▶ What is 57 minus 13?
五十七減十三是多少？

▶ One minus of this plan is it is very expensive.
這計畫的一個缺點是太過昂貴。

▶ It's so cold today! It must be at least minus 10!
今天好冷喔！一定至少有負十度以下！

---

minute [ˈmɪn.ɪt] *n.* 分鐘

▶ The speaker spoke for 30 minutes.
這位演講者講了三十分鐘。

mirror [ˈmɪr.ɚ]

① *n.* 鏡子

② *v.* 反射；反映（引申為模仿）

▶ The evil queen looked into the magic mirror and asked it a question.
這個邪惡女王看著魔鏡問了一個問題。

▶ Alice mirrors all of her older sister's actions.
艾莉絲模仿所有她姊姊的動作。

miss [mɪs]

① *v.* 錯過

實用片語與搭配字

miss out 錯過

② *n.* 小姐

▶ Don't miss the meeting or the boss will be mad.
別錯過會議，不然老闆會生氣。

▶ If you are scared of everything, you will miss out on a lot of fun things in life.
若你對很多事情都感到害怕，那你會錯過生命中許多有趣的事。

▶ Miss Broderson is Annie's favorite teacher.
伯德森小姐是安妮最喜歡的老師。

---

mistake [mɪˈsteɪk]

① *n.* 錯誤

實用片語與搭配字

correct mistake; by mistake
糾正錯誤；錯誤地

② *v.* 弄錯

▶ Carl made two mistakes on his exam.
卡爾在他的考試錯了兩題。

▶ Someone took my suitcase by mistake at the airport and I had to wait a week to get it back.
有人在機場錯拿了我的行李箱，所以我必須等一個禮拜才能取回來。

▶ Charlie mistook the stranger for his friend.
查理錯把陌生人當成他的朋友。

---

mix [mɪks]

① *v.* 混合

實用片語與搭配字

mix together / mix up （使）混合

② *n.* 結合；混合

▶ Mix the sugar with butter and add some flour.
將奶油和糖混合然後加一些麵粉。

▶ There was a mix-up at the hotel because they gave our reserved room to another person with the same last name.
飯店搞錯了，他們將我們預定的房間給了另一個同姓氏的人。

▶ That album has a really good mix of fast and slow songs.
那張專輯有快歌與慢歌，是很棒的結合。

95

model [ˈmɑː.dəl]

① *n.* 模特兒；模型

② *v.* 以…為榜樣；做模型；作模特兒

▶ We need six models for the fashion show at the mall.
購物中心的這場時尚秀需要六個模特兒。

▶ Anna modeled good behavior in her class.
安娜在她班上示範好的行為。

104

modern [ˈmɑː.dɚn] *adj.* 現代的；新式的

實用片語與搭配字

modern art 現代藝術

▶ The best feature of this house is its modern kitchen.
這房子最棒的特色就是它現代化的廚房。

▶ Many people do not like modern art because they cannot understand it.
許多人不喜歡現代藝術，因為他們看不懂。

---

moment [ˈmoʊ.mənt] *n.* 片刻

▶ Let's take a picture to remember this moment.
讓我們拍張照來紀念這個時刻。

---

mommy / momma / mom / mam(m)a / ma / mummy

[ˈmɑː.mi / ˈmɑː.mə / mɑːm / ˈmɑː.mə / mɑː / ˈmʌm.i]

n. 媽媽

▶ Mom works really hard to take care of her children.
媽媽非常努力工作來照顧她的孩子。

Monday / Mon. [ˈmʌn.deɪ] *n.* 星期一

▶ Are you free Monday night for dinner?
你星期一晚上有空一起吃晚餐嗎？

---

money [ˈmʌn.i] *n.* 錢

實用片語與搭配字

save money; time is money; money laundering

存錢；時間就是金錢；洗錢

▶ Stella makes a lot of money in her business.
史黛拉做生意賺了很多錢。

▶ We're not going on holiday this year because we're trying to save money.
今年我們不會去度假，因為我們想省錢。

---

monkey [ˈmʌŋ.ki] *n.* 猴子

▶ Steve saw some cute monkeys at the zoo.
史提夫在動物園裡看見了一些可愛的猴子。

---

monster [ˈmɑːn.stɚ] *n.* 怪物

▶ The little girl was afraid there was a monster under her bed.
這小女孩很害怕在她床底下有一隻怪物。

month [mʌnθ] *n.* 月份

▶ What month were you born?
你幾月出生？

---

moon [muːn] *n.* 月亮

實用片語與搭配字

full moon 滿月

▶ The moon is really bright tonight.
今晚的月亮非常皎潔。

▶ There is often a full moon around the time of the Moon Festival.
中秋節前後都會出現滿月。

---

moonlight [ˈmuːn.laɪt] *n.* 月光

▶ They walked along the road in the moonlight.
他們在月光下沿著馬路走。

Exercise 40

I. Choose and write the correct word. Change the form of the word when necessary.

1	middle (adj.) military (adj.)	According to the Constitution of the country, all the young men have to do a year's __________ service.
2	method (n.) million (n.)	I don't think hitting children is a very effective __________ of teaching them anything.
3	motion (n.) monster (n.)	The swaying __________ of the ship was making me feel seasick.
4	modern (adj.) most (adj.)	Katie was soon tired of classical ballet, and decided to try a __________ dance course at the academy.
5	mistake (n.) mirror (n.)	There are important lessons for you to learn from this __________.

II. Multiple choices.

(　　) 1. The smooth surface of the lake reflected back the brilliant __________.
(A) minus　(B) moonlight　(C) mistake　(D) model

(　　) 2. This photo is a wonderful happy __________ caught with perfect timing.
(A) moment　(B) mistake　(D) model　(D) mine

(　　) 3. An anonymous businesswoman donated one __________ dollars to the charity.
(A) mine　(B) meter　(D) method　(D) million

(　　) 4. She's going to take an exam next week, so she's burning the __________ oil.
(A) military　(B) middle　(D) metal　(D) midnight

(　　) 5. She worked as an artist's __________ when she was a college student.
(A) model　(B) miss　(D) mirror　(D) mix

Unit 41

more [mɔːr]

① *adj.* 更多的
② *pron.* 更多的人、事、物
③ *adv.* 更

▶ There are more people here today than yesterday.
今天在這裡的人比昨天還多。

▶ Would you like some more?
要不要再來一些？

▶ After talking to Francis for an hour, Amanda liked him even more.
和法蘭西斯談話一小時後，亞曼達更喜歡他了。

---

morning [ˈmɔːr.nɪŋ] *n.* 早晨

▶ Good morning! How did you sleep?
早安！你睡得好嗎？

---

mosquito [məˈskiː.t̬oʊ] *n.* 蚊子

▶ It's hard to sleep when there is a mosquito in your room at night.
晚上的時候有蚊子在房間裡飛來飛去很難入睡。

---

most [moʊst]

① *adj.* 最多的
② *pron.* 最多數；最大量
③ *adv.* 最；非常

▶ The team with the most points wins.
最高分的隊伍獲勝。

▶ Most of the students passed the test.
大部分的學生都通過了考試。

▶ Which flower is most beautiful?
哪一朵花最美麗？

---

moth [mɑːθ] *n.* 蛾

▶ At night, you can see moths flying around the lights on the street.
夜晚時，你可以看到很多蛾在街燈周圍飛。

---

mother [ˈmʌð.ɚ]

① *n.* 母親
② *v.* 像母親一般的照顧

▶ My mother's mother is my grandmother.
我母親的母親就是我的外婆。

▶ Please don't mother me. I can take care of myself.
請別像媽媽一樣照顧我，我能照顧我自己。

---

motion [ˈmoʊ.ʃən]

① *n.* （物體的）運動；動作

▶ What can you learn from studying the motion of birds?
你從研究鳥兒的行動可以學到什麼？

② *v.* 做手勢；點（或搖）頭示意

▶ The interviewer motioned for me to sit down.
這位面試官作勢要我坐下。

---

motorcycle [ˈmoʊ.t̬ɚ͵saɪ.kəl]
n. 摩托車；機車

▶ Motorcycle safety is important to learn before you start driving.
在你開始騎摩托車前，學習行車安全很重要的。

---

mountain [ˈmaʊn.tən] *n.* 山脈

實用片語與搭配字

go mountain-climbing 爬山

▶ Mount Everest is the tallest mountain in the world.
聖母峰是世界上最高的山。

▶ I usually go mountain-climbing with my hiking club on weekends.
我通常會在週末的時候和登山社一起爬山。

---

mouse [maʊs] *n.* 老鼠

▶ Naomi screams every time she sees a mouse.
娜俄米每次見到老鼠都會尖叫。

---

mouth [maʊθ]

① *n.* 嘴

實用片語與搭配字

keep sb's mouth shut 保持緘默

② *v.* 裝腔作勢地說

實用片語與搭配字

mouth off about sth; mouth off to / at sth
（在公開場合毫無顧忌的）發表意見；（跟某人）頂嘴

▶ Arthur, don't talk with your mouth full!
亞瑟，嘴裡有食物時不要講話！

▶ I wish my brother would keep his mouth shut, but instead he tells my mom everything I do wrong.
我希望哥哥能保密，但他還是告訴了媽媽我做錯的每一件事。

▶ Albert mouthed off his opinions to anyone who would listen.
亞伯特裝腔作勢地對每個聽他說話的人發表意見。

▶ When my friend is angry at her boyfriend, she would mouth off about him and talk about all his bad points.
當我朋友對她的男友感到不滿，她會毫無顧忌地說他的不是。

---

movable [ˈmuː.və.bəl] *adj.* 可移動的

▶ Kids love this toy because it has a lot of movable parts.
孩子很喜歡這個玩具，因為它有很多可移動的零件。

move [mu:v] *v.* 移動；改變位置

實用片語與搭配字

move on; move off sth / on (to sth)
繼續前進；轉移話題

- James moved the furniture around his bedroom.
  詹姆士重置他臥室裡的傢俱。
- My friend could not move on after she broke up with her boyfriend and she still cries herself to sleep every night.
  我的朋友無法放下上一段感情，她每天晚上還是哭著入睡。

104

movement [ˈmu:v.mənt] *n.* 動作；行動

實用片語與搭配字

civil rights movement 民權運動

- Krista's movements are very slow today. Is she hurt?
  克莉絲塔今天的動作非常緩慢，她受傷了嗎？
- The civil rights movement in that country ensured equality for all black people.
  國家的民權運動確保該國黑人有平等的權益。

---

movie / motion picture

[ˈmu:.vi / ˈmoʊ.ʃən ˌpɪk.tʃɚ] *n.* 電影

- Let's go see a movie this weekend.
  我們這個週末去看電影吧。

Mr. / mister [ˈmɪs.tɚ] *n.* 先生

- Hello, Mr. Yeh! How are you today?
  哈囉，葉先生！你今天好嗎？

Mrs. [ˈmɪs.ɪz] *n.* 太太

- Mrs. Ma is Mr. Ma's wife.
  馬太太是馬先生的妻子。

MRT / mass rapid transit / subway / underground / metro

[mæs ˈræp.ɪd ˈtræn.zɪt / ˈsʌb.weɪ / ˌʌn.dɚˈgraʊnd / ˈmet.roʊ]

n. 捷運

- The MRT system in Taipei can take you to most areas of town.
  台北捷運可以帶你到城裡的各個區域。

Ms. [məz / mɪz] *n.* 女士；小姐

- Ms. Wintour is a successful businesswoman.
  溫圖爾女士是一位成功的女企業家。

---

much [mʌtʃ]

① *adj.* 很多的

② *pron.* 大量

- Poor people don't have much money.
  窮人沒有太多錢。
- Not much is happening at school today.
  今天在學校沒有發生什麼事。

③ *adv.* 非常

▶ Grace is much more talented than I am.
葛莉絲比我更有才華。

mud [mʌd] *n.* 泥巴

▶ The kids played in the mud after the rain.
下雨後孩子們在泥巴中玩耍。

mug [mʌg] *n.* （有柄的）馬克杯；大杯子

▶ Anne drank her coffee from a mug.
安用一個馬克杯喝咖啡。

mule [mju:l] *n.* 騾子

▶ The farmer was so poor that the only animal he had was an old mule.
這位農夫很窮，他僅有的牲畜是一頭老騾子。

multiply [ˈmʌl.tə.plaɪ] *v.* 乘；（使成倍）增加

▶ To find the answer, multiply this number by six.
用六乘以這個數字來找出答案。

museum [mjuːˈziː.əm] *n.* 博物館

▶ There's an exhibit about Egyptian history at the museum.
這博物館有一個關於埃及歷史的展覽。

Exercise 41

I. Choose and write the correct word. Change the form of the word when necessary.

1	mosquito (n.) motion (n.)	The __________ of a moving car always makes me fall asleep when I'm sitting in the back.
2	more (adj.) most (adj.)	In order to achieve your goal, you should put __________ effort into your study.
3	mouse (n.) mouth (n.)	A cat will bring home a live __________ to teach her kittens how to catch it.
4	multiply (v.) move (v.)	The wardrobe was too heavy for me to __________ on my own.
5	mud (n.) mug (n.)	The mark of this man's shoe was clearly printed in the __________.

II. Multiple choices.

( ) 1. After hiking all day, we finally reached the the summit of the __________.
(A) mouth (B) movement (C) mountain (D) motion

( ) 2. Someone broke into the __________ and stole several paintings.
(A) mosquito (B) museum (C) mountain (D) mule

( ) 3. Video cameras with night vision can be activated by __________.
(A) movement (B) mud (C) mugs (D) mules

( ) 4. The germs __________ quickly in the heat, and can produce food poisoning.
(A) motion (B) mouth (C) mother (D) multiply

( ) 5. A __________ woke me up while it was flying around in my room.
(A) mosquito (B) mud (C) mug (D) mouse

Unit 42

music [ˈmjuː.zɪk] *n.* 音樂

實用片語與搭配字

compose music; face the music
創作音樂；接受批評，承擔自己行為的後果

▶ Jazz is Caroline's favorite kind of music.
爵士樂是凱洛琳最喜歡的音樂。

▶ You cheated on your test and now have to face the music and accept the punishment.
因為你考試作弊，所以必須承擔後果，接受懲罰。

---

musician [mjuːˈzɪʃ.ən] *n.* 樂手；音樂家

▶ Shaun is a talented musician; his specialty is guitar.
希恩是個很有天賦的樂手，他的專長是吉他。

---

must [mʌst / məst / məs]

① *aux. v.* 必須

② *n.* 必須做的事

▶ We must be at school by 8:00 or we'll be late.
我們八點以前必須到校，不然會遲到。

▶ Being on time for work is a must.
準時上班是必須的事。

---

my [maɪ] *pron.* 我的（所有格）

▶ My brother and I are really great friends.
我和我弟弟是非常好的朋友。

---

myself [maɪˈself] *pron.* 我自己

▶ I like to relax by myself sometimes.
有時候我想要自己放鬆一下。

---

nail [neɪl]

① *n.* 爪 ；指甲

② *n.* 釘子

③ *v.* 將…釘牢；使…集中於…

▶ Lynn had a difficult time cutting her cat's nails.
琳費了很大的力氣才剪了她貓咪的爪子。

▶ Can you hold this nail while I hammer it into the wall?
我要把這根釘子鎚進牆的時候，你可以握住它嗎？

▶ Darren nailed some boards over the broken window.
戴倫在那個壞掉的窗戶上釘了一些木板。

naked [ˈneɪ.kɪd] *adj.* 未穿衣的；裸體的

▶ Please put some clothes on the naked baby.
請幫這個沒穿衣服的小寶寶穿衣服。

---

name [neɪm]

① *n.* 名字

② *v.* 給…取名

▶ What is your name?
你叫什麼名字？

▶ The parents named their daughter Charlotte.
這對父母為他們的女兒取名叫夏綠蒂。

---

napkin [ˈnæp.kɪn] *n.* 餐巾（紙）

▶ I need a napkin to clean up this tea I spilled.
我需要一張餐巾紙來清理我翻倒的茶。

---

narrow [ˈner.oʊ]

① *adj.* 狹窄的

實用片語與搭配字

narrow-minded 心胸狹窄的

② *v.* 使變窄；縮小（範圍）

實用片語與搭配字

narrow sth down 把…縮減

▶ That road is too narrow for more than one car to pass at a time.
這條路太窄不能同時讓兩台車通過。

▶ In the 21st Century there are still narrow-minded people who believe that women should stay home and take care of the children.
到了二十一世紀，仍有些心胸狹窄的人認為女人應該待在家照顧小孩。

▶ Let's narrow down our choices to our two favorites.
將選項縮減到我們最喜愛的兩個吧！

▶ In order for us to make a final decision, we have to narrow our options down to just the best three.
為了做最後的決定，我們必須將選項縮減到最佳的三個。

---

nation [ˈneɪ.ʃən] *n.* 國家

實用片語與搭配字

United Nation (UN) 聯合國

▶ The United States is a powerful nation.
美國是一個強大的國家。

▶ The United Nations was founded after World War II to work towards world peace.
聯合國是在二次世界大戰後成立，以世界和平為宗旨。

---

national [ˈnæʃ.ən.əl / ˈnæʃ.nəl]

adj. 國家的；國民的

▶ The national colors of Turkey are red and white.
土耳其國旗的顏色是紅色與白色。

實用片語與搭配字

national anthem 國歌

- Every country has its own national anthem; a national song that can be recognized all over the world.
  每個國家都有一首全世界都認識的國歌。

---

natural [ˈnætʃ.ɚ.əl] *adj.* 天然的；自然的

實用片語與搭配字

natural beauty; natural selection
自然景觀；物競天擇

- This dish contains all natural ingredients.
  這道菜的食材都是天然的。
- Natural selection is nature's way to ensure that only the strongest survive by killing off the weak and the sick.
  物競天擇是大自然要確保適者生存，不適者淘汰的方法。

---

nature [ˈneɪ.tʃɚ] *n.* 大自然

實用片語與搭配字

human nature
人性

- Let's go for a hike and enjoy nature.
  我們去健行享受大自然吧。
- It is human nature to be greedy, but many people understand that it is not a good way to live.
  貪婪雖是人性，但許多人知道這不是生存的好方法。

M

99

naughty [ˈnɑː.t̬i] *adj.* 頑皮的

- Charles is a naughty boy who always runs away from his mother at the store.
  查爾斯是個頑皮的男孩，他在店裡總是離開媽媽跑來跑去。

---

near [nɪr]

① *adj.* 近的

實用片語與搭配字

in the near future 在不久的將來

② *adv.* 接近；幾乎

實用片語與搭配字

nowhere near
（距離、時間、數量或質量）遠遠沒有

- Tiffany hopes to see her family in the near future.
  蒂芬妮希望能在不久的將來見到她的家人。
- In the near future, experts predict that robots will take over many existing jobs.
  在不久的將來，專家指出機器人會取代許多現有的工作。
- Alison lives near her parents.
  艾莉森跟她父母住得很近。
- Even though we have been working on our school project for two weeks, it is nowhere near to completion and the deadline is tomorrow.
  儘管我們已經花兩週的時間做報告，距離完成還很遙遠，而明天就是截止日。

③ *prep.* 在…的附近

④ *v.* 靠近

▶ Bobby lives in a city near London.
巴比住在倫敦附近的城市。

▶ Carl got more nervous as his interview neared.
越接近卡爾面試的時間，他就越緊張。

---

nearby [ˌnɪrˈbaɪ]

① *adj.* 附近的

② *adv.* 在附近

▶ If you stay downtown, you can shop at the nearby stores.
如果你住在市中心，就可以在附近的商店逛街購物。

▶ Are there any hospitals nearby? I'm not feeling well.
這附近有醫院嗎？我不太舒服。

nearly [ˈnɪr.li] *adv.* 幾乎；差不多

實用片語與搭配字

not nearly enough 遠不夠

▶ It took Miriam nearly a year to finish writing her book.
米瑞安花了將近一年的時間完成她的著作。

▶ We have been saving for the past year, but we still do not have nearly enough money to pay for a holiday abroad.
我們已經花了一年的時間存錢，但還是不夠支付一趟海外度假之旅。

---

neat [niːt] *adj.* 整潔的；工整的

▶ Please leave the books in a neat pile after you're finished reading them.
在你讀完這些書後，請將它們堆疊整齊。

necessary [ˈnes.ə.ser.i] *adj.* 必需的

▶ Making a reservation is necessary at this restaurant.
這家餐廳一定要事先訂位。

---

neck [nek] *n.* 脖子

▶ Giraffes have very long necks.
長頸鹿有非常長的脖子。

---

necklace [ˈnek.ləs] *n.* 項鍊

▶ Megan loves to wear the necklace she got from her grandmother.
梅根喜歡戴那條祖母送她的項鍊。

need [niːd]

① *v.* 需要

▶ How much money do you need for your vacation?
你需要多少錢去度假？

② *aux. v.* （用於疑問句和否定句）需要；必須
③ *n.* 生活需求；(食物或金錢)缺乏

▶ The students need to take the test to pass the class.
學生們必須考試才能通過這門課。

▶ Doris loves to help people in need.
桃樂絲喜歡幫助有需要的人。

---

needle [ˈniː.dəl]

① *n.* 針；注射針
② *v.* 做針線活；縫紉

▶ I need a needle and thread so I can fix this shirt.
我需要針和線才能修補這件襯衫。

▶ My grandma spent all day needling the quilt.
我奶奶花了一整天縫這件被子。

---

negative [ˈneg.ə.t̬ɪv]

① *adj.* 否定的；消極的
② *n.* 否定的回答（或觀點等）

▶ Marcy is very negative about her job.
瑪希對她的工作非常不滿。

▶ There are too many negatives to that plan. We need to make a new plan.
那個計劃有太多負面的影響，我們需要制定一個新計畫。

Exercise 42

I. Choose and write the correct word. Change the form of the word when necessary.

1	musician (n.) nation (n.)	You show promise as a __________ but your lack of practice is keeping you back.
2	naughty (adj.) naked (adj.)	The old lady was displeased with the children's __________ behavior.
3	natural (adj.) national (adj.)	The __________ football team will arrive in Tokyo tomorrow afternoon.
4	needle (n.) necklace (n.)	The __________ she is wearing has been handed down through several generations.
5	need (v.) near (v.)	You'll __________ to calculate how much time this assignment will take.

II. Multiple choices.

(　　) 1. She was taking tiny bites of a hot dog and gently wiping her lips with a __________.
(A) needle　(B) napkin　(C) necklace　(D) nature

(　　) 2. If you care about __________, you should work to stop pollution of our environment.
(A) nation　(B) napkin　(C) nail　(D) nature

(　　) 3. Why are you always so __________? Can't you look at the bright side for once ?
(A) necessary　(B) negative　(C) nearby　(D) neat

(　　) 4. To really learn vocabulary, it's __________ to study it in a variety of ways.
(A) necessary　(B) negative　(C) nearby　(D) naughty

(　　) 5. It's very difficult to find shoes to fit Sophie because she has very __________ feet.
(A) naked　(B) narrow　(C) naughty　(D) natural

Unit 43

neighbor [ˈneɪ.bɚ]

① *n.* 鄰居；鄰近的人

② *v.* 與…鄰接；住在附近

▶ I don't like our new neighbors! They're really noisy.
我不喜歡我們的新鄰居！他們真的很吵。

▶ The parking lot neighbored a shopping mall.
這個停車場鄰接著一個購物中心。

101

neither [ˈnaɪ.ðɚ / ˈniː.ðɚ]

① *adj.* 兩者都不

② *adv.* 既不…也不…；…和…都不

③ *pron.* （兩者中）無一個

④ *conj.* 既不…也不…

▶ Neither computer is working right now.
現在這兩台電腦都壞了。

▶ Emma is neither ready nor willing to perform on stage.
艾瑪既還沒準備好也沒有意願要上台表演。

▶ Neither of those options sounds good to me.
這些選項沒有一個是我喜歡的。

▶ Neither June nor Albert went to the party.
瓊與亞伯都沒有去那個派對。

---

nephew [ˈnef.juː / ˈnev.juː] *n.* 姪兒；外甥

▶ My nephew plays soccer on the school team once a week.
我姪兒每週一次在校隊中踢足球。

---

nest [nest]

① *n.* 鳥巢；昆蟲的窩

② *v.* 築巢；窩居

▶ Do you see that small bird's nest up in the tree?
你看到那樹上的小鳥窩了嗎？

▶ The little boy sleeps nested in the blankets with his teddy bear.
這個小男孩和他的泰迪熊窩在毯子裡睡覺。

---

net [net]

① *n.* 網

② *v.* 用網捕

▶ Let's try to catch some fish with this net.
讓我們試著用這個網捕一些魚。

▶ What is the best way to net good employees?
什麼是網羅人才最好的方法？

never ['nev.ɚ] *adv.* 從未；決不

▸ Esther has never met Pat before.
愛絲特以前從沒見過派特。

new [nu:] *adj.* 新的

▸ Tony bought a new car yesterday.
湯尼昨天買了一輛新車。

news [nu:z] *n.* 新聞

實用片語與搭配字

break the news; be in the news
說出實情，透露壞消息；被報導

▸ Did you hear the news?
你聽說那則新聞了嗎？

▸ We had to break the news to Mary that her pet hamster had died, and she was very sad.
我們不得已向瑪莉透露她的倉鼠過世的消息，她為此感到非常難過。

newspaper ['nu:z,peɪ.pɚ] *n.* 報紙

▸ Dad reads the newspaper every morning at breakfast.
爸爸每天早上吃早餐時會看報紙。

102

next [nekst]

① *adj.* 其次的；緊鄰的

② *adv.* 然後

▸ The baby is sleeping in the next room.
寶寶正在隔壁房間睡覺。

▸ What should we do next?
我們接下來該做什麼？

nice [naɪs] *adj.* 好的；宜人的

▸ Rob and Amy had a nice time on vacation.
羅伯和艾咪度過了愉快的假期。

niece [ni:s] *n.* 姪女；外甥女

▸ Fiona loves to read stories to her niece.
費歐娜喜愛為她的姪女讀故事書。

night [naɪt] *n.* 夜晚

實用片語與搭配字

night and day; night after night; a night out
夜以繼日；每夜；出去玩樂的夜晚

▸ What are you doing tomorrow night?
你明天晚上要做什麼？

▸ My sister and I worked on our family business night and day.
我和妹妹為家族事業日以繼夜地打拼。

nine [naɪn]

① *n.* 九

② *adj.* 九的

▸ Eight plus one equals nine.
八加一等於九。

▸ Cats have nine lives.
貓有九條命。

nineteen [ˌnaɪnˈtiːn]

① *n.* 十九

② *adj.* 十九的

▸ We have a group of nineteen going on the trip.
我們一行有十九個人要去旅遊。

▸ Alex is going on vacation for nineteen days.
艾力克斯要去度假十九天。

---

ninety [ˈnaɪn.t̬i]

① *n.* 九十

② *adj.* 九十人的；九十個的

▸ This is a room for ninety.
這是個九十人的房間。

▸ Ninety people can sit in this room.
這個房間能坐九十個人。

---

no / nope [noʊ / noʊp]

① *adj.* 沒有；不要

② *adv.* 不；不是；沒有

③ *n.* 拒絕；否定

▸ No food is left.
沒有剩下食物。

▸ No, you're wrong.
不，你錯了。

▸ Sales people often hear many noes, before they hear a yes.
業務人員在聽到一聲同意之前，經常會先聽到許多拒絕的回答。

---

nobody [ˈnoʊ.bɑː.di]

① *pron.* 沒有人

② *n.* 無足輕重的人

▸ Nobody knows when the world will end.
沒有人知道世界末日是什麼時候。

▸ Bill was a nobody until his music was discovered by a record producer.
比爾在被一位音樂製作人發掘前是一個無名小卒。

---

nod [nɑːd]

① *v.* 點頭；點頭贊同；點頭致意

② *n.* 點頭；打盹

▸ During Sam's speech, many people nodded in agreement.
山姆演講時，有許多觀眾點頭同意。

▸ Penny greeted her teacher with a nod as she passed him in the hallway.
佩妮在走廊上與老師擦身而過時，向他點頭打招呼。

noise [nɔɪz] *n.* 噪音

▸ Steve and Ashley hear a strange noise.
史提夫和艾胥莉聽見奇怪的噪音。

N

實用片語與搭配字

make some noise about sth 不停地抱怨

► Whenever the government is doing something that people don't like, the people will make some noise about it, usually by protesting.
每當政府做與民意背道而馳的事，人民通常會透過抗議來發聲。

---

noisy [ˈnɔɪ.zi] *adj.* 喧鬧的；吵雜的

► Kids can be really noisy when they are playing.
孩子們在玩耍時都會很吵鬧。

---

none [nʌn]

① *pron.* 一點兒也沒；沒有任何一人（物）

② *adv.* 毫無；決不

► Andy ate all the cake! Now there's none left.
安迪吃了全部的蛋糕！現在連一丁點兒也沒剩。

► Louise walked away from the accident none the worse.
露易絲在這場車禍中絲毫未傷。

---

noodle [ˈnuː.dəl] *n.* 麵條

► Beef noodles are one of the well-known dishes of Taipei.
牛肉麵是台北最有名的食物之一。

---

noon [nuːn] *n.* 正午

► Let's have lunch together at noon.
我們中午一起吃飯吧。

---

nor [nɔːr] *conj.* 也不（通常與 neither 連用）

► Neither Lindsay nor Christina liked the restaurant.
琳賽和克莉絲緹娜都不喜歡這間餐廳。

---

north [nɔːrθ]

① *n.* 北方

實用片語與搭配字

the North Pole 北極

② *adj.* 北方的

③ *adv.* 向北方；在北方

► Brook lives in the north of the city.
布魯克住在這城市的北邊。

► The North Pole is warming up and its ice is melting, all due to the effects of global warming.
全球暖化使北極溫度上升，冰逐漸融化。

► The restaurant is north of Adam Street.
這家餐廳在亞當街北方。

► Drive north for one mile.
往北開車開一英里。

Exercise 43

I. Choose and write the correct word. Change the form of the word when necessary.

1	neighbor (n.) newspaper (n.)	You may ask your __________ to take any deliveries while you're on vacation.
2	next (adv.) never (adv.)	Knowledge is the most precious treasure of all things, because it can __________ be given away.
3	nobody (pron.) neither (pron.)	Fortunately, __________ the driver nor the passengers in the accident were hurt.
4	north (adj.) noisy (adj.)	It's terribly __________ living near the airport; planes are flying over all the time.
5	nod (v.) nest (v.)	At times his head would __________ sleepily at formal dinners, and he lost the thread of conversations.

II. Multiple choices.

( ) 1. A __________ reader can select what he's interested in and skip what he thinks is boring.
(A) nest (B) newspaper (C) neighbor (D) none

( ) 2. I took my two-year-old __________ down to the beach with his spade and bucket.
(A) niece (B) news (C) nephew (D) nest

( ) 3. The match was postponed to the __________ day because of the bad weather.
(A) never (B) nineteen (C) noisy (D) next

( ) 4. In the __________, the ground becomes very cold as the winter snow and ice covers it.
(A) northern (B) noon (C) north (D) noise

( ) 5. Pour the boiling water into the bowl, put the __________ into the soup and serve yourself immediately.
(A) noodles (B) nod (C) noise (D) net

Unit 44

northern [ˈnɔːr.ðɚn] *adj.* 北方的；面北的

▶ People from northern countries are used to cold weather.
從北方國家來的人習慣寒冷的天氣。

---

nose [noʊz]

① *n.* 鼻子

實用片語與搭配字

be (right) under sb's nose; keep sb's nose out of sth
就在（某人）眼前；不干預，不過問

② *v.* 嗅；聞出

實用片語與搭配字

nose sth out 打探出，查出

▶ Dogs have very sensitive noses.
狗有非常靈敏的鼻子。

▶ My father could not find his glasses, but they were right under his nose on the table.
爸爸找不到他的眼鏡，但就在他眼前的桌上。

▶ The dogs were able to nose out the fox.
這些狗能夠嗅出狐狸的味道。

▶ The reporter is very good at nosing out scandals because she has very good informants.
那位記者非常會打聽八卦，因為他有很厲害的消息提供者。

---

not [nɑːt] *adv.* 不；沒有

▶ That shirt is not red.
那件襯衫不是紅色的。

---

note [noʊt]

① *n.* 筆記

實用片語與搭配字

make / take a note 紀錄，記住，記下

② *v.* 注意；留意

實用片語與搭配字

note sth down 把…記下來

▶ Ethan takes a lot of notes in class.
伊森在課堂上寫了很多筆記。

▶ If you work hard, your boss will take note and your chances of getting a promotion will be much higher.
你若努力工作，老闆會記得，也會大大提高你升遷的機會。

▶ Did you note the difference between the two cars?
你注意到了這兩輛車的不同嗎？

▶ I will note your birthday down in my schedule so that I do not forget to buy you a gift.
我會記下你的生日，以免忘記買禮物給你。

notebook [ˈnoʊt.bʊk]

n. 筆記本；筆記型電腦

▶ I can't find my notebook anywhere! Can I borrow some paper?
我到處找不到我的筆記本！可以借我一些紙嗎？

---

nothing [ˈnʌθ.ɪŋ]

① *pron.* 沒有東西；沒有事情

實用片語與搭配字

have nothing to do with sb; be / have nothing to do with sb / sth; be / mean nothing
不關（某人）的事；與…毫不相干，對…無關重要；毫無價值，並不重要

② *n.* 微不足道的人或事

▶ There is nothing in the box.
這個盒子裡沒有東西。

▶ In the world we live in today, what you know means nothing if you do not also have good relationships with others.
如今，若沒有好的人際關係，懂再多也不重要。

▶ Sam is so rich, $500 to him is nothing.
山姆非常富有，五百美元對他來說微不足道。

notice [ˈnoʊ.t̬ɪs]

① *n.* 通知；公告

實用片語與搭配字

give sb notice; take notice; at short notice
（通常指提前）向（某人）發出解雇通知；注意，在意；在短時間內

② *v.* 看到；注意到

▶ The secretary sent her boss a notice for his meeting.
這位秘書發送了一份會議通知給她的老闆。

▶ Firefighters have to be able to make life-saving decisions at short notice or people might get hurt.
消防員必須能夠在短時間內做出救援的決定，否則會造成人員傷害。

▶ Did you notice the new restaurant in our neighborhood?
你注意到我們附近新開的餐廳了嗎？

---

novel [ˈnɑː.vəl]

① *adj.* 新奇的；新穎的

② *n.* （長篇）小說

▶ That's a really novel idea for a dessert!
那真是個做甜點的新點子！

▶ This weekend, Katie is going to stay home and read a novel.
這週末凱蒂要待在家讀小說。

November / Nov. [noʊˈvem.bɚ] *n.* 十一月

▶ Thanksgiving in the United States is in November.
在美國感恩節是在十一月。

---

now [naʊ]

① *adv.* 此刻

② *n.* 現在

▶ Tickets are now on sale for Celine's concert.
席琳的演唱會門票現正銷售中。

▶ Now is the best time to go to the mountains.
現在就是上山最佳的時間。

實用片語與搭配字

it's now or never; (every) now and then / again; now (that)...
機不可失；有時，偶爾；既然，由於

- ▶ I have never traveled abroad by myself, but if I want to be more independent it is now or never.
  我從未獨自出國旅行，所以如果要變得更獨立，現在就該立刻行動，機不可失。

number ['nʌm.bɚ]

① *n.* 數字

實用片語與搭配字

a number of; beyond number; any number of
若干；多不勝數；許多，大量

② *v.* 共計有；(數量)多達

- ▶ Caleb loves to study math and numbers.
  迦勒喜歡學算術和數字。
- ▶ The stars in the heavens are beyond number and even scientists can only guess at how many there are.
  天上的星星多不勝數，即使科學家也只能猜測大約的數量。
- ▶ Did you number all the pages of the book?
  你算過這本書有幾頁了嗎？

---

nurse [nɝːs]

① *n.* 護士

② *v.* 照顧(生病的人或動物)

- ▶ Ivy works as a nurse in a hospital.
  艾薇在一家醫院擔任護士的工作。
- ▶ Eugene's wife nursed him back to health.
  尤金的妻子照顧他直到他恢復健康。

---

nut [nʌt] *n.* 堅果

- ▶ Do these cookies have nuts in them?
  這些餅乾裡有堅果嗎？

O.K. / OK / okay [ˌoʊˈkeɪ]

① *adj.* 可以的；不錯的

② *adv.* 尚可；還算滿意

③ *n.* 許可；認可

④ *v.* 批准；同意

- ▶ Was everything OK with your dinner?
  晚餐還可以嗎？
- ▶ My cellphone still works OK even though it's old.
  我的手機雖老舊，且仍然運作順暢。
- ▶ Mom gave Chris the OK to go to the party.
  媽媽同意讓克里斯參加派對。
- ▶ The boss OK'ed the project.
  老闆批准了這項專案計畫。

---

o'clock [əˈklɑːk] *n.* …點鐘(整點鐘)

- ▶ Daniel comes home from work at 6 o'clock every day.
  丹尼爾每天六點下班回家。

obey [oʊˈbeɪ] *v.* 服從；遵守

▶ It's important to obey the rules at school.
在學校遵守校規是很重要的。

102

object [ˈɑːb.dʒɪkt] *n.* 物體；實物

▶ Can anyone guess what object I have in this box?
有誰可以猜猜看這個盒子裡有什麼東西？

object [əbˈdʒekt] *v.* 反對；有異議

▶ Does anyone object to this decision?
有人反對這個決定嗎？

96

occur [əˈkɝː] *v.* 發生

▶ When did the accident occur?
這個意外什麼時候發生的？

實用片語與搭配字

occur to sb
（想法或主意）出現在（某人）頭腦中

▶ It has never occurred to me that I could actually rent out a room in my house to overseas travelers and earn extra money.
我從未想過，原來可以把自己的房間出租給外國旅遊者賺些外快。

O

ocean [ˈoʊ.ʃən] *n.* 海洋

▶ Andrea loves to swim in the ocean.
安卓雅喜歡在海裡游泳。

October / Oct. [ɑːkˈtoʊ.bɚ] *n.* 十月

▶ Campbell and Simon's birthdays are in October.
坎柏爾和賽門的生日都在十月。

of [ɑːv] *prep.* 屬於…的

▶ Julia loves the traditions of her family.
茱莉亞喜歡她家的傳統。

off [ɑːf]

① *adv.* 離開

② *prep.* 離開…

③ *adj.* 情況不好的

▶ The couple drove off into the sunset.
這對夫妻開車駛進了夕陽。

▶ The children stepped off the school bus.
孩子們走下了校車。

▶ Henry wants to go on a trip that is off road.
亨利想要去越野旅行。

offer [ˈɑː.fɚ]

① *n.* 出價；提議

② *v.* （主動）給予；提出

► If you want to bargain, you can start by making an offer.
如果你要議價，你要先出一個價錢。

► What is the highest salary you can offer?
你可以給的最高薪水是多少？

---

office [ˈɑː.fɪs] *n.* 辦公室

► The boss has a very big office.
這位老闆有一間非常大的辦公室。

---

officer [ˈɑː.fɪ.sɚ] *n.* 官員

► Police officers help keep the law.
警察幫忙維持法律秩序。

Exercise 44

I. Choose and write the correct word. Change the form of the word when necessary.

1	notebook (n.) nothing (n.)	He took a small __________ from his jacket pocket and tore out a page.
2	notice (v.) obey (v.)	Did you __________ the guy standing behind us at the movie? He looked just like your brother.
3	occur (v.) object (v.)	Some people still __________ to teaching children about sex in public schools
4	offer (n.) object (n.)	Some guy made Sharon an __________ of 1,500 bucks for her car, but she wants at least $2,000.
5	nurse (n.) officer (n.)	He gave up his job as a police __________ after his partner was killed.

II. Multiple choices.

( ) 1. A __________ of potential buyers have expressed interest in this company.
(A) novel (B) note (C) number (D) notice

( ) 2. Although the main characters in the __________ are so true to life, they are imaginary indeed.
(A) number (B) novel (C) note (D) notice

( ) 3. According to the report, most accidents __________ when young children are left unattended in the home.
(A) obey (B) object (C) offer (D) occur

( ) 4. There's __________ worse than going out in the cold with wet hair.
(A) nothing (B) note (C) novel (D) object

( ) 5. All citizens must __________ the law and be loyal to the Constitution.
(A) offer (B) obey (C) occur (D) object

Unit 45

official [əˈfɪʃ.əl]

① *adj.* 正式的；官方的

② *n.* 官員；公務員

▶ Tom's official title is 'managing editor.'
湯姆正式的頭銜是「執行編輯」。

▶ Government officials are looking into the factory's environmental record.
政府官員正在調查這家工廠的環境紀錄。

---

often [ˈɑːf.ən] *adv.* 經常

▶ We eat at this restaurant often.
我們經常在這家餐廳吃飯。

---

oil [ɔɪl]

① *n.* 油

② *v.* 在…塗油

實用片語與搭配字

well oiled 喝醉的，運作順暢的

▶ Jamie loves to cook with oil.
傑米喜歡用油烹飪。

▶ Please oil the door. It's squeaking.
請給門上點油。它一直嘎吱作響。

▶ The government in that country functions like a well-oiled machine and each department is very efficient.
該國政府運作順暢，每個部門都非常有效率。

---

old [oʊld] *adj.* 老的；舊的

實用片語與搭配字

the old; for old time's sake
老年人，長者；看在舊日的情分上

▶ My car is old. I need a new one.
我的車舊了，我需要一輛新車。

▶ At the end of our final year in school, we celebrated for old time's sake because we were all going in different directions.
因著舊日的情份，我們在最後一年的尾聲慶祝彼此即將朝著不同方向邁進。

---

omit [oʊˈmɪt] *v.* 遺漏；排除

▶ Angie omitted mentioning her age when talking to the man.
安潔與那男人談話時沒有提到她的年齡。

---

on [ɑːn]

① *prep.* 在…上面

② *adv.* 穿上；蓋上

▶ The computer is on the table.
電腦在桌子上。

▶ Albert put his coat on.
亞伯穿上他的大衣。

once [wʌns]

① *adv.* 一次；一回

② *conj.* 一…就…

③ *n.* 一次；一回

▶ Reed talks to his mother once a day.
里德跟他媽媽一天說一次話。

▶ Once everyone leaves, we can go to sleep.
一等到大家都離開，我們就能去睡覺。

▶ Drew and Sarah ate at this restaurant more than once.
杜魯和莎拉不只一次在這家餐廳吃飯。

one [wʌn]

① *n.* 一

② *adj.* 一個的

③ *pron.* 一人

▶ One times one is still one.
一乘以一仍然是一。

▶ Christina and Steve have one child.
克莉絲緹娜和史提夫有一個孩子。

▶ Sean visited one of his relatives on the weekend.
西恩在週末拜訪了他的一位親戚。

onion [ˈʌn.jən] *n.* 洋蔥

▶ I don't like cutting onions! It makes my eyes water.
我不喜歡切洋蔥！它會讓我眼睛流淚。

only [ˈoʊn.li]

① *adv.* 只有

實用片語與搭配字

if only; not only but also; only just
只要，倘若；不但…而且…； 剛剛，剛好

② *adj.* 唯一的

③ *conj.* 要不是；若非

▶ Max has only one brother.
麥克斯只有一個弟弟。

▶ If only I could save up enough money, I would love to travel to every country in the world.
只要我存夠錢，我會想去環遊旅行。

▶ Juliet is Romeo's one and only love.
茱麗葉是羅密歐唯一所愛。

▶ We could have been here earlier, only we got lost.
要不是我們迷路，我們可能早就到這裡了。

open [ˈoʊ.pən]

① *adj.* 開著的；未關的

實用片語與搭配字

with open arms; open-minded
熱情地；心胸寬闊，能接受新思想的

▶ The door is open.
這扇門是開的。

▶ The man returned home after many years of traveling abroad and was welcomed with open arms by his family.
在外旅行多年後，男子決定回家，而他的家人也熱情地迎接他的到來。

② *adv.* 敞開地

③ *n.* 戶外

實用片語與搭配字

bring sth out into the open
把…公之於眾

▶ The door was left open.
這扇門被打開了。

▶ The children like to play in the open.
孩子們喜歡在戶外玩耍。

▶ The reporter was applauded for bringing the corruption scandal out into the open.
記者因為將貪汙醜聞公諸於世而獲得讚許。

operate [ˈɑː.pə.reɪt] *v.* 操作

▶ You need a license to operate that machine.
你需要有執照才能操作那台機器。

opinion [əˈpɪn.jən] *n.* 意見；看法；主張

實用片語與搭配字

have an opinion about / on sth
對…有看法

▶ In my opinion, mangoes are the most delicious fruit.
對我來說，芒果是最美味的水果。

▶ It is important for everyone to have an opinion about politics, but it is not always a good idea to say what you think in public.
人人都該對政治有自己看法，但在公開場合暢所欲言並不全然妥當。

---

or [ɔːr / ɚ] *conj.* 或者

▶ Do you want pizza or pasta for dinner?
你晚餐要吃披薩或義大利麵？

---

orange [ˈɔːr.ɪndʒ]

① *n.* 柳橙

② *adj.* 橘色的

▶ I ate an orange for breakfast.
我早餐吃了一個柳橙。

▶ My little sister wore an orange shirt.
我的妹妹穿了一件橘色的襯衫。

order [ˈɔːr.dɚ]

① *n.* 整齊有序

實用片語與搭配字

put sth in order （使）整齊

② *v.* 下命令

▶ I like to have order in the house.
我喜歡屋內整齊有序。

▶ The old man put his affairs in order before he died so that his family would not fight over who inherited his fortune.
老先生在過世前將自己的事打理好，希望家人不要為他的遺產而爭吵。

▶ The officer ordered us to stop moving.
這位警察命令我們不要動。

實用片語與搭配字

order sb around; order sth in
使喚（某人）; 叫外賣

▶ I don't like it when my boss orders me around, especially when she asks me to serve tea.
我不喜歡老闆使喚我做事，尤其是叫我倒茶。

---

ordinary [ˈɔːr.dən.er.i] *adj.* 平常的；普通的

▶ This looks like an ordinary purse, but it can also become a backpack.
這個包包看起來很普通，但它可以變成背包。

實用片語與搭配字

out of the ordinary 不同凡響，反常

▶ Our family trip to the jungle was out of the ordinary and it was unlike anything I had ever done.
我們家的叢林之旅不同凡響，是前所未有的經驗。

---

organ [ˈɔːr.ɡən] *n.* 內臟；器官

▶ Justin likes meat, but he doesn't eat animal organs.
賈斯汀喜歡吃肉，但他不喜歡吃動物的內臟。

97

organization [ˌɔːr.ɡən.əˈzeɪ.ʃən]
n. 機構；組織

▶ Joanna works for a non-profit organization in Africa.
喬安娜在非洲的一個非營利機構工作。

---

103 100

organize [ˈɔːr.ɡən.aɪz] *v.* 整理；安排

▶ I will organize my files this weekend.
我這週末會整理我的資料夾。

---

other [ˈʌð.ɚ]
① *adj.* 其他的
② *pron.* （兩者中的）另一人、事、物

▶ I can carry that with my other hand.
我可以用另一隻手來提。

▶ Myself and one other will meet together.
我會跟另一個人碰面。

---

our(s) [ˈaʊ.ɚ(z) / aʊr(z)] *pron.* 我們的（所有格）

▶ Our classmates are working hard.
我們的同學們正努力工作著。

---

out [aʊt]
① *adv.* 向外

▶ She walked out to go shopping.
她走出去逛街。

實用片語與搭配字

out of 耗盡，用完，沒有

▶ We are out of milk, so please buy a bottle when you come home tonight.
牛奶都喝完了，所以請你今晚回家時買一瓶回來。

② *prep.* 通過…而出

實用片語與搭配字

out and about 活躍的，正常行動的

③ *n.* 藉口；理由

④ *adj.* 外側的

▶ The little puppy ran out the door.
那隻小狗跑出門去。

▶ Matthew broke his leg, but he was out and about in no time despite the doctor's advice to stay home.
雖然馬修跌斷他的腿，但他不顧醫生的建議，在很短時間內就出門走動。

▶ I'm tired of all this. I need an out.
我對這一切感到厭倦，我需要一個藉口離開。

▶ The out surface of the boat shined beautifully in the sun.
這艘船的外側在陽光下美麗地閃耀著。

---

outside [ˌaʊtˈsaɪd / ˈaʊt.saɪd]

① *n.* 外部

② *adj.* 外面的

實用片語與搭配字

the outside world 外界

③ *adv.* 在外面

實用片語與搭配字

outside of 除了

④ *prep.* 在…外；向…外

▶ The outside of the car was clean.
這部車子的外部是乾淨的。

▶ The flowers outside need more water.
外面的花需要澆更多水。

▶ Many people live their lives in ignorance without really knowing what is happening in the outside world.
許多人的無知是因為他們活著卻不知道外界發生什麼事。

▶ We all ran outside to the park.
我們都往外跑去公園。

▶ There are many things to do in your free-time outside of sitting in front of your computer playing online games.
在空閒之餘，你除了可以在家打電動之外，還可以出門做很多事。

▶ He spoke to the woman outside the building.
他在這棟大樓外面和那個女人說話。

---

oven [ˈʌv.ən] *n.* 烤箱；爐子

▶ Put the cookies on the pan and bake them in the oven for ten minutes.
把餅乾放在烤盤上，然後放進烤箱烤十分鐘。

Exercise 45

I. Choose and write the correct word. Change the form of the word when necessary.

1	often (adv.) once (adv.)	I __________ get headaches, but they seem to pass off in a little while.
2	onion (n.) opinion (n.)	That's only someone's personal __________, and we don't have to write it into the document.
3	operate (v.) omit (v.)	We __________ the pork from the recipe because our guests were Muslims.
4	outside (adj.) ordinary (adj.)	She may be a super-model, but when she takes off all her make-up, and puts on her jeans and a T-shirt, she actually looks quite __________.
5	order (n.) organ (n.)	He made sure everything in his office was in __________ before leaving for the conference.

II. Multiple choices.

( ) 1. Badminton was not recognized as an __________ sport in the Olympics until 1992.
(A) open (B) only (C) official (D) ordinary

( ) 2. I spent the afternoon in the office trying to __________ all the files on my computer.
(A) operate (B) order (C) organize (D) over

( ) 3. There were two security guards on duty __________ the building when the robbery happened.
(A) out (B) outside (C) only (D) once

( ) 4. It doesn't take long to learn the basics of how to set up the machine and __________ it.
(A) omit (B) order (C) operate (D) organize

( ) 5. She started the __________ with the aim of helping local people in need.
(A) organ (B) order (C) opinion (D) organization

Unit 46

over ['oʊ.vɚ]

① *prep.* 在…之上

實用片語與搭配字

all over somewhere 到處，遍及

② *adv.* 在上方

實用片語與搭配字

over and over (again) 一再地，再三地

▶ I grabbed the picture over the table.
我拿了在桌上的照片。

▶ Your books are all over the place! Please put them back on the shelves.
到處都是你的書！請將他們放回書架。

▶ The horse jumped over the fence.
馬跳過了柵欄。

▶ The girl has been listening to that new pop song over and over again and I am sick of hearing it.
那女孩不停重複聽那首新的流行歌曲，我都聽膩了。

---

overpass ['oʊ.vɚ.pæs] *n.* 天橋；高架道

▶ My house is just on the other side of that overpass.
我家就在那座天橋的另一邊。

---

overseas [ˌoʊ.vɚˈsiːz]

① *adj.* 在國外的；海外的

② *adv.* 在（或向）國外；在（或向）海外

▶ Jocelyn has been living overseas for five years.
喬絲琳住在國外已經五年了。

▶ Sam and Alice moved overseas after they got married.
山姆和艾麗絲結婚後就搬到國外住。

---

owl [aʊl] *n.* 貓頭鷹

▶ Owls can hunt at night because they have very good eyesight.
貓頭鷹可以在夜間獵食，因為牠們眼力很好。

99

own [oʊn]

① *adj.* 自己的

② *v.* 擁有

實用片語與搭配字

own up to sth 承認（錯誤）

▶ She likes to cook her own food.
她喜歡自己烹煮食物。

▶ My family owns a nice house.
我家擁有一棟很好的房子。

▶ You made a mistake and you have to own up to it or people will lose respect for you.
你若不承認自己犯的錯，你會失去別人對你的尊重。

③ *pron.* 自己（代名詞）

實用片語與搭配字

(all) on your own; in sb's own time; come into sb's own

獨自，獨立地；不慌不忙地；（在某種情況下）所長得到充分的發揮，展現自己的本事

▶ Our company really looks after its own.
我們公司很照顧自己的員工。

▶ John was never a good student, but after leaving school he really came into his own and become a successful businessman.
約翰從來就不是個好學生，但畢業後他發揮所長，成為一位很成功的商人。

---

owner [ˈoʊ.nɚ] *n.* 主人；擁有者

▶ Who is the owner of this dog? It should be on a leash!
誰是這隻狗的主人？牠應該要戴鍊條！

---

ox [ɑːks] *n.* 牛

▶ Mandy was born in the year of the ox.
曼蒂是牛年出生的。

pack [pæk]

① *n.*（一）包

② *v.* 打包行李；裝箱

實用片語與搭配字

pack a punch; pack sth away

有巨大作用（或影響）; 將…收拾起來放好

▶ Can you please get two packs of cookies when you go to the supermarket?
你去超級市場時，可以幫我買兩包餅乾嗎？

▶ Teresa is packing for her trip to Japan tomorrow morning.
泰瑞莎正為了明天早上到日本的旅程打包行李。

▶ Indian food can surely pack a punch if you are not used to such spicy dishes.
如果你吃不慣辛辣的食物 ，印度菜一定能令你留下強烈的印象。

---

package [ˈpæk.ɪd]

① *n.* 包裹

實用片語與搭配字

good things come in small packages

好東西不在個頭大

② *v.* 包裝成盒（袋）

▶ Meg was so excited to receive a package in the mail from Australia.
梅格很興奮收到一個從澳洲寄來的包裹。

▶ When I complained about being so short, my mother always told me good things come in small packages.
每當我抱怨自己太矮時，母親總對我說：「好東西不在個頭大。」

▶ Please package these cups carefully so they don't break.
請小心包裝這些杯子才不會打破。

---

page [peɪdʒ] *n.* （書等的）頁

▶ Please turn to the first page of the book.
請翻到這本書的第一頁。

pain [peɪn]

① *n.* 疼痛

實用片語與搭配字

a pain in the neck 極其討厭的人（或事物）

② *v.* 使痛苦；感到疼痛

▶ Back pain is common among adults who spend most of the day sitting.
背痛很常見於整天久坐的成人身上。

▶ My younger brother is a pain in the neck because he follows me everywhere I go.
我的弟弟真討厭，因為他總是當我的跟屁蟲。

▶ It pains me to hear that you can't come to my birthday party.
聽到你不能來我的生日派對真令我痛苦。

---

painful [ˈpeɪn.fəl] *adj.* 疼痛的

▶ That cut looks painful! Do you want some medicine?
那傷口看起來很痛！你要一些藥嗎？

paint [peɪnt]

① *n.* 顏料；油漆

② *v.* 塗以顏色

▶ The artist uses different colors of paint.
這位畫家使用不同顏色的顏料。

▶ My older brother likes to paint pictures.
我哥哥喜歡畫圖。

---

painter [ˈpeɪn.t̬ɚ] *n.* 畫家；油漆工

▶ Who is your favorite Italian painter?
誰是你最喜愛的義大利畫家？

---

painting [ˈpeɪn.t̬ɪŋ] *n.* 繪畫；油畫

▶ Andrea hung the painting from her nephew on the fridge.
安卓雅把她姪子的畫作掛在冰箱上。

---

pair [per]

① *n.* （一）雙

② *v.* 使成對

實用片語與搭配字

pair sb off; pair sb up
使（兩人）結成一對情侶，介紹（兩個人）認識；（為做某事）成搭檔

▶ I am wearing a pair of gloves.
我戴著一雙手套。

▶ All the shoes were paired on the rack.
所有鞋子都成對地擺在架上。

▶ Our science teacher paired me up with this cute boy and we have to do our project together.
我的自然老師把我和一個可愛的男孩安排在同一組，我們必須一起做專題。

---

pajamas [pəˈdʒɑːməz] *n.* 睡衣

▶ Children, please put on your pajamas and get ready for bed!
孩子們，請穿上你們的睡衣準備上床睡覺！

palm [pɑːm] *n.* 手掌；手心

▸ John wrote the pretty girl's phone number on the palm of his hand.
約翰將這個漂亮女生的電話號碼寫在他手掌上。

---

pan [pæn] *n.* 平底鍋

實用片語與搭配字

pan-fry 用平底鍋煎

▸ Heat up the pan with oil before adding the garlic.
在加進大蒜之前，先在鍋子裡放油加熱。

▸ Pan-frying your food is one method of cooking, but you have to be careful not to use too much oil.
煎是一種烹煮方法，但你必須克制油的用量。

---

panda [ˈpæn.də] *n.* 貓熊

▸ There is a pair of pandas at the zoo. They are so cute!
這個動物園有一對貓熊，牠們好可愛！

---

pants [pænts] *n.* 長褲（一件）

▸ That young man is wearing black pants.
那位年輕男士穿著一件黑色長褲。

---

papa / pop [ˈpɑː.pə / pɑːp] *n.* 爸爸

▸ My papa is a hard working man.
我爸爸是個認真工作的人。

---

papaya [pəˈpaɪ.ə] *n.* 木瓜

▸ Faith's favorite drink is a shake with papaya, milk and honey.
費斯最愛的飲料是奶昔加木瓜、牛奶和蜂蜜。

---

paper [ˈpeɪ.pɚ]

① *n.* 紙

實用片語與搭配字

on paper 未經實踐，在理論上

② *v.* 在…貼壁紙；用紙包

實用片語與搭配字

paper over sth 掩蓋（尤指問題或分歧）

▸ Can I borrow some paper from you?
我能跟你借一些紙嗎？

▸ The deal I signed with the company looked much better on paper than in real life and now I want to change jobs again.
我實際的工作不如當初與公司所簽的合約，現在我想重新找工作。

▸ We can paper the walls with drawings!
我們可以用這些圖畫貼在牆上當壁紙！

▸ The government papered over the damage caused by the financial crisis, leading people to believe it was not so serious.
政府掩蓋事實，讓人民覺得金融危機所造成的傷害並不嚴重。

pardon [ˈpɑːr.dən]

① *n.* 原諒；寬恕

② *v.* 原諒；饒恕

► After the accident, Ronald asked the man he had injured for a pardon.

這場車禍後，羅瀾向那位被他弄傷的男子請求原諒。

► Pardon me, can you say your name again?

不好意思，可以再說一次你的名字嗎？

Exercise 46

I. Choose and write the correct word. Change the form of the word when necessary.

1	overpass (n.) owner (n.)	I had no ID so I couldn't prove I was the ________ of the car.
2	own (v.) pack (v.)	Early in the morning, the hikers ________ everything they would need for the hike.
3	paint (n.) painting (n.)	It's the first time this original ________ has been displayed to the public.
4	pajamas (n.) papaya (n.)	I don't drink any alcohol, but I love ________ juice and I drink mineral water.
5	palm (n.) paper (n.)	Pour some lotion into the ________ of your hand, and then smooth it over your arms and neck.

II. Multiple choices.

(　　) 1. After studying ________ for a few years, he returned to Taiwan, and got a great job.
(A) over　(B) overseas　(C) painful　(D) outside

(　　) 2. The children have received a big ________ from their uncle in New York, and are dying to open it.
(A) paint　(B) palm　(C) panda　(D) package

(　　) 3. I hope you'll ________ the state of the house; I haven't had time to clean it up.
(A) pardon　(B) pair　(C) pack　(D) paint

(　　) 4. It must have been very ________ for you to tell her about the accident.
(A) own　(B) overseas　(C) painting　(D) painful

(　　) 5. The new city government is going to build a pedestrian ________ over the highway.
(A) pain　(B) owl　(C) overpass　(D) pack

Unit 47

parent [ˈper.ənt] *n.* 父或母；父母

▶ I spend time with my parents every day.
我每天花時間和我的父母相處。

---

park [pɑːrk]

① *n.* 公園

② *v.* 停車

▶ I like to take long walks at the park.
我喜歡在公園散步。

▶ Let's park the car in the garage.
我們把車停在車庫裡吧。

---

parrot [ˈper.ət]

① *n.* 鸚鵡

② *v.* 像鸚鵡學舌般地複述；機械地複述

▶ I saw a beautiful parrot in the pet store downtown.
我在市中心的寵物店看到一隻美麗的鸚鵡。

▶ Little children parrot what adults say.
小孩子會像鸚鵡般地模仿大人說話。

---

part [pɑːrt]

① *n.* 部分

② *v.* 梳分（頭髮）；使分開

▶ That handle is a part of the door.
門把是門的一部分。

▶ Andy parts his hair down the middle.
安迪把頭髮梳中分。

101

particular [pɚˈtɪk.jə.lɚ] *adj.* 特別的

實用片語與搭配字

in particular 特別，尤其

▶ Do you have a particular restaurant that you want to eat at today?
你今天有特別想要去哪家餐廳用餐嗎？

▶ It is good to learn a new skill, in particular a skill that no robot would be able to do because then you will always have a job.
學習新技能是好事，尤其是機器人無法具備的能力，如此你才能一直有工作。

---

partner [ˈpɑːrt.nɚ] *n.* 夥伴；搭檔

▶ For this project, everyone should work with a partner.
在這個計畫，每個人應該和一位夥伴一起進行。

---

party [ˈpɑːr.t̬i]

① *n.* 派對

▶ There is a party at my friend's house.
有個派對在我朋友家舉行。

實用片語與搭配字

party animal 熱愛社交聚會的人

② *v.* 狂歡；吃喝玩樂

▶ My roommate in college is such a party animal. She did not study enough and failed her first year.
我大學室友是愛社交的人，但她不夠用功讀書，所以第一年的成績不及格。

▶ I will party after the exam is over.
考試結束後我會大肆慶祝一番。

96

pass [pæs]

① *v.* 通過；經過

實用片語與搭配字

pass sth on; pass through; pass sth around; pass for sth / sb
傳遞；通過，經歷；分發；看起來像，被當作

② *n.* 通行證

▶ The bus will pass through the city.
這輛巴士會經過城裡。

▶ Teachers are important because they pass on their knowledge and wisdom to younger generations.
老師很重要，因為他們將自己的智慧和知識傳承給新的一代。

▶ You can't come in here without a pass.
你需要通行證才能進來這裡。

passenger ['pæs.ən.dʒɚ] *n.* 乘客；旅客

▶ How many passengers were on the plane?
那班飛機上有多少乘客？

P

past [pæst]

① *prep.* （時間）超過

② *adv.* 經過

③ *adj.* 過去的

④ *n.* 昔日

▶ I stayed awake past my bedtime.
我過了睡覺時間就睡不著了。

▶ We drove past the coffee shop.
我們開車經過了這間咖啡店。

▶ Let's not talk about our past mistakes.
我們不要再談論過去的錯誤了。

▶ Smart phones did not exist in the past.
以前沒有智慧型手機。

paste [peɪst]

① *n.* 漿糊

② *v.* 用漿糊黏貼

▶ For art class tomorrow, please bring scissors, pencils and paste.
明天的美術課請帶剪刀、鉛筆與膠水。

▶ Be sure to paste the stamp on the envelope before you mail your letter.
務必在你寄件之前將郵票貼在信封上。

pat [pæt]

① *v.* 輕拍；輕撫

▶ Santa patted the little girl's head and asked her what she wanted for Christmas.
聖誕老公公輕拍這小女孩的頭並且問她聖誕節想要什麼禮物。

實用片語與搭配字

pat sb on the back 稱讚（某人）

② *n.* 輕拍；輕打

▶ Jonathan signed a profitable deal for his company and his boss patted him on the back for his achievement.
喬納森為公司簽了一個利潤不錯的合約，他老闆為此讚許他一番。

▶ Don't be afraid of the dog; just give him a light pat.
不要怕這隻狗；只要輕輕拍牠。

---

path [pæθ] *n.* 小徑

▶ Let's follow this path and see where it goes.
讓我們沿著這條小徑看看會到哪裡去。

---

patient [ˈpeɪ.ʃənt]

① *adj.* 有耐心的；能容忍的

② *n.* 病人

▶ If you want to be a kindergarten teacher, you need to be patient and kind.
如果你想當幼稚園老師，你必須有耐心和親切和藹。

▶ Dr. Klein sees over 100 patients every day.
克雷恩醫生每天看超過一百個病人。

---

pattern [ˈpæt̬.ɚn]

① *n.* 圖案

② *v.* 以圖案裝飾；仿造；模仿

▶ Kellie follows a pattern to make the dress for her daughter.
凱莉依照一個圖案為她女兒做了這件洋裝。

▶ Her design for the laptop is patterned after other well-known designs.
她這台筆電是照一些知名的樣式所設計的。

---

pay [peɪ] *n.* 付費

實用片語與搭配字

pay the price; pay for sth; pay off; pay sb back
付出代價；為…付出代價，因…得到報應；得到好結果；還（某人）錢

▶ Do not forget to pay at the counter.
別忘了在櫃台付錢。

▶ Humans are dumping tons of plastic into the oceans and sealife is paying the price for this.
人類將許多塑膠製品投入海中，而海洋生物正在為此付出代價。

---

payment [ˈpeɪ.mənt] *n.* 支付的款項

▶ The payment for the hat was settled.
這頂帽子的錢已經付了。

---

peace [piːs] *n.* 和平；太平

▶ After two years of war, the two countries finally declared peace.
經過兩年的戰爭，這兩個國家終於宣布和平。

實用片語與搭配字

at peace with sth / sb
感到平靜、與世無爭

▶ She seems very easygoing and at peace with everything that she encounters.
她看起來很隨和，對於遭遇的每件事情都很平靜。

---

peaceful [ˈpiːs.fəl] *adj.* 平靜的；和平的

▶ Caleb looks so peaceful sleeping like that.
迦勒睡著時看起來十分平靜。

---

peach [piːtʃ] *n.* 桃子

▶ The peaches from this area are very large and sweet.
這地區產的水蜜桃又大又甜。

---

peanut [ˈpiː.nʌt] *n.* 花生

▶ Peanuts are a good snack to eat when camping.
露營時花生是很好的零食。

---

pear [per] *n.* 梨子

▶ Would you like a slice of this pear?
你要來片梨子嗎？

---

pen [pen]

① *n.* 筆

② *v.* 寫

▶ Should I use a pen or a pencil?
我該用原子筆還是鉛筆寫？

▶ Please pen your signature right here.
請在這裡簽名。

---

pencil [ˈpen.səl]

① *n.* 鉛筆

② *v.* 用鉛筆寫

▶ I usually write things with a pencil.
我通常用鉛筆寫東西。

▶ He penciled a very long essay.
他用鉛筆寫了一篇非常長的文章。

---

penguin [ˈpeŋ.gwɪn] *n.* 企鵝

▶ Penguins are birds that cannot fly.
企鵝是不會飛的鳥。

Exercise 47

I. Choose and write the correct word. Change the form of the word when necessary.

1	pay (v.) pat (v.)	Thankfully, I managed to __________ off all my debts before we got married.
2	partner (n.) passenger (n.)	A number of __________ on the ferry threw up when the boat met with high waves.
3	patient (n.) pattern (n.)	The more positive a __________ is about his treatment, the better his chances for recovery.
4	pass (v.) part (v.)	You must get a minimum of 30 questions right to __________ the examination.
5	path (n.) past (n.)	Sharp stones on the __________ made walking barefoot rather uncomfortable.

II. Multiple choices.

(　　) 1. Is there any __________ kind of cheese you want for the pizza or should I just buy whatever is on sale?
(A) patient　(B) past　(C) particular　(D) peaceful

(　　) 2. He spent the afternoon __________ posters announcing the concert on walls and utility poles around town.
(A) patting　(B) pasting　(C) parting　(D) passing

(　　) 3. We must have the patience to continue to work until we find a __________ solution.
(A) peace　(B) peaceful　(C) patient　(D) past

(　　) 4. This picky child refused anything but __________ butter and jelly sandwiches.
(A) pen　(B) pear　(C) penguin　(D) peanut

(　　) 5. Last night I met an emperor __________ at the shore; it looked as though it was lost.
(A) peach　(B) pencil　(C) penguin　(D) peach

Unit 48

people [ˈpiː.pəl]

① *n.* 人（們）

實用片語與搭配字

the people 人民

② *v.* 充滿著（某種類型的人）

▶ There were a lot of people in the room.
這個房間裡有很多人。

▶ The people of the world need to come together and work out a plan to fight global warming.
人類必須一起解決地球暖化的問題。

▶ The mountains were peopled by many different groups.
這片山區住滿了不同族群的人。

---

pepper [ˈpep.ɚ]

① *n.* 椒；胡椒

② *v.* 加胡椒粉

▶ Can you please pass the salt and pepper?
可以幫我拿鹽和胡椒嗎？

▶ For dinner, I'm making peppered beef and pasta.
晚餐我要做黑胡椒牛肉和義大利麵。

---

per [pɝː / pɚ] *prep.* 每；每一

▶ Bananas cost $3.00 per kilogram at this market.
這市場的香蕉每公斤三美元。

---

perfect [ˈpɝː.fekt]

① *adj.* 完美的；百分百的

實用片語與搭配字

be perfect for 對⋯是十分理想的

② *v.* 使完美；改善

③ *n.* （文法）完成式

▶ Cindy has always been the perfect student.
辛蒂一直以來都是最優秀的學生。

▶ When Cindy saw the red dress in the shop, she knew it would be perfect for wearing to her sister's wedding.
辛蒂在店裡一見到那件紅裙，就知道穿去姊姊的婚禮一定很棒。

▶ Jamie stayed up all night perfecting her painting.
潔咪熬了一整夜就為了使她的畫作達到完美。

▶ To form the past perfect, use the verb had with the past participle.
過去完成式的組成，需要用 had 加上過去分詞。

---

perhaps [pɚˈhæps] *adv.* 或許；可能

▶ My boss will perhaps give me more work.
我的老闆或許會給我更多工作。

period [ˈpɪr.i.əd] *n.* 期間

▶ Esther and Harvey dated for a short period of time in high school.
愛絲特與哈雷高中的時候交往過一小段時間。

---

person [ˈpɝː.sən] *n.* 人；傢伙

實用片語與搭配字

in person; person-to-person
親自，本人；面對面地，直接地

▶ That person is our new instructor.
那個人是我們新的教練。

▶ The skill of person-to-person communication is dying out as more and more teenagers get addicted to social media.
面對面溝通的能力逐漸消失，因為越來越多青少年沉迷於社群媒體。

96

personal [ˈpɝː.sən.əl] *adj.* 個人的；私人的

實用片語與搭配字

get personal 進行人身攻擊

▶ It's not polite to ask too many personal questions when you first meet someone.
當你初見某人就問太多私人問題是不禮貌的。

▶ When having a conversation on social media, it is not a good idea to get personal because you do not really know the other person.
當使用社群媒體時，不要對對方有太多批判，因為你並不瞭解他。

---

pet [pet]

① *n.* 寵物

② *v.* 撫摸；輕拍

▶ Her family owns a lot of pets.
她家有很多寵物。

▶ I pet my dog whenever I get home.
我一回到家都會摸摸我的狗。

---

photograph / photo

[ˈfoʊ.t̬oʊ.græf / ˈfoʊ.t̬oʊ]

① *n.* 照片；攝影

② *v.* 拍照；攝影

實用片語與搭配字

photograph well / badly 上鏡 / 不上鏡

▶ Who is the boy next to you in that photograph?
照片中在你旁邊的男孩是誰？

▶ Ellen always photographs her food before she takes a bite.
愛倫總是在吃之前先替食物拍照。

▶ My sister photographs well and she always looks good no matter where the photo is taken.
我的妹妹很上鏡，不管照片在哪裡拍，她拍起來都很好看。

photographer [fəˈtɑː.grə.fɚ] *n.* 攝影師

▶ Richard is a wildlife photographer whose pictures have been in many magazines.
理查是位野生生態攝影師，許多雜誌裡都有他的照片。

---

phrase [freɪz]

① *n.* 片語；成語

② *v.* 用言語表達；用詞

▶ Please write one phrase to describe yourself.
請寫一個詞句來形容你自己。

▶ I don't like the way she phrased that question.
我不喜歡她表達那問題的方式。

---

piano [piˈæn.oʊ] *n.* 鋼琴

▶ My older sister plays the piano.
我的姊姊會彈鋼琴。

---

pick [pɪk]

① *v.* 挑選；選擇

實用片語與搭配字

pick and choose; pick on sb; pick sb / sth up; pick sth up

精挑細選；對（某人）刁難挑剔；舉起，抱起，提起，接（某人）;（透過練習而）學會

② *n.* 挑選；選擇

▶ Please pick one soup and one salad from the menu.
請從菜單上選一種湯和一種沙拉。

▶ If you have enough money to travel, you can pick and choose from hundreds of places to go.
若你有足夠的錢旅行，你可以從幾百個地點中精挑細選。

▶ This movie is the top pick to win an Oscar this year.
這部電影是今年贏得奧斯卡的首選。

---

picnic [ˈpɪk.nɪk]

① *n.* 野餐

② *v.* 去野餐

▶ Can we go on a picnic in the park this weekend?
這週末我們可以去公園野餐嗎？

▶ Jack and Amy picnic in the park every Saturday.
傑克與艾咪每個週六都去公園野餐。

---

picture [ˈpɪk.tʃɚ]

① *n.* 圖畫

實用片語與搭配字

get the picture; every picture tells a story

瞭解情況；不言而喻

▶ You can see my picture on the wall.
你可以在那面牆上看到我的畫。

▶ Jane found some old photographs of her family and looking at them she realized that every picture tells a story.
珍找到一些舊的家庭照，發現每張照片都訴說著一段故事。

② *v.* 想像

▶ I was pictured as a strong fighter.
我被想像成一位強壯鬥士的樣子。

---

pie [paɪ] *n.* 餡餅；派

▶ My mom will bake a pie for everyone.
我媽媽會烤一個派給大家吃。

piece [pi:s]

① *n.* (一) 張；塊；片

實用片語與搭配字

in one piece; come / fall into pieces; piece of cake
完整地；成為碎片；容易之事

② *v.* 拼合；湊集

實用片語與搭配字

piece sth together 拼合

▶ Write your name on a piece of paper.
在一張紙上寫你的名字。

▶ Every time Erin backpacks to a foreign country, her mom always tells her to come back home safely in one piece.
每次艾琳要去外國自助旅行時，她媽媽總是提醒她要平安的回來。

▶ I'm able to piece a computer together.
我能把一台電腦拼裝起來。

▶ If you can piece this table together from the store instructions, I will be very impressed.
若你可以根據指示組裝這個桌子，我將對你刮目相看。

---

pig [pɪg]

① *n.* 豬

② *v.* 狼吞虎嚥；大吃大喝 (pig out)

▶ That farmer raises pigs in his ranch.
那位農夫在他的農場裡養豬。

▶ I pig out every time I eat ice cream.
我每次吃冰淇淋時都狼吞虎嚥。

---

pigeon [ˈpɪdʒ.ən] *n.* 鴿子

▶ Kristin gave her daughter some small pieces of bread to feed the pigeons.
克莉絲汀給她女兒一小塊麵包去餵鴿子。

---

pile [paɪl]

① *n.* (一) 堆；疊；垛

② *v.* 疊；堆積；把…裝車

▶ Please shovel the snow from the driveway into a pile so I can drive to work.
請將車道上的雪鏟成一堆，這樣我才能開車上班。

▶ We're going to build a campfire with that wood, so please pile it close to the pit.
我們要用木材作營火，請將它堆疊靠近這個坑。

pillow [ˈpɪl.oʊ]

① *n.* 枕頭

② *v.* 把頭枕在…

▶ Danielle put three orange pillows on her blue sofa.
丹妮爾將三個橘色枕頭放在她的藍色沙發上。

▶ Noah pillowed his head on the grass.
諾亞將頭枕在草地上。

---

pin [pɪn]

① *n.* 別針；胸針

② *v.* （用針）別住

實用片語與搭配字

pin sb down; pin sth down
使（某人）動彈不得，（使）（某人）明確說明；清楚地知道，確認

▶ May I please borrow a pin for my hair?
我可以借一支髮夾夾我的頭髮嗎？

▶ Please pin this name tag to your shirt and keep it on for the whole conference.
請將名牌別在你的衣服上，並且整場會議都要戴著。

▶ The police officer pinned the thief down, and took his gun away from him.
警察制伏了盜賊，並且奪走他的槍。

---

pineapple [ˈpaɪnˌæp.əl] *n.* 鳳梨

▶ Pineapples grow best in a tropical country.
鳳梨在熱帶國家中長得最好。

---

ping-pong [ˈpɪŋ.pɑːŋ] *n.* 桌球

▶ Jack bought a ping-pong table so he could practice at home.
傑克買了一張桌球桌，這樣他就可以在家練習。

Exercise 48

I. Choose and write the correct word. Change the form of the word when necessary.

<table>
<tr><td rowspan="2">1</td><td>phrase (n.)</td><td rowspan="2">The Great Depression was once of the most difficult ________ in the history of the United States.</td></tr>
<tr><td>period (n.)</td></tr>
<tr><td rowspan="2">2</td><td>picnic (v.)</td><td rowspan="2">You can take boat rides, walk the wharf, or ________ along the river's grassy bank.</td></tr>
<tr><td>picture (v.)</td></tr>
<tr><td rowspan="2">3</td><td>piece (n.)</td><td rowspan="2">My children never wash their clothes; they just leave a ________ of dirty laundry on the floor in their bedrooms.</td></tr>
<tr><td>pile (n.)</td></tr>
<tr><td rowspan="2">4</td><td>pick (v.)</td><td rowspan="2">The trucks waited at the warehouse to ________ up their loads.</td></tr>
<tr><td>piece (v.)</td></tr>
<tr><td rowspan="2">5</td><td>pillow (n.)</td><td rowspan="2">I was feeling so weak that I could hardly lift my head from the ________.</td></tr>
<tr><td>pigeon (n.)</td></tr>
</table>

II. Multiple choices.

( ) 1. The gymnast, Nadia Commanechi, received ________ scores in her gold medal winning performance in the Olympics.
(A) personal (B) particular (C) patient (D) perfect

( ) 2. Taste the soup and adjust the seasoning, adding more salt or ________ as desired.
(A) pears (B) peanuts (C) pepper (D) peaches

( ) 3. You must not let your ________ reactions interfere with your professional judgement.
(A) perfect (B) personal (C) people (D) phrase

( ) 4. I thought she was leaving the company, but ________ it may be just a rumor.
(A) perhaps (B) personal (C) perfect (D) phrase

( ) 5. We all grouped together around the bride for a family ________.
(A) phrase (B) picnic (C) photograph (D) picnic

Unit 49

pink [pɪŋk]

① *adj.* 粉紅色的；桃紅色的

② *n.* 粉紅色；桃紅色

- Who lives in that pink house? It's so unique!
  誰住在那間粉紅色的房子裡？真特別！
- Most little girls like to wear pink.
  大部分的小女孩都喜歡穿粉紅色的衣服。

---

pipe [paɪp]

① *n.* 管子；管道

② *v.* 用管道輸送

- I think a pipe is broken in my bathroom. There's water everywhere!
  我想我浴室裡的水管壞了，現在到處都是水！
- Water is piped into the city in the desert.
  在沙漠中，水是由管道輸送進城的。

---

pitch [pɪtʃ]

① *v.* 投擲；扔

實用片語與搭配字

pitch in 投入，參與，支援

② *n.* 投球

- Adam hopes to pitch in his next baseball game.
  亞當希望能在下一場棒球賽中投球。
- It's our boss's birthday next week, and we can buy her a nice gift if everyone pitches in a few dollars.
  下週是老闆的生日，若大家願意花一些錢，我們可以送她一個不錯的禮物。
- Luke has been invited to make the first pitch at a baseball tournament.
  路克應邀在一場棒球錦標賽中開球。

---

pizza [ˈpiːt.sə] *n.* 披薩

- Mom made some delicious homemade pizza for lunch.
  媽媽午餐做了一些好吃的手工比薩。

---

place [pleɪs]

① *n.* 地方

實用片語與搭配字

out of place; in place
錯位，不協調；處於正確的位置，準備妥當

② *v.* 放置

- This place has a lot of night markets.
  這個地方有很多夜市。
- Nathan went to his school reunion, but he felt out of place because he was dressed too formally.
  內森參加同學會時覺得自己很突兀，因為他穿得太正式。
- Can you place the book over here?
  你能把書放在這兒嗎？

P

實用片語與搭配字

take place; take the place of sb / sth
發生；代替，取代

- The Olympic Games take place every four years and it is in a different country each time.
  奧林匹克每四年會在不同國家舉辦。

plain [pleɪn]

① *adj.* 樸素的

② *n.* 平原

- My stomach isn't feeling well, so I'll just have some plain rice for dinner.
  我的胃不太舒服，所以晚餐只會吃些白飯。
- Many wild animals live on this plain.
  有許多野生動物生活在這平原上。

plan [plæn]

① *n.* 計畫

實用片語與搭配字

go according to plan 按計畫進行

② *v.* 計畫；打算

實用片語與搭配字

plan on doing sth; plan sth out
打算做⋯; 精心安排，籌劃

- I have a plan for winning this game.
  我有一個能贏這場比賽的計畫。
- We have been working on the new product for months and if everything goes according to plan, we will launch the product next week.
  我們已投注數個月的心血在這項產品上，如果一切按照計劃進行，可以在下週正式發表產品。
- Let's plan a vacation trip for next week.
  我們計劃下週去度假吧。
- Many people plan on doing adventurous things when they are young, but they never actually do it.
  許多人在年輕時打算做冒險的事，但總是沒達成。

---

planet ['plæn.ɪt] *n.* 行星

- Mars is the planet after Earth in our Solar System.
  火星在太陽系中是排在地球之後的一顆行星。

---

plant [plænt]

① *n.* 植物

② *n.* 工廠

③ *v.* 栽種

- Many plants grow in the forest.
  許多植物生長在森林裡。
- Someone from the plant called and asked for Dr. Robinson.
  有人從工廠打電話來找羅賓森博士。
- My grandpa likes to plant trees in the yard.
  我的爺爺喜歡在院子裡種樹。

plate [pleɪt]

① *n.* 盤子；一盤食物

② *v.* 鍍上；用（金、銀等）電鍍

▶ Please set out four plates on the table for dinner.
請在桌上擺四個晚餐用的盤子。

▶ On his retirement, Daniel received a watch plated in gold.
他退休時，丹尼爾領到一只鍍金的手錶。

platform [ˈplæt.fɔːrm] *n.* 平台；月台；講台

▶ We can see the entire valley from this platform.
我們可以從這平台上看到整個村莊。

---

play [pleɪ]

① *v.* 玩耍

實用片語與搭配字

play with sth; play along; play fair; play your cards right
考慮（想法或計畫），玩弄，假意順從；公平競爭，公平待遇；處理得當

② *n.*（輕）歌劇；戲劇

實用片語與搭配字

come into play
開始活動，投入使用，起作用

▶ I like to play with my dog after school.
我喜歡在放學後和我的狗玩。

▶ Benjamin played his cards right and he managed to get the promotion even though many candidates were better suited.
儘管有更合適的升遷人選，但班傑明因處事得當獲得升遷的機會。

▶ We are watching a play at the theater.
我們在歌劇院觀賞一場戲劇。

▶ The law to protect animals will come into play next year, and then police will be able to arrest any person who abuses an animal.
保障動物權益的法律即將在明年生效，到時警察就能逮捕任何虐待動物的人。

---

player [ˈpleɪ.ɚ] *n.* 選手

▶ That baseball player is very famous.
那位棒球選手非常有名。

99

playful [ˈpleɪ.fəl] *adj.* 愛玩的；嬉戲的

▶ Our little puppy is very playful, and the kids love him.
我們的小狗非常愛玩，這些小孩很愛牠。

---

playground [ˈpleɪ.ɡraʊnd]

n.（兒童的）遊樂場；運動場

▶ All the kids will meet at the playground.
所有小孩都會在遊樂場聚集。

pleasant [ˈplez.ənt]

adj. 宜人的；愉快的；和氣的

▶ The weather is very pleasant today; let's go outside!
今天的天氣非常舒服，我們出去吧！

P

please [pli:z] *v.* 使高興；取悅

實用片語與搭配字

please yourself 請便

► It is not easy to please my parents.
要取悅我的父母並不容易。

► You can stay at home, or you can come with us to the party. Please yourself. I don't care either way.
你可以待在家或跟我們去派對。你選哪個都可以，請隨意。

---

pleased [pli:zd] *adj.* 高興的；滿意的

實用片語與搭配字

be pleased to do sth 樂於做

► The cook was pleased with the meal he made.
廚師對自己做的餐點感到滿意。

► My mom is always pleased to help the church collect old blankets for the homeless.
我媽媽總是樂意幫助教會蒐集舊毛毯給無家可歸的人。

---

pleasure [ˈpleʒ.ɚ] *n.* 愉快；樂事

實用片語與搭配字

with pleasure 非常樂意

► It will be my pleasure to host Dr. Ridge when he visits our city.
瑞居博士來訪時，我很樂意接待他。

► It is with pleasure that we welcome you to the university as first year students, the dean said.
系主任說：「我們非常開心歡迎你們成為本校的大一新鮮人。」

---

plus [plʌs]

① *prep.* 加上；外加

② *n.* 優勢；好處

③ *adj.* 正的；有利的

► This travel package includes airfare plus three nights in a hotel.
這個旅遊套裝行程包含了機票，再加上三晚的旅館費。

► If you want to get this job, speaking a second language is a plus.
如果你想得到這個工作，會說第二語言是個優勢。

► We missed our bus, but on the plus side, now we have time to look around.
我們錯過了巴士，但是往好處看，現在我們有時間到處看看。

---

pocket [ˈpɑː.kɪt]

① *n.* 口袋

► He put his cell phone in his pocket.
他把他的手機放在口袋裡。

實用片語與搭配字

in sb's pocket 被（某人）控制

▶ The police officer was in the mafia boss' pocket and he was paid a lot of money to give information to the criminals.
警察受黑手黨控制，他接受賄賂將許多訊息透露給罪犯。

② *v.* 把…裝入口袋

▶ I always pocket my wallet away.
我總是把錢包放進口袋收好。

---

poem [ˈpoʊ.əm] *n.* 詩

▶ Eric wrote a poem for his girlfriend on her birthday.
艾瑞克在他女友生日時為她寫了一首詩。

---

poet [ˈpoʊ.ət] *n.* 詩人

▶ This literature class will focus on poets from the 16th century.
這堂文學課會專注在十六世紀的詩人。

---

poetry [ˈpoʊ.ə.tri] *n.* 詩文

▶ She loves to read and write poetry.
她喜愛讀詩和寫詩。

---

point [pɔɪnt]

P

① *v.* 指出；把…指向

▶ I pointed a flashlight in the dark.
我在黑暗中用手電筒指出方向。

實用片語與搭配字

point (sb / sth) out 指明，指出

▶ The scientist pointed out that previous research on the age of the dinosaur fossil was wrong.
科學家指出，之前這份針對恐龍化石年代的研究有誤。

② *n.* 尖端

▶ The point of a sword is sharp.
劍的尖端是銳利的。

Exercise 49

I. Choose and write the correct word. Change the form of the word when necessary.

1	pipe (n.) plain (n.)	The city is putting new water __________ into old neighborhoods to reduce the amount of water lost through leaks in the old system.
2	player (n.) pitch (n.)	That was an impressive performance from such a young tennis __________.
3	pocket (n.) plan (n.)	The manager thought Mr. Lee was a reliable person and told him all about the new __________.
4	please (v.) point (v.)	To take a picture, simply __________ your camera at the subject and press the button.
5	poem (n.) poet (n.)	A __________ can convert ordinary words into a meaningful and effective piece of writing.

II. Multiple choices.

(　　) 1. If we don't do something to stop pollution, we may eventually kill most of the life forms living on our __________ today.

(A) plain　(B) plant　(C) planet　(D) pitch

(　　) 2. Polar bears use sea ice as a floating __________ to stand on when they catch seals to eat.

(A) platform　(B) plain　(C) plate　(D) plant

(　　) 3. I accidentally sat on my cell phone and broke it because I forgot it was in the back __________ of my jeans.

(A) plain　(B) pocket　(C) planet　(D) pleasant

(　　) 4. The children spent a __________ afternoon playing outside in the back yard.

(A) plus　(B) pleased　(C) pleasant　(D) plain

(　　) 5. A visit to a good __________ is a real treat; offering our children fun and adventure.

(A) play　(B) platform　(C) plant　(D) playground

poison [ˈpɔɪ.zən]

① *n.* 毒；毒藥

② *v.* 在…下毒；使中毒

▶ How can you tell which snakes have poison and which don't?
你如何分辨哪種蛇有毒而哪種沒有？

▶ The evil witch poisoned an apple and gave it to Snow White.
壞巫婆將蘋果下了毒然後給白雪公主吃。

---

police [pəˈliːs]

① *n.* 警察

② *v.* 維持…的治安；巡查

▶ We saw police all around the city.
我們在整個城市到處都看到警察。

▶ The big crowd was policed by officers.
警察在這一大群群眾中維持治安。

---

policeman / cop [pəˈliːs.mən / kɑːp]

n. 警察

▶ The policeman caught the thief.
這位警察抓到了那個小偷。

---

policy [ˈpɑː.lə.si] *n.* 政策；方針

實用片語與搭配字

policy-making 制定政策

▶ What is the company's policy on taking vacation time?
這家公司對於休假的政策是什麼？

▶ Policy-making is the job of government, but they will sometimes ask public opinion before making a final decision.
制定政策是政府的工作，但有時在做最終決策前，政府會詢問大眾的意見。

95

polite [pəˈlaɪt] *adj.* 有禮貌的；客氣的

▶ It's important to be polite to your elders.
對長者有禮貌是很重要的。

---

pond [pɑːnd] *n.* 池塘

▶ There are lots of fish in the pond.
這個池塘裡有許多魚。

---

pool [puːl]

① *n.* 游泳池

② *v.* 為…集合（資金、資源）

▶ Everybody went to swim in the pool.
大家都到游泳池裡游泳。

▶ My parents pool their money together.
我的父母把他們的錢集中起來。

poor [pʊr] *adj.* 可憐的；貧窮的

實用片語與搭配字

be poor in sth 在…方面貧乏

▶ The poor man had nothing to eat.
這個可憐的男人沒有東西可以吃。

▶ I am poor in Math and I always need my friend to help me to understand the problems.
我的數學不好，所以總是需要朋友幫我解題。

---

popcorn [ˈpɑːp.kɔːrn] *n.* 爆米花

▶ I eat popcorn at the movie theater.
我在電影院吃爆米花。

101 100 98

popular [ˈpɑː.pjə.lɚ] *adj.* 流行的；受歡迎的

▶ This is the most popular song of the year.
這是今年最流行的歌。

---

98 97

population [ˌpɑː.pjəˈleɪ.ʃən] *n.* 人口

▶ The population of Canada is more than 30 million.
加拿大的人口超過三千萬。

---

pork [pɔːrk] *n.* 豬肉

▶ Is the meat in this sandwich beef or pork?
這個三明治中的肉是牛肉還是豬肉？

---

port [pɔːrt] *n.* 港口

▶ Let's go to the port and watch the ships come in.
我們一起到港口去看船進港吧。

---

pose [poʊz]

① *v.* 擺姿勢

② *n.* 姿勢

▶ During the fashion show, you will walk to the end of the runway and pose there.
在時尚秀中，你要走到伸展台的盡頭擺姿勢。

▶ Audrey didn't like her pose in the first picture.
奧茱莉不喜歡她在第一張照片中的姿勢。

103

position [pəˈzɪʃ.ən]

① *n.* 地點

實用片語與搭配字

be in a position to do sth 能做…

▶ His position was near the stadium.
他的位置離體育場很近。

▶ The rich man was in a position to help the poor students and he did so by paying for their tuition.
這位富人有能力幫助貧困的學生，他幫他們付學費。

② *v.* 安放；使駐紮

▶ All the players were positioned behind the line.
所有選手被安置在這條線的後方。

---

positive [ˈpɑː.zə.t̬ɪv]

① *adj.* 積極的；正面的

② *n.* 優點；正面

▶ Andrew is a very positive person. He always expects good things to happen.
安德魯是一個很正面積極的人，他總是期待有好事發生。

▶ One positive of taking the train is that we can stand up and walk around.
搭火車的好處之一就是我們可以站起來到處走動。

---

possibility [ˌpɑː.səˈbɪl.ə.t̬i] *n.* 可能性

▶ Imagine the possibilities if we added another floor to our house!
想像在我們的房子增建一層樓的可能性。

possible [ˈpɑː.sə.bəl] *adj.* 可能的

實用片語與搭配字

anything's possible 一切皆有可能

▶ It is possible that the machine is broken.
這台機器有可能壞掉了。

▶ James was a sickly child, but when he became an astronaut, he truly believed that anything was possible.
詹姆斯曾是個病懨懨的小孩，但當他成為太空人後，他真心相信一切皆有可能。

---

post [poʊst]

① *n.* 郵件；郵寄

② *v.* 郵寄；投寄

③ *n.* 杆；樁

④ *v.* 貼公告；宣告

⑤ *adv.* 火速地

▶ I'll send the package by post tomorrow.
我明天會郵寄這個包裹。

▶ Please post this letter as soon as possible.
請盡快寄出這封信。

▶ You can tie the dog's leash to that fence post so he won't run away.
你可以將這隻狗的鍊子綁在那個欄杆上，讓牠不會亂跑。

▶ The political ads were posted all over the city.
在城裡到處都張貼著這則政治廣告。

▶ Please finish this task post haste! It was due yesterday!
請火速完成這項工作！昨天已經是截止日了！

⑥ *n.* 崗位；職位

⑦ *v.* 使駐守；派駐

▶ Luke's father spent three years at a military post in Japan.
路克的父親在日本的軍事基地服務了三年。

▶ Guards were posted outside the hospital room to protect the president.
保鑣駐守在醫院病房外保護總統。

---

postcard [ˈpoʊst.kɑːrd] *n.* 明信片

▶ Can you please send me a postcard when you go on vacation?
你去旅行時可以寄給我一張明信片嗎？

---

postman [ˈpoʊst.mən] *n.* 郵差

▶ She gave her mail to the postman.
她把她的郵件交給了郵差。

---

pot [pɑːt]

① *n.* 鍋；壺

實用片語與搭配字

pots of sth 大量的…

② *v.* 把（植物）栽入盆中

▶ How can you cook without any pots?
你煮東西怎麼能不用任何鍋子？

▶ Some people believe that there are pots of gold at the end of the rainbow.
有些人相信在彩虹尾端有大量的黃金。

▶ Lisa keeps potted plants on the balcony of her apartment.
麗莎把植物栽在花盆裡放在她公寓的陽台上。

---

potato [pəˈteɪ.t̬oʊ] *n.* 馬鈴薯

實用片語與搭配字

couch potato 愛窩在沙發裡看電視的人

▶ Annie makes a delicious potato salad.
安妮會做好吃的馬鈴薯沙拉。

▶ It is time for you to stop being a couch potato watching hours of TV everyday, and to start exercising.
你應該停止每天在沙發上看電視，該開始運動了。

---

pound [paʊnd]

① *n.* （重量）磅；英鎊

② *v.* 連續重擊；猛烈襲擊

實用片語與搭配字

pound away at sth / sb
對…施加壓力，指責，批評，勸說

▶ Our Thanksgiving turkey weighs 12 pounds!
我們的感恩節火雞足足有十二磅重！

▶ I can hear the rain pounding on the roof, so I don't want to go outside.
我可以聽見屋頂上的滂沱雨聲，所以我不想出門。

▶ The miners pounded away at the rock bit by bit to reveal the huge diamond inside.
採礦者一點一點擊打礦石，直到裡頭的鑽石出現。

power [ˈpaʊ.ɚ]

① *n.* 力量；能力

實用片語與搭配字

with great power comes great responsibility

能力越強，責任越大

② *v.* 給…提供動力

實用片語與搭配字

power sth up

（使）起動，（使）積蓄能量，（使）養精蓄銳

▸ She has the power to carry heavy things.

她有力氣提重物。

▸ Leaders should remember that with great power comes great responsibility, but many just like the power.

領導者應該將「能力越強，責任越大」這個格言謹記在心，但多數人只想掌權。

▸ The batteries will power the remote controller.

這些電池能啟動遙控器。

▸ The large ship powered its engines up and started sailing out of the port for its journey around the world.

大船啟動引擎，準備出港開始環遊世界之旅。

P

Exercise 50

I. Choose and write the correct word. Change the form of the word when necessary.

1	postman (n.) postcard (n.)	He tried many different jobs; in the end he became a __________.
2	pound (n.) power (n.)	How would you feel about them building a nuclear __________ plant in this area?
3	positive (adj.) popular (adj.)	Your __________ attitude towards life will contribute to ensuring your success in all you do.
4	popcorn (n.) population (n.)	Growing levels of pollution represent a serious health hazard to the local __________.
5	poison (v.) position (v.)	The air around our cities is being increasingly __________ by the fumes from automobiles.

II. Multiple choices.

(　　) 1. We __________ the plants on our balcony so that they would hang over the railings.
(A) posted　(B) posed　(C) positioned　(D) pooled

(　　) 2. New technology has made it __________ to communicate more easily.
(A) positive　(B) possible　(C) popular　(D) polite

(　　) 3. Please __________ up this advertisement for our concert in your shop window.
(A) post　(B) pose　(C) pool　(D) power

(　　) 4. The government is being roundly criticized by the citizens for its education __________.
(A) position　(B) population　(C) policy　(D) popcorn

(　　) 5. It's not __________ to interrupt a speaker with frequent questions.
(A) positive　(B) popular　(C) possible　(D) polite

Unit 51

96

powerful [ˈpaʊ.ɚ.fəl]

adj. 強大的；有力量的；有權威的

▶ This medicine is very powerful, so don't take too much.
這藥是很強效的，所以不要服用過量。

practice [ˈpræk.tɪs]

① *n.* 養成…的習慣

② *v.* 練習；訓練

實用片語與搭配字

practice makes perfect 熟能生巧

▶ I have a practice of cleaning my room daily.
我有每天整理房間的習慣。

▶ We must practice what we learn in class.
我們必須要練習在課堂上所學到的東西。

▶ If you fail at doing something right the first time, always remember that practice makes perfect.
如果你第一次嘗試就失敗，要謹記「熟能生巧」的道理。

---

praise [preɪz]

① *v.* 讚美；歌頌

② *n.* 稱讚；讚揚

▶ Jane likes to praise God at church.
珍喜歡在教堂裡讚美神。

▶ Children need regular praise from their parents.
小孩子需要父母經常稱讚他們。

103

pray [preɪ] *v.* 祈禱

▶ We need to pray for those affected by the earthquake.
我們需要為那些被地震影響的人們禱告。

---

prefer [prɪˈfɝː] *v.* 更喜愛；寧可

▶ Do you prefer fish or chicken for dinner?
你晚餐比較喜歡吃魚還是雞？

prepare [prɪˈper] *v.* 準備

實用片語與搭配字

prepare the ground for sb / sth
做好準備

▶ The pastor will prepare a message for Sunday.
牧師要為週日準備一篇講道信息。

▶ The president's aides left earlier to prepare the ground for his visit abroad to make sure everything went according to plan.
總統的助理提早離開為出國參訪做好準備，以確保計畫能順利進行。

P

presence [ˈprez.əns] *n.* 出席；存在

▶ Your presence is requested at our wedding next month.
我們下個月的婚禮需要你出席。

---

present [ˈprez.ənt]

① *adj.* 出席的；在場的

② *n.* 現在；目前

實用片語與搭配字

at present 現在，目前

③ *n.* 禮物

④ *v.* 贈送

實用片語與搭配字

present sth to sb 把…贈送給…

▶ How many club members were present at the last meeting?
上個會議有多少社團會員出席呢？

▶ At present, Gina is a high school teacher.
現在吉娜是位高中老師。

▶ One of the most talked about topics at present is global warming and what people can do to reduce CO_2 emissions.
現今最熱門的話題之一是全球暖化和人類如何減少二氧化碳的排放。

▶ Did you get Christine a present for her birthday?
你買生日禮物給克莉絲汀了嗎？

▶ Kris was presented with an award for citizen of the year.
克里斯被頒贈年度優良公民獎。

▶ The mayor presented the medal for bravery to the fire-fighter for risking his life to save a family from a burning house.
市長頒發英勇獎牌給消防員，以表彰他們在一場火災中英勇搶救困在房子的一家人。

---

president [ˈprez.ɪ.dənt]

n. 總統；會長；董事長

▶ Did you hear the president's speech about the war last night?
昨晚你聽了總統對於這個戰爭的演說嗎？

102

press [pres]

① *n.* 記者；報刊；新聞界；熨燙

② *v.* 按壓

▶ The actress couldn't escape the press anytime she left her house.
無論何時離開家，這位女演員都無法躲開記者。

▶ If you want to open the door, just press this button.
如果你想打開這扇門，只要按下這個按鈕就可以。

實用片語與搭配字

press on / ahead （不顧困難地）繼續進行

▶ Some of the climbers on Mount Everest decided to take a rest during the storm, but a few climbers decided to press on.
有些在聖母峰的登山者決定在暴風雪中暫時歇息，有些則決定繼續前進。

---

pretty ['prɪt̬.i]

① *adj.* 漂亮的

實用片語與搭配字

be not just a pretty face 不只是虛有其表

② *adv.* 相當；頗

實用片語與搭配字

pretty well / much 差不多，幾乎全部地

▶ A pretty girl stood across the street.
一位漂亮的女孩站在對街。

▶ Miss Universe for 2017 has a PhD in Economics, so she is not just a pretty face.
2017 年的環球小姐有經濟學博士學位，所以她不只是有張美麗的臉蛋。

▶ He is a pretty good drummer.
他是一位相當棒的鼓手。

▶ I know my neighbors pretty well and I am sure they will rent you a room for a few months.
我跟我的鄰居很熟，我確定他們會把房間租給你住幾個月。

100

price [praɪs]

① *n.* 價錢；價格

實用片語與搭配字

at any price 不惜任何代價

② *v.* 給…定價

▶ The price for this meal is cheap.
這頓飯的價錢很便宜。

▶ Some people will try to get what they want at any price, even if they have to do something criminal.
有些人會不惜任何代價，只為了得到想要的東西，甚至可能做涉及犯罪的事。

▶ These hats are priced with a discount.
這些帽子的價錢都有打折。

---

pride [praɪd]

① *n.* 自豪；得意；驕傲

實用片語與搭配字

take pride in sth; pride onself on sth
為…自豪；對…引以為榮

② *v.* 以…自豪；得意

▶ Most parents take pride in their children.
大部分的父母會以孩子自豪。

▶ The new community center is a huge hit and the mayor can take pride in this project to bring people together.
新的社區中心很成功，能凝聚居民的向心力，市長也為此感到自豪。

▶ Terry prides himself in his classic car, which he restored himself.
泰瑞以他那輛自己修復的經典老爺車為傲。

P

prince [prɪns] *n.* 王子；親王

▸ The handsome prince rode away on his horse.
這個英俊的王子騎著他的駿馬離開了。

princess [prɪnˈses / ˈprɪn.ses] *n.* 公主；王妃

▸ Many men asked the king for permission to marry Princess Elizabeth.
許多男士徵求國王的同意要娶伊莉莎白公主。

principal [ˈprɪn.sə.pəl]

① *adj.* 首要的

② *n.* 校長

▸ Your principal focus will be to create online ads.
你首要的重點是要建立網路廣告。

▸ The principal stood up and gave a speech to the whole school.
這位校長站起來對著全校發表談話。

principle [ˈprɪn.sə.pəl] *n.* 原則

▸ He is an honest man with strong principles.
他是個誠實又堅持原則的人。

102

print [prɪnt]

① *v.* 列印

② *n.* 印刷

▸ I printed the report for my boss to read.
我把這份報告印出來給老闆閱讀。

▸ The invitations were done by hand and not by print.
這些邀請函是用手寫的，不是印刷的。

printer [ˈprɪn.t̬ɚ] *n.* 印表機

▸ My printer is broken; can I use yours to print this document?
我的印表機壞了；我可以用你的印這份文件嗎？

prison [ˈprɪz.ən] *n.* 監牢

▸ If you are caught with drugs, you will go to prison.
如果你被捉到攜帶毒品，是會進監牢的。

prisoner [ˈprɪz.ən.ɚ] *n.* 囚犯

▸ Three prisoners escaped from the jail last night.
昨晚有三名囚犯從監獄裡逃出來。

private [ˈpraɪ.vət] *adj.* 私人的；私下的

▸ You can't go in here; it's private property!
你不能進去，這裡是私人地產！

實用片語與搭配字

in private 私下的

▶ When my supervisor asked to talk to me in private, I knew something was wrong.
當我的上司要求與我私下約談，我就知道大事不妙了。

---

prize [praɪz]

① *n.* 獎品；獎金

② *v.* 重視；珍視

▶ Everyone who enters the contest has a chance to win a prize.
每個進到比賽的人都有機會贏得獎項。

▶ Jack prized his new sports car.
傑克很重視他的新跑車。

---

probably [ˈprɑː.bə.bli]

adv. 大概；或許；很可能

▶ He probably studies hard every day.
他大概每天都很用功讀書。

---

problem [ˈprɑː.bləm] *n.* 數學習題；問題

實用片語與搭配字

have a problem with sth / sb; no problem

認為…令人討厭（或無禮）; 沒問題，沒什麼

▶ Here are some math problems to solve.
這裡有一些數學問題要解決。

▶ The best thing to do if you have a problem with your supervisor, is to discuss it in private and not go behind their back.
如果你對上司有意見，最好私下和他溝通，而不是在背後議論。

Exercise 51

I. Choose and write the correct word. Change the form of the word when necessary.

1	practice (n.) praise (n.)	All the guests are full of __________ for the staff and service they received.
2	prefer (v.) prepare (v.)	The girl studied for three solid days in order to __________ for her final exam.
3	president (n.) present (n.)	Everyone was silent as the __________ announced the winner of the competition.
4	powerful (adj.) pretty (adj.)	A __________ earthquake struck the north of this island early this morning.
5	principal (n.) principle (n.)	The school is based on the fundamental __________ that each child should develop his or her full potential.

II. Multiple choices.

( ) 1. It is difficult for movie celebrities to have a __________ life away from the cameras.
(A) principal (B) private (C) pretty (D) powerful

( ) 2. The __________ reason why she quit her job was because she didn't feel she had any future there.
(A) principal (B) powerful (C) present (D) private

( ) 3. The little girl smiled with __________ when her grandmother complimented her on the skirt she had made in sewing class.
(A) prize (B) price (C) presence (D) pride

( ) 4. This morning, the guards found a __________ who had hung himself in his jail cell.
(A) prison (B) presence (C) prisoner (D) printer

( ) 5. I don’t see the point of waiting for her; she’s __________ not coming.
(A) private (B) principal (C) probably (D) pretty

Unit 52

103 100

produce [prə'du:s] *v.* 生產；創作

▶ It takes a lot of hard work to produce a magazine.
製作一本雜誌需要許多的努力。

produce ['prɑ:.du:s] *n.* 農產品；產品

▶ Max Supermarket sells the best fresh produce in town.
邁克思超級市場在鎮上銷售最好的新鮮農產品。

---

producer [prə'du:.sɚ]
n. 製作人；生產者；製造者

▶ Who is the producer of this hit TV series?
這部熱門電視劇的製作人是誰？

---

101 97 95

progress ['prɑ:.gres] *n.* 進展；前進

實用片語與搭配字

in progress 正在進行中

▶ The hiker's progress up the mountain was slow because of the weather.
因為天氣的關係，這位登山者爬山的進度很慢。

▶ The reporter heard there was a robbery in progress at the bank and she rushed over to cover the story.
記者接到有銀行搶案正在進行中的消息，為了撰寫報導，她立刻直奔而去。

progress [prə'gres] *v.* 進步；改進

▶ How do you expect to progress if you don't practice.
你若不練習，怎能期待會進步。

103

project ['prɑ:.dʒekt] *n.* 方案；企劃

▶ There will be three students in each group for this project.
這個研究案中，每一組會有三名學生。

project [prə'dʒekt]
① *v.* 預計；推算
② *v.* 放映；投射（影、像或光）

實用片語與搭配字

project one's voice 扯開喉嚨，放聲

▶ Who do you project will win the competition?
你預計誰會贏得這場比賽？

▶ I need a machine to project my presentation for the group.
我需要一台機器來向這個小組播放我的簡報。

▶ During a presentation you should project your voice towards the audience in a loud and clear manner.
報告的時候，你應該放聲拉高分貝並清晰地傳遞給觀眾。

P

promise ['prɑː.mɪs]

① *n.* 承諾；諾言

實用片語與搭配字

keep / break a promise 遵守 / 違背諾言

② *v.* 允諾；答應

▶ I'll try to finish all my homework and that's a promise!
我保證我會盡力完成我全部的功課！

▶ If you make a promise to a friend, you should keep that promise no matter what.
若你答應了朋友，無論如何都應該遵守諾言。

▶ Sally promises to love Jim forever.
莎莉承諾會永遠愛吉姆。

pronounce [prə'naʊns] *v.* 發音

▶ Please pronounce your words more clearly.
請將你的單字發音更清楚一點。

  100

propose [prə'poʊz] *v.* 提議；求婚

實用片語與搭配字

propose a toast 提議為…乾杯

▶ Charles proposes we wait for the whole team to arrive.
查爾斯提議我們等整個隊伍抵達。

▶ During the year-end party we proposed a toast to my boss, who was retiring, and wished him good luck.
我們在吃尾牙時向即將退休的老闆敬酒，並給予他祝福。

protect [prə'tekt] *v.* 保護；防護

▶ Wear something warm to protect you from the cold.
穿暖和一點來保護你不會受風寒。

proud [praʊd] *adj.* 驕傲的；自負的

實用片語與搭配字

do sb proud 為…爭光

▶ Jaclyn is very proud of all her art work.
賈克琳對她所有的藝術作品都感到非常自豪。

▶ Bill did his parents proud when he graduated from medical school.
比爾從醫學院畢業，他為父母爭光。

prove [pruːv] *v.* 證明

實用片語與搭配字

prove sb wrong 證明（某人）錯了

▶ I can prove that this is real.
我能夠證明這是真的。

▶ Paul proved his peers wrong when he graduated from college despite their predictions that he would fail.
儘管同儕預測保羅不會從大學畢業，但他證明他們錯了。

provide [prəˈvaɪd] *v.* 提供

實用片語與搭配字

provide for sb 為（某人）提供生活所需

▶ This webpage provides all the prices of these hotels.
這個網頁提供了這些旅館的全部住房價格。

▶ If you want to get married and have a family, you have to make sure that you can provide for them financially.
如果你想結婚成家，你必須確定你可以做為家庭的經濟支柱。

---

public [ˈpʌb.lɪk]

① *adj.* 公共的

實用片語與搭配字

be in the public eye 廣為人知

② *n.* 公眾；大眾

實用片語與搭配字

in public 公開地

▶ Please close the doors for public safety.
為了公共安全，請關上門。

▶ Politicians are always in the public eye and they face a lot of criticism every day.
政治家總是廣為人知，他們每天都面臨許多批判。

▶ The public is very happy right now.
群眾現在都非常快樂。

▶ Never humiliate or scold someone in public.
絕對不要公開地羞辱或對他人說教。

P

---

pudding [ˈpʊd.ɪŋ] *n.* 布丁

▶ I'd like to eat another bowl of pudding.
我想要再吃一碗布丁。

---

pull [pʊl]

① *v.* 拉；拖

實用片語與搭配字

pull sth / sb apart; pull back; pull together
使分開；改變主意，退出；同心協力

② *n.* 拉力；引力

▶ She pulled the table to the corner.
她把那張桌子拉到角落。

▶ Employees and managers decided to pull together as a team to solve the issue in the company.
經理和員工決定同心協力，一起解決公司的問題。

▶ I felt a strong pull on my jacket.
我感到有股強大的力量拉扯我的夾克。

---

pump [pʌmp]

① *n.* 打氣筒；唧筒；幫浦

② *v.* 打氣；用幫浦抽（水等）

▶ I need to buy a bicycle pump before tomorrow morning.
我需要在明早前買一個自行車打氣筒。

▶ Can you help pump up my bicycle tires?
你能幫我的自行車輪胎打氣嗎？

pumpkin [ˈpʌmp.kɪn] *n.* 南瓜

▶ You can cook a pumpkin in so many ways.
你可以用好多種方法來烹煮南瓜。

punish [ˈpʌn.ɪʃ] *v.* 懲罰；處罰

▶ The judge punished the robber by putting him in prison.
法官將這搶匪關進監獄裡做為懲罰。

punishment [ˈpʌn.ɪʃ.mənt] *n.* 處罰

▶ After the student received his punishment, he never cheated again.
這名學生受到處罰後，就再也不作弊了。

pupil [ˈpjuː.pəl] *n.* 學生；學徒

▶ Carol's pupil won first prize in a music competition.
卡蘿的學生在一場音樂比賽中得了第一名。

puppet [ˈpʌp.ɪt] *n.* 木偶；玩偶

▶ Hannah wants to use puppets in her skit.
漢娜想要在她的短劇中用木偶表演。

puppy [ˈpʌp.i] *n.* 小狗

▶ Laura's puppy is so cute and active.
蘿拉的小狗可愛又活潑。

purple [ˈpɝː.pəl]

① *adj.* 紫色的

② *n.* 紫色

▶ Everyone must wear purple socks.
每個人都要穿紫色的襪子。

▶ Purple is my favorite color!
紫色是我最喜歡的顏色！

102 97

purpose [ˈpɝː.pəs] *n.* 目的

實用片語與搭配字

on purpose; serve a purpose
故意地；適合需要，管用

▶ His purpose for traveling was to visit friends.
他旅遊的目的是要拜訪朋友。

▶ Mike told a lie on purpose and regretted doing so afterwards.
麥可故意撒謊，事後卻感到懊悔不已。

purse [pɝːs] *n.* 錢包；手提包

▶ Oh no, I left my purse in the restaurant.
糟糕！我把錢包掉在餐廳裡了。

push [pʊʃ]

① *v.* 推

▶ John pushed the table closer to the wall.
約翰將桌子推至靠牆的地方。

實用片語與搭配字

push sb around; push for sth

擺布 (某人); 努力爭取

② *n.* 推；推動

▸ When people push you around, you should push back or they will start taking advantage of you.
你不該受人擺佈，否則你將會開始被人利用。

▸ The door is stuck; give it a little push.
這門卡住了，推一下。

P

Exercise 52

I. Choose and write the correct word. Change the form of the word when necessary.

1	progress (n.) project (n.)	We are currently working on a ＿＿＿＿＿ about the effect of pollution on plankton for our biology class.
2	promise (v.) propose (v.)	After he got arrested for drunk driving, he ＿＿＿＿＿ to stop drinking, but two weeks later he was at the bar again.
3	proud (adj.) public (adj.)	The government aims to improve ＿＿＿＿＿ services, especially education.
4	punishment (n.) purpose (n.)	Many professionals believe that spanking a child is no longer an acceptable form of ＿＿＿＿＿.
5	protect (v.) prove (v.)	Dennis tried to ＿＿＿＿＿ to his girlfriend that he had changed, but she wouldn't believe him.

II. Multiple choices.

(　　) 1. These documents will ＿＿＿＿＿ you with all the information you need to write your report.

(A) propose　(B) promise　(C) produce　(D) provide

(　　) 2. Teachers should always explain the ＿＿＿＿＿ of the activities they have their students take part in.

(A) propose　(B) purpose　(C) project　(D) promise

(　　) 3. It took the two men over three hours to ＿＿＿＿＿ all the water out of their flooded basement.

(A) push　(B) pull　(C) pump　(D) provide

(　　) 4. We're very proud that a ＿＿＿＿＿ from our school has won the prize.

(A) pupil　(B) producer　(C) puppy　(D) puppet

(　　) 5. I don't think there's any difference in the way you ＿＿＿＿＿ these two words.

(A) protect　(B) progress　(C) pronounce　(D) puzzle

Unit 53

put [pʊt] *v.* 放置

實用片語與搭配字

put oneself in sb's shoes; put sth aside; put sth / sb before sb
處在（某人的）角度考慮；擱置；把…看得比…重要

▶ Where did you put the textbook?
你把教科書放在哪裡？

▶ You should always put yourself into others' shoes because it is important to be empathetic.
你應該要處在別人的角度思考，因為同理他人很重要。

---

puzzle [ˈpʌz.əl]

① *n.* 拼圖；解謎遊戲；智力遊戲

② *v.*（使）感到迷惑

▶ I'm trying to finish my 5000 piece puzzle.
我正試著完成我的五千片拼圖。

▶ Jacob looks puzzled as he watches someone park in his space.
雅各看見某個人要把車停在他的車位上時，他看起來很困惑。

---

quality [ˈkwɑː.lə.t̬i] *n.* 質量；品質

實用片語與搭配字

quality time; quality control
寶貴時光；品質管制

▶ This smartphone is not expensive because its quality is not very good.
這隻智慧型手機不貴，因為它的品質不是很好。

▶ It is important to spend quality time with your parents as they grow older.
當父母逐漸老去時，和他們在一起的寶貴時光很重要。

---

quantity [ˈkwɑːn.t̬ə.t̬i] *n.* 量；數量；分量

▶ If you want to have a big party, you'll need a large quantity of food.
如果你想辦一個大型派對，你會需要大量的食物。

---

quarter [ˈkwɑː.t̬ɚ]

① *n.* 一刻鐘；四分之一

② *v.* 把…分成四等分

▶ Let's meet at quarter past twelve.
我們十二點十五分見。

▶ Can you quarter this piece of beef?
你可以把這塊牛肉切成四份嗎？

---

queen [kwiːn] *n.* 皇后

實用片語與搭配字

drama queen 小題大做的人

▶ The queen was loved by the people.
這位皇后深受百姓愛戴。

▶ Mary is such a drama queen; she always overreacts when things are not going her way.
瑪莉是小題大作的人，當事情不順她的意，她總是反應過度。

question ['kwes.tʃən]

① *n.* 問題

實用片語與搭配字

be out of the question;
be a question of doing sth
不可能；有必要做…

② *v.* 詢問；審問

▶ The student wanted to ask many questions.
學生想要問很多問題。

▶ Going out on a school night is out of the question; my parents would never allow it.
父母從不允許我在上學日晚間外出。

▶ My mother questioned me about my homework.
我母親詢問有關我的作業。

quick [kwɪk]

① *adj.* 快速的

實用片語與搭配字

be quick to do sth; have a quick bite
立即做…; 迅速地吃了點東西

② *adv.* 迅速地

▶ My sister is good at basketball because she is quick.
我妹妹擅長打籃球，因為她動作很快。

▶ People who are quick to judge others usually have something to hide.
會迅速評斷他人的人通常都有不為人知的一面。

▶ Run quick to get that ball!
快跑去拿那顆球！

quiet ['kwaɪ.ə]

① *adj.* 安靜的

實用片語與搭配字

keep sth quiet （對…）守口如瓶

② *n.* 安靜；靜謐

③ *v.* （使）安靜；（使）平靜

實用片語與搭配字

Quiet down! 安靜下來！

▶ I like to study in quiet places.
我喜歡在安靜的地方讀書。

▶ The company tried to keep the debt scandal quiet, but someone leaked it to the media and now everyone knows.
公司試圖對負債醜聞守口如瓶，但還是被透漏給媒體，而現在已眾所皆知。

▶ Grandma doesn't like noise; she likes the quiet much more.
奶奶不喜歡吵鬧，她比較喜歡安靜。

▶ The father quieted his crying daughter.
這位父親安撫正在哭的女兒。

▶ The teacher asked the students to quiet down when the principal walked into the classroom.
當校長走進教室時，老師請學生們安靜下來。

quit [kwɪt] *v.* 離開；退出；放棄

▶ Kelly told me that she quit her job last Friday
凱莉告訴我她上星期五離職了。

quite [kwaɪt] *adv.* 相當地；很；頗

▶ Rebekah was quite right about everything.
蕾貝卡處理每件事都相當正確。

---

quiz [kwɪz]

① *n.* 小考；測驗

② *v.* 考問；對 ... 進行測驗

▶ The next math quiz will be held next week.
下次的數學小考將在下週。

▶ The teacher quizzed her students for more than one hour.
這位老師對她的學生進行超過一小時的測驗。

---

rabbit [ˈræb.ɪt] *n.* 兔子

▶ The man bought his children several rabbits to raise.
這位男士買了幾隻兔子給他的孩子飼養。

---

race [reɪs]

① *n.* 賽跑（比賽）

② *v.* 賽跑；速度競賽

③ *n.* 民族；人種

▶ Maggie ran in a race last Saturday.
瑪姬上個星期六參加了一場賽跑。

▶ Do you want to race me to the top of the hill?
你想要跟我賽跑看誰先跑到山頂嗎？

▶ We should treat all races with respect.
我們應該尊重所有的人種。

---

radio [ˈreɪ.di.oʊ]

① *n.* 廣播節目；收音機

② *v.* 用無線電發送（資訊）

▶ I listen to the radio every day.
我每天都收聽廣播節目。

▶ She radioed the station for help.
她用無線電向站台尋求幫助。

---

railroad [ˈreɪl.roʊd] *n.* 鐵路

▶ The new railroad makes travel much more convenient.
這條新鐵路讓旅行更方便。

---

railway [ˈreɪl.weɪ] *n.* 鐵路

▶ They are building a railway across the country.
他們在建造一條橫跨全國的鐵路。

---

rain [reɪn]

① *n.* 雨

② *v.* 下雨

▶ You should stay out of the rain.
你應該躲一下雨。

▶ It rained a lot last week.
上個禮拜下了很多雨。

rainbow [ˈreɪn.boʊ] *n.* 彩虹

實用片語與搭配字

come rain or shine; take a rain check (on sth); it's raining cats and dogs
無論如何；(婉拒邀請)下次吧；傾盆大雨

▶ Did you see that rainbow after the storm yesterday?
你昨天看見了暴風雨後的那道彩虹嗎？

▶ This event is important to your career; you should come rain or shine.
這個活動對你的事業很重要，無論如何你都該參加。

---

rainy [ˈreɪ.ni] *adj.* 多雨的；下雨的

▶ The weather has been rainy and cold for three weeks.
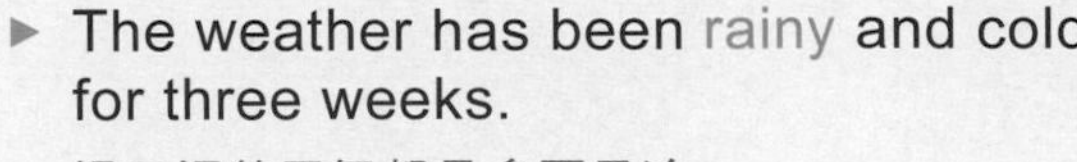
這三週的天氣都是多雨又冷。

---

101 98

raise [reɪz]

① *v.* 舉起

實用片語與搭配字

raise (a few) eyebrows;
raise sb's game
令人吃驚；努力改進

② *n.* 加薪；加價

▶ Raise your hand if you know the answer.
如果你知道答案就舉手。

▶ Amy's revealing outfit raised a few eyebrows at the party, but she did not seem to care.
艾咪的清涼穿著讓派對裡的人感到吃驚，但她似乎並不在意。

▶ Josh got a raise at work.
賈許在工作上獲得加薪了。

100

range [reɪndʒ]

① *n.* 系列；範圍

② *v.* (數量、種類等變化的)範圍

▶ The bank offers a wide range of services.
這個銀行提供很多樣的服務。

▶ The price of a new computer ranges from $100 to $300.
一台新電腦的價格介於一百美元到三百美元之間。

100

rapid [ˈræp.ɪd] *adj.* 迅速的；快的

▶ The children were excited as a rapid train went by.
當火車迅速開過的時候，孩子們都很興奮。

---

rare [rer] *adj.* 罕見的；不常發生的

▶ It's rare to see you in this exercise class.
我很少在這堂運動課看到你。

---

rat [ræt] *n.* 老鼠；大家鼠

▶ Is that a rat or a mouse?
那是一隻大鼠還是小鼠？

Exercise 53

I. Choose and write the correct word. Change the form of the word when necessary.

1	quality (n.)	Market research has shown us that customers want ________, not just low prices.
	quarter (n.)	
2	puzzle (v.)	I was ________ when my friend suddenly decided she didn't want to go to the concert because she had been talking about it all week.
	question (v.)	
3	quit (v.)	He's going to ________ his job next month because his salary is too low.
	quiz (v.)	
4	rapid (adj.)	It's difficult to keep up with the ________ pace of change.
	rare (adj.)	
5	radio (n.)	Guests at the health spa receive a ________ of beauty and fitness treatments.
	range (n.)	

II. Multiple choices.

(　　) 1. I'm sorry to bother you, but can you direct me to the ________ station?

(A) radio　(B) railway　(C) quarter　(D) rainbow

(　　) 2. Her coach encouraged her throughout the marathon ________ to keep on running.

(A) question　(B) quiz　(C) race　(D) quantity

(　　) 3. When I was at high school, I was ________ good at arts, but hopeless at science.

(A) quiet　(B) quality　(C) quarter　(D) quite

(　　) 4. The school has to rely on the goodwill of the parents to help it ________ money.

(A) raise　(B) range　(C) rapid　(D) rain

(　　) 5. When the sun shines through a light rain, it makes a ________.

(A) railway　(B) range　(C) rainbow　(D) quarter

Unit 54

101

rather [ˈræð.ɚ] *adv.* 寧願；而不是；更喜歡

實用片語與搭配字

rather than 寧願，而不是

▶ I'd rather go to the movies than to my math class.
我寧願去看電影也不想去上數學課。

▶ Rather than complaining about how lazy others are, why don't you just do it yourself.
與其抱怨他人懶惰，你為何不自己動手做。

---

reach [riːtʃ]

① *v.* 伸出手臂（去拿或觸摸）；伸手及到

實用片語與搭配字

reach out to sb; reach for the stars
向（某人）伸出援手；追求難以實現的東西

② *n.* （手臂的）伸出；伸手可及的距離

實用片語與搭配字

a reach of the imagination
大膽的想像

▶ Can you reach that box up there?
你可以伸手拿到上面那個盒子嗎？

▶ When May lost her husband in the car accident, all her friends reached out to comfort her.
當瑪莉的先生在車禍中過世，她所有的朋友都向她伸出援手。

▶ The basketball player used his long reach to grab the ball.
這名籃球選手伸長手飛身去抓球。

▶ The movie was so dramatic it took a reach of the imagination to believe the story.
這部電影太戲劇化，必須要有大膽的想像才能看懂這個故事。

---

read [riːd] *v.* 閱讀；讀到

實用片語與搭配字

read sb's mind; read sth into sth; read sth through
看出（某人的）心思；對…想得太多；快速瀏覽

▶ My father reads the newspaper every day.
我爸爸每天看報紙。

▶ Please tell me what you think about the idea because I can't read your mind.
我無法讀你的心思，所以請告訴我你對這點子的看法。

---

reader [ˈriː.dɚ] *n.* 讀者；讀物

▶ The reader was glued to his book.
這位讀者目不轉睛地讀他的書。

---

reading [ˈriː.dɪŋ] *n.* 閱讀

▶ Everyone did the reading in class today.
大家今天在課堂上都閱讀了。

ready [ˈred.i]

① *adj.* 準備好的；有準備的

實用片語與搭配字

be ready to do sth 隨時，願意做

② *v.* 預備

▶ Are you ready to go to the store?
你準備好要去那家店了嗎？

▶ Once you are ready to try out the new bicycle, let me know and we can go biking together.
當你準備好要試騎新的腳踏車時，和我說一聲，我們可以一起騎車。

▶ The test is coming, so you should ready yourself.
這場考試快到了，你應該預備好自己應試。

real [ˈriː.əl] *adj.* 真實的

▶ Do you believe Santa Claus is real?
你相信聖誕老公公是真的嗎？

reality [riˈæl.ə.tj] *n.* 現實

實用片語與搭配字

reality check; reality TV
面對現實，反思現實；電視真人秀

▶ We need to train young people to face reality.
我們必須訓練年輕人面對現實。

▶ Students who are good at studying might face a reality check when they start working because it is so different.
很會讀書的學生在出社會後，可能會了解到現實和學校很不同。

realize [ˈriː.ə.laɪz] *v.* 意識到；明白；認識到

▶ Tommy realized his car would run out of gas very soon.
湯米很快就察覺他的車子汽油快要用完了。

really [ˈriː.ə.li] *adv.* 真正地；確實地

▶ There really was a cat in the hat!
帽子裡真的有一隻貓！

reason [ˈriː.zən]

① *n.* 原因；理由

實用片語與搭配字

be reason of; within reason; see reason
由於，因為；合情合理，有道理；明白事理

② *v.* 推斷；判斷

▶ I had a reason to go downstairs, but now I forgot what it was!
我本來為了某事要下樓，但我現在忘了是為了什麼！

▶ During the holidays, it is wise to spend money within reason or you will run into a lot of debt.
度假時，合理的花錢才是睿智的選擇，否則你可能會陷入負債危機。

▶ I reasoned that she was telling the truth, so I believed her.
我推斷她說的是事實，所以我相信她了。

實用片語與搭配字

reason with sb 與（某人）講道理

▶ It is not worth it to reason with somebody who is not willing to listen to your opinion.
一個不願聆聽的人，不值得你對他說道理。

99

receive [rɪˈsiːv] *v.* 收到；得到

實用片語與搭配字

receive sth from sb 獲得

▶ Did you receive any mail today?
你今天收到任何郵件了嗎？

▶ The greatest gift I received from my parents is the ability to think independently.
我父母給我最好的禮物是教會我如何獨立思考。

---

recent [ˈriː.sənt] *adj.* 最近的；最新的

▶ I saw your photo in a recent copy of our magazine.
我在我們最新一期的雜誌上看到你的照片。

recently [ˈriː.sənt.li] *adv.* 最近；近來

▶ Those fresh cookies were baked recently.
那些新鮮的餅乾是最近才烘培的。

record [ˈrek.ɚd] *n.* 記錄；記載

▶ I need a record of every conversation you had with the criminal.
我需要一份你和這個罪犯所有談話的紀錄。

record [rɪˈkɔːrd] *v.* 錄（影、音）；記錄

▶ We recorded the concert in two hours.
我們用兩小時錄了這場演唱會。

---

rectangle [ˈrek.tæŋ.gəl] *n.* 長方形

▶ Please arrange the chairs like a rectangle.
請將椅子排成長方形。

---

red [red]

① *adj.* 紅色的

② *n.* 紅色

▶ Don't write your name with a red pen.
不要用紅筆寫你的名字。

▶ Red is my favorite color.
紅色是我最喜歡的顏色。

---

refrigerator / fridge [rɪˈfrɪdʒ.ə.reɪ.t̬ɚ]

n. 冰箱

▶ We can put all the fish in the bottom of the refrigerator.
我們可以把所有的魚放到冰箱的底層。

refuse [rɪˈfjuːz] *v.* 拒絕

▶ How could you refuse my invitation to the zoo?
你怎麼能拒絕一起去動物園的邀請？

---

101 95

regard [rɪˈgɑːrd]

① *v.* 將…認為；看待

② *n.* 看重；尊敬；敬重

實用片語與搭配字

as regards 關於，至於

▶ Lisa regards Sally as her best friend since elementary school.
從小學開始，麗莎就把莎莉當成她最好的朋友。

▶ Everyone on the basketball team holds Ian in high regard.
籃球隊裡的每一個隊友都很看重伊恩。

▶ As regards to our telephone discussion, our company wants to confirm your order for 1000 cups.
關於我們上次在電話中討論的內容，公司要確認你的訂單為一千個杯子。

---

region [ˈriː.dʒən] *n.* 地區；區域

▶ This plant is native to this region of Canada.
這種植物是加拿大這個地區的原生植物。

98

regular [ˈreg.jə.lɚ]

① *adj.* 固定的；正常的

② *n.* 常客；老顧客

▶ Hannah goes to the dentist for regular checkups.
漢娜去找牙醫做定期檢查。

▶ Jim is a regular in this gym class.
吉姆是這堂健身課的常客。

99

reject [rɪˈdʒekt] *v.* 拒絕

▶ Kelly rejected my marriage proposal last night.
凱莉昨晚拒絕了我的求婚。

---

relation [rɪˈleɪ.ʃən] *n.* 關係；聯繫；往來

實用片語與搭配字

in / with relation to; blood relation
關於，至於，就…而言；血親，骨肉

▶ There's a relation between eating too much sugar and diabetes.
吃太多糖和糖尿病有關聯。

▶ There were no questions from the audience in relation to the presentation by the speaker.
觀眾對講者的報告內容沒有任何問題。

---

relationship [rɪˈleɪ.ʃən.ʃɪp] *n.* 關係；關聯

▶ Joe and his dad's relationship has improved a lot recently.
最近喬和他爸爸的關係有很大的改善。

實用片語與搭配字

have a relationshp with sb
與（某人）有關係

▶ I have a very good relationship with my aunt and we can talk about everything under the sun.
我和阿姨的關係很好，彼此可以坦誠交流。

Exercise 54

I. Choose and write the correct word. Change the form of the word when necessary.

1	reach (v.) realize (v.)	Some people just don't ＿＿＿＿＿ how much their words can hurt someone.
2	reason (n.) record (n.)	Before you give up, think of the ＿＿＿＿＿ why you held on so long.
3	refuse (v.) regard (v.)	Some people ＿＿＿＿＿ to buy goods that are overpackaged, because they feel that it's harmful to the environment.
4	regular (adj.) recent (adj.)	If you want to retain youthful vigor, you have to take ＿＿＿＿＿ exercise.
5	receive (v.) reject (v.)	If there's a delay of twelve hours or more, you'll ＿＿＿＿＿ a full refund of the price of your trip.

II. Multiple choices.

(　　) 1. The most important thing in any ＿＿＿＿＿ is not what you get but what you give.
(A) regard　(B) region　(C) relationship　(D) reason

(　　) 2. ＿＿＿＿＿ people have moved from the city centers to suburbs because of the poor air quality downtown.
(A) Recently　(B) Really　(C) Quick　(D) Quiet

(　　) 3. For years, this ＿＿＿＿＿ has been torn apart by armed conflicts.
(A) relation　(B) record　(C) reason　(D) region

(　　) 4. Steve went quietly into the kitchen; Sally heard him opening the ＿＿＿＿＿ door.
(A) refrigerator　(B) reason　(C) rectangle　(D) ready

(　　) 5. We had a huge party, and hired a photographer to ＿＿＿＿＿ the event.
(A) realize　(B) reason　(C) record　(D) read

Unit 55

remember [rɪˈmem.bɚ] *v.* 記得

實用片語與搭配字

be remembered for
因…而被記住；因…而名垂青史

- Did you remember to buy eggs at the store?
你記得去那家店買蛋嗎？
- The soldier will be remembered for his heroic deed to save his friends' lives.
這位士兵會因拯救朋友性命的英勇事蹟而被他人紀念。

104 99

repeat [rɪˈpiːt]

① *v.* 重複

實用片語與搭配字

repeat oneself 重複說

② *n.* 重播節目；重複

- I'm going to tell you something and you must not repeat it to anyone.
我要告訴你一些事，但你絕不可以跟任何人說。
- I get angry when people do not listen to me and I have to repeat myself.
當別人不聽我說話以至於我必須重述時，我會感到生氣。
- The TV will show repeats of Jack's show every Monday and Friday.
每個星期一和星期五，電視都會重播傑克秀。

---

reply [rɪˈplaɪ]

① *v.* 回覆；回答

② *n.* 答覆；回答

- Rachel replied to the boss's questions in less than ten minutes.
瑞秋不到十分鐘就回覆了老闆的問題。
- I have not received a reply from the airline company.
我還沒接到航空公司的答覆。

102

report [rɪˈpɔːrt]

① *v.* 報告；匯報；報導

實用片語與搭配字

report back; report to
回報；向（某人）報告，向（某人）負責

② *n.* 報告

- The police reported that there was a thief in the area.
警方說那地區有個小偷。
- The teams were sent out to collect insects in the forest before they had to report back on their findings.
這些團隊必須先外出至森林採集昆蟲，再回報他們的發現。
- You will have to give your report to the class today.
你今天必須將你的報告交到班上。

reporter [rɪˈpɔːr.t̬ɚ] *n.* 記者

▶ Only one reporter was allowed to interview the famous singer.
只有一名記者被允許可以採訪這位知名歌手。

103

require [rɪˈkwaɪr] *v.* 要求；需要

▶ My boss requires me to get to work by 8 a.m.
我的老闆要求我早上八點上班。

---

requirement [rɪˈkwaɪr.mənt]
n. 必要條件；要求

▶ The requirements needed to enter this university are not easy to fulfill.
進入這間大學的必要條件不容易達到。

---

respect [rɪˈspekt]

① *n.* 器重；尊敬

實用片語與搭配字

in respect of sth; self-respect; with (all due) respect
就…而言；自重；恕我直言

② *v.* 尊敬；尊重

▶ Tom has great respect for Adam's work in physics and chemistry.
湯姆很敬重亞當在物理和化學的成就。

▶ With all due respect, Mr. Smith, I do not believe a word you are saying.
史密斯先生，恕我直言，我不相信你說的任何一個字。

▶ Jim is respected in the community.
吉姆在這個地區備受尊重。

responsible [rɪˈspɑː.n.sə.bəl] *adj.* 負責任的

實用片語與搭配字

be responsible to sb / sth; hold sb / sth responsible; be responsible for one's actions
向…負責；歸咎於…；對（某人的行為）負責

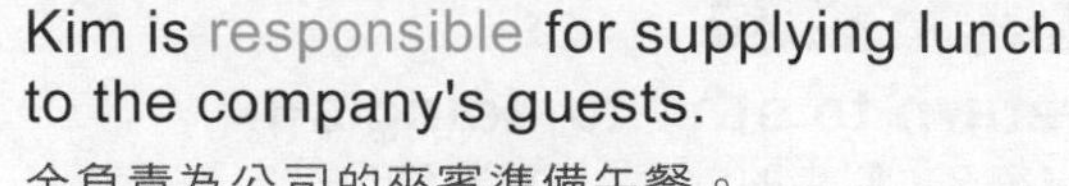

▶ Kim is responsible for supplying lunch to the company's guests.
金負責為公司的來賓準備午餐。

R

▶ As an adult you have to be responsible for your actions and accept the consequences of what you do.
身為成年人，你必須為自己的行為負責，並接受任何後果。

103

rest [rest]

① *v.* 休息

實用片語與搭配字

rest on sb / sth; rest on / upon sth
（目光在環顧四周後）落在…上；以…為基礎

② *n.* 休息；暫停

▶ I'm exhausted; I should go rest for a while.
我覺得筋疲力盡，應該要去休息一會兒。

▶ We have all completed our parts of the project; the final part now rests on the designer.
我們已完成自己該負責的工作，專案最後的部份則落在設計師的手上。

▶ Do you want to get some rest before we eat?
你想要在我們吃飯前休息一下嗎？

restaurant ['res.tə.rɑ:nt] *n.* 餐廳

▶ Irene recommended eating at the French restaurant on the corner.
艾琳推薦去吃轉角那家法式餐廳。

---

restroom ['rest.ru:m / 'rest.rʊm] *n.* 洗手間

▶ Does this restaurant have more than one restroom we can use?
這家餐廳有一間以上的洗手間供我們使用嗎？

---

103 95

result [rɪ'zʌlt]

① *n.* 結果

實用片語與搭配字

as a result of sth; result in sth
由於…; 導致

② *v.* (因…) 導致；(隨…) 產生

▶ Sam's test results will come out tomorrow.
山姆的化驗結果明天將出來。

▶ The young boy was bullied at school and as a result he became very depressed.
年幼的男孩在學校被霸凌，導致他變得很消沈。

▶ Ken's smoking resulted in bad health.
肯恩因抽菸導致健康狀況不佳。

return [rɪ'tɝ:n]

① *v.* 返回

實用片語與搭配字

return to sth / to doing sth
恢復至(原來的狀態)，重新做

② *n.* 返回；回來

實用片語與搭配字

in return; point of no return
作為交換；無退路的地步

▶ He'll be in Japan for a week and then return home.
他會在日本待一週再回家。

▶ The New Year holiday is over and all the employees have to return to doing their jobs.
新年假期已結束，所有員工必須回到自己的工作崗位。

▶ I can't wait for my brother's return from the hospital!
我等不及哥哥從醫院回來了！

▶ Could you please help me with my math homework; in return I will teach you to play the guitar.
你能幫我一起做數學作業嗎？我可以用教你彈吉他做為交換。

review [rɪ'vju:]

① *n.* 再檢查；評論；複習

② *v.* 複習；再檢查

▶ The government will perform a review of all health care starting next month.
政府將於下個月對健保展開全面的檢討。

▶ Jaclyn reviewed all her science notes at home while on vacation.
賈克琳趁著假期在家複習所有的自然科筆記。

rice [raɪs] *n.* 米

▶ Do you want some rice with your meal?
你想要吃一些米飯嗎？

---

rich [rɪtʃ] *adj.* 富有的

實用片語與搭配字

rich in sth 富含…的

▶ The person who owns that expensive car must be very rich.
擁有那輛昂貴汽車的人一定很有錢。

▶ Oranges are rich in vitamin C and prevent you from getting colds.
柳橙富含維他命 C，能預防感冒。

---

riches [ˈrɪtʃ.ɪz] *n.* 財富；財產

▶ Solomon was a king known for all his riches.
所羅門是一位以財富聞名的君王。

---

ride [raɪd]

① *v.* 坐（車）；騎（馬或腳踏車）

實用片語與搭配字

let sth ride; ride on sb / sth
聽之任之，觀望；依賴，指望

② *n.* 乘便車；搭乘免費車

實用片語與搭配字

take sb for a ride 欺騙（某人）

▶ Do you want to ride in the car with us?
你要跟我們一起搭這輛車嗎？

▶ I was angry about crashing my car, but my Mom said I should let it ride because at least I was not hurt.
我因撞壞自己的車子而感到生氣，但媽媽說我該放下了，因為至少我沒受傷。

▶ I can give you a ride to the bus station.
我可以載你一程到公車站。

▶ Scammers will often take elderly people for a ride and steal all their life savings.
詐騙者常欺騙年長者，並竊取他們的畢生積蓄。

---

rider [ˈraɪ.dɚ] *n.* 騎乘者

▶ The rider traveled far away on his horse.
這位騎士騎著他的馬走了很遠的路。

---

right [raɪt]

① *adj.* 正確的；對的

實用片語與搭配字

be not in sb's right mind; be on the right track; in the right place at the right time
精神不正常的；方法、方向正確；在恰當的時機出現在恰當的地點

▶ I don't know what's the right thing to do.
我不知道什麼是正確該做的事。

▶ I was the new store's 300th customer and won an overseas trip; truly a case of being in the right place at the right time.
因為我是這家新店的第三百位顧客，所以我贏得一趟海外之旅，這真是名符其實「在恰當的的時機出現在恰當的地點」的例子。

R

② *adv.* 向右；向右方

③ *n.* 正確；合法

④ *n.* 權利

實用片語與搭配字

in sb's own right
依靠自己的能力，根據自己的權利

- Turn right at the next traffic lights.
  在下一個紅綠燈右轉。
- I often have trouble telling the difference between right and wrong.
  我常常很難分辨對與錯之間的差別。
- Every person has basic rights.
  每個人都有基本人權。
- David became a successful businessman in his own right without his father's money to help him.
  大衛不靠父親的經濟支援，而是靠自己的能力成為一位成功的商人。

---

ring [rɪŋ]

① *n.* 戒指；指環

② *v.* 環繞；圍住

③ *v.* 響起鈴聲；響個不停

④ *n.* 鈴聲；鐘聲

- The man gave his girlfriend a ring.
  那個男人給他女朋友一枚戒指。
- We all ringed around the birthday girl and sang to her.
  我們環繞這位過生日的女孩並且為她唱歌。
- The phone rang, but no one picked up.
  電話響了，但沒有人接聽。
- That ring doesn't sound like my phone.
  那鈴聲聽起來不像是我的手機。

rise [raɪz]

① *v.* 上升；升高

實用片語與搭配字

rise above sth; rise and shine
克服；起床

② *n.* 增加

實用片語與搭配字

on the rise; give rise to
在生長、增長；引起，導致

- Because the man worked so hard, he rose to a high position in the company.
  因為那男人很努力工作，他在這家公司升到很高的職位。
- If people could rise above their desire to be rich, there would be much less greed in this world.
  如果人能克服想致富的慾望，世上的貪婪就會少一些。
- There has been a rise in crime lately.
  最近犯罪率持續增加。
- The high cost of new cars gave rise to more and more people choosing to cycle or use public transportation.
  買新車所要付出的高成本，讓越來越多人選擇腳踏車或坐大眾交通工具。

river [ˈrɪv.ɚ] *n.* 河流

▶ My dad likes to go fishing in the river.
我爸爸喜歡在河裡釣魚。

R

Exercise 55

I. Choose and write the correct word. Change the form of the word when necessary.

1	repeat (v.) reply (v.)	Please don't __________ what I've just told you to anyone else.
2	require (v.) respect (v.)	I __________ your point of view, but I'm not sure I agree with you.
3	review (n.) result (n.)	The failure of the company was a direct __________ of bad management.
4	right (n.) rise (n.)	The __________ in crime is mainly due to the social and economic factors.
5	restroom (n.) restaurant (n.)	The manager of the __________ has trained the waitress to serve correctly at table.

II. Multiple choices.

(　　) 1. I can still vividly __________ my grandfather teaching me to play cards.

(A) reply　(B) repeat　(C) remember　(D) require

(　　) 2. The newspaper __________ has to turn in his story before midnight.

(A) rider　(B) review　(C) reporter　(D) result

(　　) 3. The hotel isn't __________ for any loss or damage to guests' personal property.

(A) responsible　(B) reply　(C) require　(D) repeat

(　　) 4. The students __________ in September for the start of the new academic year.

(A) review　(B) return　(C) rest　(D) respect

(　　) 5. We should be grateful if you could __________ at your earliest convenience.

(A) reply　(B) repeat　(C) review　(D) require

road [roʊd] *n.* 馬路

實用片語與搭配字

on the road; all roads lead to Rome; on the road to sth
在途中；殊途同歸；在…的過程中

▶ Look both ways before you cross the road.
過馬路前先看左右兩邊。

▶ On the road to success, it is often necessary to make difficult decisions which could hurt someone's feelings.
在往成功的路上，時常需要做出可能會傷人的困難決定。

97

robot [ˈroʊ.bɑːt] *n.* 機器人

▶ Do you know how to build robots?
你知道怎麼做機器人嗎？

---

rock [rɑːk]

① *n.* 石頭

實用片語與搭配字

rock bottom （生活中的）最低點

② *v.* 使震動；搖動

實用片語與搭配字

sth / sb rocks …棒極了

▶ We sat on the rock and watched the sunset.
我們坐在這個大石頭上看夕陽。

▶ After Jack lost his job, he hit rock bottom and became depressed about having no money.
傑克失業後跌入谷底，他因沒有錢而陷入沮喪。

▶ The earthquake rocked the whole area of New York City.
地震震動了整個紐約地區。

▶ Our Chinese teacher rocks; she does not give us any homework.
我們的中文老師棒極了，她不會給我們任何作業。

---

rocky [ˈrɑː.ki] *adj.* 崎嶇難行的；多岩石的

實用片語與搭配字

rocky road 困難重重

▶ Be careful because this path is very rocky.
小心，因為這條步道崎嶇難行。

▶ His road to fame was a rocky road and he had to overcome many challenges.
他的成名之路難行，途中他必須克服許多挑戰。

---

role [roʊl] *n.* 角色

▶ I can't believe Brian got the role of Batman in this new movie.
我無法相信布萊恩在這部新電影裡拿到了蝙蝠俠的角色。

實用片語與搭配字

role model; role play
楷模；（尤指在學習新技巧過程中作為練習的）角色扮演

▶ Role models like pop stars should be more responsible because they have so many young fans who copy what they do.
身為楷模，如時下偶像應該更有責任感，因為許多年輕的粉絲會仿效他們的行為。

---

roll [roʊl]

① *v.* 滾動

▶ We rolled the ball on the floor to each other.
我們在地板上滾球給彼此。

實用片語與搭配字

roll up sb's sleeves
捲起袖子（準備行動）；躍躍欲試

▶ If you want to achieve your goals, you have to roll up your sleeves and start working to make your dreams come true.
若想達成目標，你必須開始努力才能讓夢想成真。

② *n.* 打滾；翻滾

▶ The kids went for a roll in the field.
這群孩子在田野上打滾。

---

roof [ru:f]

① *n.* 屋頂

▶ This house looks nice, but the roof has a leak.
這棟房子看起來很棒，但是屋頂有裂縫。

② *v.* 給（建築物）蓋屋頂；覆蓋

▶ My dad had to roof our house again after the storm.
我爸爸需要在暴風雨後把屋頂再重新整修。

---

room [ru:m / rʊm]

① *n.* 房間

▶ Our house has four rooms.
我們房子有四間房間。

② *v.* 為…提供住宿

▶ Can the guests room in your house for the weekend?
這週末你的房子可以提供給這些客人住宿嗎？

---

rooster [ˈru:.stɚ] *n.* 公雞

▶ The rooster woke me up early in the morning.
這隻公雞早上很早就叫我起床。

---

root [ru:t]

① *n.* 根

▶ A tree cannot live without strong roots.
一顆樹沒有強壯的根是無法生長的。

② *v.* 生根；長出根來

▶ Many weeds are rooting in my garden.
在我花園裡有很多野草生根。

實用片語與搭配字

root for sb 給（某人）以支援；為（某人）助威

- ▶ My family supports our school's soccer team, but I have always rooted for the other team because there is a cute boy I like.
  我的家人支持我們學校的足球隊，但我總是為另一隊助陣，因為隊中有我喜歡的男生。

---

rope [roʊp]

① *n.* 繩子

② *v.* （用繩索）捆；紮

- ▶ You need to use a strong rope when rock climbing.
  攀岩的時候，你需要用一條堅固的繩子。
- ▶ The cowboy roped the cow while riding his horse.
  這個牛仔邊騎馬邊用繩索套上那頭牛。

---

rose [roʊz] *n.* 玫瑰

- ▶ My husband gave me a dozen roses on my birthday.
  我先生在我生日時送我十二朵玫瑰花。

---

round [raʊnd]

① *adj.* 圓形的

實用片語與搭配字

all-round 全能的

② *n.* 一場；一回合；一局

實用片語與搭配字

round-up; round of applause

聚集；一陣掌聲

③ *adv.* 到各處；在…各處

④ *prep.* 在…周圍；在…附近

⑤ *v.* 使變圓

- ▶ Everyone now knows that the Earth is round.
  現在每個人都知道地球是圓的。
- ▶ The movie star is such an all-round actress that she can play any role, from drama to comedy.
  那位全能的電影明星能演任何角色，從劇情戲到喜劇都可以。
- ▶ Marvin and I played three rounds of golf.
  我和馬文打了三場高爾夫球。
- ▶ Following the opera singer's amazing performance, the round of applause lasted for 10 minutes.
  在歌劇演唱家精采的演出後，掌聲持續超過十分鐘。
- ▶ We walked round for hours.
  我們到處走了好幾個小時。
- ▶ The children ran round the park.
  這些孩子繞著公園跑。
- ▶ She rounded the dough into balls and put them in the oven.
  她將麵團揉成圓球狀再放進烤箱烤。

實用片語與搭配字

round sth off 把…磨光修圓，圓滿完成

▶ We had a delicious lunch at the restaurant and we rounded it off with coffee and dessert at a coffee shop.
在餐廳享用美味的中餐後，我們用咖啡和甜點劃下完美的句點。

---

row [roʊ]

① *n.* 一排；一行；一列

② *v.* 划（船）

▶ The first row of chairs are taken.
第一排的這些椅子已經被佔滿了。

▶ In his free time, Steve likes to row a boat around the lake.
閒暇時，史提夫喜歡去湖邊划船。

---

royal [ˈrɔɪ.əl] *adj.* 王室的；高貴的

▶ Did you know William is a member of the royal family?
你知道威廉是皇室成員嗎？

---

rub [rʌb]

① *v.* 揉搓；摩擦

② *n.* 揉搓；摩擦

▶ Rub your shirt with soap to get that stain out.
用肥皂搓揉你的襯衫將那個污漬去除。

▶ My back is sore. I need a rub.
我的背很痠痛。我需要按摩一下。

---

rubber [ˈrʌb.ɚ] *n.* 橡膠

▶ This ball is made of rubber.
這顆球是橡膠做的。

rude [ruːd] *adj.* 無禮的；粗魯的

▶ I can't believe Lily was so rude to her mom.
我不敢相信莉莉對她媽媽這麼無禮。

---

rule [ruːl]

① *n.* 規則

實用片語與搭配字

golden rule
（尤指在某種情況下使用的）重要的原則

② *v.* 統治

▶ On the first day of school, the teacher told us the rules.
開學的第一天，這位老師告訴我們一些規則。

▶ According to the Bible there is one golden rule to follow; love one another.
根據聖經記載，彼此相愛是重要的原則。

▶ The king ruled the kingdom for twenty years.
這位國王統治這個王國已有二十年。

96

ruler [ˈruː.lɚ] *n.* 統治者；管理者

▶ King John was the ruler of England for many years.
約翰國王曾是英格蘭多年的統治者。

---

run [rʌn] *v.* 跑步；奔跑

實用片語與搭配字

run into sb; run after sb / sth
偶然遇到(某人); 追逐…

▶ Do you often run for exercise?
你是否常常以跑步作為運動？

▶ Today at the supermarket, I ran into an old classmate I have not seen in ages and she recognized me.
今天我在超市偶然遇到一個許久不見的老同學，她居然還認得我。

---

runner [ˈrʌn.ɚ] *n.* 跑步者；參加賽跑的人

實用片語與搭配字

front-runner; runner-up 領先者；第二名

▶ Peter is a runner and enjoys running every evening.
彼得是一名跑者，他喜歡每天晚上跑步。

▶ Jim is the front-runner for the manager's position in our company, but Jenny also really wants the job.
吉姆在經理職缺的競選中為領先者，但珍妮也很想要這份工作。

---

running [ˈrʌn.ɪŋ] *n.* 跑步；運轉；管理

實用片語與搭配字

running shoes 運動鞋

▶ Running seemed like a boring exercise to Brian.
跑步對布萊恩來說似乎是個無聊的運動。

▶ Brian bought a pair of running shoes after his New Year's resolution to go jogging every day.
布萊恩在新年時期望自己能每天跑步，所以後來買了一雙慢跑鞋。

---

97 95

rush [rʌʃ]

① *v.* 衝；(使)趕緊；(使)急速行進

實用片語與搭配字

rush into sth 倉促做

② *n.* 激增；(交通)繁忙

▶ Emma rushed to the bus stop straight after class.
艾瑪在下課後馬上衝向公車站。

▶ It would be a big mistake to rush into this deal without thinking about the consequences.
毫不考慮後果就倉促做決定將會是個大錯誤。

▶ There was a sudden rush to catch the subway after the show ended.
在表演結束後，搭地鐵的人潮突然激增。

R

實用片語與搭配字

rush hour　（上下班）交通高峰時間

▶ I hate riding on the buses during rush hour because there are so many people.

我很討厭在交通尖峰時間搭公車，因為人很多。

---

sad [sæd] *adj.* **難過的；悲傷的**

▶ Don't be sad; tomorrow will be a better day.

不要難過，明天會更好。

實用片語與搭配字

sadder but wiser　經一事，長一智

▶ Paul lost many of his friends after he was fired; he was sadder but wiser about who his true friends were.

許多保羅的朋友在他失去工作後紛紛離他而去，雖然他很傷心，但也更清楚誰是真正的朋友。

Exercise 56

I. Choose and write the correct word. Change the form of the word when necessary.

1	robot (n.) role (n.)	The ________ business began to look brighter as we built up experience in putting the machine to work.
2	round (adj.) royal (adj.)	A media circus surrounded the ________ couple wherever they went.
3	root (n.) roof (n.)	The helicopters rescued nearly 20 people from the ________ of the burning building.
4	rule (v.) rush (v.)	There's plenty of time, so we don't need to ________ at finishing the job.
5	rude (adj.) rocky (adj.)	This misbehaving student was punished because he was ________ to the teacher.

II. Multiple choices.

(　　) 1. Most tires are made of ________ compounded with other chemicals and materials.
(A) rules　(B) rulers　(C) rubber　(D) ropes

(　　) 2. She threw her arms ________ his neck and hugged him warmly.
(A) round　(B) roll　(C) row　(D) rub

(　　) 3. He held on to the ________ and slipped down the cliff slowly.
(A) rose　(B) root　(C) rooster　(D) rope

(　　) 4. The ________ flew up to a big rock and started to crow.
(A) rooster　(B) ruler　(C) rubber　(D) runner

(　　) 5. In our office building, there's a hard ________ against smoking.
(A) rubber　(B) runner　(C) ruler　(D)rule

Unit 57

safe [seɪf]

① *adj.* 安全的

實用片語與搭配字

safe and sound; in safe hands
安然無恙；受到妥善照管

② *n.* 保險箱

▸ Is it safe to walk there by myself?
我自己一個人走到那裡安全嗎？

▸ My mother was so anxious when she heard there was a fire at our school, but we were safe and sound already on our way home.
當媽媽聽到我們學校有火災時心急如焚，但其實我們已經安然無恙地在回家的路上。

▸ The rich man kept all his money in a safe.
這個有錢人將他所有的錢都放在保險箱中。

99

safety [ˈseɪf.ti] *v.* 安全；平安

實用片語與搭配字

safety first; safety belt
安全第一；安全帶

▸ Tim has been working on improving safety within the schoolyard.
提姆持續在校園內進行改善安全的工作。

▸ These days, it is law in many countries to wear a safety belt even when you are sitting in the back seat of a car.
現在許多國家都規定車子後座的乘客也要繫上安全帶。

---

sail [seɪl]

① *n.* 帆

② *v.* 行駛；（船）航行

實用片語與搭配字

sail through sth 順利通過（考試）

▸ Boats with sails need wind in order to move.
帆船需要風推動才能航行。

▸ My uncle taught me how to sail his boat on the lake.
我舅舅教了我如何在湖上行駛他的船。

▸ I was so scared to take the test for my driver's licence, but I sailed through it without any mistakes.
我很害怕考駕照，但還是順利地通過測驗。

---

sailor [ˈseɪ.lɚ] *n.* 水手；船員

▸ Hank has been a sailor for more than forty years.
漢克已經當了超過四十年的船員。

---

salad [ˈsæl.əd] *n.* 沙拉

▸ Can you put some more tomatoes in my salad?
你可以多放一些番茄在我的沙拉裡嗎？

sale [seɪl] *n.* 廉價出售；降價銷售

▶ The store is having a sale this week; everything is very cheap!
這家店這週有特賣會，每樣東西都非常便宜！

---

salt [sɑːlt]

① *n.* 鹽

② *adj.* 鹹水的

③ *v.* 給…加鹽

▶ There's too much salt on this fish.
這道魚太鹹了。

▶ This kind of fish only lives in salt water.
這種魚只能生活在海水中。

▶ The cook salted the soup too much.
這位廚師在這道湯裡加太多鹽了。

---

salty [ˈsɑːl.t̬i] *adj.* 鹹的

▶ Do you think this pumpkin soup is too salty?
你覺得這南瓜湯會太鹹嗎？

---

same [seɪm]

① *adj.* 同樣的

實用片語與搭配字

be in the same boat; all the same
面臨同樣的困境；照樣，依然

② *prop.* 一模一樣；完全一樣的人、事、物

實用片語與搭配字

same here 我同意

③ *adv.* 同樣地

▶ We are wearing the same shirt!
我們穿著同樣的襯衫！

▶ During the 2008 financial crisis many people were in the same boat; they were poor because they all lost their jobs.
2008 年的金融海嘯讓許多人面臨同樣的困境，他們都因為失去工作而非常貧困。

▶ She wants a hot coffee, and I'll have the same.
她想要一杯熱咖啡，我也想要一樣的。

▶ My friend said she liked the new English teacher. I agreed and said "same here."
我朋友說她喜歡新的英文老師，我也說：「我同意」。

▶ You look the same as you did twenty years ago!
你現在跟二十年前看起來一樣！

---

sample [ˈsæm.pəl]

① *n.* 樣品；試用品

② *v.* （少量）品嘗；體驗

▶ I have some makeup samples for you to take home.
我有一些化妝品樣品讓你帶回家。

▶ Did you get to sample Chris' delicious chocolate cake?
你嚐過克里斯美味的巧克力蛋糕了嗎？

sand [sænd]

① *n.* 沙子

② *v.* （尤指用砂紙）打磨；磨光

▶ Maggie likes to go to the beach and play in the sand.
瑪姬喜歡到沙灘上玩沙。

▶ He sanded the table until it was smooth and beautiful.
他用砂紙拋光桌子直到它變光滑又美麗。

---

sandwich [ˈsæn.wɪtʃ]

① *n.* 三明治

② *v.* 把…夾在中間

▶ Can I have a bite of your roast chicken sandwich?
我可以嚐一口你的烤雞三明治嗎？

▶ Ian is sandwiched between Andy and Fred in the back seat of the plane.
伊恩坐在飛機後排，夾在安迪和佛萊德中間。

---

satisfy [ˈsæt̬.ɪs.faɪ] *v.* 使滿意；使滿足

▶ Were you satisfied with the customer service in this restaurant?
你對這家餐廳的客戶服務滿意嗎？

Saturday / Sat. [ˈsæt̬.ɚ.deɪ] *v.* 星期六

▶ I like to rest at home on Saturdays.
星期六我喜歡在家休息。

---

sauce [sɑːs]

① *n.* 調味醬

② *v.* 給…加調味醬

▶ Can you pass me the sauce from the end of the table?
你可以幫我把調味醬從桌子那一端傳過來嗎？

▶ Did you sauce the chicken with herbs and spices?
你是用香草和香料將這塊雞肉調味嗎？

---

save [seɪv] *v.* 挽救

實用片語與搭配字

save the day 扭轉劣勢

▶ The police saved the dog from the fire.
這個警察將狗從火場中救出來。

▶ Our office party was so boring at first, but Janet arrived and saved the day with her outgoing personality.
我們辦公室的派對原本很無聊，但外向的珍妮特別到場扭轉局勢，炒熱了派對的氣氛。

---

saw [sɑː]

① *n.* 鋸子

② *v.* 鋸成；鋸開

▶ Jack used a saw to cut down the tree.
傑克用鋸子鋸斷這棵樹。

▶ I can saw the wood in half, then it will be easier to carry.
我可以將木頭鋸成兩半，那會比較容易扛。

say [seɪ] *v.* 說；講；陳述

實用片語與搭配字

it goes without saying 不證自明

▶ I couldn't hear you; what did you say?
我聽不到你，你剛剛說什麼？

▶ Chinese Lunar New Year is celebrated in many countries and it goes without saying that it is a very important holiday.
許多國家慶祝中華農曆新年，此節慶的重要性不證自明。

scare [sker]

① *v.* （使）害怕；受驚嚇

實用片語與搭配字

scare sth / sb away 把…嚇跑

② *n.* 驚嚇；驚恐

▶ My brother always tries to scare me.
我弟弟總是想要嚇我。

▶ When watching wild animals you have to be very quiet or you will scare them away.
觀察野生動物時必須要很安靜，否則你會把牠們嚇跑。

▶ That loud noise gave me a scare and made me jump!
那巨大聲響嚇到我，讓我跳了起來！

---

scared [skerd] *adj.* 驚嚇的；恐懼的

▶ The scared boy saw a big spider.
這個害怕的男孩看見了一隻大蜘蛛。

---

scene [siːn] *v.* 景象

實用片語與搭配字

set the scene; behind the scenes
鋪路，做好準備；不公開地

▶ That accident is a terrible scene!
那場意外是很可怕的景象！

▶ People who work behind the scenes at music concerts work harder than the singers, but they get less money.
演唱會的幕後工作人員其實比歌手更辛苦，但他們領比較少薪水。

---

school [skuːl]

① *n.* 學校

實用片語與搭配字

old-school 舊式的，老派的

② *v.* 訓練；培養；教育

▶ I go to school to learn.
我到學校學習。

▶ When it comes to food, my dad is pretty old-school and he does not like to try new dishes.
說到食物，我爸爸比較老派，他不喜歡嘗試新菜色。

▶ She was schooled by some very famous teachers.
她接受一些名師的訓練。

S

science [ˈsaɪ.əns] *n.* 科學；自然科學

▸ Julia received awards in science and math during her final year of high school.
茱莉亞在高中最後一年裡獲得了科學和數學的獎項。

scientist [ˈsaɪən.tɪst] *n.* 科學家

▸ Carl wants to be a scientist when he grows up.
卡爾長大後想要成為一名科學家。

scissors [ˈsɪz.ɚz] *n.* 剪刀

▸ I put the scissors in the top drawer of your desk.
我把剪刀放在你書桌最上層的抽屜。

Exercise 57

I. Choose and write the correct word. Change the form of the word when necessary.

1	safety (n.) sailor (n.)	The factory was closed for failing to comply with government __________ regulations.
2	sale (n.) safe (n.)	The increasing __________ of luxury goods is an index for the country's prosperity.
3	satisfy(v.) scare (v.)	I can't believe that this enormous meal wasn't enough to __________ your hunger.
4	sample (n.) sauce (n.)	The shop is giving away a __________ pack to every customer.
5	salty (adj.) scared (adj.)	The small animals are __________ when they see a tiger walking towards them.

II. Multiple choices.

( ) 1. This young __________ has put forth a new theory in his research field.
(A) scene (B) scientist (C) school (D) scare

( ) 2. Cook and gently stir the __________ over a medium heat until it thickens.
(A) sand (B) sample (C) sauce (D) salt

( ) 3. The main drawback to these products is that they tend to be too __________.
(A) same (B) safe (C) scared (D) salty

( ) 4. A __________ threw a rope ashore and we tied the boat to a post.
(A) sailor (B) sample (C) saw (D) scene

( ) 5. Several items of clothing were found near the __________ of the crime.
(A) scientist (B) safety (C) sailor (D) scene

Unit 58

scooter [ˈskuː.t̬ɚ]

n. （小型）摩托車；(速克達)機車

▶ Everybody drove a scooter to work.
大家都騎摩托車去上班。

---

score [skɔːr]

① *n.* 得分；成績

② *v.* 成功；贏

▶ Helen, could you keep score at tonight's basketball game?
海倫，你可以為今晚的籃球比賽計分嗎？

▶ Grace scored a success with her latest album.
葛瑞絲最新的專輯很成功。

104

screen [skriːn]

① *n.* 銀幕；螢幕

② *v.* 遮護；掩蔽

▶ The movie theatre has big screens.
這個電影院銀幕很大。

▶ We need to screen this area to keep the bugs out.
我們需要防範這個區域不讓蟲子入侵。

---

sea [siː] *n.* 海；海洋

實用片語與搭配字

a sea of sth 大量的…

▶ She prefers to swim in the sea, not in pools.
她比較喜歡在海裡游泳，而不是在游泳池。

▶ There was a sea of people who went to watch the New Year's fireworks, but I decided not to go because I don't like crowds.
大批群眾去觀賞新年煙火，但我決定不去，因為我不喜歡人擠人。

---

search [sɝːtʃ]

① *v.* 搜查；尋找

② *n.* 搜尋；調查

實用片語與搭配字

in search of sth 尋找

▶ Eve searched her office for her missing ring.
伊芙在她的辦公室裡找她遺失的戒指。

▶ Robin joined the search for the missing campers after the snowstorm.
羅賓在暴風雪後加入了搜尋失蹤露營者的工作。

▶ After the fire, the family went in search of their two dogs and found them at a nearby shelter.
火災後，這家人去找尋兩隻家犬，並且在附近的收容所找到牠們。

season [ˈsiː.zən] *n.* 季節

實用片語與搭配字

in season （水果和蔬菜）當季的

▸ It's almost the Christmas season.
聖誕季節快到了。

▸ It is cheaper to buy fruits and vegetables that are in season, for example, buy oranges in winter.
當季生產的蔬菜及水果比較便宜，像是冬天的柳橙。

---

seat [siːt]

① *n.* 座位

② *v.* 給…安排座位

▸ Is this seat taken, or may I sit here?
這個位子有人坐嗎？還是我可以坐這裡？

▸ He seated the guests when they arrived.
當貴賓抵達時，他為他們安排了座位。

---

second [ˈsek.ənd]

① *adj.* 第二的

② *n.* 第二名

③ *adv.* 居第二位

④ *n.* 秒

▸ We knew the second song, but not the first.
我們熟悉第二首歌，但不知道第一首。

▸ She studied so well that she was second in her class.
她用功讀書而且在班上是第二名。

▸ He wanted to win the race, but came in second instead.
他想要在這場賽跑中得冠，但是卻只位居第二名。

▸ There are sixty seconds in a minute.
一分鐘有六十秒。

95

secret [ˈsiː.krət]

① *adj.* 祕密的

② *n.* 秘密

實用片語與搭配字

in secret; your secret's safe with me
秘密地；我會守口如瓶

▸ Kim's team found a secret passage at the back of the old church.
金的團隊在老教堂的後面找到了一條秘密通道。

▸ Nina had several secrets she needed to tell her mother.
妮娜有幾個需要告訴她媽媽的秘密。

▸ You are my best friend and you can tell me anything; your secret is safe with me.
你是我最好的朋友，任何秘密都可以跟我說，我會守口如瓶。

---

secretary [ˈsek.rə.ter.i] *n.* 秘書

▸ Mark had to hire another secretary after Hannah got sick.
漢娜生病後，馬克需要聘用另一個秘書。

section [ˈsek.ʃən]

① *n.* 章節；部份

② *v.* 把…分段；切片

▶ Dan completed five sections of his research paper after lunch.
丹恩在午餐後完成了他研究報告中的五個章節。

▶ We'll section this piece of land before selling it.
在賣出這塊土地前，我們會先進行分割。

---

see [siː] *n.* 看見

實用片語與搭配字

see sb off; see eye to eye
為（某人）送行；（兩人）意見一致

▶ I can't see because it's too dark.
我看不見因為太暗了。

▶ My new boss and I could not see eye to eye on the new project, so eventually I had to quit.
我和新老闆無法在計劃上達成共識，所以最後我必須退出計畫。

---

seed [siːd]

① *n.* 種子

② *v.* 在…播種

▶ Plants begin as little seeds.
植物是從小種子開始長大的。

▶ Did you seed those tomatoes in good soil?
你是在好的土壤裡種植這些番茄嗎？

---

seem [siːm] *v.* 似乎

▶ Tony seems happy; he's been smiling all day.
湯尼似乎很快樂，他整天都掛著笑容。

---

seesaw [ˈsiː.sɑː]

① *n.* 蹺蹺板

② *v.* 上下（來回）搖動不定

▶ The children played on the seesaw.
孩子們在玩蹺蹺板。

▶ The boat seesawed through the rough water.
這艘船在狂風巨浪中搖擺不定。

---

select [səˈlekt]

① *v.* 挑選；選拔

② *adj.* 精選的；最優秀的

▶ Ben was selected to speak at the graduation ceremony.
班恩被選上在畢業典禮中致詞。

▶ A select group of athletes got into the Winter Olympics.
這群最優秀的運動員參加了冬季奧運會。

---

selection [səˈlek.ʃən]

n. 選擇；挑選出的人（物）

▶ The store has a large selection of dresses.
這家店有很多洋裝的選擇。

self [self] *n.* 自己

▶ I'm in the process of discovering my true self.
我正在探索真正自我的過程中。

---

selfish [ˈsel.fɪʃ] *adj.* 自私的

▶ The father taught his children how to share and not be selfish.
這個爸爸教他的孩子如何無私與人分享。

---

sell [sel] *v.* 販賣

實用片語與搭配字

sell sb off; sell sth off
為背叛，出賣；減價出售

▶ Do you sell raincoats here?
你這裡賣雨衣嗎？

▶ The company went bankrupt and had to sell stocks off at very cheap prices.
這家公司破產了，不得不以非常便宜的價格出售股票。

---

semester [səˈmes.tɚ] *n.* 學期

▶ The end of the school semester is next Monday.
下星期一是這學期的尾聲。

---

send [send] *v.* 發送；（尤指）郵寄

實用片語與搭配字

send sth back; send word; send for sb
退回；傳話；請（某人）來

▶ I want to send a present to my brother.
我想寄一個禮物給我弟弟。

▶ Todd got seriously injured while playing basketball and we had to send word to his mother that he was in the hospital.
陶德在打籃球時受了重傷，我們必須傳話給他媽媽說他人在醫院。

---

sense [sens]

① *n.* 節慶的氣氛；感官

實用片語與搭配字

sixth sense; talk sense; in every sense; in a sense
第六感，直覺；說得有理；從任何意義上來看；從某種意義上來看

② *v.* 感覺到

▶ Christmas always comes with a sense of excitement.
聖誕節總是伴隨著歡樂的氛圍。

▶ My grandmother always said you should listen to your sixth sense because it could save your life.
外婆總是說，你應該相信第六感，因為它也許能救命。

▶ She sensed that he had a surprise for her.
她感覺到他要給她一個驚喜。

---

sentence [ˈsen.təns]

① *n.* 句子

▶ We can practice saying these sentences out loud.
我們可以練習將這些句子大聲唸出來。

② *v.* （法官）宣佈判決

▶ He will be sentenced in court next week.
他下個星期將會被判刑。

---

separate ['sep.ɚ.ət]

① *adj.* 個別的；分開的

實用片語與搭配字

go separate ways 分道揚鑣

② *v.* 使分離；分隔

實用片語與搭配字

separate from 分開

▶ The eggs and fruit were placed on separate shelves in the refrigerator.
蛋和水果被放在冰箱裡的分隔架上。

▶ After many years as a couple, Adam and Sarah decided to break up and go their separate ways.
交往許多年後，亞當和莎拉決定分手，各走各的。

▶ The twins were separated at birth and never knew their real parents.
這對雙胞胎一出生就被分開，他們從不認識他們的親生父母。

▶ It is important to keep your work separate from your private life and not mix the two things.
把工作和私生活分開很重要，不要混為一談。

Exercise 58

I. Choose and write the correct word. Change the form of the word when necessary.

1	screen (n.) score (n.)	Your computer ___________ should be at eye level so that you can work with your neck straight.
2	search (v.) sense (v.)	She decided to ___________ for her biological mother after her adoptive parents died.
3	section (n.) semester (n.)	A student will probable attend four or five courses during each ___________.
4	send (v.) select (v.)	It's important to ___________ a software package that suits your requirements.
5	selfish (adj.) secret (adj.)	She never considers anyone but herself; she's completely ___________.

II. Multiple choices.

( ) 1. Summer is a pleasant ___________ for all kinds of cold foods and juicy fruits.
(A) search (B) second (C) season (D) score

( ) 2. The ___________ is trying to schedule this month's appointments for the manager.
(A) semester (B) selection (C) seesaw (D) secretary

( ) 3. The central ___________ of the book is a historical overview of drug use.
(A) section (B) semester (C) secret (D) sense

( ) 4. The two dogs started to snarl at each other, so I had to ___________ them.
(A) sentence (B) send (C) sell (D) separate

( ) 5. By analyzing the parts of the ___________, we learn more about English grammar.
(A) sentence (B) secretary (C) sense (D) selection

Unit 59

September / Sept. [sep'tem.bɚ] *n.* 九月

▶ Autumn starts in September.
秋天自九月開始。

---

99 95

serious ['sɪr.i.əs] *adj.* 認真的；嚴肅的

▶ Peter is very serious about his work.
彼得非常認真面對他的工作。

---

servant ['sɝː.vənt] *n.* 僕人

實用片語與搭配字

public servant 公務員

▶ The royal family has many servants.
這個皇室家庭有許多僕人。

▶ My father was a public servant his whole life, but I decided never to work for the government.
我父親一生都是公務員，但我決定不為政府工作。

103

serve [sɝːv] *v.* 工作；服務

實用片語與搭配字

serve sb right （某人）罪有應得

▶ Judy served the company faithfully for fifty years.
茱蒂忠心地為這家公司服務了五十年。

▶ Failing your exam serves you right because I told you not to go to that party the night before the test.
考試不及格是你應得的，因為我曾告訴你考試前一天晚上不要去參加那個派對。

---

service ['sɝː.vɪs]

① *n.* 服務；效勞

實用片語與搭配字

be of service (to sb); lip service
幫助(某人); 口頭上同意

② *v.* 為…服務

▶ Laura received a gift for her years of service at the company.
蘿拉因為在這家公司服務多年而收到了一個禮物。

▶ You can't take Joe seriously because he only pays lip service to his deeds and he never does what he says he will do.
你不要把喬當回事，因為他只是口頭說說，他從來沒有完成承諾的事。

▶ The waiter serviced us the food.
那位服務生為我們服務上菜。

---

set [set]

① *n.* (一) 套；組

▶ I bought a new set of clothes for the trip.
我為這趟旅行買了一套新衣服。

② *v.* 布置；設置

▶ John set the food on the table.
約翰將食物擺好在桌上。

settle [ˈset̬.əl] *v.* 安頓；解決

實用片語與搭配字

settle down; settle in
安頓下來；適應新環境

▶ Claire and Sam settled their argument.
克萊兒和山姆解決了他們的爭論。

▶ Most people want to settle down and have a family, but I am happy just traveling around the world, living day by day.
許多人想要組織家庭安頓下來，但我喜歡環遊世界，日復一日地過日子。

---

settlement [ˈset̬.əl.mənt] *n.* 協定；庭外和解

▶ Many residents were unhappy with the government's settlement.
許多住戶對政府的協調結果感到不滿意。

---

seven [ˈsev.ən]

① *n.* 七

② *adj.* 七的；七個的

▶ In some countries, seven is a lucky number.
在某些國家，七是個幸運數字。

▶ There are seven visitors coming today.
今天有七位訪客要來。

---

seventeen [ˌsev.ənˈtiːn]

① *n.* 十七

② *adj.* 十七的；十七個的

▶ Sixteen plus one equals seventeen.
十六加一等於十七。

▶ We put seventeen candles on the cake.
我們在蛋糕上放了十七根蠟燭。

---

seventy [ˈsev.ən.t̬i]

① *n.* 七十

② *adj.* 七十的；七十個的

▶ Seventy is a big number.
七十是個大數字。

▶ Seventy houses were destroyed in the flood.
在那場水災中有七十間房子被摧毀。

103

several [ˈsev.ɚ.əl]

① *adj.* 幾個的

② *pron.* 幾個；數個

▶ I ate several cookies, so I'm not hungry anymore.
我吃了幾塊餅乾，所以我不餓了。

▶ There were deer in the park today; I saw several!
今天我在公園裡看到了幾隻鹿！

shake [ʃeɪk]

① *v.* 搖動

實用片語與搭配字

shake sth / sb off; shake sb up
擺脫，甩掉；使震驚

② *n.* 搖動；抖動；使顫動

▶ He shook the tree, but the apples didn't fall.
他搖了搖那棵樹，但蘋果沒有掉下來。

▶ We gave Jerry the bad news about crashing his car, but he just shook it off and said it was OK.
我們告訴杰瑞，他的車被撞壞的消息，但他不在意，直說沒關係。

▶ The boy gave the box a shake to hear what was inside.
這男孩把盒子搖一搖聽聽裡面有什麼。

---

shall [ʃæl / ʃəl] *aux. v.* 將會

▶ I shall forgive you.
我會原諒你。

---

shape [ʃeɪp]

① *n.* 形狀

實用片語與搭配字

be in good shape; in the shape of sth
保持良好狀態；以…的形式

② *v.* 塑造；使成形

實用片語與搭配字

shape up 進展，發展

▶ I baked cookies of different shapes.
我烤了很多不同形狀的餅乾。

▶ My grandfather ran marathons until he was 88 and he was in good shape for a man his age.
我爺爺到了八十八歲還在跑馬拉松，對這個年齡的男人來說，他有著很好的體態。

▶ He shaped the clay into a beautiful bowl.
他將陶土塑成一個美麗的碗。

▶ We are planning to go mountain-climbing during the summer holidays so I better shape up or I won't be able to do it.
我們計畫在暑假去爬山，所以我要好好鍛鍊，否則可能沒辦法完成。

---

share [ʃer]

① *n.* 一份

② *v.* 分享

▶ The children argued over their share of the Laura's birthday cake.
孩子們為了分蘿拉的生日蛋糕吵了起來。

▶ Linda shared the chocolates she got from Hawaii with her friends.
琳達將她從夏威夷帶回來的巧克力分享給她的朋友們。

---

shark [ʃɑːrk] *n.* 鯊魚

▶ Watch out for sharks while you swim!
你游泳的時候要小心鯊魚！

sharp [ʃɑ:rp]

① *adj.* 尖銳的

② *adv.* 整（指時間）

▶ Be careful with that sharp knife.
小心那把尖銳的刀。

▶ I arrived at seven o'clock sharp.
我七點整抵達。

---

she [ʃi: / ʃi]

① *pron.* 她（主格）

② *n.* 女性；雌性

▶ She is my sister.
她是我的姊姊。

▶ Is your dog a he or a she?
你的狗是公的還是母的呢？

---

sheep [ʃi:p] *n.* 綿羊

▶ There are many sheep in New Zealand.
紐西蘭有很多羊。

---

sheet [ʃi:t] *n.* 床單

▶ Put clean sheets on the bed for the guest.
幫客人在床上鋪乾淨的床單。

---

shelf [ʃelf] *n.* 架子；書架層版

▶ Greg put up new shelves in his bedroom after he painted his wall.
葛瑞克將臥室的牆粉刷之後，再搭起了新層架。

---

shell [ʃel]

① *n.* 外殼；貝殼

② *v.* 剝…的殼；為…去殼

▶ The snail died because its shell was cracked.
這隻蝸牛死了，因為牠的殼破了。

▶ Have you finished shelling all these oysters?
你已經把全部的牡蠣剝殼了嗎？

---

shine [ʃaɪn]

① *v.* 照耀；發光

② *n.* 光澤；光

▶ The sun is shining in my eyes.
陽光在我眼睛裡閃耀著。

▶ I want my hair to have more shine.
我想讓我的頭髮更有光澤。

---

ship [ʃɪp]

① *n.* 船

② *v.* 用船運；運送

▶ He took a ship to Japan.
他搭了船去日本。

▶ The store shipped their products overseas.
這間店將他們的產品船運到國外去。

實用片語與搭配字

ship sb off 送走（某人）

▶ The mother shipped her children off to their grandmother on the farm for the holidays so that she could take a break.

這位母親將她的小孩送到在農場的奶奶家過節，這讓她能好好休息。

Exercise 59

I. Choose and write the correct word. Change the form of the word when necessary.

1	serious (adj.) several (adj.)	Using a seat belt will reduce the likelihood of __________ injury in a car accident.
2	servant (n.) service (n.)	In the beach resort, the apartments and villas have daily maid __________.
3	settle (v.) share (v.)	They've been unable to __________ the dispute over working conditions.
4	shine (v.) shake (v.)	When the earthworm appears in the morning, the sun will __________ brightly.
5	shelf (n.) shape (n.)	Please put the book back on the __________ when you've finished with it.

II. Multiple choices.

( ) 1. Use a pair of __________ scissors and make a small cut in the material for the shape you want.

(A) sharp (B) shine (C) several (D) shark

( ) 2. __________ countries have expressed their strong disapproval of the law.

(A) Shine (B) Several (C) Shake (D) Sharp

( ) 3. She didn't know whether to __________ her hands or kiss her cheek when she first met the foreigner.

(A) shake (B) shark (C) shine (D) shape

( ) 4. How much do men __________ housework and the care of the children?

(A) shine (B) shell (C) settle (D) share

( ) 5. The old __________ fulfilled his master's charge to care for the children.

(A) servant (B) service (C) shape (D) share

Unit 60

shirt [ʃɝ:t] *n.* 襯衫

▶ I need a new shirt to go with my pants.
我需要一件新襯衫來配我的褲子。

97

shock [ʃɑ:k]

① *n.* 衝擊；震驚

實用片語與搭配字

culture shock 文化衝擊

② *v.* 使震驚；使震動

▶ The shock of the bomb caused everyone to run out of their houses.
炸彈的衝擊力讓每個人都從他們的屋子裡跑了出來。

▶ Many people who live in cultures different from their own can suffer from culture shock.
許多生活在不同文化中的人會受到文化衝擊。

▶ Everyone was shocked when Phil quit his high-paying job.
大家都對菲爾辭去高薪的工作感到震驚。

---

shoe [ʃu:] *n.* 鞋子

實用片語與搭配字

be in sb's shoes; step into sb's shoes
設身處地；取代（某人）

▶ Are those shoes good for running?
這雙鞋適合用來跑步嗎？

▶ To understand what it is to be homeless, step into a homeless person's shoes and live on the street for a while.
要體會什麼是無家可歸的感受，就設身處地如街友般在街上住一陣子。

---

shoot [ʃu:t]

① *v.* 射擊；發射

實用片語與搭配字

shoot for sth 爭取

② *v.* 射擊

▶ The police shot all the criminals dead.
警方射殺了所有的罪犯。

▶ There was an opening for a job on a cruise ship and Tom decided to shoot for it.
郵輪公司開放了職缺，湯姆決定爭取看看。

▶ Bryan got shot in the leg during his time in Iraq.
布萊恩在伊拉克作戰時腿部中彈。

---

shop [ʃɑ:p] *v.* 逛街購物

▶ Do you want to shop for some new clothes?
你想要去逛街買新衣服嗎？

實用片語與搭配字

shop around 貨比三家

▶ Buying a new cellphone is not easy and you really have to shop around to find the best price and brand.
買新手機並不簡單，你真的必須貨比三家，才能買到最優惠的價格以及最好的品牌。

shop / store [ʃɑːp / stɔːr] *n.* 商店

實用片語與搭配字

be in the shops 上市

▶ This shop is closed.
這家商店關門了。

▶ The latest product will be in the shops by Thanksgiving.
最新的產品將在感恩節前到貨。

shore [ʃɔːr] *n.* （海、湖或大河的）岸

▶ I like to sit by the shore and watch boats.
我喜歡坐在岸邊欣賞船隻。

short [ʃɔːrt] *adj.* 短的

實用片語與搭配字

short and sweet; in short; be short on / of sth; short-term
簡潔明瞭；總之；缺乏的；暫時的

▶ Tom is short for his age.
湯姆按他的年紀長得算矮小。

▶ I wanted to go to the movies, but I am short on cash and decided to just stay home and watch TV.
我想去看電影，但我錢不夠，所以我決定待在家看電視就好。

shorts [ʃɔːrts] *n.* 短褲

▶ Bring your shorts because the weather is going to be sunny and clear.
帶你的短褲來，因為天氣會很晴朗。

104

shot [ʃɑːt] *n.* 射擊；開槍

▶ His first shot missed the deer, but his second one hit it.
他第一槍射擊沒打中那隻鹿，但第二發就射中了。

should [ʃʊd / ʃəd]
aux. v. 應該；將會（shall 的過去式）

▶ I should rest, but I'm having too much fun!
我應該休息一下，但我玩得太開心了！

shoulder [ˈʃoʊl.dɚ]

① *n.* 肩膀

實用片語與搭配字

sb's shoulders （責任在）…的肩上

▶ Sam put his son on his shoulders and carried him around.
山姆把他的兒子放在肩膀上並帶著他到處走。

▶ Peter has so many responsibilities that it seems he is carrying the world on his shoulders..
彼得有著許多的責任，他似乎肩負著整個世界。

② *v.* 承擔職責；承受重負

▶ He shouldered a lot of responsibility at the office.
他在辦公室裡擔負很多責任。

---

shout [ʃaʊt]

① *v.* 叫喊

② *n.* 呼喊聲

▶ The kids all shouted during the game.
這些孩子玩遊戲時都大聲叫喊。

▶ Shouts of excitement fill the streets on New Year's Eve.
興奮的歡呼聲洋溢在跨年夜的街道上。

---

show [ʃoʊ]

① *v.* 給…看；顯示

實用片語與搭配字

show sb around; show sb / sth off
帶（某人）參觀；炫耀

② *n.* 展覽

實用片語與搭配字

get this / the show on the road; the show must go on
開始行動、著手；事情還得繼續做下去

▶ He showed me how to fish.
他示範如何釣魚給我看。

▶ On her first day at the new job, the boss showed Rita around and introduced her to all the staff.
麗塔上班的第一天，老闆帶她參觀公司，並且將她介紹給所有同事。

▶ There were many new products at the technology show.
在科技展上有很多新產品。

▶ The company designed a new electronic device, but they had to get the show on the road and market it before the competition found out.
這家公司設計了一款新的電子產品，他們要在競爭對手發現之前著手行銷。

---

shower [ˈʃaʊ.ɚ]

① *n.* 陣雨

② *v.* 洗淋浴

實用片語與搭配字

shower sb with sth
大量給予（某人）（禮物或讚美）

▶ Bring an umbrella. There might be showers this afternoon.
帶把傘，今天下午可能會下雨。

▶ Tom showers before going to work.
湯姆上班前會先淋個浴。

▶ The famous singer's admirers showered her with flowers when she walked onto the stage.
那位知名歌手的仰慕者們在她走上舞台時獻給她許多束花。

---

shrimp [ʃrɪmp] *n.* 蝦

▶ They have a lot of shrimp on this restaurant's menu.
在這家餐廳的菜單上有很多蝦子料理。

shut [ʃʌt] *v.* 關閉

實用片語與搭配字

shut (sb) up; shut (sth) down; shut sb / sth out

（使某人）閉嘴；（使）停止運作；把…關在外面

▶ Please shut the door.
請關門。

▶ The police raided the illegal casino and shut it down so that it could not do any further business.
警察查緝了非法賭場，並強制他們停止營業，如此他們就沒辦法再做生意了。

---

shy [ʃaɪ] *adj.* 害羞的

▶ He's shy and doesn't like to talk to strangers.
他很害羞而且不喜歡跟陌生人交談。

---

sick [sɪk] *adj.* 生病的

實用片語與搭配字

sick to sb's stomach; sick leave

噁心的，非常難過；病假

▶ If you're sick, you should rest and take some medicine.
如果你生病了，應該休息並吃藥。

▶ Watching that extremely violent horror movie made me sick to my stomach.
看極為暴力的恐怖電影讓我感到噁心不舒服。

---

side [saɪd] *n.* (一) 邊；面

實用片語與搭配字

side by side; take sides; take sb's side

肩並肩地；(在爭論或戰爭中)表明立場；(在爭論中)支持(某人)

▶ A square has four sides.
正方形有四個邊。

▶ In an argument, I want my friends to take my side even if they think I am wrong.
在爭論中，我希望我的朋友能站在我這邊，儘管他們認為我是錯的。

---

sidewalk [ˈsaɪd.wɑːk] *n.* 人行道

▶ Don't ride your bicycle on the sidewalk. It's for pedestrians.
別把你的自行車騎上人行道，那是給行人走的。

---

sight [saɪt]

① *n.* 視力；視覺

實用片語與搭配字

out of sight, out of mind; lose sight of sth

眼不見，心不念；忘記，忽略

② *v.* 看到

▶ I wear glasses because I have very poor sight.
我戴眼鏡，因為我視力很不好。

▶ A government can easily lose sight of its real purpose -- taking care of society.
政府很容易忽略掉真正的宗旨：造福社會大眾。

▶ We sighted some interesting animals during our trip.
我們在旅途中看到一些有趣的動物。

sign [saɪn]

① *n.* 標誌；招牌

實用片語與搭配字

sign of the times 時代特徵

② *v.* 簽名於

實用片語與搭配字

sigh for sth; sign sth off 簽收；結束

▶ Follow the road signs and you'll see where the race begins.
跟著路標走，你就會看到起跑點。

▶ War, global warming, pollution and floods are all signs of the times we live in.
戰爭、全球暖化、汙染以及水災都是我們這個時代的特徵。

▶ The accountant is waiting for you to sign these financial documents.
這名會計正等著你簽這些財務文件。

▶ I wanted to go the summer camp, but my father did not want to sign for permission.
我想要去參加夏令營，但我爸不願意簽同意書。

---

silence [ˈsaɪ.ləns]

① *n.* 寂靜；沈默

② *v.* 使安靜

▶ The sound of the woman's scream interrupted the silence of the night.
這女人的尖叫聲劃破了夜晚的寂靜。

▶ The president silenced the crowd by raising his hand.
總統舉起他的手讓群眾安靜下來。

silent [ˈsaɪ.lənt] *adj.* 沉默的；寂靜無聲的

▶ The house was silent after all the guests left.
所有賓客離開後，屋子安靜了下來。

Exercise 60

I. Choose and write the correct word. Change the form of the word when necessary.

1	shock (v.) shout (v.)	When I call your name, __________ out so that we know you're here.
2	shoulder (n.) shorts (n.)	He wore a vest top and a pair of luminous __________ to the beach party.
3	sick (adj.) shy (adj.)	I tried to make a conversation with the three __________ people round the table.
4	sign (n.) sight (n.)	The injured man, with blood all over his face, was a gruesome __________.
5	silence (n.) sidewalk (n.)	He stood on the __________ with his hands buried in the pockets of his dark overcoat.

II. Multiple choices.

( ) 1. The guards were ordered to __________ on sight anyone trying to escape.
(A) shout (B) show (C) shoot (D) ship

( ) 2. The students __________ various degrees of skill in doing the experiments.
(A) show (B) shout (C) shoot (D) shop

( ) 3. The boat was about a mile off __________ when the engine suddenly died.
(A) shop (B) ship (C) shorts (D) shore

( ) 4. It was a real __________ to hear that the factory would have to close.
(A) shoulder (B) show (C) shock (D) shoot

( ) 5. __________ your name in the blank space at the bottom of the form.
(A) Sign (B) Shop (C) Ship (D) Shoot

Unit 61

silk [sɪlk] *n.* 絲綢；絲線

▶ This material is made of high quality silk and will be ideal for your jacket.
這布料是由高品質的絲綢做成的，拿來做你的外套最好。

---

silly [ˈsɪl.i] *adj.* 愚蠢的；傻的

▶ Be serious; don't be so silly!
正經一點，別那麼愚蠢！

---

silver [ˈsɪl.vɚ]

① *n.* 銀色

② *adj.* 銀色的

▶ Silver and blue look good together.
銀色和藍色看起來很配。

▶ I need to buy some silver shoes.
我需要去買一雙銀色的鞋子。

similar [ˈsɪm.ə.lɚ] *adj.* 相像的；類似的

▶ Karen and Jade are wearing similar dresses today.
今天凱倫和潔德穿了很相似的洋裝。

---

simple [ˈsɪm.pəl] *adj.* 簡單的

實用片語與搭配字

simple-minded 頭腦簡單的，愚蠢的

▶ I can only play simple songs on the guitar.
我只會用吉他彈一些簡單的歌曲。

▶ You should not make fun of simple-minded people just because they are not as smart as you are.
你不應該取笑頭腦簡單的人，只因為他們不像你一樣聰明。

simply [ˈsɪm.pli] *adv.* 簡單地

▶ Carl now dresses simply because he is no longer in the banking industry.
因為不在銀行業工作了，卡爾現在都穿著簡便。

---

since [sɪns]

① *prep.* 自從…；從…以來

實用片語與搭配字

since when; ever since
從甚麼時候起；從那以後一直

▶ I've loved swimming since my childhood.
我從小就熱愛游泳。

▶ Ever since I told my mother that I failed my exam, she has been pushing me to study for hours every day.
自從我告訴媽媽我考試不及格，她就開始督促我每天要念好幾小時的書。

② *conj.* 既然；因為

③ *adv.* 從那時到現在

▶ Since he's going, I'll go too.
既然他要去，那我也要去。

▶ He moved, and I haven't spoken with him since.
從他搬走後，我就沒再跟他講過話。

---

sing [sɪŋ] *v.* 唱歌

實用片語與搭配字

sing along
跟著（別人的演唱或演奏的音樂）一起唱

▶ She sings all my favorite songs.
她唱著所有我最愛的歌。

▶ During the Christmas festivities, our family usually joins the Christmas Carol sing-along in the park.
聖誕節時，我們家通常會加入唱詩班跟著公園報佳音。

---

singer [ˈsɪŋ.ɚ] *n.* 歌手；歌唱家

▶ I don't consider myself a singer, but I do like to sing.
我並不認為自己是位歌手，但我的確喜歡唱歌。

---

singing [sɪŋ] *n.* 演唱；歌唱；歌聲

▶ The singing at that concert was beautiful.
那場音樂會裡的演唱很美。

---

single [ˈsɪŋ.gəl]

① *adj.* 單一的；單身的；唯一的

② *n.* 單個；單身者

③ *v.* 選出；挑出

▶ I need to buy a single ticket for the concert tonight.
我需要去買一張今晚音樂會的票。

▶ My sister Louise is still single and doesn't want to get married.
我姊姊露易絲仍然是單身，而且不想結婚。

▶ Tom was unhappy because his teacher had singled him out.
湯姆因為他的老師單獨挑選他而感到不高興。

100

sink [sɪŋk]

① *v.* 下沉；落

實用片語與搭配字

sink in; sink in / into sth; sink or swim
（事實或想法）逐漸被完全理解；逐漸滲入；成敗全憑自己

▶ The boat began to sink as water leaked onto the deck.
當水滲進甲板時船開始下沉。

▶ When Maggie started her new job, she had no idea what to do, but she was told to sink or swim by her new boss.
瑪姬開始她的新工作時，完全沒有頭緒要做什麼，但她被新上司告知成敗全靠她自己。

S

② *n.* 水槽；洗臉槽

▶ Can you put all the dishes into the kitchen sink?
你可以把所有碗盤放進廚房的水槽裡嗎？

---

sir [sɝː] *n.* 先生

▶ Sir, are you Mr. Johnson?
先生，你是強生先生嗎？

---

sister [ˈsɪs.tɚ] *n.* 姊或妹

▶ My sister and I look very much alike.
我姊姊和我長得很像。

---

sit [sɪt] *v.* 坐

實用片語與搭配字

sit around; sit in
閒坐，無所事事；（在公共建築物內）靜坐示威

▶ I sat on the empty chair.
我坐在一張空的椅子上。

▶ When we go camping we like to sit around the fire and tell ghost stories.
我們去露營的時候喜歡圍坐在營火旁講鬼故事。

---

six [sɪks]

① *n.* 六

② *adj.* 六個的；六的

▶ Six comes after five.
六在五後面。

▶ My brother can eat six eggs at once.
我哥哥一次可以吃六顆蛋。

---

sixteen [ˌsɪkˈstiːn]

① *n.* 十六

② *adj.* 十六個的；十六的

▶ Eight plus eight equals sixteen.
八加八等於十六。

▶ My family is big; there are sixteen of us!
我有個大家庭，我們總共有十六個人！

---

sixty [ˈsɪk.sti]

① *n.* 六十

② *adj.* 六十個的；六十的

▶ Thirty plus thirty is sixty.
三十加三十等於六十。

▶ Sixty men followed the president to guard him.
六十個人貼身保護總統。

---

size [saɪz]

① *n.* 尺寸；大小

實用片語與搭配字

king-size
比正常（或標準）尺寸長（或大）的

▶ This size is too small for me.
這個尺寸對我來說太小了。

▶ My sister has two children and three dogs, so she and her husband bought a king-size bed that everyone could fit in.
我姊姊有兩個小孩及三隻狗，所以她和她老公買了特大號的床，所有人才能同時擠得上去。

② *v.* 按尺寸製作

▶ Please size the ring for me.
請你幫我量戒圍做這個戒子。

實用片語與搭配字

size sth / sb up 打量，估計，判斷

▶ The first day on my new job as a manager, I could feel everyone sizing me up to see if I could do the job.
在我上任經理的第一天，我可以感受到大家都在打量我是否能夠勝任。

---

skiing [ˈskiː.ɪŋ] *n.* 滑雪

▶ My mom loves to go skiing in the snow.
我媽媽喜歡在雪地裡滑雪。

---

skill [skɪl] *n.* 技巧

▶ Working with others is an important skill to have.
和他人合作是個很重要的技巧。

---

skilled [skɪld] *adj.* 熟練的；有技術的

▶ We are trying to keep Kelly in the company as she is a skilled IT worker.
因為凱莉是位熟練的資訊工程人員，我們想要把她留在在公司裡。

---

skin [skɪn]

① *n.* 皮膚

▶ Take good care of your skin, and you won't get wrinkles!
好好照顧你的皮膚，才不會有皺紋！

實用片語與搭配字

be skin and bone(s) 瘦得皮包骨

▶ Some girls are always on a diet despite the fact that some of them are already skin and bones and did not need to lose any weight.
有些女孩總是在節食，儘管她們中的一些已經瘦得皮包骨不需要減肥。

② *v.* 剝掉…的皮；去掉…的皮

▶ In the old days, people skinned animals for their fur.
以前人們會剝動物的皮來取牠們的軟毛。

實用片語與搭配字

skin sb alive 狠狠責罰（某人）

▶ I went to the party last night after my parents told me not to go; they found out and I am sure they are going to skin me alive.
我父母叫我別去參加昨晚的派對，但我還是去了；他們發現了，肯定會狠狠責罰我一頓。

103

skinny [ˈskɪn.i] *adj.* 極瘦的；皮包骨的

▶ Did you see that group of skinny cows?
你看到那群骨瘦如柴的牛了嗎？

skirt [skɝːt]

① *n.* 裙子

② *v.* 位於…的外圍；繞過…的邊緣

▶ Cindy likes to wear skirts.
辛蒂喜歡穿裙子。

▶ The airport skirts the border of our house.
這個機場緊臨我家房子外圍。

Exercise 61

I. Choose and write the correct word. Change the form of the word when necessary.

1	silver (adj.) similar (adj.)	The pictures are ________, but there are subtle differences between them.
2	simply (adv.) since (adv.)	Many people come to the resort ________ to enjoy the fresh mountain air.
3	single (n.) singer (n.)	The ________ used a microphone so that everyone in the hall could hear him.
4	sink (n.) size (n.)	Water from the kitchen ________ overflowed onto the floor.
5	skill (n.) skin (n.)	________ is acquired through repeated practice, and practice makes perfect.

II. Multiple choices.

(　) 1. As a ________ father, he found it a struggle bringing up three children.
(A) skilled (B) single (C) simple (D) sixty

(　) 2. ________ I started jogging, I've lost three and a half inches from my waistline.
(A) Single (B) Simply (C) Since (D) Similar

(　) 3. Her ideas are fundamentally sound, even if she says ________ things sometimes.
(A) silver (B) single (C) silk (D) silly

(　) 4. Computers and electronics are growing industries and need ________ technicians.
(A) skilled (B) silver (C) singing (D) similar

(　) 5. Despite the warm weather, we searched out some snow and went ________.
(A) skiing (B) singing (C) skill (D) sleeping

Unit 62

sky [skaɪ] *n.* 天空

實用片語與搭配字

the sky's the limit 沒有限制

▶ What a beautiful blue sky today!
今天的天空藍得好美！

▶ Young people today have so many opportunities; they can do everything, really, the sky is the limit.
現今的年輕人有許多機會；他們可以去做任何事情，真的，沒有限制。

---

sleep [sliːp]

① *n.* 睡眠

② *v.* 睡覺

實用片語與搭配字

sleep like a log; sleep on sth; sleep in; oversleep
睡得很香；延遲對…作出決定；睡懶覺；睡過頭

▶ You look tired; you need more sleep.
你看起來很疲累，需要更多睡眠。

▶ Abby was so tired that she slept most of the weekend.
艾比很累，所以她大半個週末都在睡覺。

▶ James stayed up all night last night to study for his final exam and I am sure he will sleep like a log tonight.
昨晚詹姆士熬夜準備期末考，我很確定他今晚會睡得很香。

---

sleepy [ˈsliː.pi] *adj.* 睏倦的；想打瞌睡的

▶ Elle and Tom are sleepy after listening to the professor's lecture all afternoon.
整個下午聽教授講課後，艾莉和湯姆覺得很睏。

---

slender [ˈslen.dɚ] *adj.* 苗條的；修長的

▶ The thief is a slender man with brown hair.
這個扒手是一個有著褐色頭髮瘦瘦的男子。

---

slide [slaɪd]

① *v.* 滑動

② *n.* 溜滑梯

▶ Can you help me slide this note under Kate's door?
你能幫我把這個字條塞進凱特的門裡嗎？

▶ The council plans to buy a new slide for the local playground.
議會計劃替當地的遊樂場買一個新的溜滑梯。

---

slim [slɪm]

① *adj.* 苗條的；纖細的

▶ Kenneth has become slim since he started running every morning.
自從凱妮絲每天早晨開始跑步之後就變苗條了。

② *v.* 減輕體重

▶ This exercise machine will slim your legs if you use it every day.
如果你每天使用這個運動器材的話就能瘦腿。

---

slip [slɪp]

① *v.* 溜；悄悄走

▶ Holly slipped into class without the teacher seeing her.
荷莉溜進教室沒被老師看見。

實用片語與搭配字

slip sb's memory / mind; slip through sb's fingers; slip away; slip of the tongue
被（某人）忘記;（機會或某人）被錯過; 秘密地離開，（時間）很快地過去，（權力、能力或實現或贏取的可能性）消失; 口誤

▶ The teacher asked me the name of a famous leader in history, but I did not know because it had slipped my mind.
老師問了一位歷史上知名領袖的姓名，但我不知道，因為我忘了。

② *n.* 滑跤；失足

▶ Dennis began to walk more carefully after he had that slip in the hallway.
丹尼斯在走廊滑了那一跤後，他開始更加小心走路。

---

slipper [ˈslɪp.ɚ] *n.* 拖鞋

▶ The dog ate my slippers so I need to buy a new pair.
狗咬壞了我的拖鞋，所以我需要買一雙新的。

---

slow [sloʊ]

① *adj.* 慢的

▶ Karl is a slow driver.
卡爾開車很慢。

② *v.* （使）減速；（使）放慢速度

▶ He slowed down, so I could enjoy the view.
他減速下來，這樣我才能欣賞美景。

實用片語與搭配字

slow (sb / sth) down / up; slow-witted
（使）慢下來; 反應遲緩的

▶ We went hiking yesterday, but I was not fit enough and I slowed everyone down; I feel bad about it.
我們昨天去健行，但我不太習慣，拖慢了大家的速度，我覺得很抱歉。

---

slowly [ˈsloʊ.li] *adv.* 緩慢地

▶ Drive slowly, so I can follow you!
開慢點，我才能跟得上你！

實用片語與搭配字

slowly but surely 緩慢但確實地

▶ If you have too much work to do, the best is to just start doing it and slowly but surely, you will see progress.
若你有很多工作要完成，最好的方式就是馬上著手開始，你會緩慢但確實地看見成效。

---

small [smɑːl]

① *adj.* 小的

▶ I want a small cup, please.
請給我一小杯。

S

實用片語與搭配字

it's a small world; small-scale
這世界真小；小規模的

② *n.* 細小的部分

③ *adv.* 小地；不大地

▶ In Africa, many people farm on small-scale because they cannot afford to have large farms.
在非洲，很多人僅在小規模的農場耕作，因為他們無法負擔大型農地的開支。

▶ The small of the project is finished, but there's still a lot more to do.
這個專案的一小部分已完成，但還有更多部分要做。

▶ Cut the pie small because we have many people.
因為我們有很多人，請把這個派切小片一點。

---

smart [smɑːrt] *adj.* 聰明的

▶ Smart people listen to the advice of older people.
聰明人會聽長者的建議。

---

smell [smel]

① *n.* 氣味

② *v.* 聞；嗅

實用片語與搭配字

smell sth / sb out 聞出，嗅出

▶ I like the smell of rain; the air is so fresh!
我喜歡雨的味道，空氣變得很清新！

▶ Breathe in and smell this flower!
深呼吸聞一聞這朵花吧！

▶ My mother can smell lies out no matter how small, so I have learned never to lie to her.
不論謊言多小，我媽媽就是能夠察覺，所以我學會絕不對她說謊。

---

smile [smaɪl]

① *v.* 笑；微笑

實用片語與搭配字

smile on sth / sb 積極對待；眷顧

② *n.* 笑容；微笑

實用片語與搭配字

be all smiles 笑容滿面

▶ Katherine smiled when she saw the kitten.
當凱薩琳看到這隻小貓就笑了。

▶ The family lost everything during the storm, but luck smiled on them when a kind person gave them a home.
那個家庭在暴風雨中失去一切，但幸運之神眷顧，有一位好心人給了他們一個家。

▶ Brock has a big smile on his face.
布羅克的臉上掛著燦爛的笑容。

▶ My brother has been all smiles today after he got news that he had won a free trip to France.
我哥哥自從知道自己獲得去法國旅行的免費機票後，整天都笑容滿面。

smoke [smoʊk]

① *n.* 煙；煙霧

實用片語與搭配字

go up in smoke
化成了煙，化為泡影（未達到預期的效果）

② *v.* 抽菸

實用片語與搭配字

smoke sb / sth out 用煙把（動物或人）熏出

▶ There is too much smoke in the kitchen.
廚房裡冒著太多煙。

▶ After working at the company for years, John's dream of a promotion went up in smoke when he was laid off.
在公司工作多年後，約翰想升遷的夢想在他被裁員時都化成了泡影。

▶ Please don't smoke in the restaurant.
請不要在餐廳裡抽菸。

▶ The criminals were hiding in the department store, so the police tried to smoke them out by sending in sniffer dogs.
那些犯人藏匿在百貨公司裡，警察用煙引他們出來，並派出警犬搜索。

---

smoking [ˈsmoʊ.kɪŋ] *n.* 抽菸

實用片語與搭配字

non-smoking （地方）禁煙的，不准吸煙的

▶ Smoking is very bad for your health.
抽菸對你的健康非常不好。

▶ Most restaurants today are non-smoking places, so you have to go outside if you want to smoke.
現在多數餐廳都是禁菸場所，若你想要抽菸必須出去外面。

---

snack [snæk]

① *n.* 點心；小吃

② *v.* 吃點心

▶ Eat a snack before you head back to class.
在你回教室之前先吃個點心。

▶ I've been snacking on this new cereal all day.
我一整天都在吃這個新的穀片點心。

---

snail [sneɪl] *n.* 蝸牛

▶ Be careful not to step on all the snails that came out after the heavy rain.
小心不要踩到大雨過後出現的蝸牛。

---

snake [sneɪk]

① *n.* 蛇

② *v.* 蜿蜒伸展

▶ There are many dangerous snakes in Australia.
在澳洲有很多危險的蛇。

▶ The line snaked around the street corner.
隊伍沿著街角蜿蜒著。

snow [snoʊ]

① *n.* 雪

② *v.* 下雪；飄雪

▶ When snow melts, it turns into water.
當雪融化時就變成了水。

▶ It snows a lot in Canada.
加拿大下很多雪。

---

snowy [ˈsnoʊ.i] *adj.* 似雪的；雪白的

▶ Grandpa's hair is snowy white.
爺爺有著一頭雪白的鶴髮。

---

so [soʊ]

① *adv.* 那麼；非常

實用片語與搭配字

so be it; so much so; so what?
（用於表示有必要接受目前的處境）就接受吧；到…程度；那又怎樣？

② *conj.* 所以；因此

▶ He was so tired that he fell asleep immediately.
他實在太累，所以立刻睡著了。

▶ Mason liked eating ice-cream so much so that he started his own ice-cream business.
梅森很喜歡吃冰淇淋，所以他自己開創了冰淇淋事業。

▶ It's Brandon's birthday, so we should celebrate.
今天是布蘭登的生日，所以我們應該慶祝一下。

---

soap [soʊp]

① *n.* 肥皂

② *v.* 用肥皂（清潔液）擦洗

▶ I use soap and water to wash my hands.
我用肥皂和水洗手。

▶ I soaped all the dishes, but I haven't rinsed them yet.
我用洗碗精洗了碗盤，但還沒用水沖乾淨。

---

soccer [ˈsɑː.kɚ] *n.* 足球

▶ The whole family is going to watch Ian play soccer this afternoon.
今天下午全家人都要去看伊恩踢足球。

104

social [ˈsoʊ.ʃəl] *adj.* 社會的

實用片語與搭配字

social network; social media; social welfare
（網站或電腦程式）社交網路；社群媒體；社會福利

▶ The social problems in our community have been increasing over several years.
我們社會裡的社會問題年年增加。

▶ One should not underestimate the power of social media like Facebook to influence people.
人們不應該低估像 Facebook 這樣的社群媒體對人的影響。

Exercise 62

I. Choose and write the correct word. Change the form of the word when necessary.

1	sleepy (adj.) slim (adj.)	We arrived at the hotel late last night, and were too ________ to notice how beautiful it was.
2	slide (v.) soap (v.)	I locked the front door and started to ________ the key automatically into my purse.
3	slipper (n.) smell (n.)	For people who don't drink, alcohol has a very distinctive ________.
4	smoke (v.) slow (v.)	The threat of global warming will eventually force us to ________ down the energy consumption.
5	snowy (adj.) social (adj.)	The rapid expansion of cities can cause ________ and economic problems.

II. Multiple choices.

( ) 1. Gabriel is a tall, ________ young man with a light, brown mustache.
(A) sleepy (B) slide (C) slender (D) slow

( ) 2. There was a marked improvement in my health when I gave up ________.
(A) smoking (B) sleeping (C) sliding (D) slowing

( ) 3. The ________ player was seeing red after being ejected from the game.
(A) snail (B) smoke (C) smile (D) soccer

( ) 4. It's healthier to ________ on fruit rather than chocolate or chips.
(A) snack (B) snake (C) smoke (D) smell

( ) 5. Sometimes they just drive ________ down the lane, enjoying the scenery.
(A) slipper (B) snowy (C) slowly (D) sleepy

Unit 63

society [sə'saɪ.ə.t̬i] *n.* 社會

▶ Modern society has adapted to the use of smartphones quickly.
現代社會已經快速適應智慧型手機的使用。

---

sock [sɑːk] *n.* 襪子

▶ Please put your socks into the laundry basket now.
請馬上把你的襪子放進洗衣籃裡。

---

soda ['soʊ.də] *n.* 汽水；蘇打水

▶ My mom likes to drink soda on a hot summer day.
我媽媽喜歡在炎熱的夏天喝汽水。

---

sofa ['soʊ.fə] *n.* 沙發

▶ We bought a new sofa for the living room.
我們買了一張新沙發放客廳。

---

soft [sɑːft] *adj.* 柔軟的

實用片語與搭配字

soft on sb / sth 十分喜歡（某人），太寬大，不夠嚴厲（某事）

▶ The kitten's fur is very soft. Feel it!
這隻小貓咪的毛非常柔軟，摸摸看吧！

▶ My father refused to have a dog until I brought a puppy home one day and he went all soft on it.
我父親拒絕養狗，直到有天我帶了一隻小狗回家，他徹底愛上牠了。

---

soil [sɔɪl]

① *n.* 土壤

② *v.* 弄髒

▶ This soil is good for growing vegetables.
這種土壤適合種蔬菜。

▶ The little boy soiled his pants, so his mother had to put new ones on him.
這小男孩弄髒了他的褲子，所以他的媽媽必須幫他穿上新的。

---

soldier ['soʊl.dʒɚ] *n.* 士兵

▶ The soldiers were happy to go home after the war was over.
士兵們在戰事結束後很高興能返鄉。

solution [sə'luː.ʃən] *n.* 解決方法；答案

▶ Our committee hopes to find a solution to the slowing economy.
我們的委員會希望能找到針對經濟趨緩的解決方案。

103

solve [sɑːlv] *v.* 解答；思考

▶ Everyone's trying to solve the mystery of the missing girl.
每個人都正試著解開失蹤女孩之謎。

---

some [sʌm / səm]

① *adj.* 某些的；一部分的

② *pron.* 一些；若干；一部分

▶ Some people are tall, and others are short.
某些人長得高，某些人長得矮。

▶ Some of the students will go to the event, but others will stay home.
有一些學生會參加活動，但有一些會待在家。

---

somebody [ˈsʌm͵bɑː.di / ˈsʌm͵bʌ.di]

① *pron.* 某人；有人

② *n.* 重要人物

▶ Somebody needs to stop that alarm because it's hurting my ears.
需要有人按掉警鈴，因為我的耳朵被弄得很痛。

▶ She was somebody important because the Queen greeted her.
她是個重要人物，因為女王都來問候她。

---

someone [ˈsʌm.wʌn]

① *n.* 重要人物

② *pron.* 某人

▶ She thinks she is someone because she has a lot of money.
因為她很有錢，所以自認是個重要人物。

▶ Can you find someone who will help me?
你可以找誰來幫我嗎？

---

something [ˈsʌm.θɪŋ]

① *n.* 具有某種特點的人（或事物）

實用片語與搭配字

be (really) something 了不起

② *pron.* 某物；某事；某個東西

▶ Did you see that show? Wasn't that something?
你看到那場表演了嗎？是不是很棒很有特色？

▶ I don't know if you saw the amazing full moon on New Year's Eve; it was really something.
我不知道你有沒有看到除夕時的滿月，真的是很了不起。

▶ Something is bothering her.
有些事正讓她煩心。

---

sometimes [ˈsʌm.taɪmz] *adv.* 有時候

▶ Sometimes, I eat bananas for breakfast.
有時候我吃香蕉當早餐。

somewhere [ˈsʌm.wer] *adv.* 在某處

▶ Carl found the book somewhere in the library.
卡爾在圖書館的某處找到了那本書。

---

son [sʌn] *n.* 兒子

▶ Mr. Brown has two sons and three daughters.
布朗先生有兩個兒子和三個女兒。

---

song [sɑːŋ] *n.* 歌曲

▶ I like to sing English songs.
我喜歡唱英文歌。

---

soon [suːn] *adv.* 不久；很快地

實用片語與搭配字

sooner or later; no sooner said than done; see you soon; as soon as; as soon as possible
遲早；馬上就做；稍後再見；一…就；盡快

▶ I'm going to bed soon; I just need to brush my teeth first.
我就要睡了，要先去刷牙。

▶ If you do not change your ways and stop dealing in drugs, the police will catch you sooner of later.
你若不嘗試改變，並且停止買賣毒品，警察遲早會抓到你。

---

sorry [ˈsɔːr.i] *adj.* 感到難過的

實用片語與搭配字

I'm sorry to say; feel sorry for yourself; better safe than sorry
我很遺憾的說；（因發生的倒楣事而）憤憤不平；有備無患

▶ He was sorry for lying to me, so I forgave him.
他對跟我說謊感到很抱歉，所以我原諒了他。

▶ When you travel to Africa, it is a good idea to get a malaria vaccine; better safe than sorry.
去非洲旅行前建議先施打瘧疾疫苗，有備無患。

---

sort [sɔːrt]

① *n.* 種類

實用片語與搭配字

sort of 有點

② *v.* 分類；區分

▶ Theresa and Katie both like the same sort of cheese.
泰瑞莎和凱蒂兩人喜歡同樣種類的起司。

▶ May asked me if I liked roses or sunflowers, but I couldn't choose because I sort of like both.
梅問我喜歡玫瑰還是向日葵，我無法決定，因為我兩種都有點喜歡。

▶ I need some help sorting through all these shoes.
我需要有人幫忙把這些鞋子分類。

實用片語與搭配字

sort sth out 挑出

▶ After the death of her husband, the widow had to sort his business out but everything was confusing.
自從她的丈夫過世，那個寡婦必須處理他公司的事務，但所有事情都很混亂。

---

soul [soʊl] *n.* 靈魂

實用片語與搭配字

soul-searching; soulmate
自我反省；靈魂伴侶

▶ What happens to our souls after we die?
我們死後靈魂會發生什麼事呢？

▶ Every person wishes to find their soulmate, a person who understands them and can share everything with them.
每個人都希望找到靈魂伴侶，一位能夠理解他們並分享所有事情的人。

---

sound [saʊnd]

① *adj.* 完好的；健康的

② *n.* 聲音

實用片語與搭配字

the sound of sth …給人的印象（或感覺）

③ *v.* 聽起來

實用片語與搭配字

sound like 聽起來像

▶ The building is sound; it won't fall.
這棟建築很完好，不會倒。

▶ We heard a loud sound outside and ran to see what happened.
我們聽到外面有很大的聲音，所以跑出去看發生什麼事。

▶ The sound of the church bells ringing outside my apartment reminds me of my childhood.
公寓外頭教堂的鐘聲，使我回憶起我的童年。

▶ This job sounds like a good opportunity for you.
這個工作聽起來對你是個好機會。

▶ My friend was very upset over the phone and it sounded like she had an accident.
我朋友在電話那頭聽起來相當難過，她聽起來好像發生了事故。

---

soup [suːp] *n.* 湯

▶ Ken wants to eat soup and bread for lunch.
肯恩午餐想喝湯配麵包。

---

sour [saʊr]

① *adj.* 酸的；有酸味的

② *n.* 酸味

▶ This lemon juice is very sour.
這檸檬汁非常酸。

▶ I like sweet but not sour.
我喜歡甜的而不是酸的。

③ *v.* 變酸

- The milk is so old that it soured.
  這牛奶已經放太久變酸了。

---

source [sɔːrs] *n.* 源頭；來源

- The source of heat came from the fire Tony lit.
  這高溫的熱源是從湯尼點的火引起的。

Exercise 63

I. Choose and write the correct word. Change the form of the word when necessary.

1	society (n.) soldier (n.)	The increase in crime is a sad reflection on our ________ today.
2	solve (v.) sort (v.)	We need to get to the root of the problem before we can ________ it.
3	soon (adv.) sometimes (adv.)	People who can't have a baby of their own ________ foster one.
4	sound (n.) soul (n.)	Anything is possible, as long as you set your heart, mind, and ________ to it.
5	source (n.) someone (n.)	Many of the villagers rely on fishing as their primary ________ of income.

II. Multiple choices.

( ) 1. We haven't found the ________ yet, but I'm sure we're on the right track.
(A) society (B) solution (C) soul (D) sound

( ) 2. It's important to use ________ pickle chips; this is what gives the burger its distinctive taste.
(A) soft (B) soil (C) sour (D) sound

( ) 3. Happiness is to find ________ who can give you warmth and share your life with you.
(A) someone (B) something (C) somewhere (D) solutions

( ) 4. A business can only be built and expanded on a ________ financial base.
(A) soul (B) soft (C) something (D) sound

( ) 5. After the harvest, the peasants began to prepare the ________ for seeding.
(A) soil (B) soup (C) soul (D) sort

Unit 64

south [saʊθ]

① *n.* 南方

② *adj.* 南方的

③ *adv.* 向南方；在南方

▶ Birds fly to the south for the winter.
鳥兒飛到南方過冬。

▶ I live in the south part of the city.
我住在城南。

▶ We drove south for several hours before we arrived.
我們向南開了好幾個小時才抵達。

---

southern [ˋsʌðən] *adj.* 南方的；向南的

▶ Brady is from the southern part of the United States.
布萊迪來自美國南部。

---

soybean / soya bean / soy
[ˋsɔɪˏbin / ˋsɔɪ.əˏbi:n / sɔɪ] *n.* 黃豆；大豆

▶ I need to go and buy some soybean from the local market.
我需要去本地市場買一些黃豆。

---

space [speɪs]

① *n.* 空間

實用片語與搭配字

open space （尤指城市中的）空地，開闊地

② *v.* 把…以一定間隔排列；在…中留間隔

▶ Is there space in your car for my bags?
你的車子有空間放我這些袋子嗎？

▶ I love the open space of the countryside where I can enjoy nature and go walking with my dogs.
我喜歡鄉村的開闊空地，在那裡我可以享受自然並且跟我的狗一起散步。

▶ Make sure to space the photos out on the wall.
要確定掛在牆上的照片有一樣的間隔。

---

speak [spi:k] *v.* 説話

實用片語與搭配字

speak out / up; not be on speaking terms; speak your mind
公開發表意見，坦率說出；（因生氣）互不理睬；說出心裡話

▶ Please don't speak when your mouth is full of food.
當你嘴裡都是食物時請不要說話。

▶ After our big fight two years ago, I have not been on speaking terms with my best friend; I really miss her.
自從兩年前我們大吵一架，我和最好的朋友就不理對方了，我真的很想念她。

speaker [ˈspiː.kɚ] *n.* 說話者；演說者

實用片語與搭配字

native speaker 母語使用者

▶ My friend is the main speaker at this conference.
我的朋友是這場研討會的主講人。

▶ If you want to teach English as a foreign language, you should be a native speaker of English.
若你想要教英語這個外語，你應該是英語的母語人士。

97

special [ˈspeʃ.əl] *adj.* 特殊的

實用片語與搭配字

special education 特殊教育

▶ We ate a special meal to celebrate my mother's birthday.
我們吃了一頓特別的餐點來慶祝我媽媽的生日。

▶ These days, many children have behavior problems and they require special education to change their ways.
現今許多兒童有行為障礙，他們需要特殊教育去幫助改變這樣的情況。

---

speech [spiːtʃ] *n.* 演說

▶ The president's speech was full of promises.
總統的演說充滿了各種承諾。

---

speed [spiːd]

① *n.* 速度；速率

實用片語與搭配字

speed-up 加速

② *v.* 迅速前進；加速

▶ The speed of that car definitely exceeded the road limit.
那輛車的車速絕對超過道路速限。

▶ The project manager told us to speed-up the testing of the new computer to make our deadline.
專案負責人告訴我們要加快新款電腦的測試，才能趕上完成的最後期限。

▶ Alex sped to the hospital as soon as he heard that Louis was in the emergency room.
艾力克斯一聽到露易絲在急診室，就盡快趕往醫院。

---

spell [spel] *v.* 拼字

實用片語與搭配字

spell sth out 詳細地說明

▶ Do you know how to spell this word?
你知道要如何拼這個字嗎？

▶ The criminal was in court for the third time and the judge spelled a warning out to him that the next time he would go to jail for life.
那名犯人已經第三次上法院，法官鄭重警告他，若是再一次，他就得坐牢一輩子。

spelling [ˈspel.ɪŋ] *v.* 拼字

實用片語與搭配字

spelling bee
（正確拼出單詞數量最多者獲勝的）拼字比賽

▶ Casey's spelling has improved since her parents employed a tutor.
自從她的父母請了家教，凱西的拼字進步了許多。

▶ My 6-year-old niece won the national spelling bee and we are all proud of her ability to spell so well.
我六歲的姪女贏得了全國拼字比賽，我們都為她的優秀拚字能力感到驕傲。

---

spend [spend] *v.* 花費

▶ How much time do you spend studying every night?
你每天晚上花多少時間讀書？

---

spider [ˈspaɪ.dɚ] *n.* 蜘蛛

▶ Can you help me remove several spiders hiding under my bed?
你能幫我把藏在我床鋪下面的幾隻蜘蛛弄走嗎？

---

spinach [ˈspɪn.ɪtʃ] *n.* 菠菜

▶ This salad also contains one cup of spinach and carrots.
這道沙拉含有一杯菠菜和胡蘿蔔。

---

103 95

spirit [ˈspɪr.ət] *n.* 心靈；精神

實用片語與搭配字

kindred spirit; team spirit; free spirit; that's the spirit
志同道合的人；團隊精神；無拘無束的人；用於表示贊同或鼓勵）這就對了

▶ Although I can only see Frank through the webcam, I feel like he's here in spirit.
雖然我只能透過網路攝影機見到法蘭克，但我感覺他的心也在這裡。

▶ Janet found a kindred spirit in Michael, and the two of them fell in love very quickly.
珍妮特和麥可是志同道合的人，他們很快就墜入愛河。

---

spoon [spuːn]

① *n.* 湯匙

② *v.* 用杓舀；用匙盛

▶ I need a spoon to eat this soup.
我需要湯匙喝這碗湯。

▶ He spooned up the ice cream for each person.
他用杓子挖冰淇淋給大家吃。

---

sport [spɔːrt]

① *n.* 運動

▶ Basketball is my brother's favorite sport.
籃球是我弟弟最愛的運動。

② *v.* 遊戲；玩耍

▶ He sported with his new puppy in the yard.
他跟新養的小狗在後院裡玩耍。

---

spot [spɑːt]

① *n.* 斑點；汙點

② *v.* 弄髒；玷污

▶ I got several oil spots on my new shirt.
我的新襯衫上弄到了幾個油污。

▶ John spilled coffee and spotted his shirt.
約翰把咖啡灑了，還弄髒了他的襯衫。

---

spread [spred]

① *v.* 攤開；散佈；傳播

實用片語與搭配字

spread your wings; spread the word
展翅高飛，初試身手；散佈消息

② *n.* 使擴散；使蔓延

▶ I need you to help me spread the blanket out onto the ground.
我需要你幫我把毯子攤開在地上。

▶ Every student should spread their wings after high school and see the world before going to university.
每個學生在高中畢業後都應該展翅高飛，並在上大學前好好看看這個世界。

▶ The spread of this cold has affected the whole city this winter.
這個冬天感冒的擴散已經影響了整個城市。

---

spring [sprɪŋ]

① *n.* 春天

② *v.* 彈開；跳躍

實用片語與搭配字

spring to life; spring to mind
突然活躍（或忙碌）起來；腦海瞬間浮現…

③ *n.* 彈簧

▶ In the spring, the weather turns warm.
春天時天氣變暖。

▶ I sprang out of my chair when the president walked into the room.
當總統走進房間時，我從我的椅子上跳了起來。

▶ There are many great classical books; one that springs to mind is The Catcher in the Rye.
有許多很棒的經典書籍，腦海中浮現的一本就是《麥田捕手》。

▶ The springs in this sofa need to be replaced.
這張沙發的彈簧該換了。

---

square [skwer]

① *adj.* 正方形的

② *n.* 正方形

▶ The builder recommends you put a square shaped box in that corner.
這個建商建議你放一個正方形的盒子在那個角落。

▶ Draw four squares on your piece of paper.
在你的紙上畫四個正方形。

squirrel [ˈskwɝː.əl] *n.* 松鼠

▶ The squirrel darted up the tree and away from me.
這隻松鼠衝上樹並跳離了我。

stage [steɪdʒ]

① *n.* 舞台

▶ We need all the performers to meet on the stage in ten minutes.
我們要所有的表演者在十分鐘內到舞台上集合。

實用片語與搭配字

take the stage; be on the stage; early-stage
登臺表演；當演員；早期

▶ After winning the award for her great performance, the actress took the stage to make her acceptance speech.
在她精湛的演出獲獎後，那名女演員登上舞台發表得獎感言。

② *v.* 舉辦

▶ The charity event was staged in the city center.
這場慈善活動曾在市中心舉辦。

---

stair [ster] *n.* 樓梯

▶ Go up these stairs to the second floor.
上樓梯到二樓。

---

stamp [stæmp]

① *v.* 貼郵票；蓋章

▶ Please stamp the envelopes before you mail them.
在你寄出這些郵件前，先在信封貼上郵票。

實用片語與搭配字

stamped on sb's memory
銘刻於（某人）的記憶中

▶ The horrors of the war were stamped on people's memory and they vowed to try and prevent future wars.
戰爭的可怕深深刻在人們的記憶中，他們誓言要阻止未來發生戰爭。

② *n.* 郵票；印章

▶ Tina collects stamps from around the world.
緹娜收集世界各地的郵票。

Exercise 64

I. Choose and write the correct word. Change the form of the word when necessary.

1	speed (n.) speech (n.)	His first __________ as president made a strong impression on his audience.
2	speaker (n.) spider (n.)	We couldn't hear the __________ at the back of the hall because her voice didn't carry very well.
3	stamp (v.) spend (v.)	The government has promised to __________ more on health and education.
4	special (adj.) square (adj.)	Rescuers used a __________ device for finding people trapped in collapsed buildings.
5	soybean (n.) spinach (n.)	Popeye, the sailor man, eats green, leafy __________ to make him strong.

II. Multiple choices.

( ) 1. She was a very brave girl and everyone who knew her admired her __________.
(A) spoon (B) spider (C) spring (D) spirit

( ) 2. The long, cruel winter came to an end at last, yielding to a gentle and warm __________.
(A) spring (B) spirit (C) square (D) squirrel

( ) 3. The starting point for the guided tour of the town is in the market __________.
(A) spring (B) spirit (C) square (D) sport

( ) 4. My doctor says I should start playing __________ because my lifestyle is too sedentary.
(A) spiders (B) sports (C) springs (D) spoons

( ) 5. The tourists sought out a shady __________ to sit down and rest.
(A) spring (B) sport (C) spot (D) spider

Unit 65

stand [stænd]

① *v.* 站立

實用片語與搭配字

can't stand the sight of sb / sth; know where you stand; stand your ground; stand by sb

受不了；知道自己的立場；堅持立場；繼續支持（或幫助某人

② *n.* 攤位；貨攤

- Jeffrey hurt his leg and cannot stand for a long time.
  傑佛瑞的腳受傷無法久站。
- Many teenagers are bullied on social media today, but they should be taught to stand their ground and fight back.
  許多青少年在社群媒體上遭受霸凌，但他們應當學會堅持立場並且反擊。
- I like to buy tea from the stand across the street.
  我喜歡去對街的那家飲料攤買茶。

99

standard ['stæn.dɚd]

① *n.* 標準；規格

實用片語與搭配字

double standard 雙重標準

② *adj.* 標準的；一般性的

- The teacher told me my homework was not of an acceptable standard.
  老師告訴我，我的功課未達到可接受的標準。
- I cannot stand people who have double standards; people who say one thing and then does exactly the opposite thing.
  我無法忍受有著雙重標準的人，說一套做一套。
- The standard procedure for opening the store is contained in this document.
  這份文件包含了開設這家店的標準流程。

---

star [stɑːr]

① *n.* 星星；明星

實用片語與搭配字

co-star; superstar 合演者；超級巨星

② *v.* 主演

- I love looking at all the beautiful stars.
  我喜歡晚上出去看美麗的星星。
- The actress and her co-star were honored for their roles in the award-winning drama.
  這齣獲獎戲劇的女主角和配角都因他們在劇中的角色而受到表彰。
- My favorite actor stars in many old movies.
  我最愛的演員主演很多老電影。

---

start [stɑːrt]

① *v.* 開始；出發

- Let's start our lesson today; please open your books to page ten.
  現在開始我們今天的課程，請翻開課本第十頁。

實用片語與搭配字

start (sth) off （使）（以…）開始

- If you start something off, then you have to finish it because quitting is not good.
  你若是開始了一件事，那就去完成它，半途而廢是不好的事情。

② *n.* 開始，開端

- At the start of her trip, she was excited, but she soon became bored.
  在她旅程剛開始時，她很興奮，但很快地就覺得無聊。

實用片語與搭配字

from start to finish 自始至終

- From start to finish, it took them only two weeks to build the house.
  從頭到尾，這幢房子只花了他們兩個禮拜建造。

---

state [steɪt]

① *n.* 狀況；情形

- Rick was sick and in a terrible state when I last saw him.
  我上次看見瑞克時，他生病而且狀況很糟。

② *v.* 陳述

- Please state all the facts.
  請陳述所有事實。

102

statement [ˈsteɪt.mənt] *n.* 聲明；說明；表態

- I agree with your statement.
  我同意你的聲明。

100

station [ˈsteɪ.ʃən]

① *n.* 車站；（各種機構的）站，所，局

- Please meet me at the train station at 1 p.m.
  請下午一點和我在火車站碰面。

② *v.* 駐紮

- Many soldiers were stationed in other countries during the war.
  很多軍兵在戰爭中駐紮於其他國家。

---

stay [steɪ]

① *v.* 停留；暫住

- We stayed in a hotel during our vacation.
  我們度假時都住在飯店裡。

實用片語與搭配字

stay away from sb / sth; stay out of sth
避開某人事物；置身於…之外

- Gemma's family warned her to stay away from Peter because he was a bad influence, but she did not listen.
  蓋瑪的家人警告她遠離彼得，因為他會給她帶來不好的影響，但她不聽勸。

② *n.* 停留時間，逗留時間

- We hope you enjoy your stay here in Canada.
  我們期待你享受在加拿大的這段時間。

S

steak [steɪk] *n.* 牛排

▶ Francis requested steak at his birthday barbecue.
法蘭西斯要求他的生日烤肉會要有牛排。

---

steal [sti:l] *v.* 偷竊；侵佔

▶ Thieves stole several luxury watches from the jewelry store.
小偷從珠寶店裡偷走了好幾隻昂貴的手錶。

---

steam [sti:m]

① *n.* 蒸氣；水氣

實用片語與搭配字

run out of steam 忽然失去動力

② *v.* 蒸煮（食物）

▶ The steam rose from my bowl of rice.
蒸氣從我的飯碗裡冒了出來。

▶ We had been trying to finish our homework, but by midnight we ran out of steam and went to bed.
我們一直努力想要完成作業，但到了半夜，我們失去動力就上床睡覺了。

▶ Becky eats healthy. She steams her vegetables.
貝姬吃得很健康，她的蔬菜都是用蒸的。

---

steel [sti:l]

① *n.* 鋼；鋼鐵

② *v.* 使堅強；使像鋼

▶ This artwork is made of steel.
這件藝術品是用鋼做成的。

▶ John steeled himself for the bad news.
約翰讓自己堅強起來以接受壞消息。

---

step [step]

① *n.* 台階；腳步

實用片語與搭配字

step by step 按部就班地

② *v.* 踩踏；跨步

實用片語與搭配字

step forward; step back
站出來；退一步（考慮問題）

▶ There are 1000 steps to the top of this hill.
要上這座山頂必須爬一千個台階。

▶ The best way to learn a new skill is by doing it step-by-step, otherwise, you will not learn.
學習新技能最好的方式就是按部就班地做，否則你學不會。

▶ The floor is wet, step carefully.
地板濕滑，請小心腳步。

▶ It is important to sometimes take a step back from our busy lives and reflect on what we are doing.
重要的是，我們有時需要從忙碌的生活中退一步，反思我們正在做的事情。

stick [stɪk]

① *n.* 枝條；棍棒

② *v.* 黏住；刺；戳

實用片語與搭配字

stick around; stick out

逗留，停留；探出，突出

- I need a stick to lean on while hiking up the mountain.
  登山的時候我需要靠著一根手杖爬。
- Dan stuck a note on your desk.
  丹恩在你書桌上黏了一張紙條。
- For Halloween, my brother decided to dress like a princess. He will sure stick out and everyone will notice him.
  我哥哥決定在萬聖節裝扮成一位公主，他肯定會是最突出的，所有人都會注意到他。

---

still [stɪl]

① *adj.* 靜止的；不動的

② *adv.* 仍然；仍舊

實用片語與搭配字

hold still; time stands still

別動；時間彷彿凝固了

- In the morning, the lake is still and quiet.
  清晨時，這湖是靜止安寧的。
- She is still going to Spain even though her friends aren't going.
  雖然她的朋友都不去，她仍然要去西班牙。
- My grandfather always said that time stood still for no-one and that we have to use every minute we have.
  我爺爺總是說時間不為任何人停留，我們都應該好好運用所擁有的每分每秒。

---

stomach [ˈstʌm.ək] *n.* 胃；肚子

實用片語與搭配字

stomach ache 胃痛

- The spicy food from last night's dinner upset my stomach.
  昨晚的辣味食物讓我的胃不舒服。
- Mavis had a stomach ache after eating the oysters, so we rushed her to see the doctor.
  梅維斯在吃了生蠔後開始胃痛，所以我們趕緊帶她去看醫生。

---

stone [stoʊn]

① *n.* 石頭

② *v.* 向…扔石頭

實用片語與搭配字

stone-faced 不顯露任何情緒的

- These houses are made of stones.
  這些房子是用石頭砌成的。
- In some countries, criminals are stoned to death.
  有些國家，罪犯會處石刑，被扔石頭致死。
- The two boys knew something was wrong when they arrived home past their curfew and saw their father's stone-faced expression.
  當那兩個男孩過了門禁時間才回家，看到他們的父親面色如土時，便知道大事不妙。

S

stop [stɑ:p]

① *v.* 停止

② *n.* 停留；停留時間

實用片語與搭配字

non-stop; put a stop to sth

不停頓的，不間斷的；使停止

▶ Sara needs to stop eating junk food.
莎拉要停止吃垃圾食物。

▶ We don't have time for another stop.
我們沒有時間中途再停一下。

▶ People all over the world are fighting to put a stop to animal abuse.
全球各地的人都在為禁止動物虐待的議題發聲。

---

store [stɔ:r]

① *n.* 商店

② *v.* 儲存

實用片語與搭配字

store sth up 儲存，牢記

▶ Tony went to the store to buy some drinks.
湯尼去這家店買飲料。

▶ My mother stored all my baby photos in a book.
我媽媽把我所有嬰孩時的照片都存放在一本簿子裡。

▶ In summer, many animals will work hard to store food up so that they have enough to eat during the winter.
夏季時，許多動物會忙於儲存糧食，以便有足夠的食物過冬。

95

storm [stɔ:rm]

① *n.* 暴風雨

實用片語與搭配字

take sb / sth by storm; cook up, dance up, talk up, etc. a storm

在（某處）大獲成功；奮力地燒飯做菜 / 充滿激情地跳舞 / 熱烈地談話等

② *v.* 起風暴

▶ The storm damaged many houses and trees.
暴風雨摧毀了許多房屋和樹木。

▶ The scientist took the medical world by storm when he announced that he had found a cure for cancer.
當那位科學家宣布他發現癌症解藥時，他在藥學界造成轟動。

▶ It stormed through the night and all of the next day.
一整晚颳風又下雨，隔天一整天也是這樣。

---

story [ˈstɔ:r.i]

① *n.* 故事

實用片語與搭配字

cover story; it's / that's the story of my life

封面報導；（表示經常遇到類似的倒楣事）我就是這個命

▶ Grandpa loves to tell stories of his childhood.
爺爺最愛說他小時候的故事。

▶ The cover story in the magazine is about becoming a successful businessman and it could be useful; you should read it.
雜誌的封面故事是有關如何成為成功的企業家，這或許有幫助；你應該閱讀一下。

② *v.* 樓層

▶ My house has three stories, but we only use the first and second.
我家有三層樓，但是我們只用一樓和二樓。

---

stove [stoʊv] *n.* 爐子

▶ I left some soup on the stove for you.
我在爐子上留了一些湯給你。

straight [streɪt]

① *adj.* 筆直的

▶ You need to ride your scooter in a straight line for six seconds.
你需要在筆直的一條線上騎著你的摩托車持續六秒鐘。

實用片語與搭配字

straight out 不拐彎抹角地

▶ The man was accused of stealing money from the company, but he denied it straight out and hired a lawyer.
那位男士被指控挪用公款，但他直接否認，並聘用了一位律師。

② *n.* 直線

▶ The winning horse raced past the other horses on the straight.
這匹冠軍馬在直線衝刺時超越了其他馬匹。

③ *adv.* 挺直地

▶ Continue straight along this road and the post office is next to the library.
沿著這條路繼續直行，郵局就在圖書館旁邊。

實用片語與搭配字

straight away / off 立即，馬上

▶ My mom asked me to take out the garbage and I said I'd do it straight away.
我媽媽叫我把垃圾拿出去，我說我馬上去做。

100

strange [streɪndʒ] *adj.* 奇怪的

▶ It is strange to see snow in summer.
夏天見到雪真的很奇怪。

實用片語與搭配字

feel strange 感覺不舒服，感覺不正常

▶ Eve was not used to the new house and she felt strange in the place.
依芙不太習慣她的新家，這個地方讓她覺得不舒服。

---

stranger [ˈstreɪn.dʒɚ] *n.* 陌生人

▶ Be careful not to talk to strangers.
小心不要和陌生人交談。

S

Exercise 65

I. Choose and write the correct word. Change the form of the word when necessary.

<table>
<tr><td rowspan="2">1</td><td>state (n.)</td><td rowspan="2">When all passengers are on board, the train pulls out of the ________.</td></tr>
<tr><td>station (n.)</td></tr>
<tr><td rowspan="2">2</td><td>steal (v.)</td><td rowspan="2">The man sneaked around the place watching for a chance to ________ something.</td></tr>
<tr><td>stick (v.)</td></tr>
<tr><td rowspan="2">3</td><td>store (n.)</td><td rowspan="2">Their fishing boats were tied together before the ________ came.</td></tr>
<tr><td>storm (n.)</td></tr>
<tr><td rowspan="2">4</td><td>strange (adj.)</td><td rowspan="2">She shivered as she heard the ________ noise in the night.</td></tr>
<tr><td>straight (adj.)</td></tr>
<tr><td rowspan="2">5</td><td>stomach (n.)</td><td rowspan="2">I woke up this morning with a fever and an upset ________.</td></tr>
<tr><td>statement (n.)</td></tr>
</table>

II. Multiple choices.

( ) 1. This used to be my favorite restaurant, but the ________ of cooking has fallen off recently.
(A) steak (B) start (C) standard (D) stand

( ) 2. What the witness said in court was not consistent with the ________ he made to the police.
(A) start (B) stand (C) station (D) statement

( ) 3. It can be difficult to strike up a conversation with a complete ________.
(A) stranger (B) store (C) storm (D) step

( ) 4. We'd better get off the lake before the ________ breaks, or we'll get soaked.
(A) stove (B) storm (C) stone (D) steel

( ) 5. At 86, he's quite active, although he walks with the aid of a ________.
(A) stick (B) storm (C) station (D) story

Unit 66

straw [strɑ:] *n.* 稻草；麥桿

▶ In the story of the three little pigs, one pig's house was made of straw.
三隻小豬的故事裡，有一隻豬的房子是稻草蓋的。

---

strawberry [ˈstrɑ:ˌber.i] *n.* 草莓

▶ The fruit salad contains strawberries, kiwi fruit and bananas.
這份水果沙拉裡有草莓、奇異果和香蕉。

---

stream [stri:m]

① *n.* 小河

② *v.* 流；流動

▶ Our house is located next to a small stream.
我們的房子位在小河邊。

▶ Kelly had tears streaming down her face as she said goodbye to her parents.
當凱莉和父母說再見時，淚水從臉上流了下來。

---

street [stri:t] *n.* 街道

實用片語與搭配字

take to the streets 上街遊行示威

▶ This street has many interesting shops.
這條街上有許多有趣的商店。

▶ The workers were upset with the new laws by the government so they took to the streets to show their anger.
員工對於政府新的法令感到不滿，所以他們上街遊行示威，表達憤怒。

---

stress [stres]

① *n.* 壓力

② *v.* 強調；著重

實用片語與搭配字

stress sb out 令（某人）緊張

▶ Tony's job gives him a lot of stress.
湯尼的工作給他很大的壓力。

▶ The doctor stressed to Joan she needs to exercise more.
這位醫生向瓊安強調說她需要做更多的運動。

▶ The constant noise next door stressed me out, so I went to work in a coffee shop.
隔壁持續不斷的噪音讓我感到緊張，所以我到咖啡店工作。

96

stretch [stretʃ]

① *v.* 伸展；伸直

實用片語與搭配字

stretch (yourself) out 舒展四肢躺下

② *n.* 伸展

▶ John tried to stretch the sheet across the whole bed.
約翰試著要把床單拉開可以鋪整張床。

▶ I just want to go home and stretch out on the sofa.
我只想回家攤開四肢舒服地躺在沙發上。

▶ Make sure you have a good stretch before and after you go for a run.
你跑步前後務必要做伸展操。

---

strict [strɪkt] *adj.* 嚴格的；嚴謹的

▶ There are strict rules to follow in this warehouse due to the dangerous chemicals here.
因為這間倉庫有危險的化學物品，所以要遵守嚴格的規定。

---

strike [straɪk]

① *v.* 攻擊

實用片語與搭配字

strike out; strike a pose / attitude; strike back
自立謀生；擺出姿勢；反擊

② *n.* 攻擊

實用片語與搭配字

hunger strike 絕食抗議

▶ Sally didn't strike one ball today during her baseball game.
今天莎莉在棒球比賽中沒有擊出任何一球。

▶ The author received a lot of criticism over his book, but he decided to strike back by proving he wrote the truth.
那位作者收到許多對於他的著作的批評，但他決定反擊，證明他寫的內容皆屬實。

▶ Electricity is out due to the lightening strikes earlier this evening.
因為今晚早些時候的雷擊，電力中斷了。

▶ The prisioners received such bad treatment that they went on a hunger strike and stopped eating for two weeks.
犯人受到很差的待遇，所以他們開始絕食抗議，兩週都沒吃東西。

---

string [strɪŋ]

① *n.* 細繩

實用片語與搭配字

strings attached
（協議等的）附加條件，限制條款

▶ I need some strings to tie these balloons to the chairs.
我需要一些細繩把氣球綁在椅子上。

▶ If you help someone, there should be no strings attached; in other words, don't expect anything in return.
如果你幫助別人，就不應該有附加條件。換句話說，不要期望任何回報。

② *v.* （用線、繩）綁、縛

實用片語與搭配字

string sth together; string sth out
把…說清楚；拖延…的時間

▶ Can you string these flowers together?
你可以把這些花綁在一起嗎？

▶ The lawyer was able to string the truth together after talking to the thief and witnesses.
在與竊賊和證人談話後，律師能將真相釐清。

---

strong [strɑːŋ] *adj.* 強壯的

實用片語與搭配字

be going strong 依然運行良好

▶ My dad is so strong that he can lift a car!
我爸爸很強壯，他可以舉起一輛車！

▶ The financial crisis left a lot of companies in trouble, but our restaurant is still going strong thanks to our customers.
金融危機使得許多公司碰到困難，但我們的餐廳仍然營運得很好，這都要感謝我們的顧客。

---

struggle [ˈstrʌg.əl]

① *v.* 奮鬥；努力；拚搏

實用片語與搭配字

struggle on 竭力堅持下去

② *n.* 努力；奮鬥

▶ Frank struggled with his math homework.
法蘭克努力要完成他的數學作業。

▶ The coffee-shop was not doing a lot of business, but the owner decided to struggle on for another year.
這間咖啡店生意並不好，但店主決定要再奮鬥一年。

▶ Henry's terrible struggle with cancer ended when he passed away last night.
當亨利昨晚病逝，他與癌症的艱苦奮鬥終於結束了。

---

student [ˈstuː.dənt] *n.* 學生

▶ The teacher helped the students prepare for the test.
這位老師幫學生準備考試。

95

study [ˈstʌd.i]

① *n.* 書房

實用片語與搭配字

case study 個案研究

▶ We have a study in our house.
我家有個書房。

▶ The case study presented by the professor showed that it is possible to be a small-scale farmer and still earn a good living.
教授的個案研究指出，小規模農場的主人仍有機會過上很好的生活。

② *v.* 學習；研讀

實用片語與搭配字

study under sb 師從（某人）

▶ The test is coming, so I need to study harder.
考試快到了，所以我要更用功讀書。

▶ Over the years, many students have studied under the famous math professor.
多年來，許多學生都在著名數學教授的指導下學習。

---

stupid [ˈstuː.pɪd] *adj.* 笨的

▶ Pigs are not stupid. They are smart animals.
豬並不笨，牠們其實很聰明。

---

subject [ˈsʌb.dʒekt] *n.* 主題

實用片語與搭配字

change the subject; subject matter
改變話題；主要內容

▶ The subject of this novel is love.
這本小說的主題是愛。

▶ Elon felt uncomfortable talking about marriage with his girlfriend, so he always changes the subject.
伊隆對於和女朋友談論結婚這件事感到不自在，所以他總是轉移話題。

---

103 102

subtract [səbˈtrækt] *v.* 減去；扣除

▶ If we subtract Kim from the list of conference workers, how many people remain?
如果我們把金從研討會工作人員名單中剔除，還剩下多少人？

---

subway [ˈsʌb.weɪ]
n. （美）地下鐵；（英）地下道

▶ I need to run and catch the subway this morning.
我今早得快跑去搭地鐵。

101

succeed [səkˈsiːd] *v.* 實現目標；成功

▶ Cathy succeeded in her goal of becoming class president.
凱西成功達成做班代的目標。

---

102 95

success [səkˈses] *n.* 成功；成就

實用片語與搭配字

success story 成功的事例（或人）

▶ The success of the meeting depends on whether an agreement can be reached.
會議的成功取決於是否可以達成協議。

▶ The survival of the elephants in Africa is a success story in nature conservation despite many challenges.
非洲象的存活是自然保育的成功案例，儘管有許多挑戰。

successful [sək'ses.fəl]

adj. 成功的；有成就的

▸ Chris' second attempt to pass his driver's test was successful.

克里斯第二次嘗試考駕照終於成功了。

---

such [sʌtʃ]

① *adj.* 這樣的

實用片語與搭配字

such as 例如

② *pron.* 這樣的人、事、物

實用片語與搭配字

as such 從字面意義來看，嚴格地說

▸ No such promise was made.

我們並沒有做這樣的承諾。

▸ You can choose from many European travel destinations to go skiing, such as Norway or Switzerland.

你可以選擇許多歐洲國家做為去滑雪旅行的目的地，像是挪威或瑞士。

▸ There are no such hospitals in this town.

這城裡並沒有你說的那家醫院。

▸ I have been waiting to see the doctor for a long time and as such, I should be first in line.

我為了看醫生而等了很長的時間，嚴格來說，我應該是隊伍中的第一位。

---

sudden ['sʌd.ən] *adj.* 突然的；意外的

實用片語與搭配字

all of a sudden 突然間

▸ The boss made a sudden announcement this afternoon that will affect hundreds of people's jobs.

老闆今天下午突然發布了一項將會影響數百人工作的公告。

▸ Everything was quiet, but all of a sudden there was a loud crash as the heavy rock fell on the roof.

一切都悄然無聲，突然間，一聲巨響伴隨著巨石掉落在屋頂上。

suddenly ['sʌd.ən.li] *adv.* 突然地；意外地

▸ His computer suddenly stopped working.

他的電腦突然停止運作。

---

sugar ['ʃʊg.ɚ]

① *n.* 糖

實用片語與搭配字

sugar cane; sugar-free 甘蔗；無糖的

▸ I always drink coffee with cream and sugar.

我喝咖啡都加奶精和糖。

▸ It is better to drink sugar-free drinks because too much sugar is not healthy.

喝無糖飲料是最好的，因為過多的糖分對身體不健康。

② *v.* 給…加糖

► She sugared the pies.
她在這些派裡加了糖。

---

suit [su:t]

① *n.* (一套)西裝

② *v.* 適合;與…相配

實用片語與搭配字

suit yourself! 你想怎麼樣就怎麼樣吧!

► Alan wore a suit to his job interview yesterday.
艾倫昨天穿著西裝去面試工作。

► That chair doesn't suit the design of the living room.
那張椅子並不適合這個客廳的設計。

► You can either get up and come with me to the party, or you can stay here and be bored; suit yourself.
你可以起身跟我一起參加派對,又或者是無聊地待在這裡,你想怎麼樣就怎麼樣吧!

Exercise 66

I. Choose and write the correct word. Change the form of the word when necessary.

1	stream (n.) stress (n.)	________ has an effect on both of your physical and mental health.
2	stretch (v.) strike (v.)	After a long drive, it was good to get out of the car and ________ our legs.
3	strong (adj.) sudden (adj.)	While talking excitedly to one another, the students were surprised by the ________ entry of their teacher.
4	succeed (v.) subtract (v.)	Do your work with your whole heart and you'll ________.
5	sugar (n.) subject (n.)	The ________ may be full of interest to you, but it holds no interest for me.

II. Multiple choices.

( ) 1. My parents were very ________ with me when I was young because they thought it was the right thing to do.
(A) successful (B) stupid (C) strict (D) strong

( ) 2. During a ________ business career, she accumulated a great amount of wealth.
(A) strict (B) successful (C) such (D) sudden

( ) 3. The ________ you're in today is developing the strength you need for tomorrow, so don't give up on your task.
(A) success (B) struggle (C) string (D) strike

( ) 4. Her grandfather was taken into hospital last week when his condition ________ deteriorated.
(A) sudden (B) suddenly (C) strike (D) stretch

( ) 5. The only time he got his parents' attention was when he brought home ________ A's on his report card.
(A) strike (B) straw (C) straight (D) strict

Unit 67

summer [ˈsʌm.ɚ] *n.* 夏天

實用片語與搭配字

summer camp 夏令營

▸ Summer is my favorite season.
夏天是我最喜歡的季節！

▸ Many students all over the world attend summer camps in other countries to learn about new cultures.
全世界許多學生會在暑假到其他國家去參加夏令營，藉此認識新的文化。

---

sun [sʌn]

① *n.* 太陽

② *v.* 曬太陽；做日光浴

▸ The sun is out today.
今天出太陽。

▸ She was sunning herself by the pool.
她在泳池邊曬太陽。

Sunday / Sun. [ˈsʌn.deɪ] *n.* 星期天

▸ I go to church every Sunday.
每週日我都去教堂做禮拜。

---

sunny [ˈsʌn.i] *adj.* 陽光普照的

▸ Today's weather has turned out to be really sunny.
今天的天氣變得非常晴朗。

---

sunrise [ˈsʌn.raɪz] *n.* 日出；黎明

▸ I watch the sunrise early in the morning.
我一大早去看日出。

---

sunset [ˈsʌn.set] *n.* 日落

▸ Let's see the sunset before it's too dark.
讓我們在天黑前去看日落吧。

---

super [ˈsuː.pɚ]

① *adj.* 超級的

② *adv.* 特別地

▸ This price is really super; you can't find a better one!
這價錢超級划算，你無法找到更便宜的！

▸ Tim was super careful in carrying the expensive vase.
提姆特別小心地拿那個昂貴的花瓶。

---

supermarket [ˈsuː.pɚˌmɑːr.kɪt] *n.* 超級市場

▸ I need to go to the supermarket to pick up some laundry detergent.
我需要去超級市場買一罐洗衣精。

supper [ˈsʌp.ɚ] *n.* 晚餐

▶ It was already very late when we finished supper.
當我們吃完晚餐時，時間已經很晚了。

99

supply [səˈplaɪ]

① *v.* 供應；提供

② *n.* 供應量；供應

實用片語與搭配字

in short supply; supply and demand
供應不足；供求

▶ The teacher will supply all the students with a new notebook and pen.
這位老師將會提供所有學生新的筆記本和筆。

▶ We need a regular supply of fresh vegetables for the restaurant.
我們需要為餐廳固定供給新鮮蔬菜。

▶ These days, good service is in short supply and I often complain about waiters not doing a good job.
現在很少有好的服務，我經常抱怨服務生做得不夠好。

support [səˈpɔːrt]

① *v.* 支撐

② *n.* 支持

實用片語與搭配字

support group; support network
（尤指經歷過相同苦難的人組成的）互助協會；（為處境艱難的人提供情感和實際幫助的）支援網絡

▶ He used his suitcase to support his laptop.
他用他的公事包來撐住筆電。

▶ Jennifer needed a lot of support in the office after her manager left.
珍妮佛在她的經理離開之後需要很多辦公室同仁的支援。

▶ It is important for everyone to have a support network of friends and family to help you in times of need.
每個人都應該要有朋友和家人的支援網絡，以在需要時幫助你，這很重要。

---

sure [ʃʊr]

① *adj.* 確定的

實用片語與搭配字

for sure; be sure of sth; make sure (that)
肯定的（地）；肯定；確保

② *adv.* 的確；當然

實用片語與搭配字

sure thing; sure enough
（表示同意）當然；不出所料

▶ Are you sure that you have enough money to take a trip to Europe?
你確定你有足夠的旅費去歐洲旅行？

▶ Before you quit your job, make sure that you have another job or you will be sorry.
在你離職前，先確定你有另一份工作，不然你會後悔的。

▶ Wow! It sure is hot outside.
哇！外面一定很熱。

▶ Meg looked for her cat everywhere before looking in his favorite spot, and sure enough, there he was.
梅姬到處找她的貓咪，不出所料地，牠就在牠最喜歡待著的地方。

surface ['sɜːfɪs]

① *n.* 表面；面

② *v.* 對……進行表面處理

▶ The kitchen tiles have a slippery surface so be careful when you walk on them.
廚房磁磚的表面很滑，所以走在上面要小心。

▶ The workers will surface the road from midnight to six o'clock in the morning.
工作人員將會在午夜到早上六點鐘之間鋪設路面。

surprise [sɚ'praɪz]

① *n.* 驚喜；驚奇

實用片語與搭配字

take sb by surprise 令（某人）大吃一驚

② *v.* 使…感到驚訝

▶ Should we plan a surprise for Luke's birthday?
我們應該為路克辦一個生日驚喜派對嗎？

▶ My sister organized a birthday party for me, and I was completely taken by surprise when I saw all my friends there.
我妹妹為我計畫了生日派對，當我看到所有朋友都在場時，我嚇了一大跳。

▶ I was really surpised he is quitting his job.
我對他辭職感到非常驚訝。

---

surprised [sɚ'praɪzd] *adj.* 感到驚訝的

▶ The surprised cat jumped backwards.
那隻驚訝的貓往後跳了起來。

  96

survive [sɚ'vaɪv] *v.* 生存；倖存

▶ Roger survived the plane crash but broke both legs.
羅傑在墜機中倖存下來，但卻摔斷了雙腿。

---

swallow ['swɑː.loʊ]

① *n.* 燕子

② *v.* 吞嚥

實用片語與搭配字

swallow your words
被迫承認自己說的話不對

③ *n.* 吞嚥；一次吞嚥之物

▶ Lizzy saw that a swallow had made its nest in the tree outside her bedroom window.
麗絲看見一隻燕子在她臥室窗外的樹上築巢。

▶ Please swallow all your food before you try to speak.
你要講話前，請先把食物全部吞下去。

▶ Wisdom has it that you have to be careful about what you say or you might have to swallow your words later.
智慧是必須小心說出口的話，否則你可能必須為自己的失言道歉。

▶ Liam gave a swallow every time he got nervous before speaking in public.
利亞姆每次在公開講話前都會緊張得吞一下口水。

swan [swɑːn] *n.* 天鵝

▶ Peter has a pond in the backyard that contains five swans and ten ducks.
彼得家後院有個池塘，裡面有五隻天鵝和十隻鴨子。

---

sweater [ˈswetə] *n.* 毛衣；毛線衫

▶ I left my sweater on the train on my way to work today.
我今天去上班的途中把毛衣掉在火車上了。

104

sweep [swiːp]

① *v.* 打掃；清除

實用片語與搭配字

sweep sb off their feet 使（某人）為之傾倒

② *n.* 清掃

▶ Did the students finish sweeping the auditorium floor?
學生們清掃完禮堂的地板了嗎？

▶ The charming man swept the girl off her feet and she fell completely in love with him.
那位迷人的男士使她傾倒，她完全愛上他了。

▶ I gave the living room floor a sweep before the guests arrive.
我在客人抵達前掃了客廳的地板。

---

sweet [swiːt] *adj.* 甜的

實用片語與搭配字

sweet spot; be sweet on sb
最佳打擊點；深愛

▶ This cake is too sweet; I can't eat it.
這蛋糕太甜，我無法吃。

▶ My brother was sweet on the neighbor's daughter, but he was too afraid to ask her out on a date.
我哥哥很喜歡鄰居家的女兒，但他不敢約她出去。

S

---

swim [swɪm]

① *v.* 游泳

② *n.* 游泳

▶ Once every year, many people swim across Sun Moon Lake.
每年一次，許多人會游泳橫渡日月潭。

▶ Is it safe to take a swim at this beach?
在這個海邊游泳安全嗎？

---

swimming [ˈswɪm.ɪŋ] *n.* 游泳（運動）

▶ Swimming is a great way to exercise.
游泳是一種很棒的運動方式。

---

swing [swɪŋ]

① *v.* 搖擺；擺動

實用片語與搭配字

swing (sth / sb) around （使）迅速轉身

▶ The kite swung from side to side.
這個風箏左右搖擺。

▶ The company was facing bankruptcy, but the new manager was able to swing things around to make it successful.
公司面臨破產之際，新來的經理人卻能夠挽回頹勢，使之成功。

② *n.* 擺動；搖擺

實用片語與搭配字

swing voter 中間遊離選民

▶ Sam needs to practice his golf swing.
山姆需要練習打高爾夫球的擺動姿勢。

▶ Swing voters are not sure yet who to vote for, so they can still be convinced to vote for the other party.
中間選民還不確定要投給誰，所以其他黨派還有空間遊說他們。

---

104 99

symbol [ˈsɪm.bəl] *n.* 象徵；標誌

▶ The eagle is a symbol of bravery and courage.
老鷹是勇氣與膽量的象徵。

Exercise 67

I. Choose and write the correct word. Change the form of the word when necessary.

1	sunrise (n.) symbol (n.)	A wedding ring is a __________ of eternal love between a married couple.
2	supply (v.) survive (v.)	The company found it hard to __________ in a changing marketplace.
3	support (n.) surprise (n.)	Mothers are often the ones who provide emotional __________ for the family.
4	super (adj.) sweet (adj.)	For fruit juice, I prefer either guava or grapefruit because they aren't too __________.
5	swallow (v.) sweep (v.)	He had a sore throat and found it difficult to __________ the food.

II. Multiple choices.

( ) 1. If this bill isn't paid within a week, your gas __________ will be cut off.
(A) supper (B) supply (C) support (D) sunrise

( ) 2. The air was so still that there was hardly a ripple on the pond's __________.
(A) surface (B) swallow (C) sweep (D) surprise

( ) 3. Much to my __________, it had stopped raining by the time I wanted to go out.
(A) sweep (B) surface (C) swan (D) surprise

( ) 4. Let's pile up the fallen leaves in the corner and __________ up the floor.
(A) support (B) sweep (C) surprise (D) survive

( ) 5. When I heard the door __________ shut behind me, I knew that I was locked out.
(A) sweep (B) supply (C) swing (D) support

Unit 68

T-shirt [ˈtiː.ʃɝːt] *n.* 短袖圓領衫

▶ You don't need to dress up; a T-shirt and jeans are fine.
你不需要特別打扮，穿 T 恤和牛仔褲就可以。

---

table [ˈteɪ.bəl] *n.* 桌子

實用片語與搭配字

set the table; round-table
擺飯桌；（討論或會議）圓桌的（指參與者身分平等）

▶ We have a table in our dining room, but we need more chairs.
我們的飯廳有張桌子，但是我們需要更多椅子。

▶ Every Sunday, my sister and I have to set the table so that our family can sit down for a home-cooked meal.
我和我姊姊每週日都會負責擺碗筷，讓家人們能夠坐下一起吃一頓家常便飯。

---

table tennis [ˈteɪ.bəl ˌten.ɪs] *n.* 桌球

▶ Our class is having a table tennis tournament this week.
我們班即將在這禮拜舉行一場桌球比賽。

---

tail [teɪl]

① *n.* 尾巴

實用片語與搭配字

be on sb's tail 緊緊跟隨（某人）

② *v.* 跟隨；追蹤

▶ That cat's tail is so short! What happened to it?
那隻貓的尾巴好短！牠發生了什麼事？

▶ The criminal escaped from jail only minutes ago, but police were already on his tail and might arrest him again soon.
罪犯幾分鐘前才從監獄脫逃，但警察已經緊跟著他，可能很快就會再次逮捕他。

▶ We all tailed after the leader during the parade.
我們在遊行中伴隨這個指揮官。

---

take [teɪk] *v.* 拿；取用

實用片語與搭配字

take sth away 拿走

▶ Did you take my favorite book? I can't find it.
你是否拿了我最喜歡的書？我找不到。

▶ The students did not do their homework so their teacher took their privileges away.
那些學生沒有完成作業，所以老師取消了他們的特別待遇。

tale [teɪl] *n.* 傳說；故事

▶ My grandfather told me many exciting tales when I was a child.
當我還小時，祖父告訴我許多精彩的傳說。

99

talent [ˈtæl.ənt] *n.* 天才

▶ Jack has a talent for singing and performing on stage.
傑克有在舞台上唱歌表演的天份。

talk [tɑːk]

① *v.* 說話；談論

實用片語與搭配字

talk business; talk sb into sth; talk sb out of sth; talk around sth

談論正事；說服（某人）做…; 說服（某人）放棄；拐彎抹角地說

② *n.* 談話；交談

實用片語與搭配字

be all talk (and no action); talk show

光說不做；脫口秀

▶ The two of them talked about the problem, but they couldn't solve it.
他們兩個人討論這個問題，卻無法解決。

▶ My father wanted to buy a restaurant and he had several meetings with the owner to talk business.
我父親想要買下一間餐廳，他和老闆見了好幾次面談生意。

▶ I need to have a talk with my daughter; she isn't doing well in school.
我需要跟我女兒談談；她在學校功課不是很好。

▶ Most politicians make promises to get votes, but they are all talk and no action.
大部分的政治人物為了贏得選票而承諾許多事情，但他們都光說不做。

102

talkative [ˈtɑː.kə.t̬ɪv] *adj.* 健談的

▶ Lisa is outgoing and talkative so she will be perfect for this sales job.
麗莎外向又健談，所以她會很適合這份業務工作。

tall [tɑːl] *adj.* 高的

實用片語與搭配字

stand / walk tall 充滿自信地做事

▶ I am tall, but both my parents are short!
我很高，但我的父母都很矮！

▶ It does not matter what kind of job you do, you always have to walk tall and do it to the best of your ability.
無論做什麼工作，總要充滿自信，並發揮自己最佳的能力。

tangerine [ˈtæn.dʒə.riːn] *n.* 橘子

▶ I need to put some tangerines in this salad.
我需要放一些橘子在這沙拉裡。

tank [tæŋk] *n.* （蓄水）罐、箱、槽；坦克

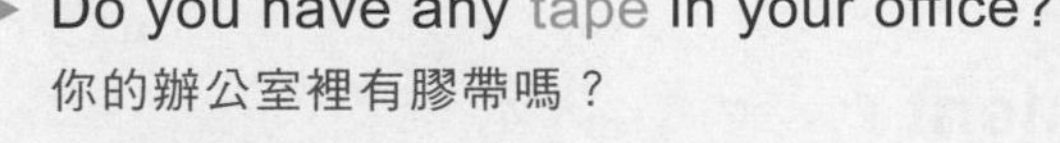

▶ Do you think one tank of water is enough for everyone at the party?
你認為一箱水足夠在派對上讓每個人喝嗎？

---

tape [teɪp]

① *n.* 膠帶；（影音）磁帶；捲尺

② *v.* 用帶子捆；用膠布黏

實用片語與搭配字

tape sth up 包紮

▶ Do you have any tape in your office?
你的辦公室裡有膠帶嗎？

▶ We're going to tape the photos to the wall as decorations for the party.
我們要把照片貼在牆上做為派對的裝飾。

▶ He injured himself playing basketball and his arm was taped up.
他打籃球受了傷，手臂纏了繃帶。

103

target [ˈtɑːr.gɪt]

① *n.* 靶子；目標 / 把…作為目標

② *v.* 靶子；目標 / 把…作為目標

▶ Russell managed to hit the target twenty times.
羅素設法擊中目標二十次。

▶ Soldiers targeted the department store in their attack.
士兵們將百貨公司作為他們的攻擊目標。

---

task [tæsk]

① *n.* 工作

② *v.* 指派…任務

▶ Leonard finished all the tasks his manager had given him before lunch.
李奧納德在午餐前完成了所有他的經理交付的工作。

▶ Rita is tasked with writing up the report.
瑞塔負責撰寫這份報告。

---

99 95

taste [teɪst]

① *n.* 味道

實用片語與搭配字

give sb a dose / taste of their own medicine
對（某人）以牙還牙

② *v.* 嚐…的味道

▶ Do you like the taste of stinky tofu? I think it's delicious!
你喜歡臭豆腐的味道嗎？我覺得很美味！

▶ I wish I could give that bully a taste of his own medicine, then he would know how it feels to be bullied.
我希望能給那些霸凌者一個教訓，如此他就能知道遭到霸凌是什麼滋味。

▶ Taste this soup. Is it ready to eat?
嚐一下這碗湯，可以喝了嗎？

---

tasty [ˈteɪ.sti] *adj.* 美味的；可口的

▶ Every dish at the dinner party was tasty.
晚餐派對上的每道菜都好美味。

taxicab / taxi / cab

[ˈtæk.si.kæb / ˈtæk.si / kæb] *n.* 計程車

▶ Buses are too slow; let's call a taxicab instead.
坐巴士太慢了；叫計程車吧。

---

tea [tiː] *n.* 茶

▶ I can't drink tea before bed, or I'll have trouble sleeping!
我不能睡前喝茶，否則我會睡不著！

96

teach [tiːtʃ] *v.* 教導

實用片語與搭配字

teach sb a lesson 教訓（某人）

▶ Parents teach their children many important life lessons.
父母教導小孩很多生命中重要的課題。

▶ Leon's father wanted to teach him a lesson for failing his test, so he took away his cellphone for a month.
因為里昂的考試成績不佳，他的父親要給他一個教訓，所以沒收了他的手機一個月。

---

teacher [ˈtiː.tʃɚ] *n.* 老師

實用片語與搭配字

substitute teacher; teacher's pet
代課教師；教師的寵兒

▶ The student asked the teacher for help.
這名學生請老師幫忙。

▶ Our Math teacher is going on honeymoon, so a substitute teacher will come to teach us.
我們的數學老師要去度蜜月，所以一位代課老師會來教我們。

---

team [tiːm]

① *n.* 團隊

實用片語與搭配字

dream team 夢幻組合

② *v.* 使合作；使結成一隊

實用片語與搭配字

team up 合作

▶ Cody made the rugby team for the second year in a row.
科迪連續兩年加入了橄欖球隊。

▶ Sue likes her job and she is always telling us that she is in charge of a dream team.
蘇很喜歡她的工作，她總是說她管理的是夢幻團隊。

▶ Jim teamed up with Vera hoping to win the competition.
吉姆和維拉合作希望可以贏得比賽。

▶ In science class, boys have to team up with girls in pairs, but I don't know who to choose.
上理化課時，男生必須和女生一組，但我不知道該選誰。

T

teapot [ˈtiːˌpɑːt] *n.* 茶壺

▶ The waiter poured water into the teapot.
服務生把水倒進茶壺。

---

tear [tɪr]

① *n.* 眼淚

實用片語與搭配字

burst into tears; in tears 突然哭起來；哭

② *v.* 流淚

實用片語與搭配字

tear up
（因為情緒激動）眼裡含淚（幾乎要開始哭泣）

③ *v.* 扯破；撕裂

④ *n.* 撕破處；裂口

▶ I had tears in my eyes when I saw the beautiful performance.
當我看到這麼動人的演出，我的淚水盈眶。

▶ When Grace saw her parents after being abroad for months she burst into tears and hugged them.
出國數個月後，當葛瑞絲看見她的父母時，突然哭了起來並擁抱他們。

▶ Everyone was tearing up at the wedding.
在婚禮上，每個人都感動得落淚。

▶ Susan always teared up when she talked about her parents who passed away in a car accident.
每當蘇珊提及在車禍中意外過世的父母時，總是眼框泛淚。

▶ Be careful not to tear your new dress.
小心不要扯破妳的新洋裝。

▶ Did you see the tear in the classroom curtains?
你看到教室窗簾上的破洞了嗎？

---

teen [tiːn] *n.* 十幾歲的階段；青少年

▶ Ben and Laura are in their teens.
班和蘿拉正值青少年時期。

Exercise 68

I. Choose and write the correct word. Change the form of the word when necessary.

1	talent (n.) target (n.)	At the age of five, he showed exceptional ________ as a musician.
2	taste (v.) tape (v.)	If you add some pepper and salt to the vegetables, they'll ________ better.
3	tank (n.) team (n.)	They came to the baseball field to root for their school ________.
4	tail (n.) tale (n.)	We went to the village of Hamelin, where the ________ of the Piped Piper took place.
5	teach (v.) tear (v.)	________ off this coupon and use it to get 25% off of your next cup of coffee.

II. Multiple choices.

( ) 1. The ________ driver hadn't stopped chatting from the moment I had entered the cab.
(A) talent (B) tale (C) talkative (D) tasty

( ) 2. Cars without security devices are an easy ________ for the thief.
(A) talent (B) target (C) tale (D) team

( ) 3. The students accomplished the ________ assigned by their teacher in less than ten minutes.
(A) taste (B) target (C) task (D) teapot

( ) 4. There's a hole in the bottom of the water ________ and the water has been leaking away.
(A) tank (B) tale (C) task (D) tape

( ) 5. The English usually make tea in a ________ and drink it with cream and sugar.
(A) teapot (B) taste (C) tank (D) target

Unit 69

teenage [ˈtinˌeɪdʒ] *adj.* 十幾歲的

▶ Kelly just joined a teenage singing group at her church.
凱莉剛加入她教會裡的青年詩班。

---

teenager [ˈtinˌeɪ·dʒər] *n.* 青少年

▶ We have several teenagers in our hiking club.
我們的健行社裡有幾名青少年。

---

telephone / phone [ˈtel·əˌfoʊn / foʊn]

① *n.* 電話

② *v.* 打電話

▶ Can you install a telephone into the kitchen?
你可以在廚房裡安裝一台電話嗎？

▶ I'll phone you when I have more news about Barry's surgery.
若我有巴瑞手術的進一步消息，我會打電話給你。

---

television / TV [ˈtel.ə.vɪʒ.ən]

n. 電視；電視業

▶ We need to get a new TV because our old one broke.
我們需要買一台新電視，因為舊的壞了。

---

tell [tel] *v.* 告訴

實用片語與搭配字

tell the truth; tell it like it is
說真話；實話實說

▶ This is a secret. Don't tell anyone!
這是個秘密，不要告訴任何人！

▶ My friend is very direct and if she is unhappy or angry about something, she will tell it like it is.
我的朋友很直接，若她不開心或是生氣的時候，她會實話實說。

temple [ˈtem.pəl] *n.* 寺廟；聖殿

▶ The vegetable market is next to the local temple.
菜市場就在當地寺廟的旁邊。

---

ten [ten]

① *n.* 十

② *adj.* 十的；十個的

▶ Apples were on sale, so I bought ten!
蘋果在特價，所以我買了十顆！

▶ There were ten people at the party last night.
昨晚的派對有十個人。

tennis [ˈten.ɪs] *n.* 網球

▶ David wants to play a game of tennis with us after work.
大衛想在下班後和我們打一場網球賽。

---

tent [tent] *n.* 帳篷

▶ Do you have a tent I can borrow for our camping trip next week?
我下週要去露營，你有帳篷可以借用嗎？

---

term [tɝːm]

① *n.* 期限

實用片語與搭配字

long-term; short-term; come to terms with sth
長期的；短期的；逐漸接受

② *v.* 把…稱為…

▶ Tyler's term as class president came to an end yesterday.
泰勒擔任學生會長的任期昨天圓滿結束。

▶ It is good to make long-term plans for the future, but you should also make short-term plans to enjoy your life now.
為未來制訂長程計劃是好的，但你也應該規劃短期計劃來享受你的生活。

▶ Mary was termed an expert in math by her classmates.
瑪麗被她的同學稱為數學專家。

---

terrible [ˈter.ə.bəl] *adj.* 糟糕的；可怕的

▶ Dylan received the terrible news that his younger brother drowned yesterday.
狄倫接獲他的弟弟昨天淹死的壞消息。

95

terrific [təˈrɪf.ɪk] *adj.* 極好的；特佳的

▶ Did you know Aiden was a terrific guitar player in college?
你知道艾登在大學時是個很棒的吉他手嗎？

---

test [test]

① *n.* 考試；測驗

實用片語與搭配字

put sth to the test 使經受考驗

② *v.* 試驗；測驗

實用片語與搭配字

test sth out 試驗（尤指理論或想法）

▶ Everyone has to take this test today.
每個人今天都必須參加這堂考試。

▶ To sleep better at night, you have to go to bed at 11pm; I am going to put it to the test tonight to see if it works.
為了一夜好眠，你必須在晚上十一點就寢；我今晚要試試是否有效。

▶ Peter is getting tested for the virus.
彼得正在做病毒的測試。

▶ Before my brother jumps into the water, he tests it out to feel the temperature.
我哥哥跳入水中之前，他測試了一下水溫。

textbook [ˈtekst.bʊk] *n.* 課本；教科書

▶ I need to pick up my physics textbook from my locker before my next class.
我需要在下堂課前從置物櫃裡拿物理課本。

than [ðæn / ðən]

① *prep.* 比

② *conj.* 比較（數量）

▶ Bill is taller than Jimmy.
比爾比吉米高。

▶ Paula ate more than I did.
寶拉吃的比我多。

thank [θæŋk] *v.* 感謝

實用片語與搭配字

have sb to thank (for sth); thank sb for sth
應責怪（某人）; 把…歸功（或歸咎）於（某人）

▶ Be sure to thank your mother on Mother's Day.
不要忘了在母親節感謝你的媽媽。

▶ Our class will not go on an outing on Friday, and we have Peter to thank for that because he disobeyed the teacher.
週五我們班不會去校外教學了，都怪彼得頂撞老師。

thanks [θæŋks] *n.* 謝意

▶ Let's give thanks to God for all his blessings.
我們為了上帝所賜一切的祝福來感謝祂。

that [ðæt / ðət]

① *pron.* 那個（人事物）

② *conj.* 用於引導從句（有時可省略）

▶ That umbrella belongs to May's mother.
那支雨傘是梅的媽媽的。

▶ He loved the girl so much that he asked her to marry him.
他很愛這個女孩，他向她求婚。

that [ðæt]

① *adj.* 那個

② *adv.* 那樣；那麼

▶ I want to buy that computer over there.
我想在那邊買那部電腦。

▶ We had no idea the restaunt would be that crowded.
我們並不知道那家餐廳會那麼擁擠。

the [ði: / ðə]

art. 定冠詞（用於名詞前，指聽者或讀者已知的事物或人）

▶ The newspaper has many important stories and reports.
這報紙有很多重要的故事和報導。

theater [ˈθi:.ə.t̬ɚ] *n.* 電影院；劇場

▶ We can meet you at the theater straight after work.
我們會在下班後直接去電影院和你碰面。

their(s) [ðer(z)] *pron.* 他們的（所有格）

▶ That's not my dog; it's theirs.
那不是我的狗，是他們的。

---

them [ðem / ðəm] *pron.* 他們（受格）

▶ I love my parents, and I enjoy spending time with them.
我愛我的父母，而且很喜歡花時間和他們在一起。

---

themselves [ðəmˈselvz] *pron.* 他們自己

▶ They wanted to look around by themselves.
他們想要自己四處看看。

---

then [ðen]

① *adv.* 在那時

實用片語與搭配字

but then (again) 不過話又說回來

② *adj.* 在當時的

實用片語與搭配字

from then on 從那時起

③ *n.* 那時

④ *conj.* 接著；然後；後來

▶ I finish work at six o'clock; do you want to get dinner then?
我六點會完成工作，你那時想去吃晚餐嗎？

▶ We can go to the movies on Saturday, but then again it will probably be very crowded.
我們週六可以去看電影，不過話又說回來，到時可能人擠人。

▶ My dad looks really young in the photo; he was then twenty years old.
我爸爸在照片上看起來很年輕；他當時才二十歲。

▶ Jade had a bad experience with a dog and from then on, she has been scared of them.
婕德對狗有陰影，從那時起，她就很怕狗。

▶ I can't drive until I turn 18; until then, my parents have to drive me.
我十八歲才能開車；在此之前，我父母必須載我。

▶ He graduated from college. Then, he married his girlfriend.
他從大學畢業，接著就娶了他的女朋友。

---

there [ðer]

① *adv.* 往那裡；在那裡；到那裡

② *n.* 那裡；那個地方

▶ There's a new restaurant in town; let's go there Saturday.
城裡新開了一家餐廳，我們星期六去那裡吧！

▶ This bread is from the bakery; I always buy something from there.
這個麵包是那家麵包店的；我總是在那裡買東西。

Exercise 69

I. Choose and write the correct word. Change the form of the word when necessary.

1	temple (n.) tent (n.)	You mustn't wear your shoes in a __________ in Thailand; it's a great insult.
2	teenager (n.) textbook (n.)	The __________ has a Q&A section at the end of each chapter.
3	thank (v.) phone (v.)	The first thing I did when I got home last night was to __________ up Joe and tell him about my day.
4	term (n.) theater (n.)	Crowds flocked after the singer as he was leaving the __________.
5	terrible (adj.) terrific (adj.)	Hiking is a __________ way to keep your body and mind in top shape.

II. Multiple choices.

(　　) 1. There's no need to push the meeting ahead because we still have three weeks before the end of the __________.

(A) then　　(B) term　　(C) tent　　(D) test

(　　) 2. I would like to express my appreciation and __________ to you all for helping me going through the hard time.

(A) themselves　　(B) thank　　(C) thanks　　(D) that

(　　) 3. I saw them at Christmas but haven't heard a thing from them since __________.

(A) that　　(B) than　　(C) then　　(D) term

(　　) 4. He was a bit of rebel when he was a __________; he dyed his hair blue and had his nose pierced.

(A) teenager　　(B) teenage　　(C) temple　　(D) term

(　　) 5. My right ankle is rather weak, so I always put a bandage on it to support it when I play __________.

(A) tent　　(B) term　　(C) textbook　　(D) tennis

Unit 70

therefore [ˈðer.fɔːr] *adv.* 因此

▶ I didn't remember to bring my tennis racket and therefore missed our practice after school.

我忘了帶我的網球拍，因此錯過了我們放學後的練習。

---

these [ðiːz]

① *pron.* 這個；這些

② *adj.* 這些的

▶ Don't buy those pants; I think these are better.

不要買那條褲子，我想這條比較好看。

▶ Who made these cookies? They are delicious!

誰做了這些餅乾？很好吃！

---

they [ðeɪ] *pron.* 他們（主格）

▶ They plan to get married in France.

他們計畫到法國結婚。

---

thick [θɪk] *adj.* 厚的；粗的

實用片語與搭配字

thick-skinned 厚臉皮的，感覺遲鈍的

▶ My living room walls are thick so I can't hear my neighbors when they come home.

我客廳的牆壁很厚，所以我的鄰居回家時我是無法聽見的。

▶ The salesman was so thick-skinned (that) he did not take no for an answer even after the woman got angry.

那個銷售員很厚臉皮，即使婦人發怒了，他也不把拒絕當一回事。

---

thief [θiːf] *n.* 小偷

▶ The old man caught the thief stealing money from his kitchen drawers.

這位老先生抓到了從他廚房抽屜偷錢的小偷。

---

thin [θɪn] *adj.* 薄的；細的；瘦的

實用片語與搭配字

paper-thin 極薄的

▶ I should not have worn thin pants in this cold weather.

我不應該在這麼冷的天還穿薄褲子。

▶ Be careful! The butterfly's wings are paper-thin and you could break them if you pick it up.

小心！蝴蝶的翅膀相當薄，若你撿起來，可能會弄壞它。

thing [θɪŋ] *n.* 東西

▶ I need to clean my room; there are things all over the floor!
我需要清理我的房間，地板上到處都是東西！

---

think [θɪŋk] *v.* 認為；覺得；思考

實用片語與搭配字

think of sth / sb; think big; think ahead; think sth out
認為；立大志；仔細為未來做打算；仔細考慮

▶ What do you think? I want your opinion.
你覺得如何？我需要你的意見。

▶ If you cannot think ahead in business today and make plans for the future, you will not succeed.
如果你今天不能在商業中有前瞻思考，並為未來做計畫，你就不會成功。

thinking [ˈθɪŋ.kɪŋ] *n.* 想法；觀點

實用片語與搭配字

critical thinking; wishful thinking
批判性思考；癡心妄想

▶ Everyone got together to share their thinking.
每個人聚在一起分享了他們的想法。

▶ Critical thinking is important because it teaches you to solve problems in a creative way.
批判性思考很重要，因為它能幫助你用有創意的方式解決問題。

---

third [θɝːd]

① *adj.* 第三的；第三個的

實用片語與搭配字

third party 第三人，協力廠商，第三者

② *n.* 第三

▶ If you get a third strike in baseball, you are out.
在棒球賽中，如果你被三振，就出局了。

▶ The two families have been arguing for months, so finally they asked the help of a third party to resolve their argument.
那兩家人已經爭吵數個月了，所以他們終於尋求第三方來解決彼此之間的紛爭。

▶ I'm the third child in my family.
我是我家的老三。

---

thirsty [ˈθɝː.sti] *adj.* 口渴的

實用片語與搭配字

thirsty work 重體力工作

▶ I am so thirsty after running ten kilometers this afternoon.
今天下午跑了十公里後我覺得很渴。

▶ Working in the fields all day planting crops is thirsty work and I usually go to bed very early.
整天在田裡幹活是很耗費體力的工作，我通常很早就上床睡覺。

thirteen [θɝːˈtiːn]

① *n.* 十三

② *adj.* 十三個的；十三的

▶ Thirteen is considered an unlucky number.
十三被視為是個不幸運的數字。

▶ Thirteen people were hired this year.
今年僱用了十三個人。

thirty [ˈθɝːṭɪ]

① *n.* 三十

② *adj.* 三十個的；三十的

▶ Is thirty too many people to invite to our house?
邀請三十個人到我們家來會太多嗎？

▶ Thirty dogs were rescued from the shelter; that's great!
三十隻狗從收容所被救了出來，太棒了！

this [ðɪs]

① *pron.* 這個（人、事、物）

② *adj.* 這個

③ *adv.* 這麼

▶ Whose is this? There's no name on it.
這是誰的？上面沒有名字。

▶ This new car isn't mine; it belongs to my neighbor.
這輛新車不是我的，是我鄰居的。

▶ Why are you acting this way? Are you OK?
你為什麼要這麼做？你還好嗎？

those [ðoʊz]

① *pron.* 那些（人、事、物）

② *adj.* 那些的；那些個的

▶ Are those your parents? You look just like them!
那兩位是你的父母嗎？你跟他們好像！

▶ When you go to the zoo, don't touch those animals!
當你去動物園時，不要摸那些動物！

though [ðoʊ]

① *conj.* 雖然

實用片語與搭配字

as though 好像

② *adv.* 儘管（常放在句尾）

▶ Though she was busy, she still made time to spend with her kids.
雖然她很忙，但她還是騰出時間來陪她的小孩。

▶ My boss talked to me as though I was a child and that made me very angry.
我老闆跟我說話，好像我還是個孩子，這讓我很生氣。

▶ I'm tired; I might still go out though.
儘管我累了，我可能還是會出去。

thought [θɑːt] *n.* 想法；考慮

實用片語與搭配字

well thought of; second thought; that's a thought

受好評的；改變主意；那是個好主意

▶ I don't know what to do; do you have a good thought?
我不知道該怎麼做，你有好的看法嗎？

▶ I think I will just relax at home for the weekend; on second thought, I might actually go see a movie.
我想我週末只會待在家放鬆；或許我會改變心意出去看電影。

---

thousand [ˈθaʊ.zənd]

① *n.* （一）千

② *adj.* （一）千的

▶ A thousand is more than a hundred but less than a million.
千大於百，但小於百萬。

▶ A thousand students entered the competition.
有一千名學生來參加這項比賽。

---

three [θriː]

① *n.* 三

② *adj.* 三的；三個的

▶ One plus two is three.
一加二是三。

▶ My family has three dogs at home.
我家有三隻狗。

---

throat [θroʊt] *n.* 喉嚨；咽喉

實用片語與搭配字

force sth down sb's throat

強迫（某人）接受

▶ Greg keeps coughing and can't seem to clear his throat.
葛瑞克一直咳嗽，似乎無法清除他喉嚨的不適。

▶ The government is trying to force the new law down people's throats, but there are already protests in the street.
政府正試圖迫使人民接受新的法律，但街上已經出現抗議活動了。

through [θruː]

① *prep.* 完成；做完

② *adv.* 穿過；穿越

實用片語與搭配字

see-through; drive-through; through and through

透明的；無需下車即可接受服務的場所；完全地

▶ The students went through the museum in one morning.
這些學生一個早上就參觀完這個博物館了。

▶ Hikers carved an opening in the cave's wall and went through.
登山客在洞穴牆上開了一個通道，並且走了過去。

▶ If you are in a hurry, you can always just order from the restaurant's drive-through in your car.
若你趕時間，你可以開車到餐廳得來速點餐。

throughout [θru:ˈaʊt]

① *prep.* 從頭到尾

② *adv.* 處處

▶ The factory fire burned throughout the night.
那個工廠大火燒了一整晚。

▶ The bread has molded throughout.
麵包已經整個發霉了。

---

throw [θroʊ]

① *v.* 投；擲；拋

實用片語與搭配字

throw sth away / out 丟棄

② *n.* 投；擲

▶ I can catch the ball, but I can't throw it well.
我可以接球，但我投球投得不好。

▶ Before you throw something out, like clothes or shoes, check to see if you can give it to charity.
在你扔掉東西，比如衣服或鞋子之前，看看你是否能把它捐給慈善機構。

▶ During the football game, John made a lot of good throws.
在這場美式足球賽當中，約翰擲了許多好球。

---

thumb [θʌm]

① *n.* 拇指

② *v.* 用拇指翻動；迅速翻閱

▶ I injured my right thumb when I hit it with a hammer.
我用鐵槌敲東西時傷了我的右拇指。

▶ I thumbed through your script but I need more time to read it in detail.
我翻閱了你的腳本，但我需要更多時間來細讀。

---

thunder [ˈθʌn.dɚ]

① *n.* 雷；雷聲

② *v.* 打雷

▶ The thunder and lightening kept the whole family from falling asleep.
雷聲和閃電讓全家無法睡著。

▶ The sky started to thunder and rain as I drove my scooter home.
正當我騎著摩托車回家時，天空開始打雷下雨。

Exercise 70

I. Choose and write the correct word. Change the form of the word when necessary.

1	thick (adj.) thin (adj.)	___________ fog has made driving conditions dangerous; you need to drive with caution.
2	thief (n.) thinking (n.)	The police will have the picture enlarged in an attempt to identify the ___________.
3	think (v.) throw (v.)	She can't bear to ___________ away anything that might come in useful one day.
4	thought (n.) throat (n.)	To live happily, wake up every morning with the ___________ that something wonderful is about to happen.
5	thunder (n.) thumb (n.)	The rain grew heavier and ___________ rumbled over the mountains.

II. Multiple choices.

(　　) 1. We do not have enough money. __________ we can't afford to buy the new car.
(A) Therefore　(B) Third　(C) Through　(D) Though

(　　) 2. The teacher drew a diagram showing how the blood flows __________ the heart.
(A) therefore　(B) though　(C) through　(D) throughout

(　　) 3. People have been intrigued by the question of whether there's intelligent life elsewhere in the universe __________ history.
(A) through　(B) throughout　(C) though　(D) therefore

(　　) 4. __________ he's not clever, he's a diligent worker and has often done well in the examinations.
(A) Though　(B) Through　(C) Throughout　(D) Therefore

(　　) 5. I always keep a bottle of water by my bedside is case I'm __________ in the middle of the night.
(A) thin　(B) thief　(C) there　(D) thirsty

Unit 71

Thursday / Thurs. / Thu. [ˈθɝːz.deɪ]

n. 星期四

▶ I usually go shopping on Thursdays.
我通常在星期四去逛街購物。

---

thus [ðʌs] *adv.* 如此；這樣

實用片語與搭配字

thus far 迄今

▶ Our shop has more customers than before. Thus, we hope to make more money.
我們的店比以前有更多顧客登門，這樣一來，我們希望能賺更多錢。

▶ People have been happy with our store's products, thus far, and we are working hard to maintain our quality.
到目前為止，人們對我們商店的產品感到滿意，我們正努力維護我們的品質。

---

ticket [ˈtɪk.ɪt]

① *n.* 車票；入場券

實用片語與搭配字

parking ticket; e-ticket

違規停車罰單；電子機票

② *v.* 售票；給…票

▶ You need to buy your train ticket before you get on the train.
上火車前你需要先買車票。

▶ I forgot to pay my parking ticket and now I have to pay a fine that is double the fee.
我忘了付停車費用，現在我得付雙倍的罰款。

▶ The event was ticketed, so we bought our tickets early.
這個活動採售票制，所以我們很早就買了票。

---

tie [taɪ]

① *n.* 領帶

② *v.* 繫；捆

實用片語與搭配字

tie sb to sth / sb; tie the knot

束縛，限制；結婚

▶ The event is very formal; you should wear a nice suit and tie!
這個活動十分正式，你應該穿正式服裝和領帶！

▶ Tie your shoes tight; you don't want to trip on your laces!
把你的鞋子繫好；你不會想要被鞋帶絆倒！

▶ After dating his high school classmate for more than ten years, Paul finally decided to tie the knot and asked her to marry him.
在和他的高中同學交往十多年後，保羅決定要向她求婚，步入婚姻。

tiger [ˈtaɪ.gɚ] *n.* 老虎

▶ There are very few tigers left in the wild.
現在只有少數老虎還生活在荒野。

---

time [taɪm]

① *n.* 時間

實用片語與搭配字

all the time; no time to lose; have / take time off; for the time being; at the time; in time; on time; from time to time; at all times; ahead of your time

不停；沒時間耽擱；抽出時間；暫且；在當時；及時；極為準時；偶爾；一直；領先時代的

② *v.* 確定…的時間；為…安排時間

▶ I know you are busy, but do you have some time to help me?
我知道你很忙，但你有時間幫我嗎？

▶ The application for scholarships will close at the end of the month and it is already the 25th, so there is no time to lose.
獎學金申請將在這個月底截止，都已經 25 日了，沒時間耽誤了。

▶ We timed the party to end at 10 p.m.
我們會在晚上十點結束這個派對。

---

tiny [ˈtaɪ.ni] *adj.* 微小的

▶ Ants are tiny insects.
螞蟻是很小的昆蟲！

---

tip [tɪp]

① *n.* 頂端；小費

② *v.* 使傾斜

實用片語與搭配字

tip (sth / sb) over （使）翻倒

▶ I scratched my hand on the tip of your pen.
你的筆尖刮傷我的手了。

▶ Sam's cat jumped on the coffee table and tipped my drink over.
山姆的貓跳上茶几翻倒了我的飲料。

▶ The truck went around the corner so fast that it tipped over and landed on its side.
那輛卡車過彎速度太快，隨後就翻倒了。

---

tire [taɪɚ] *n.* 輪胎

▶ The tires on my bike are a little flat; I need to add some air.
我腳踏車的輪胎有點漏氣，我需要打點氣。

tire [taɪr] *v.* 疲倦

實用片語與搭配字

tire sb out 使（某人）筋疲力盡

▶ While Nancy was sick, she tired easily and had to rest often.
當南西生病時，她很容易疲倦而且常常需要休息。

▶ George complained that his friends are tiring him out because they are always partying.
喬治抱怨他的朋友們讓他感到疲倦，因為他們一直開派對玩樂。

tired [taɪrd] *adj.* 感到疲倦的；厭煩的

實用片語與搭配字

grow tired of sth / sb 逐漸厭倦某人事

▶ Billy felt tired after hiking up and down the mountain.
比利爬完山後覺得很疲累。

▶ When Max and Sarah grew tired of the hectic city life, they moved to the countryside.
當麥斯和莎拉厭倦了忙碌的都市生活，他們便搬到鄉村居住。

---

tiring [ˈtaɪ.rɪŋ] *adj.* 累人的；令人疲倦的

▶ Running up a hill can be very tiring.
跑上山會是件很累人的事。

---

title [ˈtaɪ.t̬əl]

① *n.* 標題；書名

② *v.* 取書名為…；加標題於…

▶ Jeff still needs to choose a title for his new movie.
傑夫仍需要為他的新電影選擇一個片名。

▶ Carrie titled her new book *Hello Life!*
凱莉為她的新書取名「嗨！人生」。

---

to [tuː / tə / t̬ə / tu] *prep.* 向；往

▶ Let's go to the store on our way home.
我們回家時順道去那家商店吧。

---

toast [toʊst]

① *n.* 烤麵包片

實用片語與搭配字

the toast of sth; French toast
受…敬慕的人；法式吐司

② *v.* 烘烤

▶ I made everyone eggs and French toast for breakfast.
我早餐為大家做了蛋和法式吐司。

▶ My favorite breakfast food is French toast with peanut butter and coffee.
我最喜歡的早餐是法式吐司淋上花生醬配咖啡。

▶ I'm going to toast the bread and then put some avocado on it.
我要去烤麵包，然後放一些酪梨在上面。

---

today [təˈdeɪ]

① *adv.* 在今天

② *n.* 今天

▶ They are going out of town today.
他們今天要出城。

▶ Today is my birthday!
今天是我生日！

---

toe [toʊ]

① *n.* 腳趾；足尖

▶ Make sure your toes are covered when you lift heavy objects.
務必確認你在舉重物時腳趾有被包覆著。

實用片語與搭配字

on your toes; step on sb's toes

永不懈怠；得罪（某人）

② *v.* 用腳尖踢（、觸或踩）

- Doctors always have to be on their toes because one mistake could have serious consequences.
  醫生總是要有警覺，因為一個錯誤可能會造成嚴重後果。
- Jake toed the ball into the goal and won the game for his soccer team.
  傑克用腳尖把球踢進球門，為他的足球隊贏得了這場比賽。

---

tofu [ˈtoʊ.fuː] *n.* 豆腐

- I'm going to try making a new salad with tofu and peanuts tonight.
  我今晚想試著做加豆腐和花生的新式沙拉。

---

together [təˈgeð.ɚ] *adv.* 在一起；共同

實用片語與搭配字

together with 連同，加上

- My best friend and I do everything together.
  我跟我最好的朋友一起做每件事。
- A lot of rain together with strong winds caused the landslide that buried the town.
  豪雨加上強風造成了土石流，淹沒了整座城鎮。

---

toilet [ˈtɔɪ.lət] *n.* 廁所；沖式馬桶

- Can you tell me where the closest toilet is?
  你能告訴我最近的廁所在哪裡嗎？

---

tomato [təˈmeɪ.t̬oʊ] *n.* 番茄

- Lily bought five boxes of tomatoes for the pasta festival.
  莉莉為義大利麵節買了五盒番茄。

---

tomorrow [təˈmɔːr.oʊ]

① *adv.* 在明天

實用片語與搭配字

like there is / was no tomorrow

好像沒有將來似的，不顧一切的

② *n.* 明天

- What do you want to do tomorrow?
  你明天想做什麼？
- Parents should teach teenagers to save money and not to party like there is no tomorrow.
  父母應該要教育青少年存錢的觀念，不應該不顧一切的玩樂。
- The newspaper said that tomorrow will be rainy all day.
  報紙上說明天會下一整天的雨。

tone [toʊn] *n.* 音調

實用片語與搭配字

tone-deaf; tone sth down
不能辨別音調的；使緩和

▶ Jeremy isn't a good singer; he never sings the right tones.
傑瑞米不是個好歌手，他從來沒有唱準音過。

▶ James was very critical of the new CEO, but we asked him to tone it down because he could get us all into trouble.
詹姆士對於新上任的執行長很挑剔，我們希望他能夠緩和情緒，因為他會使我們都惹上麻煩。

---

tongue [tʌŋ] *n.* 舌頭

實用片語與搭配字

mother tongue; hold your tongue
母語；（使）某人閉嘴

▶ Betty bit her tongue while eating the oranges.
貝蒂在吃橘子時咬到她的舌頭。

▶ If you cannot say something nice about somebody, then it is better to hold your tongue.
若你沒辦法對某人說好話，那最好還是什麼話都別說。

---

tonight [tə'naɪt]

① *adv.* 在今晚

② *n.* 今晚

▶ The project is due tomorrow, so we need to finish it tonight.
這個專案明天截止，我們必須在今晚完成。

▶ Tonight is a good time to get together; will you be free?
今晚是聚一下的好時間，你有空嗎？

---

too [tuː] *adv.* 太；也是

▶ Susie wants to go to the concert, and I do, too.
蘇西想去參加這場演唱會，我也想去。

Exercise 71

I. Choose and write the correct word. Change the form of the word when necessary.

1	ticket (n.)	Please show your __________ to the flight attendant when you board the plane.
	tie (n.)	
2	tip (n.)	We don't need to leave a __________ for the waiter, because there's a service charge included in the bill.
	tire (n.)	
3	tired (adj..)	I don't feel like doing anything energetic tonight. I've had a __________ day.
	tiring (adj.)	
4	together (adv.)	Barbara and her mother like to listen to music __________, though their tastes don't harmonize.
	today (adv.)	
5	tone (n.)	A speaker conveys information through __________ and body language.
	toilet (n.)	

II. Multiple choices.

( ) 1. Just key in the __________ or the author's name, and then you might see the further details.

(A) tire (B) toe (C) title (D) time

( ) 2. Besides Chinese, my mother __________, I can also speak English and French.

(A) tongue (B) tip (C) tone (D) title

( ) 3. Newspaper, __________ paper or tissues are all short life items which could be made from recycled reserves.

(A) tone (B) toast (C) tire (D) toilet

( ) 4. She began frying bacon and eggs, and then filled the kettle and sliced bread for __________.

(A) tone (B) toast (C) toilet (D) tire

( ) 5. Some stars look as __________ as pinheads, but in fact, they're even bigger than the sun.

(A) tiring (B) tired (C) tiny (D) together

tool [tu:l]

① *n.* 工具

② *v.* 用工具給……加工（或造形）

▶ You need some tools to build things out of wood.
你需要一些工具來用木頭做東西。

▶ He tooled a table out of wood.
他用木頭做了一張桌子。

---

tooth [tu:θ] *n.* 牙齒

實用片語與搭配字

wisdom tooth; sweet tooth

智齒； 對甜食（尤指糖果和巧克力）的喜愛

▶ I chipped my tooth while playing soccer yesterday.
我昨天踢足球時弄斷了一顆牙齒。

▶ Amy is such a sweet tooth; she always has candy in her purse.
艾咪很熱愛甜食，她包包裡總是有糖果。

---

toothache [ˈtu:θ.eɪk] *n.* 牙痛

▶ My toothache is hurting my mouth.
牙疼讓我的嘴好痛。

---

toothbrush [ˈtu:θ.brʌʃ] *n.* 牙刷

▶ A good toothbrush can last for a long time.
一支好牙刷可以用很久。

---

toothpaste [ˈtu:θ.peɪst] *n.* 牙膏

▶ You must use toothpaste to clean your teeth.
你必用牙膏來清潔牙齒。

---

top [tɑ:p]

① *n.* 頂端

② *adj.* 頂端的

實用片語與搭配字

be on top of sth; from top to toe

能控制；（衣著等的樣式、顏色等）從頭到腳都一樣

③ *v.* 給…加蓋

▶ We climbed to the top of the mountain.
我們爬上了山頂。

▶ My sister is a top student in her high school.
我姐姐是她高中裡的頂尖學生。

▶ Frank's boss was very worried about the project, but Frank ensured his boss that he was on top of it.
法蘭克的老闆相當擔心他們的專案，但他向老闆保證一切都在掌控之中。

▶ The cook topped the ice cream with some chocolate and nuts.
這位廚師在冰淇淋上面加上巧克力與堅果。

T

實用片語與搭配字

top sth off 順利完成；圓滿完成

▶ Our year-end function was a lovely occasion with great food and to top it all off, we each got a gift.
我們的年終尾牙是個充滿美食的盛會，更棒的是，我們每個人都有禮物。

98

topic [ˈtɑː.pɪk] *n.* 題目；話題

▶ The topic of the conference hasn't been decided yet.
研討會的主題尚未決定。

---

total [ˈtoʊ.t̬əl]

① *adj.* 總計的；全部的

② *n.* 總額；總數

③ *v.* 合計為…；總數達

▶ What is the total price for all of these things?
這些東西總共多少錢？

▶ That comes to a total of $42.75.
那個總額是四十二點七五美元。

▶ We totaled the number of guests to make sure we had enough food.
我們加總客人的數量，以確認食物是否足夠。

---

touch [tʌtʃ]

① *v.* 接觸

② *n.* 觸覺

實用片語與搭配字

be, get, keep, etc. in touch; lose touch; a touch of

有 / 取得 / 保持等聯繫；（通常因身居異地）失去聯繫；少許的

▶ Touch this blanket; isn't it soft?
摸摸看這條毯子，是不是很柔軟？

▶ Blind people depend on the sense of touch more than others do.
盲人比其他人更加依賴他們的觸覺。

▶ After living abroad for many years, Jenny lost touch with many of her friends from school.
旅居國外數年，珍妮和許多同學都失去聯繫了。

---

tour [tʊr]

① *n.* 旅行；遊覽

② *v.* 旅行

▶ Andy took us on a tour of the city for free.
安迪帶我們去參加免費的市區遊覽。

▶ Kevin toured around New Zealand for one month during summer.
凱文夏天時在紐西蘭旅行了一個月。

---

toward(s) [təˈwɔːdz / twɔːdz / tɔːrdz / twɔːrdz]

prep. 朝著；對著

▶ This bus is heading toward the city center.
這輛巴士正朝著市中心開去。

towel [taʊəl]

① *n.* 毛巾；紙巾

② *v.* 用毛巾擦

▶ Please bring a towel with you when you go to the swimming pool.
當你去游泳池的時候，請帶一條毛巾。

▶ We toweled ourselves down before getting on our scooters and riding to the city.
在坐上機車到市區前，我們先用毛巾擦乾身體。

---

tower [ˈtaʊ.ɚ]

① *n.* 高樓；塔

實用片語與搭配字

ivory tower 象牙塔

② *v.* 高出；高聳

實用片語與搭配字

tower above / over sb / sth
矗立在…上

▶ Fred's office is in the tallest office tower in New York City.
佛萊德的辦公室位在紐約市最高的辦公大樓裡。

▶ It is easy to criticise from the comfort of your ivory tower, but you have no idea how poor people suffer.
在你的象牙塔裡批判他人很容易，但你不知道窮人是如何受苦的。

▶ Ian towered over everyone else in his basketball team.
伊恩比他籃球隊裡的每個人都高。

▶ The tall building towered over the downtown area and was a landmark for all to see.
那棟高聳的建築矗立在市中心，是大家都能看見的地標。

---

town [taʊn] *n.* 城鎮

實用片語與搭配字

downtown; go to town
在市中心（的）；（尤指大量花錢地）精心操持

▶ Many people from the countryside are moving to town to find work.
許多人從鄉下搬到城裡找工作。

▶ The students went to town on their school's anniversary and invited the whole town to attend festivities.
學生們去市中心參加校慶，並邀請所有市民來參與慶祝活動。

---

toy [tɔɪ]

① *n.* 玩具

實用片語與搭配字

soft toy 絨毛（動物）玩具

▶ The little boy got many toys for his birthday.
這個小男孩在生日時得到很多玩具。

▶ Soft toys like teddybears should be kept clean, especially if your child has allergies.
像泰迪熊這樣的絨毛玩具要保持清潔，尤其當你的小孩會過敏時。

② *v.* 玩弄

實用片語與搭配字

toy with sth 不太認真地考慮，擺弄

▶ Please don't toy with my emotions.
請別玩弄我的情感！

▶ Pat toyed with the idea of opening a coffee shop downtown, but then decided it would be too expensive.
派特動了在市中心開咖啡廳的念頭，但又覺得花費太高了。

track [træk]

① *n.* 足跡；行蹤

實用片語與搭配字

be on the right / wrong track; keep track
方法得當 / 判斷錯誤的；確保知道

② *v.* 追蹤；跟蹤

實用片語與搭配字

track sth / sb down 追蹤到

▶ The tiger left a track of prints in the mud.
這隻老虎在泥巴裡留下了足跡。

▶ The principal warned the boy that he was on the wrong track and would fail his grade if he did not start studying.
校長告誡那男孩他已偏離正軌，若是再不開始念書，他會把他當掉。

▶ We tracked the ducks to the Northern lake district.
我們跟蹤鴨群到了北邊的湖區。

▶ The old man wanted to track down a girl from his past, so he asked a private investigator to help him.
那個老先生想尋找一位他以前認識的女孩，所以他請了一個私家偵探協助他。

---

trade [treɪd]

① *n.* 貿易

實用片語與搭配字

fair trade; trade-off 公平貿易；協調，妥協

② *v.* 交換；做買賣

實用片語與搭配字

trade sth off; trade sth in
權衡（為獲得好的東西而接受差的方面）；以…折價換購（尤指同類的新品）

▶ The country's trade to Europe has increased by ten percent in the last year.
去年國家對歐洲的貿易已經增加了百分之十。

▶ Many large companies today ignore fair trade and pay farmers as little as possible for their products.
如今許多大型企業忽略公平貿易，盡可能用低價來向農夫購買產品。

▶ Lenny managed to get traded to the basketball team of his choice.
藍尼設法要被交易到他所選擇的籃球隊去。

▶ If you want to trade your old car in for a new one, you have to make sure that you get a good deal.
若你想要用舊車換新車，要確保你能談得一個好價錢。

tradition [trəˈdɪʃ.ən] *n.* 傳統

實用片語與搭配字

oral tradition;
in the tradition of sb / sth

口頭文化（某一群體對其信仰、習俗、歷史的傳承體系，由父母口頭傳授給孩子，代代相傳）；具有…的傳統

▶ One of our family traditions is to open our Christmas gifts on Christmas Eve.
在聖誕夜拆聖誕禮物是我們家眾多傳統之一。

▶ In the tradition of the Lunar New Year, our family will have a reunion at my uncle's house.
按農曆新年的傳統，我們家會在我叔叔家吃團圓飯。

traditional [trəˈdɪʃ.ən.əl] *adj.* 傳統的

實用片語與搭配字

non-traditional 非傳統的

▶ Ray and Marian decided to have a traditional wedding ceremony.
雷和瑪麗安決定要辦一個傳統的結婚典禮。

▶ The family is very non-traditional and they give their children a lot of freedom.
這個家庭有別於一般傳統家庭，他們給予孩子很多自由。

traffic [ˈtræf.ɪk]

① *n.* 交通

實用片語與搭配字

traffic jam 交通堵塞

② *v.* 交易；做非法買賣

▶ The traffic on the freeway increased as people finished work.
下班以後高速公路上的交通流量就增加了。

▶ Do not drive to downtown area during rush-hour because the traffic jams will drive you crazy.
不要在尖峰時間開車進市中心，因為塞車會讓你抓狂。

▶ Several criminals were arrested for trafficking drugs into the country.
幾個罪犯因為非法交易毒品到這個國家而被捕。

---

train [treɪn]

① *n.* 火車

實用片語與搭配字

train of thought / events
思路 / 一連串事件

② *v.* 訓練

▶ Buses can get stuck in traffic, but trains are usually on time.
公車會被卡在車陣中，但是火車通常是準時的。

▶ I prefer to work in quiet places because any kind of noise will disturb my train of throught and I will lose concentration.
我比較喜歡在安靜的地方工作，因為任何噪音都會干擾我的思路，讓我無法專心。

▶ If you are going to run a race, you first need to train!
如果你想參加賽跑，首先要接受訓練！

trap [træp]

① *n.* 陷阱

② *v.* 設陷阱

實用片語與搭配字

be trapped;
be trapped into (doing) sth

陷入困境；被誘騙做（某事）

▶ The farmer found several rabbits in his traps.
農夫在他設的陷阱裡找到幾隻兔子。

▶ Dennis managed to trap the mouse in the bathroom.
丹尼斯設法要在浴室裡捕捉老鼠。

▶ Alice does not like horror movies, but she accepted her friends' dare and now she is trapped into going to see the film.
艾莉絲不喜歡恐怖片，但她接受朋友的挑戰，現在她被騙去看電影了。

travel [ˈtræv.əl]

① *v.* 旅行

實用片語與搭配字

travel light 輕裝旅行

② *n.* 旅行；遊歷

實用片語與搭配字

travel agent 旅行社

▶ Suzy traveled to Germany after she graduated from university.
蘇西大學畢業後到德國去旅遊。

▶ The best advice when you go backpacking is to travel light, so just take what you need.
自助旅行最好的建議是裝備要輕便，只帶必需品就好。

▶ Joe likes to share photos from his travels.
喬喜歡分享他旅行的照片。

▶ Our company asked the travel agent to arrange a tour to Germany for employees.
我們公司委託旅行社安排到德國的員工旅遊。

treasure [ˈtreʒ.ɚ]

① *n.* 財富；貴重物品

② *v.* 珍藏；珍惜

▶ A lot of ancient treasure was found in the old ruins.
很多古老的寶藏都在廢墟中被發現。

▶ Jenny wanted the photos of her mom so she could treasure them in her memory.
珍妮想要媽媽的照片，這樣她就可以珍藏在她的回憶裡。

treat [tri:t]

① *v.* 對待

▶ Mariah didn't treat her coworkers very well.
瑪利亞沒有善待她的同事。

實用片語與搭配字

treat sb like dirt; treat sb like royalty

把（某人）視為草芥；以最高標準招待（某人）

② *n.* 難得的樂事

► After winning the singing competition, Michelle was treated like royalty by all the record companies who wanted to represent her.

在贏得歌唱比賽後，蜜雪兒被所有想簽下她的唱片公司以高規格接待。

► Seeing Bruno Mars in concert was a real treat for Laura.

在演唱會看到名歌手布魯諾．馬爾斯對蘿拉來說真是一大樂事。

T

Exercise 72

I. Choose and write the correct word. Change the form of the word when necessary.

1	toothache (n.) toothbrush (n.)	She's suffered tortures from a __________ for many days, but she hasn't gone to the dentist yet.
2	topic (n.) total (n.)	I couldn't follow the talk because she kept jumping about from one __________ to another.
3	track (v.) trade (v.)	When I was little, I liked to __________ with my classmates for something I didn't have.
4	travel (v.) treat (v..)	Although she's lived there for ten years, the villagers still __________ her as an outsider.
5	trap (n.) tower (n.)	The two __________ buildings of the World Trade Center have disappeared from the map of New York.

II. Multiple choices.

(　　) 1. If you witness a __________ accident, make sure to mark down the plate number of the car.
(A) towel　(B) tower　(C) traffic　(D) tradition

(　　) 2. This village has its own __________ dress, cuisine, folklore and handicrafts.
(A) tradition　(B) traditional　(C) total　(D) top

(　　) 3. When they opened up the tomb, they found __________ buried around the coffin.
(A) tradition　(B) traffic　(C) treasure　(D) trade

(　　) 4. The country's attitude __________ government is harsher than it was a century ago.
(A) towards　(B) tower　(C) trade　(D) total

(　　) 5. If the two wires __________, the appliance will have a short-circuit and probably go up in flames.
(A) trade　(B) touch　(C) track　(D) traffic

Unit 73

treatment [ˈtri:t.mənt] *n.* 待遇；對待

▶ Oscar gets special treatment at this restaurant because he knows the owner.
因為奧斯卡認識這家餐廳的老闆，所以他們特別禮遇他。

tree [tri:] *n.* 樹

▶ This little apple seed will grow into an apple tree!
這個小小的蘋果種子會長成一棵蘋果樹！

trial [traɪəl] *n.* 審判；審理

實用片語與搭配字

trial and error 反覆試驗

▶ The trial finished quicker than expected.
這場審判結束得比預期還快。

▶ This project is the first of its kind, so it is trial and error for all of us to learn everything.
這個計畫是首開先例，所以我們透過反覆試驗學習所有的事。

triangle [ˈtraɪ.æŋ.gəl] *n.* 三角形

▶ The new office is shaped like a triangle.
這間新辦公室像是一個三角形。

trick [trɪk]

① *n.* 把戲；詭計

實用片語與搭配字

do the trick; trick question
起作用；有陷阱的問題

② *v.* 哄騙；戲弄

▶ The small boy showed his mother many magic tricks.
這個小男孩表演很多魔術給媽媽看。

▶ The history test was so difficult because the teacher asked a trick question and no one knew the answer.
這次歷史考試很難，因為老師出了一題陷阱題，沒有人知道正確答案是什麼。

▶ My friends tricked me into thinking they had forgotten my birthday.
我的朋友騙我，讓我以為他們已經忘了我的生日。

trip [trɪp]

① *n.* 旅行

▶ Our trip to Brazil was long; we were there for over two months!
我們去巴西旅遊了很長一段時間，在那裡有兩個多月之久！

實用片語與搭配字

field trip （學生的）校外考察旅行

② *v.* 絆倒

- ▶ Our class was so excited because we were going on a field trip to the amusement park.
  我們班很興奮，因為我們將要去遊樂園校外教學。
- ▶ I tripped on the stairs and fell, but I didn't get hurt.
  我在樓梯上絆倒了，但是我沒有受傷。

---

trouble [ˈtrʌb.əl]

① *n.* 麻煩；問題

實用片語與搭配字

spell trouble 預示著麻煩

② *v.* 使有麻煩；費心

- ▶ Of course I can help you; it's no trouble!
  我當然可以幫你，一點都不麻煩！
- ▶ Jane's parents warned her that her new boyfriend spelled trouble and that he would break her heart eventually.
  珍的父母警告她，她的新男友會是一個大麻煩，最後一定會傷透她的心。
- ▶ Sorry to trouble you, but can I change my drink order?
  不好意思麻煩你，我可以更換飲料嗎？

---

trousers [ˈtraʊ.zɚz] *n.* 長褲

- ▶ I need to buy another pair of trousers for work.
  我需要去買另一件上班穿的褲子。

---

truck [trʌk]

① *n.* 卡車

② *v.* 用卡車運送

- ▶ There are a lot of trucks going to the port on this road.
  這條路上有很多要去港口的卡車。
- ▶ We trucked most of the boxes to the department store before opening time.
  我們在百貨公司營業之前用卡車把大部分的箱子運送到那裡。

---

true [tru:]

① *adj.* 真實的

實用片語與搭配字

be / stay true to yourself; come true; true love
堅持自己的信念；（希望或願望）實現；真愛

② *adv.* 真實地；準確地

- ▶ His story was hard to believe; do you think it is true or false?
  很難相信他的故事，你覺得是真的還是假的？
- ▶ It does not matter what you do in life, but you need to stay true to yourself and do what makes you happy.
  你在生活中做什麼無關緊要，但你需要忠於自己，做讓自己快樂的事。
- ▶ She stayed true to what she said and fulfilled her promise.
  她持守她所說的而且實現了她的承諾。

③ *v.* 擺正；配準

▶ These boards are crooked; we need to true them until they are straight.
這些板子是歪的，我們必須將它們擺正弄直。

---

trumpet [ˈtrʌm.pət]

① *n.* 小喇叭

② *v.* 吹噓；鼓吹

▶ Nancy plays the trumpet in our school band.
南西在我們學校的樂團裡吹奏小喇叭。

▶ Tom likes to trumpet his success in front of his friends.
湯姆喜歡在朋友面前吹噓他的成功。

---

trust [trʌst]

① *n.* 信任；信賴

② *v.* 信任

▶ Ursula is trying to gain her dog's trust after he got scared by the fireworks.
娥蘇拉正試著要在她的狗被煙火驚嚇後再次取得牠的信任。

▶ Vivian didn't trust the harness to hold her as she climbed the mountain.
薇薇安不太相信安全繩具可以在她登山時撐住她。

---

truth [truːθ] *n.* 實話；實情

實用片語與搭配字

the truth; in truth 事實；事實上

▶ Please tell me the truth.
請告訴我實情。

▶ Sarah agreed to go to her ex-boyfriend's wedding, but in truth she did not want to see him at all.
莎拉說好要去參加前男友的婚禮，但事實上，她根本不想再見到他。

---

try [traɪ]

① *v.* 嘗試

實用片語與搭配字

try for sth; try sth on; try sth out
試圖獲得；試穿，試戴；試用，試試看

② *n.* 嘗試；努力

▶ You should try to do it by yourself first, and if you can't do it, I will help you.
你應該自己先嘗試做做看，如果不行，我再幫你。

▶ This summer, I am going to try out something new like scuba diving or windsurfing.
今年夏天，我想嘗試一些新的東西，例如潛水或風帆衝浪。

▶ You failed the test, but you can give it another try next week.
雖然你這次考試不及格，但是下禮拜可以再試試看。

---

tube [tuːb] *n.* 管子

▶ The rats ran from one glass box to another through a tube.
這些老鼠從一個玻璃盒經過管子跑到另一個玻璃盒。

T

Tuesday / Tues. / Tue. [ˈtu:z.deɪ]
n. 星期二

▸ On Tuesdays, I often play baseball.
我通常週二會去打棒球。

tummy [ˈtʌm.i] *n.* 肚子

▸ I need to see the doctor because my tummy hurts.
我要去看醫生，因為我肚子痛。

tunnel [ˈtʌn.əl]

① *n.* 隧道；地道

② *v.* 挖掘隧道；挖鑿地道

▸ The train went through several tunnels before arriving at my stop.
火車在抵達我這站之前穿過了好幾個隧道。

▸ The ants tunneled their way into the wall.
這群螞蟻挖出一條到牆裡的通道。

turkey [ˈtɝː.ki] *n.* 火雞

▸ Mom is planning on making turkey for dinner on Sunday night.
媽媽計畫要在星期天晚餐做火雞。

turn [tɝːn]

① *v.* （使）轉身；（使）轉向

實用片語與搭配字

turn a blind eye; turn your back on sb; turn (sb / sth) into sb / sth
視而不見；拒絕幫助（某人）；（使）變成

② *n.* 轉彎；轉向

實用片語與搭配字

take a ... turn; take turns
朝…發生變化；輪流

▸ I turned around and saw a bear behind me!
我轉過頭看見一隻熊在我後面！

▸ Many people prefer to turn a blind eye to the suffering in the world because it is easier for them than doing nothing.
許多人選擇無視這世界上的苦難，因為對他們來說，這比愛莫能助更為容易。

▸ We took a left turn at the corner.
我們在這街角左轉。

▸ My brother and I take turns to take out the garbage at night.
我哥哥和我晚上輪流去倒垃圾。

turtle [ˈtɝː.t̬əl] *n.* 海龜；烏龜

▸ I saw a lot of turtles while swimming in the ocean last weekend.
我上週末在海裡游泳時看見了很多海龜。

twelve [twelv]

① *n.* 十二

② *adj.* 十二的；十二個的

▸ Six plus six is twelve.
六加六是十二。

▸ Twelve students followed him to his office to ask questions.
十二個學生跟著他到辦公室問他問題。

twenty [ˈtwen.t̬i]

① *n.* 二十

② *adj.* 二十的；二十個的

▶ Ten plus ten is twenty.
十加十是二十。

▶ There is a twenty percent discount on coffee today.
今天咖啡打八折。

---

twice [twaɪs] *adv.* 兩次

▶ I told you twice already; do I need to tell you a third time?
我已經告訴過你兩次了，我還要告訴你第三次嗎？

---

two [tuː]

① *n.* 二

② *adj.* 兩個的；二的

▶ One plus one is two.
一加一等於二。

▶ The two musicians played a beautiful song together.
這兩位音樂家一起演奏一首美麗的歌曲。

Exercise 73

I. Choose and write the correct word. Change the form of the word when necessary.

1	trick (n.) trip (n.)	The polar explorers took every precaution to minimize the dangers of their __________.
2	trouble (n.) trumpet (n.)	Many people are now having __________ making their monthly house payments.
3	trust (v.) turn (v.)	As long as you __________ yourself, you'll know how live well and reach your goals.
4	twenty (adj.) twice (adv.)	He was sentenced to __________ years' imprisonment for poisoning and attempted murder.
5	triangle (n.) treatment (n.)	If you experience any unusual symptoms after the __________, then contact your doctor immediately.

II. Multiple choices.

( ) 1. As a witness of the incident, he took the responsibility for collecting evidence for the __________.

(A) treatment (B) trick (C) trial (D) treat

( ) 2. Remember to go through the pockets before you put those __________ in the washing machine.

(A) trumpets (B) tricks (C) trials (D) trousers

( ) 3. After being trapped for a few days, the miners came out of the __________ and thankfully breathed the fresh air.

(A) truck (B) trouble (C) trumpet (D) tunnel

( ) 4. The __________ beauty in a woman isn't in a facial mode, but is reflected in her soul.

(A) true (B) twice (C) trust (D) truth

( ) 5. In countries like America or England, __________ is traditionally eaten on Christmas Day.

(A) trumpet (B) turkey (C) tube (D) triangle

Unit 74

type [taɪp]

① *n.* 類型；典型

實用片語與搭配字

be sb's type 是（某人）喜歡的那種類型

② *v.* （用電腦鍵盤或打字機）打字

實用片語與搭配字

type sth in 輸入

- ▶ There are so many types of chocolates in this store.
  這家店裡有好多種類的巧克力。
- ▶ That guy is not Maggie's type; she does not usually like to go out with short, shy guys.
  這男生不是瑪姬喜歡的類型，通常她不喜歡和身高矮又害羞的男生約會。
- ▶ I need to type up the notes from the financial meeting this morning.
  我需要把今早財務會議的筆記打出來。
- ▶ The secretary typed the address in and then she sent the form to the HR department.
  秘書把地址輸入，隨後把表格送到人資部門。

typhoon [taɪˈfuːn] *n.* 颱風

- ▶ A typhoon is forecast to arrive in the next few days.
  天氣預報在接下來的幾天內會有個颱風。

typing [ˈtaɪ.pɪŋ] *n.* 打字

- ▶ Her typing is much faster than his!
  她打字的速度要比他快得多！

ugly [ˈʌg.li] *adj.* 難看的；醜陋的

實用片語與搭配字

ugly duckling
醜小鴨（年少或剛問世時難看平庸、日後變得漂亮或出眾的人或物）

- ▶ I wish you wouldn't wear that ugly sweater.
  我希望你別穿那件難看的毛衣。
- ▶ After her prom make-over, Ruby looked beautiful -- the ugly duckling had became a swan.
  在舞會大改造後，露比看起來很漂亮， 醜小鴨變成了天鵝。

umbrella [ʌmˈbrel.ə] *n.* 傘

- ▶ Do you have an umbrella I can borrow?
  我可以跟你借一把雨傘嗎？

uncle [ˈʌŋ.kəl] *n.* 叔叔；伯伯；舅舅

- ▶ My dad's brother is my uncle.
  我爸爸的弟弟是我的叔叔。

under [ˈʌn.dɚ]

① *prep.* 在…下面

實用片語與搭配字

be under sb's influence 受（某人）影響

② *adv.* 在下面

▶ I checked under my bed, but I still can't find my bag!
我檢查了床底下，但還是找不到我的包包！

▶ The teenager was under the gang's influence when he committed the crime, but he was still sent to jail.
那名青少年受到了幫派的影響而犯罪，但他還是被送進了監獄。

▶ The turtle stayed on top of the water for a while, then went under.
這隻烏龜停在水面上一會兒，然後就游到水面下了。

---

understand [ˌʌn.dɚˈstænd] *v.* 瞭解

實用片語與搭配字

understand each other / one another; make yourself understood
彼此理解；把自己的意思表達清楚

▶ Do you understand Korean?
你懂韓語嗎？

▶ This workshop hopes to help people of different backgrounds understand each other better.
這個工作坊的用意是要讓不同文化背景的人們更了解彼此。

---

underwear [ˈʌn.dɚ.wer] *n.* 內衣

▶ Heidi bought new underwear before she left for boarding school.
海蒂在去寄宿學校前買了新內衣。

unhappy [ʌnˈhæp.i]

adj. 不快樂的；對…不滿意的

▶ He tried to cheer up the unhappy child.
他試著要讓這個不快樂的孩子高興起來。

---

uniform [ˈjuː.nə.fɔːrm]

① *adj.* 相同的；整齊劃一的

② *n.* 制服

③ *v.* 使成一律化

▶ Every house on this block has the same uniform fence.
這個街區的每棟房子都有相同的圍籬。

▶ Mom is planning on buying my new school uniform tomorrow.
媽媽計畫明天要幫我買新學校的制服。

▶ The student desks were uniformed in the same position.
學生書桌被一致地擺成同樣位置。

---

unit [ˈjuː.nɪt] *n.* 小隊；單位

▶ This unit has fifty soldiers.
這個小隊有五十名士兵。

until / till [ənˋtɪl / ʌnˋtɪl / tɪl]

① *prep.* 直到…時候

② *conj.* 到…為止

► We drove until morning, then we stopped to rest for a few hours.
我們一直開車開到早上才停下來休息幾個小時。

► I carried her bag until we arrived home.
我背著她的包包直到我們到家。

---

up [ʌp]

① *adv.* 朝上地

實用片語與搭配字

up and down; up for sth

起起伏伏，上上下下；計劃要

② *prep.* 向…上

③ *adj.* 向上的

④ *n.* 上升

⑤ *v.* 提高；增加

實用片語與搭配字

up to 接近於

► Look up in the sky, and you can see many clouds!
朝天空看，你會看到很多雲！

► All of us agreed that bungee jumping would be an adventure, but Ryan was scared and he was not up for it.
我們都認為高空彈跳是一種冒險挑戰，但萊恩很害怕，不打算加入。

► The bank isn't here; it's up the road.
那家銀行不在這裡，要沿著路一直往上走。

► Joe is happy because his grades are up this year.
喬很高興，因為今年他的成績提升了。

► Our family had many ups and downs last year.
去年我們家經歷了許多起伏。

► Last week gas was cheap, but this week they upped the price.
上週汽油很便宜，但這禮拜他們提高了價格。

► The stadium can seat up to a thousand people, but there is plenty of place to stand if you don't mind.
這個體育場可以容納一千人，但如果你不介意的話，還有很多地方可以站。

103

upon [əˈpɑːn] *prep.* 在…上面

實用片語與搭配字

put upon 被利用的

► Jack set the cake upon the table for us to eat.
傑克把蛋糕放在桌子上讓我們享用。

► The responsibility for keeping the customers happy was put upon Rory's shoulders and he did a great job.
讓顧客感到愉快是羅瑞的責任，他做得相當好。

upper [ˈʌp.ɚ] *adj.* 較高的；上面的

實用片語與搭配字

the upper hand 有利位置

▶ Neil sustained burns to his upper body during the car accident.
尼爾還留有在車禍中上半身的燒傷。

▶ The fisherman struggled for an hour with the fish before he gained the upper hand and pulled the fish out of the water.
漁夫在獲得優勢之前與魚掙扎了一個小時，最後成功將魚從水中拉出。

---

upstairs [ʌpˈsterz]

① *adv.* 在樓上

② *adj.* 樓上的

③ *n.* 樓上

▶ Your classroom is upstairs and to the left.
你的教室在樓上的左側。

▶ The upstairs bathroom doesn't work; you can use the one down here.
樓上的洗手間壞了，你可以用樓下的。

▶ Our house doesn't have an upstairs.
我們的房子沒有二樓。

---

us [ʌs / əs] *pron.* 我們（受格）

▶ My brother and I got a puppy, and our mom is letting us name it.
我和弟弟養了一隻小狗，媽媽讓我們為牠取名。

---

use [juːz] *v.* 使用；運用

實用片語與搭配字

use your head; use sth up
（略有些生氣地告訴某人）動動腦子；用光

▶ How do you use this new tool?
你怎麼使用這個新工具？

▶ In a dangerous situation, you have to use your head to come up with a plan to save your life.
緊急情況下，你必須動腦想出一個方法來救命。

use [juːs] *n.* 使用；得到利用

實用片語與搭配字

make use of sth; be (of) (any / some) use; be (of) no use
利用；有用，有幫助；沒有幫助，不可能

▶ I didn't get a lot of use out of my new machine before it broke.
我還沒怎麼使用新機器，它就壞了。

▶ Many companies today make use of cultural experts to train their international staff.
現今許多公司會運用文化專家來訓練國際員工。

---

used [juːst] *adj.* 二手的；舊的；用過的

▶ I bought a used sofa and table at the school market.
我在學校市集買了一張二手沙發和一張桌子。

used to [ˈju:sttu:]

① *aux. v.* 過去曾經；過去慣常

② *adj.* 習慣於…

- ▶ Tammy used to live in Alaska.
  譚美過去曾住在阿拉斯加。
- ▶ The dolphins are used to humans wanting to interact with them.
  海豚習慣於那些想和牠們互動的人類。

---

useful [ˈju:s.fəl] *adj.* 有用的；有助益的

實用片語與搭配字

make yourself useful; come in useful

別閒著；派上用場

- ▶ Carrying a cellphone is useful because you may need to call someone.
  隨身帶手機很有用，因為你可能會需要打電話給別人。
- ▶ When your work is done, make yourself useful and assist Carol to send out the invitations.
  當你完成了工作，別閒著，去幫凱蘿寄出邀請函。

---

user [ˈju:.zɚ] *n.* 使用者；用戶

實用片語與搭配字

user-friendly 易於使用的

- ▶ Children under the age of seven are the users of this playground.
  七歲以下的兒童才能使用這個遊樂場。
- ▶ The new cellphone is cheap, but it is not user-friendly and really difficult to use.
  這款新手機價格便宜，但它不易上手，使用起來很困難。

Exercise 74

I. Choose and write the correct word. Change the form of the word when necessary.

1	typhoon (n.) umbrella (n.)	A powerful ________ nearly forced the plane to make an emergency landing.
2	until (prep.) upon (prep.)	Sometimes you'll never know the true value of a moment ________ it becomes a memory.
3	upper (adj.) upstairs (adj.)	They complained about the excessive noise coming from the ________ neighbors.
4	underwear (n.) uniform (n.)	I woke up before six, dressed in my ________ and went to my office to get things ready for the day.
5	useful (adj.) used (adj.)	Cars are ________, but their impact on the environment is another matter we need to be concerned about.

II. Multiple choices.

( ) 1. The teacher wants the students to feel confident about asking questions when they don't ________.
(A) type (B) uniform (C) understand (D) use

( ) 2. He was ________ in his job for years but felt too shy to tell his boss.
(A) upstairs (B) unhappy (C) useful (D) used

( ) 3. The system has been designed to give the ________ quick and easy access to the required information.
(A) used (B) useful (C) user (D) uncle

( ) 4. We're looking for somebody with direct experience in this ________ of work.
(A) type (B) typing (C) used (D) ugly

( ) 5. The air pollution caused ________ brown clouds that brought on smog alerts and left residents wheezing.
(A) useful (B) ugly (C) used (D) typing

Unit 75

usual [ˈjuː.ʒu.əl] *adj.* 通常的

實用片語與搭配字

(it's) business as usual
（儘管情況困難）一切照常

▶ Carl drove the bus, as usual, to the swimming pool.
卡爾如同往常一樣開著巴士去游泳池。

▶ Two days after the earthquake, it was business as usual for many companies despite the damage they had suffered.
地震發生兩天後，許多公司儘管遭受了損失，仍然照常營運。

101

vacation [veɪˈkeɪ.ʃən]

① *n.* 休假；假期

② *v.* 度假

▶ I went to Bali Island on vacation last month.
我上個月去峇里島度假。

▶ We vacation in Greece every year.
我們每年都去希臘度假。

---

valley [ˈvæl.i] *n.* 山谷；溪谷

實用片語與搭配字

Silicon Valley （美國加利福尼亞州的）矽谷

▶ The sheep got stuck at the bottom of the valley.
那隻羊被困在山谷底下。

▶ Sally always dreamed of working as an engineer in Silicon Valley, but she ended up staying in her hometown.
莎莉總夢想著在矽谷擔任工程師，但她最後仍留在家鄉。

---

value [ˈvæl.juː]

① *n.* 價值；重要性

實用片語與搭配字

added value 附加價值

② *v.* 給…估價

▶ The value of Peggy's home went down after the earthquake.
佩吉的房子在地震後價格下跌。

▶ The electronics business is very competitive and brands try to give their products added value to increase sales.
電子產品市場競爭相當激烈，各品牌都想賦予產品附加價值，以刺激銷量。

▶ Kate valued Sean's new painting at one million dollars.
凱特估計西恩的新畫作價值一百萬美元。

---

vegetable [ˈvedʒ.tə.bəl] *n.* 蔬菜

▶ Carrots and lettuce are vegetables.
胡蘿蔔和萵苣是蔬菜。

very [ˈver.i] *adv.* 非常地

- I'm glad that the meeting went very smoothly!
  我很高興這個會議進行得非常順利！

---

victory [ˈvɪk.tɚ.i] *n.* 勝利

- Our baseball team has had ten victories and three losses this season.
  這一季我們的棒球隊已經十勝三敗了。

---

video [ˈvɪd.i.oʊ]

① *adj.* 錄影的；影像的

② *n.* 錄影；錄影機（帶）

③ *v.* 錄影

- The video recording of the two cats singing is cute.
  這兩隻貓唱歌的影片很可愛。
- Rex made a new music video and will present it to us later today.
  雷克斯今天稍晚將展示他新製作的音樂影片給我們看。
- Phoebe has volunteered to video Martin's wedding.
  菲比自願幫忙錄製馬丁的婚禮。

---

view [vjuː]

① *n.* 視野；景象

實用片語與搭配字

in view of sth; point of view
因為；（思考的）角度

② *v.* 觀看；查看

- We had a great view from the top of the mountain!
  我們從山頂上看到了很棒的景色！
- In view of the extremely cold weather, schools have decided to close for the week.
  鑒於天氣非常寒冷，學校決定停課一週。
- I view every challenge as an opportunity to learn.
  我把每個挑戰都視為學習的機會。

---

village [ˈvɪl.ɪdʒ] *n.* 村莊

實用片語與搭配字

the global village 地球村

- Alex and I have decided to trek up to the mountain village.
  艾力克斯和我已經決定要徒步到那座山裡的村莊。
- To survive in the global village, you need to have an advantage, for example, speaking Chinese.
  要在地球村生存，你需要擁有優勢，像是能夠說中文。

---

violin [ˌvaɪəˈlɪn] *n.* 小提琴

- Vera wants to start learning the violin this year.
  維拉想要在今年開始學小提琴。

visit [ˈvɪz.ɪt]

① *v.* 探望；拜訪

實用片語與搭配字

visit sth on / upon sb （使壞事）降臨到

② *n.* 作客；參觀

實用片語與搭配字

pay a visit （通常指短時間的）拜訪

▶ My friend moved away, but he still comes back to visit me sometimes.
我朋友搬走了，但他有時候還會回來拜訪我。

▶ In Greek mythology, the gods often visited their anger on their followers in the form of drought or terrible illness.
在希臘神話中，眾神會將他們的憤怒以乾旱或嚴重疾病的形式降臨在信徒身上。

▶ When will your grandma come for a visit?
你奶奶什麼時候會來看你？

▶ My grandmother is in the hospital and we will pay her a visit tonight and bring her some flowers.
我外婆住院了，我們今晚會去探病，並帶些花給她。

visitor [ˈvɪz.ɪ.t̬ɚ] *n.* 訪客

▶ The government visitors will arrive in the reception area in the next thirty minutes.
這些政府訪客將在三十分鐘後抵達接待區。

---

vocabulary [voʊˈkæb.jə.ler.i] *n.* 字彙；語彙

▶ This semester we will be expected to learn a lot more vocabulary.
這個學期我們預計將會學到更多字彙。

---

voice [vɔɪs]

① *n.* 嗓音；聲音

實用片語與搭配字

give voice to sth 表達（觀點或情感）

② *v.* 表達；吐露

▶ Lee has a great voice; you should hear him sing!
李有很好的聲音，你應該聽聽他唱歌！

▶ Do not be afraid to speak, give voice to your ideas during the meeting so that people can discuss them.
不要害怕在會議中表達你的想法，如此大家可以一起討論。

▶ Sarah wasn't afraid to voice her opinion to everyone in the room.
莎拉毫無畏懼地向房間裡的每一位說出她的意見。

---

volleyball [ˈvɑː.li.bɑːl] *n.* 排球

▶ Sandra decided to play volleyball this year.
珊卓決定今年要打排球。

V

vote [voʊt]

① *n.* 投票；選舉

實用片語與搭配字

cast vote; vote sth down
投票；投票否決

② *v.* 投票；選舉

- Billy won the election because he had the most votes.
  比利贏得了選舉，因為他獲得最多票數。
- The school's decision to allow students more free-time for sport was voted down by the parents.
  家長們投票否絕了學校要讓學生有更多的時間進行體育活動的提議。
- Jill voted against the building of a new chemical factory in her village.
  吉兒投票反對新的化學工廠蓋在她的村莊裡。

---

voter [ˈvoʊ.t̬ɚ] *n.* 投票者；選舉人

- The voters have been lining up outside the school since five o'clock in the morning.
  從早上五點就已經有選民在學校外面排隊了。

---

waist [weɪst] *n.* 腰；腰部

- The tailor needs to measure your waist before he begins making your trousers.
  這位裁縫師在製作你的褲子前需要量你的腰圍。

---

wait [weɪt]

① *v.* 等待；等候

實用片語與搭配字

can't wait; wait and see 迫不及待；等著瞧

② *n.* 等待；等候

- I'll be ready soon; can you wait for me?
  我快準備好了，你可以等我嗎？
- We have done all we could to prepare for this event, now, we have to wait and see what happens.
  我們已經盡全力籌備此次的活動，現在我們只能等著看結果如何了。
- We stood in line for an hour, but the wait was worth it.
  我們排隊排了一個小時，但是等待是值得的。

---

waiter / waitress [ˈweɪ.t̬ɚ / ˈweɪ.trəs]

n. （男）服務生 / 女服務生

- I'm ready to order my meal so can you call the waiter?
  我準備好要點餐了，你能叫服務生過來嗎？

---

wake [weɪk] *v.* 醒來

- I need to wake up early tomorrow as I want to go for a run before work.
  我明天需要早起，因為我想在上班前去跑步。

實用片語與搭配字

wake (sb) up; wake up to sth

叫醒（某人）；開始意識到（問題）

- After weeks of rain and cold weather, I woke up to the sun shining through my window this morning.
  連續數週下雨及寒冷的天氣後，今天早上我醒來意識到陽光透過窗戶照了進來。

---

walk [wɑːk]

① *v.* 走路

- The car is broken, so let's walk to school today.
  車子壞了，所以我們今天就走路上學吧。

實用片語與搭配字

walk away; walk away with sth

（從困境中）脫身，一走了之；輕鬆獲（獎）

- The design competition was tough, but our team walked away with the first prize.
  這場設計大賽相當艱難，但我們這隊獲得了第一名。

② *n.* 散步；行走

- The weather is so nice; do you want to go for a walk outside?
  今天天氣真好，你想到外面散散步嗎？

實用片語與搭配字

jaywalk; a walk in the park; walk of life

（不遵守交通規則）亂過馬路；簡單易做的事；各行各業，各個社會階層

- In many countries, it is illegal to jaywalk and you can only cross at the traffic lights.
  在許多國家，隨意穿越馬路是違法行為，你只能走斑馬線。

---

walkman [ˈwɑːk.mən] *n.* 隨身聽

- I use my walkman to play my favorite music.
  我用隨身聽播放我最愛的音樂。

---

wall [wɑːl]

① *n.* 牆壁

- There is a spider on the wall in my room!
  有一隻蜘蛛在我房間的牆上！

實用片語與搭配字

drive sb up the wall 令（某人）大怒

- My colleague drives me up the wall; he is always complaining about his life.
  我的同事讓我很生氣；他總是在抱怨他的生活。

② *v.* 用牆圍住

- I feel walled up in this tiny old house.
  在這又小又舊的房子裡，我感覺被困住了。

Exercise 75

I. Choose and write the correct word. Change the form of the word when necessary.

1	value (n.) victory (n.)	His previous experience gave him a big advantage over the other contestants for the final ___________.
2	visit (v.) vote (v.)	I've never been to Malaysia, but I hope to ___________ it next year.
3	wake (v.) wait (v.)	We fell asleep on the train, and ___________ up to find ourselves in another city.
4	waist (n.) visitor (n.)	As a foreign ___________ at Cambridge, I was shown the libraries, laboratories, and administrative offices.
5	vocabulary (n.) vacation (n.)	Every year my father would get all the family members together to discuss where we were going on ___________.

II. Multiple choices.

(　　) 1. From the top of the hill, there's a beautiful prospect over the __________.
(A) valley　(B) victory　(C) value　(D) view

(　　) 2. There's a __________ tournament at Sunshine Park which begins today.
(A) voter　(B) visit　(C) video　(D) volleyball

(　　) 3. In the __________ market, the stalls are piled high with local vegetables.
(A) view　(B) voice　(C) village　(D) victory

(　　) 4. After she moved to Boston, she worked as a __________ and put herself through school.
(A) waiter　(B) waitress　(C) visitor　(D) waist

(　　) 5. The performer in an evening dress played classical selections on the __________.
(A) voter　(B) waist　(C) violin　(D) video

Unit 76

wallet [ˈwɑː.lɪt] *n.* 皮夾；錢包

▶ Can you help me check if I left my wallet in your car?
你能幫我確認一下我是不是把皮夾掉在你車上嗎？

---

want [wɑːnt]

① *v.* 想要

實用片語與搭配字

want in / out of; not / never want for anything
想要加入 / 退出；什麼也不缺

② *n.* 需求；需要

▶ Do you want noodles or rice for lunch?
你午餐要吃麵還是飯？

▶ The widow's husband left her enough money so that she would never want for anything.
那位寡婦的丈夫留給她足夠的錢，所以她什麼都不缺。

▶ Kiki is very content; she doesn't have a lot of wants.
奇奇很容易滿足，她沒有太多需求。

---

war [wɔːr]

① *n.* 戰爭

② *v.* 打仗

▶ Many soldiers were killed during the terrible war.
許多軍兵在這場可怕的戰爭中遭到殺害。

▶ The king warred with his neighbors because he wanted their land.
那位國王與鄰國打仗是因為想要別人的土地。

100

warm [wɔːrm]

① *adj.* 溫暖的

② *v.* 變暖和

實用片語與搭配字

warm-up 做準備活動，熱身；熱鬧起來

▶ It's too warm to wear a sweater today!
今天太熱不適合穿毛衣！

▶ He warmed the soup until it was hot.
他加熱了這碗湯。

▶ Before we start singing, let's do some warm-up exercises for our voices.
在我們開始唱歌之前，先做一些熱身運動開嗓。

---

wash [wɑːʃ]

① *v.* 清洗；洗滌

實用片語與搭配字

wash sth away; wash sth off
沖掉；使…被洗下

▶ Did you wash these clothes, or are they still dirty?
你洗這些衣服了嗎？或是它們仍是髒的？

▶ When you hurt someone, you can wash the blood off your hands, but not the guilt.
當你傷害某人時，你可以將血洗掉，但無法將罪惡消除。

② *n.* 洗滌

▶ It took a very strong wash to get all the dirt off the car.
經過強力的沖洗才把那輛車所有的污泥都洗乾淨。

---

waste [weɪst]

① *v.* 浪費

② *n.* 垃圾；廢料

實用片語與搭配字

go to waste 被浪費掉

▶ Take that leftover food home; don't waste it.
把這些剩菜帶回家，不要浪費了。

▶ This trashcan is full of waste.
這個垃圾桶裝滿了垃圾。

▶ We should not let food go to waste, but give it to the poor instead.
我們不應該浪費食物，而是應該把它給窮人。

---

watch [wɑːtʃ]

① *n.* 手錶

② *v.* 觀看；注視

實用片語與搭配字

watch out for sb / sth 密切注意

③ *n.* 看守；觀察；監視

▶ My watch says that it's 1:30 now.
我的手錶顯示現在是一點半。

▶ Do you want to come watch a movie with us tonight?
你今晚要過來跟我們一起看電影嗎？

▶ Elderly people should watch out for scammers who steal their money by telling lies.
年長者應需要小心那些說謊騙錢的騙子。

▶ The guard wasn't allowed to sleep because it was his watch.
保全人員在輪值看守時是不准睡覺的。

---

water [ˈwɑː.t̬ɚ]

① *n.* 水

② *v.* 給…澆水；灌溉

實用片語與搭配字

water sth down 稀釋，使（觀點等）弱化

▶ Be sure to drink plenty of water when you exercise.
當你運動時，一定要多喝些水。

▶ My mom waters her flowers every day, so they can grow.
我媽媽每天澆花，所以花兒可以生長。

▶ Instead of telling the truth, Janet watered her dire financial situation down so her parents wouldn't be worried.
與其說出事實，珍妮特寧願淡化自己危急的財務狀況，這樣她的父母才不會擔心。

97

waterfall [ˈwɑː.t̬ɚ.fɑːl] *n.* 瀑布

▶ Paul is going to try to climb to the top of the waterfall.
保羅試著要爬上瀑布的頂端。

watermelon [ˈwɑː.t̬ɚ͵mel.ən] *n.* 西瓜

▸ The watermelon you gave me was so sweet and juicy.
你給我的這個西瓜又甜又多汁。

---

wave [weɪv]

① *n.* 波浪

② *v.* 揮手

實用片語與搭配字

wave / say goodbye to sth; wave sb off

向…揮手告別；與（某人）揮手道別

▸ There were big waves after the storm today so I decided not to go surfing.
今天暴風雨過後會有大浪，所以我決定不去衝浪了。

▸ George waved to his fans as he left the concert hall.
喬治離開音樂廳時向他的粉絲揮了揮手。

▸ When Ron left home for his studies abroad, his friends and family were all at the airport to wave him off.
當榮恩要離家出國念書時，他的朋友和家人都到機場向他道別。

---

way [weɪ] *n.* 道路

▸ I'm lost; can you show me the way to town?
我迷路了，你可以告訴我往城裡的方向嗎？

---

we [wiː / wi] *pron.* 我們（主格）

▸ My friend and I don't always agree, but we respect each other.
我和我的朋友不是每次都意見相同，但我們尊重彼此。

---

weak [wiːk] *adj.* 虛弱的；無力的

▸ I may look weak, but actually my muscles are very strong!
或許我看起來很弱，但其實我的肌肉很強壯！

---

weapon [ˈwep.ən] *n.* 武器

實用片語與搭配字

secret weapon 秘密武器

▸ The soldiers put their weapons into a secure location before the enemy arrived.
這些士兵們在敵人抵達前，先把他們的武器放到安全地點。

▸ Connie said her secret weapon to not get angry quickly was to count to 10 before she said anything.
康妮說她不發怒的秘密武器，是在她說話前先從一數到十。

wear [wer]

① *v.* 穿著；戴著；塗抹著

實用片語與搭配字

wear (sth) away; wear sb down

（使）磨損；使（某人）精疲力竭

② *n.* 衣服；穿著

實用片語與搭配字

wear and tear （一定時期內的）磨損

▶ It's raining today, so you should wear a raincoat.
今天下雨，所以你應該穿雨衣。

▶ Continuous criticism can wear a good person down until they feel they cannot do anything at all.
持續地批皮會消磨一個好人的自信心，直到他認為自己什麼事都做不到。

▶ Formal wear is required for the wedding.
在婚禮穿著正式服裝是必須的。

▶ Airplanes must be checked for wear and tear often and old or broken parts must be replaced.
飛機必須經常檢查磨損情況，舊的或損壞的零件必須更換。

weather [ˈweð.ɚ]

① *n.* 天氣

實用片語與搭配字

be / feel under the weather; in all weathers

覺得不舒服；無論天氣好壞

② *v.* 平安渡過（困境）；經受住

實用片語與搭配字

weather the storm 渡過難關

▶ The weather is sunny and hot now, but it might change later today.
現在天氣晴朗且炎熱，但等一下可能會變天。

▶ My dog has been feeling under the weather for the past week, so I will take him to the vet for a check-up.
過去幾週我的狗一直感到不適，所以我會帶牠到獸醫那裡做檢查。

▶ Tim is a sailor. He has weathered many storms at sea.
提姆是個水手，他在海上經歷過許多暴風雨。

▶ During the financial crisis, many companies weathered the storm and did not go bankrupt.
在金融危機期間，許多公司渡過了難關，沒有破產倒閉。

---

wed [wed] *v.* 與…結婚

▶ Larry wed Sally after coming back from the war in Iraq.
賴瑞從伊拉克戰場回來後就與莎莉結婚了。

---

wedding [ˈwed.ɪŋ] *n.* 婚禮

▶ My brother is getting married; his wedding is next month!
我哥哥要結婚了，他的婚禮在下個月！

Wednesday / Wed. / Weds. [ˈwenz.deɪ]

n. 星期三

- ▶ I'm busy on Tuesday, but I'm free on Wednesday.
  我星期二很忙，但星期三有空。

---

week [wiːk] *n.* (一) 星期；週

實用片語與搭配字

sb / sth of the week; week-long

本周最佳；一週長的

- ▶ There are usually four to five weeks in a month.
  一個月通常有四到五週。
- ▶ During my week-long vacation, I am going to just lie on the beach and relax.
  在我長達一週的假期中，我只想躺在沙灘上放鬆。

---

weekday [ˈwiːk.deɪ]

n. 平日；(非週末的) 工作日

- ▶ Jordan's clothing store is open on weekdays, except for public holidays.
  除了國定假日外，喬登服飾店平日都營業。

---

weekend [ˈwiːk.end]

① *n.* 週末

② *v.* 度週末

- ▶ Since we don't have work on the weekends, I try to get some rest.
  因為週末不用工作，我試著多休息。
- ▶ My family often weekends at the beach.
  我家人通常會在海邊度過週末。

---

weigh [weɪ] *v.* 秤重量

- ▶ People at the market use a scale to weigh vegetables before buying them.
  市場上的人在購買蔬菜前，會先用磅秤秤重量。

weight [weɪt] *n.* 重量

實用片語與搭配字

weight training; be / take a weight off your mind

舉重訓練；消除煩惱

- ▶ The doctor will ask you to tell him your height and weight.
  醫生會詢問你的身高與體重。
- ▶ It is important for older women to do weight training to ensure stronger bones.
  年長的婦女進行重量訓練以確保骨骼更強壯是很重要的。

Exercise 76

I. Choose and write the correct word. Change the form of the word when necessary.

1	warm (adj.) weak (adj.)	It's not surprising you feel __________ if you haven't eaten properly for days.
2	wallet (n.) waste (n.)	He took his __________ from his suit jacket and headed off to the cafeteria for lunch.
3	wear (v.) wave (v.)	I was driving along the road quite happily when a policeman __________ me down.
4	weapon (n.) weather (n.)	They have to cancel tomorrow's football match because of the bad __________.
5	weigh (v.) wash (v.)	We have to __________ the cost of the new system against the benefits it will bring.

II. Multiple choices.

(　　) 1. The __________ cascaded over the rocks and splashed into a pool at the bottom.
(A) weather　(B) wedding　(C) waterfall　(D) wave

(　　) 2. We'll have to buy some food at the supermarket for the __________ if we are having visitors.
(A) weapon　(B) weather　(C) weekend　(D) wedding

(　　) 3. We don't want to __________ our time trying to persuade people who aren't interested in our idea.
(A) waste　(B) wave　(C) wear　(D) wash

(　　) 4. I like to bring my friends home to a __________ welcome from my family.
(A) weak　(B) week　(C) warm　(D) wedding

(　　) 5. The plants in the garden are withering because they haven't been __________ for days.
(A) waved　(B) watered　(C) watched　(D) washed

Unit 77

welcome [ˈwel.kəm]

① *v.* 歡迎；迎接

② *adj.* 受歡迎的

實用片語與搭配字

make sb welcome 使（某人）覺得受歡迎

③ *n.* 歡迎

- When I moved into my new home, my neighbors welcomed me.
  當我搬進我的新家，鄰居都來歡迎我。
- Please tell Yvonne that she is welcome to come to the party.
  請告訴依芳歡迎她來參加派對。
- My mom has a talent for making people welcome in our house with her warm personality.
  我媽媽有一種天賦，能夠以她溫暖的個性讓來我家的人感到受歡迎。
- The class didn't give the new student a warm welcome, so he didn't feel comfortable.
  班上沒有給新同學熱情的歡迎，所以他感覺不自在。

---

well [wel]

① *adj.* 健康的；很好的

實用片語與搭配字

well done; as well (as); well known

做得好；除…之外還；著名的

② *adv.* 很好地；令人滿意地

③ *n.* 井

- My father was sick last week, but now he is well again.
  我爸爸上禮拜生病，但是現在他恢復健康了。
- The well-known author just published his latest book and it has already sold-out in some stores.
  那位知名的作家剛發表了新書，在許多商店已經賣完了。
- He speaks French quite well.
  他的法文說得很流利。
- A long time ago, people used to get water from this well.
  很久以前，人們習慣從這口井裡取水。

---

west [west]

① *n.* 西方

② *adj.* 西方的

③ *adv.* 向西方；在西方

- The sun rises in the east and sets in the west.
  太陽從東邊升起西邊落下。
- The west coast of Florida is warmer than the east coast.
  佛羅里達州的西海岸比東海岸溫暖。
- This bus is going west, not east.
  這輛巴士要往西，不是往東。

western [ˈwes.tɚn]

① *adj.* 西的；西方的

② *n.* 西部片

▶ Alex is planning to travel to western Europe during his summer vacation.
艾力克斯計畫在暑假時去西歐旅行。

▶ Clint loves to watch old western movies during his free time.
柯林特在他空閒時喜歡看老西部片。

---

wet [wet]

① *adj.* 濕的；潮溼的

實用片語與搭配字

wet blanket 掃興的人

② *v.* 把…弄濕；使潮濕

▶ I got completely wet after getting caught in the heavy rain today.
我今天遇到大雨全身都濕透了。

▶ My brother was such a wet blanket during our camping trip. He complained about everyone and everything.
我弟弟真是個掃興的人，在露營時他無論何人何事都能抱怨一番。

▶ Wet the cloth thoroughly before wiping the table clean.
先把抹布徹底弄濕再把桌子擦乾淨。

---

whale [weɪl] *n.* 鯨魚

▶ While diving in the ocean we saw turtles and whales.
我們潛在海裡時看見了烏龜和鯨魚。

---

what [wɑːt]

① *pron.* 什麼

② *adj.* 什麼

▶ I couldn't hear you; what did you say?
我聽不到，你剛剛說什麼？

▶ What homework do we have to do for tomorrow?
我們明天的家庭作業是什麼？

---

whatever [wɑːˈt̬ev.ɚ]

① *adj.* 無論什麼的；不管怎樣的

② *pron.* 任何事；不論什麼

▶ Whatever food you like we'll order it immediately.
無論你喜歡什麼樣的食物，我們都會馬上點。

▶ Do whatever you want but don't be noisy after ten o'clock at night.
你可以做任何你想做的事，但晚上十點後不要吵鬧。

---

wheel [wiːl]

① *n.* 車輪；輪子

② *v.* 推動（有輪子的東西）

▶ The wheels I ordered for my bike will arrive by mail this afternoon.
我訂購的自行車輪胎今天下午會郵寄到貨。

▶ Can you wheel the trolley into the supermarket while I park the car?
我去停車時，你能推購物推車進超市嗎？

when [wen]

① *adv.* 什麼時候
② *pron.* 什麼時候；那時
③ *conj.* 當…時

▶ When do you want to go shopping?
你什麼時候想要去逛街購物？

▶ Since when did you start walking to work?
你從什麼時候開始走路去上班？

▶ I send you a message when I arrive at their house.
當我到他們家時會傳個簡訊給你。

---

whenever [wenˈev.ɚ]

① *conj.* 無論何時；每當
② *adv.* 無論在任何時候

▶ I can help you move these boxes whenever you're free.
等你有空，我可以幫你搬這些箱子。

▶ We try to eat fresh vegetables whenever possible.
我們無論何時都儘可能吃新鮮的蔬菜。

---

where [wer]

① *adv.* 在哪裡；往哪裡
② *conj.* 在…處；到…的地方
③ *pron.* 哪裡；何處
④ *n.* 地點

▶ Excuse me, where is the bathroom?
不好意思，洗手間在哪裡？

▶ We drove to a place where we could see the sunset.
我開車到一個我們可以看到夕陽的地方。

▶ I looked where I thought I left my phone, but it wasn't there.
我查看我可能掉手機的地方，但是並不在那裡。

▶ This is where I found the lost puppy.
這是我找到走失小狗的地點。

---

wherever [werˈev.ɚ]

① *adv.* 去任何地方；無論在什麼地方
② *conj.* 無論何處；無論什麼情況

▶ Wherever I go in the city I always seem to find a coffee shop.
無論我去城裡什麼地方，都會找一間咖啡店。

▶ Gabby seems to take pictures of couples wherever she goes.
蓋比似乎無論去哪裡她都會拍戀人的照片。

---

whether [ˈweð.ɚ] *adj.* 不管…還是…

▶ I plan to go out tonight, whether you want to or not.
不管你是否想去，我計畫今晚出去。

---

which [wɪtʃ]

① *pron.* 哪個；哪些

▶ I don't know which is better, the black shirt or the white one?
我不知道哪一個比較好，黑色襯衫好還是白襯衫？

② *adj.* 哪一個

▶ Which one do you prefer, coffee or tea?
哪一種你比較喜歡，咖啡或茶？

---

while [waɪl]

① *conj.* 在…的時候；與…同時
② *n.* 一會兒
③ *v.* 消磨（時光）

▶ I painted my nails while watching TV.
我看電視的時候把指甲油都擦好了。

▶ We talked for a while.
我們談了一會兒。

▶ Since Jason was stuck at home sick, he whiled away his time with reading.
因為傑森生病在家休養，他用閱讀來消磨時間。

---

whisper [ˈwɪs.pɚ]

① *v.* 耳語；低聲說出
② *n.* 小聲說話；耳語

▶ Sheryl whispered the password of her computer to her best friend.
雪柔跟她最好的朋友小聲說她的電腦密碼。

▶ The teacher heard whispers during the test and went to investigate.
老師在考試時聽見有人竊竊私語就進行調查。

---

white [waɪt]

① *adj.* 白色的
② *n.* 白色

實用片語與搭配字

white lie 善意的謊話

▶ Polar bears have white hair, but their skin is black.
北極熊有白色的毛，但牠們的皮膚是黑色的。

▶ White is a good color for you.
白色是適合你的顏色。

▶ Sometimes it is necessary to tell a white lie, especially when you do not want to make your best friend feel bad.
有時善意的謊言是必要的，尤其是你不想讓你最好的朋友感覺不好時。

---

who [huː] *pron.* 誰；什麼人

實用片語與搭配字

says who?
（在爭執時表示不同意或不接受對方的說法）誰說的？

▶ Who ate the last cookie?
誰吃了最後一片餅乾？

▶ It is never a good idea to have too much fun… says who?
有太多樂趣並不是一個好主意……誰說的？

---

whoever [huːˈev.ɚ]

pron. 任何人；無論什麼人

▶ Whoever finishes the race the fastest will be eligible to compete in the national competition.
無論誰最快完成賽跑，就有資格在國際賽事上出賽。

97

whole [hoʊl]

① *adj.* 整個的

② *n.* 整個…；全部

▶ The whole class participated in the event.
整個班級都參加了這個活動。

▶ I didn't understand the whole of the lesson, but I could understand some parts.
我不明白這堂課全部的內容，但有些部分我懂。

---

whom [huːm] *pron.* 誰（受格）

▶ For whom did you buy those flowers?
你買了那些花要給誰？

---

whose [huːz]

pron. 誰的（who 或 which 的所有格）

▶ Whose house is this?
這是誰的房子？

---

why [waɪ]

① *adv.* 為什麼

實用片語與搭配字

why not...? 表示建議或同意）為甚麼不（呢）？

② *n.* 原因

▶ Why did you call the police?
你為什麼打電話給警察？

▶ There are many experts who say that drinking coffee is not healthy and I can't see why not...?
有很多專家說喝咖啡不健康，我不明白為什麼不……？

▶ Nobody in the company asked the whys of the surprise decision.
公司中沒人問過這個令人意外的決定是如何做出的。

---

wide [waɪd]

① *adj.* 寬闊的

實用片語與搭配字

wide-eyed; wide open
單純的；完全開放的

② *adv.* 大大地；充分地

▶ This road is very wide; there's plenty of space for cars to drive.
這條路很寬，有很大的空間給車子行駛。

▶ The kids sat in front of the television, looking at the fantasy film with wide-eyed wonder.
那群小孩坐在電視機前，純真地看著奇幻電影。

▶ He opened his mouth wide and took a big bite of the hamburger.
他張大嘴咬了一大口漢堡。

W

Exercise 77

I. Choose and write the correct word. Change the form of the word when necessary.

1	western (adj.) whatever (adj.)	__________ his shortcomings as a husband, he's a good father to his children.
2	wide (adj.) whole (adj.)	The __________ food chain is affected by the overuse of chemicals in agriculture.
3	whoever (pro.) whose (pro.)	In the film, he plays a spy __________ mission is to confirm the verity of a secret military document.
4	welcome (v.) whisper (v.)	The two girls were __________ in the corner and giggling over some private joke.
5	well (n.) wheel (n.)	While he was changing the __________ on his car, his coat had become stained with oil.

II. Multiple choices.

( ) 1. __________ countries enjoy considerable advantages in terms of technology.
(A) Wet (B) Western (C) Whatever (D) Whenever

( ) 2. A cloud of volcanic ash is spreading across __________ areas of the Philippines.
(A) white (B) while (C) wide (D) which

( ) 3. __________ you have a goal, you must sacrifice some kind of freedom to attain it.
(A) Whatever (B) Whenever (C) Whoever (D) Wherever

( ) 4. The two countries claimed the proposal wouldn't endanger the __________ populations.
(A) Well (B) whale (C) wheel (D) west

( ) 5. I babysit for Jenny on Tuesday evenings __________ she goes to her yoga class.
(A) whatever (B) wherever (C) whenever (D) whoever

Unit 78

widen [ˈwaɪ.dən] *v.* 變寬；加寬

實用片語與搭配字

widen sb's horizons 開闊（某人）的眼界

► As you go around the corner, the path begins to widen and allow more room for bicycles.
當你到轉角，這條小徑開始變寬，而且有更多空間可以騎自行車。

► Highschool students should take a gap year to travel abroad and widen their horizons.
高中生應該在空檔年出國旅行，增廣見聞。

95

width [wɪtθ / wɪdθ] *n.* 寬度

► The width of the table was very large.
這張桌子的寬度很寬。

---

wife [waɪf] *n.* 妻子；老婆

實用片語與搭配字

ex-wife 前妻

► Jack and his wife have been married for fifty years.
傑克和他太太已經結婚五十年了。

► My brother's ex-wife got married again recently and she is very happy.
最近哥哥的前妻再婚了，她看起來很快樂。

95

wild [waɪld]

① *adj.* 野生的

實用片語與搭配字

be wild about sth / sb 對…非常狂熱

② *adv.* 無控制地

③ *n.* 荒野

► He saw a wild fox wandering the forest.
他看見了一隻野狐狸漫步在森林裡。

► Kids are wild about every new thing, but they also get bored with it quickly.
孩子們對每件新事物都很狂熱，但他們也很快就厭倦了。

► The grass was growing wild in the field.
草在田地裡恣意地生長。

► She saw many creatures in the wild.
她在荒野上看見許多動物。

---

will [wɪl]

① *n.* 意志；毅力；決心

► Training for a long race requires a strong will.
長跑訓練需要很強的意志力。

實用片語與搭配字

where there's a will there's a way; free will
有志者事竟成；自由意志

② *aux. v.* 將要

- The question of free will and how free humans really are to make their own choices is a popular debate among students.
  自由意志的問題及人類自由做選擇的方式是學生們廣泛討論的熱門話題。
- I will go to Japan when I graduate.
  我畢業後會去日本。

---

willing [ˈwɪl.ɪŋ] *adj.* 願意的；樂意的

實用片語與搭配字

the spirit is willing, but the flesh is weak
心有餘而力不足

- My friend was willing to help me.
  我的朋友樂意幫助我。
- I would love to climb Mt. Everest, but I am not fit enough -- it is a case of the spirit is willing but the flesh is weak.
  我想要去爬珠穆朗瑪峰，但我體能還不夠好，這是心有餘而力不足的例子。

---

win [wɪn]

① *v.* 贏得

實用片語與搭配字

win sb over 說服（某人）

② *n.* 贏；勝利；第一名

實用片語與搭配字

win-win 雙贏的

- Paul never won a basketball game in his life.
  保羅在他一生中從沒贏過一場籃球比賽。
- To get the decision accepted in the meeting, we need to win the mayor over to our side.
  要在會議中通過這個決定，我們必須說服市長站在我們這邊。
- This game was an important win for the Chicago Cubs.
  對芝加哥小熊隊來說，贏得這場比賽很重要。
- After months of negotiation, the employer and employees finally agreed that the offer was a win-win solution for both.
  經過數個月的協商，雇主和雇員終於達成共識，創造雙贏的局面。

---

wind [wɪnd]

① *n.* 風

實用片語與搭配字

get wind of sth 得知…秘密消息

- A typhoon is coming, so the wind today is quite strong.
  颱風要來了，所以今天的風十分強勁。
- We organized a surprise party for our best friend, but we had to be careful so that she did not get wind of it beforehand.
  我們替一位好朋友籌辦了驚喜派對，但要小心不能讓她事先知道消息。

② *v.* 包裹；使纏繞成團

實用片語與搭配字

wind (sth) down （使）逐漸結束

► He wound the wire around the object.
他用電線纏繞這個物品。

► My birthday dinner was a huge success and we winded the evening down with wine next to the pool.
我的生日大餐相當成功，最後我們坐在泳池邊喝著酒結束這個夜晚。

---

window [ˈwɪn.doʊ] *n.* 窗戶

實用片語與搭配字

go out (of) the window; window seat
完全消失；（尤指公共交通工具上）靠窗子的座位

► I can see birds right outside my window.
我可以從我的窗戶外看到鳥兒。

► I prefer the window seat whenever I fly because I like to watch the clouds and the cities from above.
當飛行時我喜歡坐在靠窗的座位，因為我喜歡從上面觀看雲層和城市。

---

windy [ˈwɪn.di] *adj.* 風大的；多風的

► The air was windy near the beach.
沙灘附近的風很大。

---

wine [waɪn]

① *n.* 葡萄酒；果酒

實用片語與搭配字

red wine; white wine; table wine
紅酒；白酒；佐餐酒

② *v.* 喝酒

實用片語與搭配字

wine and dine sb 設酒宴款待（某人）

► Wine is alcohol made from grapes.
紅酒是由葡萄做的酒。

► I like to drink red wine, but in summer, it is sometimes great to have a chilled white wine.
我喜歡喝紅酒，但在夏天，有時喝一杯冰鎮的白酒會很棒。

► We wined and dined with our friends on our weekend trip.
我們週末旅行時和朋友大吃大喝。

► Our European customer is visiting and my boss has ordered me to wine and dine him at a five-star restaurant.
我們的客戶自歐洲來訪，我的老闆請我在五星級餐廳設宴款待他。

---

wing [wɪŋ]

① *n.* 翅膀

② *v.* 飛；翱翔

► That hawk has an injured wing.
那隻老鷹有一個翅膀受傷了。

► The birds will wing to their nest.
這些鳥會飛到牠們的巢。

實用片語與搭配字

wing it 即興發言 / 做

▶ I did not have time to study for my math test and I am just going to have to wing it; let's hope I pass.
我沒有時間準備數學考試，我打算即興發揮了，希望能及格。

---

winner [ˈwɪn.ɚ] *n.* 優勝者

▶ The winner of that game was excited!
那場比賽的優勝者感到非常興奮！

---

winter [ˈwɪn.t̬ɚ] *n.* 冬天

▶ This winter has been cold and snowy.
這個冬天又冷又下雪。

---

wire [waɪr]

① *n.* 金屬線

② *v.* 接電線；用金屬線連接、固定

▶ He used a wire to hold the frame together.
他用一條金屬線把框架固定在一起。

▶ Dad will wire the house with cables.
爸爸會幫家裡接電線。

---

wise [waɪz] *adj.* 有智慧的；聰明的

▶ My history teacher is very wise.
我的歷史老師非常有智慧。

---

wish [wɪʃ]

① *v.* 希望；但願

實用片語與搭配字

wish sb well; as you wish / like
祝（某人）成功；（尤指實施並不同意某人的要求時）悉隨尊便

② *n.* 願望

實用片語與搭配字

wish list 夢想清單

▶ I wish I could go to Australia, but I don't think it's possible.
我希望我可以去澳洲，可是應該是不可能的。

▶ The company boss retired and everyone wished him well.
公司老闆退休了，大家祝福他一切都好。

▶ On your birthday, you make a wish and blow out candles on a cake.
生日時，你可以許願，並且在蛋糕上吹蠟燭。

▶ Everyone should have a bucket list, a wish list of things you want to do before you are too old.
每個人都應該列一個夢想清單，在清單上是感覺太老以前想要完成的事情。

---

with [wɪð] *prep.* 和…一起

▶ I'm going to the park with my little nephew.
我要和我的小姪子一起去公園玩。

103

within [wɪˈðɪn]

① *prep.* 在…之內

② *adv.* 在裡面；在心中

▸ The pen was within her grasp.
這隻筆在她伸手可及之處。

▸ I felt the happiness within.
我心中感到幸福。

---

without [wɪˈðaʊt]

① *prep.* 沒有；不；無

實用片語與搭配字

go without (sth) 沒有…也行

② *adv.* 沒有；無；缺少

▸ She left her home without a cell phone.
她離家時沒帶手機。

▸ Halfway to the airport, my sister remembered she forgot her computer; she would have to go without it now.
在前往機場的途中，我姊姊想起來她忘了帶電腦，但現在她沒有電腦也必須走了。

▸ There are things to see at the park without paying money.
在公園裡有許多不用花錢就可欣賞的事物。

---

wok [wɑːk] *n.* （中式）炒菜鍋

▸ The cook uses a wok to make fried rice.
這位廚師用炒菜鍋來炒飯。

---

wolf [wʊlf] *n.* 狼

實用片語與搭配字

lone wolf 孤僻的人

▸ We heard the wolf howl at night.
我們在晚上聽見了狼嚎。

▸ Police said the murderer was a lone wolf who had no accomplices, so people could feel safe.
警察說殺人犯是孤僻的人，沒有同夥，所以人們可以安心。

---

woman [ˈwʊm.ən] *n.* 女人；成年女子

實用片語與搭配字

woman-to-woman 坦率的（地）

▸ Is that woman your mother or your aunt?
那位女士是你的媽媽還是阿姨？

▸ My sister and I had a woman-to-woman chat about the challenges we face as mothers who work full-time.
我和姊姊坦率談論我們做為全職母親所面臨的挑戰。

95

wonder [ˈwʌn.dɚ]

① *n.* 驚訝；驚嘆

▸ They gazed at the sky in awe and wonder.
他們帶著敬畏和驚嘆凝視著天空。

實用片語與搭配字

work / do wonders; no wonder
產生奇妙的作用；並不奇怪

▶ A day at the spa can work wonders to relax you; you will feel like a new person.
花一天時間做水療能產生奇妙的作用，讓你感覺好像一個全新的人。

② *v.* 感到驚訝；感到納悶

▶ He will wonder as he sees all the gifts.
當他看到所有的禮物時會感到驚訝的。

---

wonderful [ˈwʌn.dɚ.fəl] *adj.* 極好的

▶ Traveling the world is a wonderful experience.
環遊世界是一個極好的經驗。

---

wood [wʊd] *n.* 木頭

▶ My dad likes to build things made of wood.
我爸爸喜歡用木頭建造東西。

實用片語與搭配字

be out of the woods 脫離險境（或困境）

▶ My grandmother is very sick, and even though she is better, the doctor said she is not out of the woods yet.
我的祖母生了重病，儘管情況有好轉，但醫生仍說她並未脫離險境。

Exercise 78

I. Choose and write the correct word. Change the form of the word when necessary.

1	wild (adj.) willing (adj.)	To work effectively, you need to have positive work attitude and be __________ and able to work diligently.
2	width (n.) window (n.)	You must now decide the __________ of the columns, including the space between them.
3	wing (n.) wire (n.)	Once we have the __________, we can coil it up into the shape of a spring.
4	wonder (v.) widen (v.)	I __________ how many celebrities actually use the products they endorse.
5	within (prep.) without (prep.)	We have to get straight down to business __________ wasting time on small talk.

II. Multiple choices.

( ) 1. Modern farming methods have led to the total extinction of many species of __________ flowers.

(A) will (B) willing (C) wild (D) windy

( ) 2. Everyone was silent when the president announced the __________ of the competition.

(A) winner (B) wood (C) wire (D) width

( ) 3. Look at the weather! I think we've made a __________ decision not to go to the coast this weekend.

(A) without (B) wise (C) wish (D) winner

( ) 4. The __________ conditions made it difficult to put the tent up.

(A) wonder (B) wise (C) windy (D) wire

( ) 5. This photo is a __________ happy moment caught with perfect timing.

(A) wonder (B) wise (C) windy (D) wonderful

Unit 79

wooden [ˈwʊd.ən] *adj.* 木頭的；木製的

▶ The wooden chair was light-brown.
那把木椅是淺褐色的。

wool [wʊl] *n.* 羊毛

▶ All my shirts are made of wool.
我所有的襯衫都是羊毛製的。

word [wɝːd]

① *n.* 詞；字；單詞

實用片語與搭配字

a good word; have a word with sb; in a word; word for word

（表示贊同或支持某人或某事的）好話；與某人談話；簡而言之；一字不差地

② *v.* 措詞；用言辭表達

▶ This dictionary has ten thousand words in it.
這本字典有一萬個單字。

▶ I told my friend I would put in a good word for him with my boss if he was interested in working for our company.
我告訴我的朋友，如果他有興趣為我們公司工作，我會跟老闆說好話。

▶ I'm not sure how to word this important letter; can you help me write it?
我不知道這封重要的信該如何措詞，你可以幫我寫嗎？

work [wɝːk]

① *v.* 工作；（使）勞動

實用片語與搭配字

work against / for sb; work sth off; work on sth

使對（某人）不利 / 有利；（透過消耗體力）擺脫；改善

② *n.* 工作；勞動

實用片語與搭配字

work ethic; be at work; get to work

職業道德感；在工作，有效；開始工作

▶ We worked outside all day in the garden, so we were tired and dirty!
我們在外面花園裡工作了一整天，又髒又累！

▶ After college, I had to work off the loan from the company for 5 years.
大學畢業後，我必須在這家公司工作五年才能擺脫貸款。

▶ Having a farm is a lot of work; it's not easy.
經營農場有很多工作要做；這並不容易。

▶ Different countries have different work ethics; for example, people in Europe have more vacation days than people in Asia.
不同的國家會有不同的工作倫理，舉例來說，在歐洲國家比在亞洲國家有更多假期。

worker [ˈwɝː.kɚ] *n.* 工人；工作者

▶ There were many workers fixing the bridge.
有很多工人在修那座橋。

實用片語與搭配字

social worker 社會福利工作者

▶ The social worker stopped by to check on the family every day to ensure the children were taken care of.
社工每天到那個家庭探訪，以確保孩子們得到了照顧。

---

world [wɝːld] *n.* 世界；地球

實用片語與搭配字

make a world of difference; mean the world to sb; do sb the world of good
大大提高；對（某人）來說非常重要；使某人感到更健康或更高興

▶ We share this world, so we should take good care of it.
我們都共享這世界，所以應該要好好愛護地球。

▶ My doctor advised me to change jobs and said the change would do me a world of good.
我的醫生建議我換工作，這樣能更有益身心健康。

---

worm [wɝːm]

① *n.* 蟲；昆蟲

② *v.* 擠過；鑽過

▶ My dad uses worms on his line to catch fish.
我爸爸拿蟲當誘餌釣魚。

▶ It was crowded, but I wormed my way to the exit.
雖然這裡很擁擠，可是我鑽過人群到出口。

96

worry [ˈwɝːɪ]

① *v.* 擔心；憂慮

② *n.* 煩惱

▶ Don't worry; it'll be okay!
別擔心，沒關係的！

▶ On vacation, we forget about all our worries and just rest.
在度假時，我們忘記所有的煩惱，全然休息放鬆。

95

worse [wɝːs]

① *adj.* 更壞的

② *adv.* 更糟；更壞；更差

③ *n.* 更糟的事；更壞的情況

▶ The food at this restaurant continues to get worse.
這間餐廳的食物越來越糟。

▶ My headache is getting worse, not better.
我的頭越來越痛，沒有變好。

▶ For better or for worse, I promise to love you.
無論是好是壞，我承諾要愛你。

---

worst [wɝːst]

① *adj.* 最壞的

▶ Just go for it. What is the worst thing that can happen?
儘管去做（都已經這麼壞了），還能發生什麼最壞的情況嗎？

② *adv.* 最壞地

③ *n.* 最壞的人（或事）；最糟的情況

④ *v.* 擊敗；打敗

▶ This university ranked worst for sports.
這所大學的運動項目排名最差。

▶ The worst is that I can't even remember what happened.
最糟的是我居然不記得發生了什麼事。

▶ The famous tennis player was worsted by the other player and lost the game.
這位知名的網球選手被另一名球員擊敗，輸了這場比賽。

---

worth [wɝːθ]

① *adj.* 值…錢的

實用片語與搭配字

be worth sth; be worth having / doing sth; be worth your while

值得…; 值得擁有 / 做…; 值得去做

② *n.* 價值

▶ Gold is worth a lot more than silver.
金比銀有價值得多。

▶ If you are not interested in art, it will not be worth your while to spend money going to the fine arts museum.
你若對藝術不感興趣，就不值得花錢去美術館。

▶ The worth of this violin is very high!
這把小提琴的價值非常高！

---

would [wʊd / wəd / əd]

aux. v. 將要（will 的過去式）

▶ I knew that he would bring his running shoes.
我知道他會帶他自己的跑步鞋。

---

wound [wuːnd]

① *n.* 傷口

② *v.* 傷害；使受傷

▶ He wrapped a bandage around his wound.
他用繃帶把他的傷口包紮起來。

▶ Be careful not to wound yourself while exercising.
運動的時候要小心，不要傷到你自己。

---

write [raɪt] *v.* 書寫；寫（字）

實用片語與搭配字

write sth down; written all over sb's face

寫下，記下；（情緒）寫在（某人）臉上的

▶ Sara wants to write a book about her travels.
莎拉想要寫一本關於她旅遊的書。

▶ When he did not win the award for Businessman of the Year, disappointment was written all over Paul's face.
當保羅得知他沒有贏得年度最佳企業家獎項時，他的臉上寫滿了失望。

writer [ˈraɪ.t̬ɚ] *n.* 作家

▶ Linda's husband is a writer.
琳達的先生是個作家。

---

wrong [rɑːŋ]

① *adj.* 錯誤的

實用片語與搭配字

prove sb wrong 證明（某人）是錯誤的

② *adv.* 錯誤地

實用片語與搭配字

get sth wrong; go wrong; don't get me wrong

答錯；出問題，犯錯誤；別誤會

③ *n.* 錯誤

④ *v.* 不公正地對待；冤枉

▶ I thought I knew the right answer to the question, but I was wrong.
我以為我知道這問題的正確答案，但我錯了。

▶ Nobody ever thought that I would be successful, but I proved them all wrong by becoming CEO at 34.
沒有人認為我會成功，但我三十四歲當上執行長，證明了他們是錯誤的。

▶ You played the note wrong; try again, and follow the music carefully.
你把音符彈錯了，再試一次，並且小心地跟著樂譜彈。

▶ I cannot stand stinky tofu; don't get me wrong, I love tofu, just not stinky tofu.
我受不了臭豆腐，別誤會我的意思，我喜歡豆腐，只是不喜歡臭豆腐。

▶ We all have a choice between right and wrong; I want to choose to do right.
我們對於對或錯都有選擇；我想要選擇去做對的事。

▶ Karl wronged me by telling everyone my secret.
卡爾將我的祕密告訴了大家，讓我深受傷害。

---

yam / sweet potato [jæm / ˌswiːt pəˈteɪ.t̬oʊ]

n. 番薯

▶ Yams grow under the ground and are very healthy to eat.
番薯長在地底下，是健康食物。

---

yard [jɑːrd] *n.* （長度）碼

▶ The ball was only one yard away from her.
這顆球離她只有一碼遠。

---

year [jɪr] *n.* 年

▶ In which year were you born?
你在哪一年出生的？

---

yellow [ˈjel.oʊ]

① *adj.* 黃色的

▶ Is that yellow car a taxicab?
那輛黃色的車是計程車嗎？

② *n.* 黃色

③ *v.* （使）變黃

▶ I like the color yellow because it is bright, and it makes me happy.
我喜歡黃色，因為它很鮮亮，而且讓我很快樂。

▶ These photographs have yellowed because they are so old.
這些照片已經泛黃，因為它們很老舊了。

---

yes [jes]

① *adv.* 是的

實用片語與搭配字

yes and no 也是，也不是

② *n.* 肯定的回答

▶ Yes, that is correct.
是的，那是正確的。

▶ You ask me if I want to go to the movies? Yes and no -- I want to see the movie but I need to finish my report.
你問我是否想去看電影？是，也不是，我想要看電影，但我需要完成我的報告。

▶ Please give me a yes or no answer.
請給我一個是或不是的答案。

---

yesterday [ˈjes.tɚ.deɪ]

① *adv.* (在)昨天

實用片語與搭配字

not be born yesterday 不易上當

② *n.* 昨天

▶ I wasn't feeling well yesterday, but today I'm fine!
我昨天不舒服，但今天我好多了！

▶ Do not try and convince me that it is a smart thing to do, I was not born yesterday.
別試圖說服我這是明智的做法，我不會這麼容易上當的。

▶ Yesterday was Saturday; today is Sunday.
昨天是星期六，今天是星期日。

---

yet [jet]

① *adv.* 還沒（用於否定句）

實用片語與搭配字

have yet to 還沒有

② *conj.* 可是；然而

▶ Did you try this ice cream yet? It's delicious!
你吃過這冰淇淋了嗎？太好吃了！

▶ I have traveled to many countries in the world, but I have yet to visit Antarctica.
我已經遊歷了世界上許多國家，但還沒機會造訪南極洲。

▶ Sam didn't want to watch the movie, yet he still went.
山姆本來不想去看那場電視，可是終究他還是去了。

you [juː / jə / jʊ] *pron.* 你；你們（主格）

▶ Nice to meet you.
很高興認識你。

---

young [jʌŋ]

① *adj.* 年輕的

實用片語與搭配字

young at heart; young love
心態年輕；年輕人的愛情

② *n.* （總稱）青年人；年輕人

▶ Winnie's daughter is so young and full of energy.
薇尼的女兒很年輕又充滿活力。

▶ My grandparents might be old in years, but they are still young at heart and I enjoy doing things with them.
我的祖父母或許年事已高，但心態仍舊年輕，我很喜歡和他們在一起。

▶ Sometimes it's difficult for the young and the old to understand each other.
有時候年輕人與老年人很難了解彼此。

Exercise 79

I. Choose and write the correct word. Change the form of the word when necessary.

1	wooden (adj.) worse (adj.)	The __________ boat was built to withstand the various weather conditions at sea.
2	worker (n.) world (n.)	The very best thing you can do for the whole __________ is to make the most of yourself.
3	worth (adj.) wrong (adj.)	We could probably trust him with the information but it's just not __________ the risk.
4	write (v.) worry (v.)	Don't __________ about how we're going to pay for the new machine; we'll cross that bridge when we come to it.
5	wound (n.) yesterday (n.)	Ten people died and thirty were seriously injured in the rail crash __________.

II. Multiple choices.

(   ) 1. The trees are beginning to turn to their orange and _________ autumn colors.
(A) wrong (B) worth (C) yellow (D) yam

(   ) 2. The _________ illustrates his points by quotation from a number of sources.
(A) wrong (B) writer (C) worm (D) wound

(   ) 3. He had no office of his own and, _________ of all, he didn't have his own computer.
(A) worst (B) worry (C) work (D) word

(   ) 4. The little girl helped her grandmother to thread the _________ into the needle.
(A) work (B) worm (C) worse (D) wool

(   ) 5. There's no denying that the quality of our lives has gone from bad to _________.
(A) worse (B) world (C) word (D) wound

Unit 80

your(s) [jʊr(z)] *pron.* 你的；你們的（所有格）

▶ Is this guitar yours?
這把吉他是你的嗎？

---

yourself [jʊrˈself / jɚˈself] *pron.* 你自己

實用片語與搭配字

be yourself; (all) by yourself; not be / seem / feel yourself; do-it-yourself
不造作；獨自地；不太舒服；DIY

▶ Help yourself to the food on the table.
請隨意到桌上拿食物吃。

▶ If you are a do-it-yourself kind of person, you will love that new store where you can buy anything from tools to paint.
若你喜歡自己動手做，你會喜歡那家新的店，在那裡從工具到油漆都買得到。

---

youth [juːθ] *n.* 青少年時期

▶ His youth allowed him to do many things.
他在青少年時被容許做很多事情。

---

yucky [ˈjʌk.i] *adj.* 噁心的；令人厭惡的

▶ Look at that trash! It's so yucky.
你看那堆垃圾！真的很噁心。

---

yummy [ˈjʌm.i] *adj.* 好吃的

▶ That pie was so yummy that I ate three slices!
那派真好吃，我吃了三片！

---

zebra [ˈziː.brə] *n.* 斑馬

▶ The zebra has black and white stripes.
斑馬有著黑白條紋。

---

zero [ˈzɪr.oʊ]

① *n.* 零

實用片語與搭配字

zero-carbon 零碳的

② *v.* 把…調整歸零

▶ Zero times any number is still zero.
零乘以任何數字還是零。

▶ In some countries, households use only solar power to ensure a zero-carbon house -- no fossil fuels to generate energy.
在某些國家，住家只使用太陽能以確保零碳，就是不用石化燃料產生能源。

▶ After weighing the food, Sam zeroed the scales.
在秤完食物後，山姆將磅秤歸零。

Y

zoo [zuː] *n.* 動物園

▶ The zoo has some new animals on display, like penguins and giraffes.

這個動物園有一些新的動物在展演，像是企鵝和長頸鹿。

Exercise 80

I. Choose and write the correct word. Change the form of the word when necessary.

1	zoo (n.) zero (n.)	The temperature is expected to drop to ten degrees below ________ tonight.
2	zoo (n.) youth (n.)	In the ________, we saw many monkeys running around in the cage.

II. Multiple choices.

( ) 1. She regrets that she spent her ________ traveling and not studying.
(A) yucky (B) yummy (C) youth (D) yourself

( ) 2. Some high school students don't like the food in cafeteria because it tastes ________.
(A) yucky (B) yummy (C) youth (D) yours

( ) 3. We strongly advise you to rid ________ of the bad habit of smoking.
(A) yours (B) yourself (C) zero (D) youth

( ) 4. The ________ is a wild African horse with black and white stripes.
(A) zero (B) zoo (C) zone (D) zebra

( ) 5. The salad is not only ________ but healthy, too.
(A) yummy (B) yucky (C) youth (D) yours

解答
Answer

Answer 解答

Exercise 1

Ⅰ. ① active ② adult ③ accepted ④ ability ⑤ affair

Ⅱ. ① B ② C ③ A ④ D ⑤ C

Exercise 2

Ⅰ. ① alarm ② ahead ③ album ④ alive ⑤ alike

Ⅱ. ① C ② B ③ A ④ D ⑤ C

Exercise 3

Ⅰ. ① amount ② ankle ③ always ④ already ⑤ among

Ⅱ. ① B ② C ③ D ④ C ⑤ A

Exercise 4

Ⅰ. ① appeared ② arrive ③ appetite ④ armed ⑤ argument

Ⅱ. ① C ② A ③ D ④ B ⑤ C

Exercise 5

Ⅰ. ① article ② attend ③ assistant ④ asleep ⑤ attack

Ⅱ. ① D ② B ③ A ④ C ⑤ B

Exercise 6

Ⅰ. ① balcony ② barber ③ barbecue ④ basis ⑤ barks

Ⅱ. ① C ② B ③ A ④ D ⑤ A

Exercise 7

Ⅰ. ① beard ② bear ③ beetle ④ before ⑤ beef

Ⅱ. ① C ② B ③ A ④ D ⑤ C

Exercise 8

Ⅰ. ① believable ② bench ③ bend ④ beyond ⑤ bill

Ⅱ. ① A ② C ③ B ④ D ⑤ B

Exercise 9

Ⅰ. ① bottom ② bloody ③ block ④ blind ⑤ bomb

Ⅱ. ① C ② D ③ A ④ C ⑤ B

Exercise 10

Ⅰ. ① brightly ② bridge ③ bread ④ busy ⑤ butter

Ⅱ. ① D ② A ③ B ④ C ⑤ C

Exercise 11

Ⅰ. ① care ② cause ③ carry ④ capped ⑤ chart

Ⅱ. ① C ② A ③ D ④ C ⑤ A

Exercise 12

Ⅰ. ① check ② chief ③ close ④ clear ⑤ coast

Ⅱ. ① B ② D ③ A ④ D ⑤ B

Exercise 13

Ⅰ. ① common ② cover ③ cooking ④ cowboy ⑤ count

Ⅱ. ① D ② A ③ D ④ A ⑤ D

Exercise 14

Ⅰ. ① danger ② dates ③ different ④ digit ⑤ decide

Ⅱ. ① C ② A ③ B ④ D ⑤ B

Exercise 15

Ⅰ. ① drag ② downstairs ③ drawer ④ doubt ⑤ Drama

Ⅱ. ① D ② C ③ B ④ A ⑤ C

Exercise 16

Ⅰ. ① drug ② drop ③ duty ④ early ⑤ dress

Ⅱ. ① B ② C ③ D ④ A ⑤ B

Exercise 17

Ⅰ. ① effect ② elected ③ element ④ elder ⑤ elevator

Ⅱ. ① C ② B ③ A ④ D ⑤ A

Exercise 18

Ⅰ. ① enjoyment ② equal ③ entire ④ errors ⑤ enter

Ⅱ. ① C ② B ③ A ④ D ⑤ C

Exercise 19

Ⅰ. ① example ② except ③ exact ④ experience ⑤ exists

Ⅱ. ① C ② C ③ D ④ A ⑤ D

Exercise 20

Ⅰ. ① failure ② fear ③ false ④ fail ⑤ fault

Ⅱ. ① B ② C ③ A ④ C ⑤ C

Exercise 21

Ⅰ. ① fence ② field ③ final ④ figure ⑤ finally

Ⅱ. ① B ② C ③ A ④ D ⑤ C

Exercise 22

Ⅰ. ① fisherman ② flat ③ flash ④ flu ⑤ focus

Ⅱ. ① D ② D ③ B ④ A ⑤ B

Exercise 23

Ⅰ. ① fool ② forgive ③ formal ④ frank ⑤ form

Ⅱ. ① D ② A ③ C ④ A ⑤ C

Exercise 24

Ⅰ. ① fright ② further ③ frighten ④ garbage ⑤ full

Ⅱ. ① B ② A ③ D ④ C ⑤ A

Exercise 25

Ⅰ. ① general ② giant ③ gluing ④ goal ⑤ glad

Ⅱ. ① C ② B ③ D ④ C ⑤ B

Exercise 26

Ⅰ. ① government ② greedy ③ guarding ④ ground ⑤ grassy

Ⅱ. ① C ② D ③ A ④ B ⑤ C

Exercise 27

Ⅰ. ① guide ② guitar ③ handsome ④ hardly ⑤ handle

Ⅱ. ① C ② A ③ D ④ B ⑤ C

Exercise 28

Ⅰ. ① heater ② healthy ③ hero ④ heat ⑤ helpful

Ⅱ. ① D ② C ③ B ④ A ⑤ C

Exercise 29

Ⅰ. ① highway ② honest ③ hire ④ holiday ⑤ hop

Ⅱ. ① B ② D ③ D ④ A ⑤ B

Exercise 30

Ⅰ. ① human ② hunger ③ hunt ④ humble ⑤ husband

Ⅱ. ① C ② B ③ D ④ A ⑤ B

Exercise 31

Ⅰ. ① improve ② important ③ income

④ influence ⑤ indicated

Ⅱ. ① C ② B ③ A ④ B ⑤ C

Exercise 32

Ⅰ. ① introduce ② interview ③ interested

④ iron ⑤ item

Ⅱ. ① D ② A ③ A ④ A ⑤ C

Exercise 33

Ⅰ. ① join ② kingdom ③ kind ④ kick

⑤ judgement

Ⅱ. ① C ② B ③ A ④ D ⑤ C

Exercise 34

Ⅰ. ① knee ② lacks ③ last ④ lake

⑤ latest

Ⅱ. ① D ② B ③ A ④ C ⑤ B

Exercise 35

Ⅰ. ① lawyer ② least ③ leave ④ length

⑤ lend

Ⅱ. ① C ② A ③ C ④ B ⑤ A

Exercise 36

Ⅰ. ① lie ② library ③ limit ④ local

⑤ link

Ⅱ. ① C ② B ③ D ④ A ⑤ B

Exercise 37

Ⅰ. ① lonely ② loss ③ lock ④ located

⑤ machine

Ⅱ. ① D ② C ③ D ④ A ⑤ A

Exercise 38

Ⅰ. ① maintain ② manners ③ main ④ master

⑤ mass

Ⅱ. ① C ② A ③ D ④ A ⑤ C

Exercise 39

Ⅰ. ① materials ② measure ③ member

④ metal ⑤ message

Ⅱ. ① C ② A ③ C ④ B ⑤ B

Exercise 40

Ⅰ. ① military ② method ③ motion ④ modern

⑤ mistake

Ⅱ. ① B ② A ③ D ④ D ⑤ A

Exercise 41

Ⅰ. ① motion ② more ③ mouse ④ move

⑤ mud

Ⅱ. ① C ② B ③ A ④ D ⑤ A

Exercise 42

Ⅰ. ① musician ② naughty ③ national

④ necklace ⑤ need

Ⅱ. ① B ② D ③ B ④ A ⑤ B

Exercise 43

Ⅰ. ① neighbor ② never ③ neither ④ noisy

⑤ nod

Ⅱ. ① B ② C ③ D ④ C ⑤ A

Exercise 44

Ⅰ. ① notebook ② notice ③ object ④ offer

⑤ officer

Ⅱ. ① C ② B ③ D ④ A ⑤ B

Exercise 45

Ⅰ. ① often ② opinion ③ omitted ④ ordinary

⑤ order

Ⅱ. ① C ② C ③ B ④ C ⑤ D

Exercise 46

Ⅰ. ① owner ② packed ③ painting ④ papaya

⑤ palm

Ⅱ. ① B ② D ③ A ④ D ⑤ C

Exercise 47

Ⅰ. ① pay ② passengers ③ patient ④ pass
⑤ path

Ⅱ. ① C ② D ③ B ④ D ⑤ C

Exercise 48

Ⅰ. ① period ② picnic ③ pile ④ pick
⑤ pillow

Ⅱ. ① D ② C ③ B ④ A ⑤ C

Exercise 49

Ⅰ. ① pipes ② player ③ plan ④ point
⑤ poet

Ⅱ. ① C ② A ③ B ④ C ⑤ D

Exercise 50

Ⅰ. ① postman ② power ③ positive
④ population ⑤ poisoned

Ⅱ. ① C ② B ③ A ④ C ⑤ D

Exercise 51

Ⅰ. ① praise ② prepare ③ president
④ powerful ⑤ principle

Ⅱ. ① B ② A ③ D ④ C ⑤ C

Exercise 52

Ⅰ. ① project ② promised ③ public
④ punishment ⑤ prove

Ⅱ. ① D ② B ③ C ④ A ⑤ C

Exercise 53

Ⅰ. ① quality ② puzzled ③ quit ④ rapid
⑤ range

Ⅱ. ① B ② C ③ D ④ A ⑤ C

Exercise 54

Ⅰ. ① realize ② reason ③ refuse ④ regular
⑤ receive

Ⅱ. ① C ② A ③ D ④ A ⑤ C

Exercise 55

Ⅰ. ① repeat ② respect ③ result ④ rise
⑤ restaurant

Ⅱ. ① C ② C ③ A ④ B ⑤ A

Exercise 56

Ⅰ. ① robot ② royal ③ roof ④ rush
⑤ rude

Ⅱ. ① C ② A ③ D ④ A ⑤ D

Exercise 57

Ⅰ. ① safety ② sale ③ satisfy ④ sample
⑤ scared

Ⅱ. ① B ② C ③ D ④ A ⑤ D

Exercise 58

Ⅰ. ① screen ② search ③ semester ④ select
⑤ selfish

Ⅱ. ① C ② D ③ A ④ D ⑤ A

Exercise 59

Ⅰ. ① serious ② servant ③ settle ④ shine
⑤ shelf

Ⅱ. ① A ② B ③ A ④ D ⑤ A

Exercise 60

Ⅰ. ① shout ② shorts ③ shy ④ sight
⑤ sidewalk

Ⅱ. ① C ② A ③ D ④ C ⑤ A

Exercise 61

Ⅰ. ① similar ② simply ③ singer ④ sink
⑤ Skill

Ⅱ. ① B ② C ③ D ④ A ⑤ A

Exercise 62

Ⅰ. ① sleepy ② slide ③ smell ④ slow
⑤ social

Ⅱ. ① C ② A ③ D ④ A ⑤ C

Exercise 63

Ⅰ. ① society ② solve ③ sometimes ④ soul ⑤ source

Ⅱ. ① B ② C ③ A ④ D ⑤ A

Exercise 64

Ⅰ. ① speech ② speaker ③ spend ④ special ⑤ spinach

Ⅱ. ① D ② A ③ C ④ B ⑤ C

Exercise 65

Ⅰ. ① station ② steal ③ storm ④ strange ⑤ stomach

Ⅱ. ① C ② D ③ A ④ B ⑤ A

Exercise 66

Ⅰ. ① Stress ② stretch ③ sudden ④ succeed ⑤ subject

Ⅱ. ① C ② B ③ B ④ B ⑤ C

Exercise 67

Ⅰ. ① symbol ② survive ③ support ④ sweet ⑤ swallow

Ⅱ. ① B ② A ③ D ④ B ⑤ C

Exercise 68

Ⅰ. ① talent ② taste ③ team ④ tale ⑤ Tear

Ⅱ. ① C ② B ③ C ④ A ⑤ A

Exercise 69

Ⅰ. ① temple ② textbook ③ phone ④ theater ⑤ terrific

Ⅱ. ① B ② C ③ C ④ A ⑤ D

Exercise 70

Ⅰ. ① Thick ② thief ③ throw ④ thought ⑤ thunder

Ⅱ. ① A ② C ③ B ④ A ⑤ D

Exercise 71

Ⅰ. ① ticket ② tip ③ tiring ④ together ⑤ tone

Ⅱ. ① C ② A ③ D ④ B ⑤ C

Exercise 72

Ⅰ. ① toothache ② topic ③ trade ④ treat ⑤ tower

Ⅱ. ① C ② B ③ C ④ A ⑤ B

Exercise 73

Ⅰ. ① trip ② trouble ③ trust ④ twenty ⑤ treatment

Ⅱ. ① C ② D ③ D ④ A ⑤ B

Exercise 74

Ⅰ. ① typhoon ② until ③ upstairs ④ uniform ⑤ useful

Ⅱ. ① C ② B ③ C ④ A ⑤ B

Exercise 75

Ⅰ. ① victory ② visit ③ woke ④ visitor ⑤ vacation

Ⅱ. ① A ② D ③ C ④ B ⑤ C

Exercise 76

Ⅰ. ① weak ② wallet ③ waved ④ weather ⑤ weigh

Ⅱ. ① C ② C ③ A ④ C ⑤ B

Exercise 77

Ⅰ. ① whatever ② whole ③ whose ④ whispering ⑤ wheel

Ⅱ. ① B ② C ③ B ④ B ⑤ C

Exercise 78

Ⅰ. ① willing ② width ③ wire ④ wonder ⑤ without

Ⅱ. ① C ② A ③ B ④ C ⑤ D

Exercise 79

Ⅰ. ① wooden ② world ③ worth ④ worry
⑤ yesterday

Ⅱ. ① C ② B ③ A ④ D ⑤ A

Exercise 80

Ⅰ. ① zero ② zoo

Ⅱ. ① C ② A ③ B ④ D ⑤ A

單字索引

C

D

I

M

N

S

T

U

國家圖書館出版品預行編目(CIP)資料

完勝大考英語7000單字. 初級篇1~2500字/空中美語教室編輯群著.
-- 二版. -- 臺北市 : 笛藤出版圖書有限公司, 2023.12
面； 公分
ISBN 978-957-710-908-8(平裝)
1.CST: 英語教學 2.CST: 詞彙 3.CST: 中等教育
524.38 112020506

2024年7月27日 二版第3刷 定價330元

著　　者 | 空中英語教室編輯群
封面設計 | 王舒玗
總 編 輯 | 洪季楨
編　　輯 | 林子鈺、葉雯婷
編輯協力 | 張雅森、關蕙芯、Charmaine Pretprious
編輯企畫 | 笛藤出版
發 行 人 | 林建仲
發 行 所 | 八方出版股份有限公司
地　　址 | 台北市中山區長安東路二段171號3樓3室
電　　話 | (02) 2777-3682
傳　　真 | (02) 2777-3672
總 經 銷 | 聯合發行股份有限公司
電　　話 | (02) 2917-8022 ・ (02) 2917-8042
製 版 廠 | 造極彩色印刷製版股份有限公司
劃撥帳戶 | 八方出版股份有限公司
劃撥帳號 | 19809050